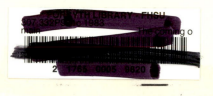

The coming of industrial order

The coming of industrial order

*Town and factory life in rural
Massachusetts, 1810–1860*

JONATHAN PRUDE

CAMBRIDGE UNIVERSITY PRESS

Cambridge
London   New York   New Rochelle
Melbourne   Sydney

This publication was supported by a grant from the Merrimack Valley
Textile Museum.

Published by the Press Syndicate of the University of Cambridge
The Pitt Building, Trumpington Street, Cambridge CB2 1RP
32 East 57th Street, New York, NY 10022, USA
296 Beaconsfield Parade, Middle Park, Melbourne 3206, Australia

First published 1983

Printed in the United States of America

Library of Congress Cataloging in Publication Data
Prude, Jonathan.
The coming of industrial order.
Bibliography: p.
Includes index.
1. Massachusetts – Industries – History – 19th century.
I. Title.
HC107.M4P78 1983   307'.332'09744   82-14599
ISBN 0 521 24824 8

To my parents

PRESIDENT JACKSON: "I understand you taught us how to spin, so as to rival Great Britain in her manufactures; you set all these thousands of spindles at work, which I have been delighted in viewing, and which have made so many happy, by a lucrative employment."

SAMUEL SLATER: "Yes, sir. I suppose that I gave out the psalm and they have been singing to the tune ever since."

George S. White, *Memoir of Samuel Slater*

Contents

List of tables, figures, and maps   *page* viii
Preface   xi

Part I. Background and beginnings   1

1   *The rural order: Dudley and Oxford in 1810*   3
2   *Samuel Slater, textile mills, and a new economic landscape*   34

Part II. The first generation   65

3   *People and work: the social structure of occupations*   67
4   *The industrial order*   100
5   *How the operatives responded*   133
6   *How the towns responded*   158

Part III. The second generation   181

7   *Society and economy in three towns*   183
8   *Workers: responses new and old*   217
9   *Communities: "the greatest good to the greatest number"*   238

Part IV. Afterwards   257

10   *The war and beyond*   259

Appendixes   265

1   A note on transiency   267
2   Tables   269

List of abbreviations used in notes   273
Notes   274
Bibliography   341
Index   355

Tables, figures, and maps

Tables

1.1	Nonagricultural establishments in Dudley and Oxford, 1791, 1801, and 1811	*page* 7
1.2	Geographical mobility and persistence of household heads and individuals in Dudley and Oxford, 1800–10	22
2.1	Geographical mobility and persistence of household heads in Dudley and Oxford, 1810–30	55
2.2	Nontextile enterprises in Dudley and Oxford, 1801, 1811, 1831	58
3.1	Average annual work force, East Village, 1813–35	85
7.1	Age distribution of antebellum Dudley, Oxford, and Webster populations, in percentages	185
7.2	Ethnic composition of Dudley, Oxford, and Webster populations, 1850 and 1860, in percentages	187
7.3	Percentage of Dudley, Oxford, and Webster labor forces in the four leading occupations, 1860	189
7.4	Average annual work force of North, South, and East villages in Webster, 1836–59	208
7.5	Average daily wage and percentage of Americans holding selected jobs, Webster cotton mills, 1860	216
A.1	Average annual work force, aggregate turnover, and estimated voluntary departure rates, Slater employees, 1814–59	270
A.2	Population of Dudley, Oxford, and Webster, 1790–1860	271
A.3	Nativity of Dudley, Oxford, and Webster inhabitants, 1860, in percentages	272

Figures

5.1	Aggregate turnover and estimated voluntary departure rates, Slater employees, 1814–35	145

8.1   Aggregate turnover and estimated voluntary
      departure rates, Slater employees, 1814–59   227

Maps

1.1   Massachusetts, ca. 1822, with detail of Dudley
      and Oxford   5
3.1   Geographical distribution of outworkers serving
      the Slater mills, 1813–16   74
3.2   Geographical distribution of outworkers serving
      the Slater mills, 1825–8   75
3.3   Ground plan of South Village, ca. 1825   97
7.1   Detail of south-central Massachusetts, ca. 1842,
      showing the new township of Webster   184

Preface

This is a study of industrialization in the antebellum New England countryside. More specifically, it is an investigation of pre–Civil War industrialization in two contiguous south-central Massachusetts townships, Dudley and Oxford, and in a third community, Webster, which was carved from them in 1832.

But "industrialization," of course, is a term of magic: It can mean anything, or everything, and so, often enough, ends up meaning almost nothing at all.[1] I am sensitive to this risk – the more so because in the pages that follow I offer no single, concise definition of industrialization. (Indeed, until Part IV I use the word itself sparingly.) Something changed between 1810 and 1860 in the communities under review; and because much of what changed related to the introduction of waterpowered textile factories, industrialization would seem to provide an appropriate summary rubric. But for the most part I am content to rely on an accumulating operational understanding of the term: Industrialization is what happened in these townships during these years.

I do not take this tack out of conceptual timidity. Rather, it is a strategy that reflects the first of two central themes in this study. For it is my contention that in the communities I am considering the emergence of industrial order must be understood not as a single homogeneous development but as a blend of different changes – or, more precisely, as a blend of changes and lack of changes. Thus, in the southern Massachusetts hinterland between 1810 and 1860, the coming of industrial order manifestly involved the construction of cotton and woolen "manufactories." But it also involved the development of small commercial and handicraft establishments shaped by ambitions, structures, and technologies initially quite distinct from those characterizing the mills. And it involved a gradual – but only gradual, and through much of this period strikingly limited – commercialization of agriculture. Finally, the coming of industrial order encompassed – at least through the first several decades under review – a stubborn retention of community-wide notions concerning appropriate forms of governance and hierarchy. Industrialization, that is, involved not just a single kind of innovation but a range of new ways of living and working. And it also involved the maintenance of old ways. Such contrasts were not by-products of the industrializing process; they were what the process was all about.

Which leads directly to the second theme of this study. Precisely because the industrial order embraced a variety of developments and experiences, it also embraced tension. The most dramatic expressions of innovation stood out against – in fact often contradicted – received attitudes and institutions that still colored vital areas of daily existence. And so, in widely differing ways, the sharpest, most far-reaching, and most emphatic changes met resistance. Or more bluntly: There was not opposition to industrialization; opposition was intrinsic to the nature of industrialization. This was true despite the fact that even major changes emerged to some degree out of trends and energies embedded in traditional mores. People still found distressing what they, or their neighbors, had helped create.

In the context of this case study, it was the textile mill that constituted the most dramatic challenge to established values and habits, and it was thus the textile mill that met the most vivid opposition. During the first period explored in these pages, two connected but discrete areas of tension emerged: one between managers and "hands" inside the mills, the other between the mills and the towns.

By the 1830s, after a generation of industrialization, the first of these struggles had produced what can be properly viewed as a class relationship between factory employees and employers. There were, to be sure, no significant strikes; and, in fact, exploring the history of mills in Dudley, Oxford, and Webster throws light on why large-scale confrontations were generally rare among antebellum textile operatives. But by the late 1820s and early 1830s there had developed between local millworkers and mill managers complex patterns of give and take, of managerial demands evoking heated and sustained efforts by operatives to win greater earnings and, equally important, greater independence.[2] The second struggle – between the towns and the mills – did not involve class tensions. But reflecting its own rhythm of frustrations and antagonisms, and inflamed further by particular personalities and personal hostilities, the town–mill struggle led ultimately to the precipitous – and vigorously protested – incorporation of Webster.

Both conflicts shifted somewhat during the 1840s and 1850s. New developments and pressures – the arrival of immigrants, the softening of contrasts between textile mills and certain nontextile business ventures, the rise of new attitudes toward town administration and leadership, and (in Webster) the powerful hold over town life by a particular manufacturing interest – all modified the play of tensions within these communities. Nonetheless, in one form or another, antagonisms continued. There are suggestions of frustrations persisting in textile mills and building up in other workplaces as well. And there are indications that various late antebellum enterprises – including mills – were targets of considerable community suspicion.

This is what the book is about. This is the shape of an investigation that I hope will illuminate what industrialization meant to people living in these towns in this period. But I should acknowledge at the outset that my analysis, simply by its focus and thematic slant, presses against certain received notions of antebellum historiography.

In the first place, this study, in company with a number of other recent monographs, challenges the proposition that antebellum America's passage into the industrial age was remarkable for its smoothness: the notion (to quote a classic investigation of early Yankee textile manufacturing) that New England's "factory system did not upset an old industrial order [or] bring with it the social conditions familiar in older countries."[3] Now it is probably true that the rise of northern cotton and woolen mills – in fact all of America's early-nineteenth-century "great transformation" – was less explosively disruptive than comparable developments in, say, Great Britain. But it also remains true – and this book certainly aims to demonstrate – that industrialization in this country was from the outset marked by significant tension. Indeed, it is my hope that by excavating local versions of such conflicts, the present study will contribute to a deeper, more nuanced appreciation of how unsmooth the coming of American industrial order actually was.

I also mean the book to challenge scholarly inclinations to probe early-nineteenth-century industrialization primarily through the experience of urban artisans. Even the most intelligent and sensitive of recent investigations into pre–Civil War social and economic change have tended to focus mainly on craftsmen in northeastern cities.[4] Because of these works, we are beginning to gain significant leverage on what happened to these people – and what they did about it. But what happened in Dudley, Oxford, and Webster reveals that urban artisans were not the only ones to feel buffeted by rapid economic change; nor were they alone in trying to resist the troubling new pressures and conditions introduced by antebellum economic change. Unskilled and semiskilled factory employees were

also protagonists in the drama. So, to some extent, were rural handicraft workers. And so also, more consistently and forcefully, were
New Englanders who remained farmers or who, whatever their
vocation, simply took their stand as citizens of rural townships.

In fact, the whole inclination to equate urbanization and industrialization may be questioned. Even if we focus on the textile factory
as a talisman of rapid economic change during these years, the
countryside must be considered. After all, at midcentury more than
half the textile manufactories and textile operatives in the Commonwealth of Massachusetts were located in settings like Dudley, Oxford, and Webster: townships of less than five thousand people.[5] It
is, to be sure, difficult – and probably fruitless – to lay down rigid
demographic standards specifying where "rural" ends and "urban"
begins.[6] But when it is recalled that formal municipal status in antebellum Massachusetts was reserved for communities of more than
twelve thousand inhabitants,[7] and when it is realized that most mills
outside such municipalities were situated in factory villages that
were in turn scattered across townships of comparatively sparse
populations – when all this is borne in mind – it becomes clear
enough that the widespread proliferation of cotton and woolen factories through the pre–Civil War Yankee hinterland represented a
decidedly non-city phenomenon.

Indeed, the rationale for considering developments outside large
cities may be pressed even further. For the fact is that we are remarkably ignorant not just about the coming of textile mills but
about virtually any aspect of life in the early-nineteenth-century
northern countryside. Although more than 60 percent of all Massachusetts residents, both operatives and nonoperatives, lived outside
major population centers as late as 1860,[8] there have been few efforts
to develop for antebellum years the studies of small towns that have
so enriched our knowledge of colonial New England. My hope is
that this project will begin to fill that gap.[9]

If the antebellum history of Dudley, Oxford, and Webster takes us
beyond cities generally and urban artisans particularly, it also sheds
light on a kind of manufactory that has been effectively ignored by
historians. The New England textile factory has probably been stud-
ied as intensely as any institution connected to American industrialization. Among both nineteenth-century commentators and recent
scholars, however, attention has been lavished mainly on the large
and heavily capitalized factories of Waltham, Lowell, and other major
or at least sizable Yankee towns: the mills clustered in northern
New England and typically owned by absentee merchant propri-

etors; the mills noted for their prompt decision to combine water-powered spinning with waterpowered weaving; and, above all, the mills famous for employing unmarried, middle-class farmers' daughters – the well-read, piano-playing, poetry-writing "Lowell girls" so astounding to foreign visitors – and housing them all together in large, tightly supervised, dormitorylike boardinghouses. The economic and cultural importance of these establishments is beyond dispute. And a number of fine studies have usefully considered their story.[10] The difficulty is that focusing exclusively on Waltham-style (or boardinghouse-style) factories has skewed our understanding of the early American textile industry.

It is not just that Yankee mills of the period were commonly built in rural communities like Dudley, Oxford, and Webster. Also important is the fact that most of these establishments were structurally distinct from Waltham-style factories but entirely similar to manufactories considered in this study. Clustered mainly in southern New England, these factories were typically small, moderately financed, and administered personally by at least some of their proprietors. For many years they "put out" certain tasks, including weaving, to outlying handworkers. They recruited workers from across the social and economic spectrum, both households and domestically unattached individuals, and they dispersed their recruits through a range of cottages and larger residences. These various organizational features are conventionally gathered under the label family- or Rhode Island-style; and early nineteenth-century "country" mills may thus be viewed as having characteristically also been family- or Rhode Island-style factories.[11]

In the final analysis, the difference between Waltham- and family-style establishments was neither permanent nor rigid. After the mid-1840s pressure within the industry and the influx of immigrants combined to reduce the distance between them; and even in the 1820s and 1830s some mills combined traits of both genres. Nor, it should be noted, did Waltham- and family-style factories exhaust the range of formats for pre–Civil War textile manufacturing: Cities like New York and Philadelphia, for example, developed their own institutional arrangements for spinning yarn and weaving cloth.[12]

Still, it is likely that through much of the antebellum era most New England mills conformed to the family-style of organization. The scholarly inclination to overlook these country factories and the distinctive social patterns they exhibited is thus an anomaly that needs to be corrected.[13]

And correcting it yields one further dividend. The man who introduced family-style mills to America was Samuel Slater, the celebrated English immigrant who helped introduce the whole process of waterpowered spinning into the country. But Slater was also directly involved in bringing the textile industry to the towns explored in this study, and he played a particularly consequential role in the town–factory conflicts that subsequently emerged. Investigating the country mills of Dudley, Oxford, and Webster thus provides added illumination to the curiously underinvestigated biography of this significant figure in early American industrial history.[14]

A word about organization. The study is basically chronological, but the boundaries of certain chapters are of necessity somewhat imprecise. Part I explores the towns before the mills were built and then examines both the genesis and overall dimension of economic change that occurred between 1810 and, roughly, the mid-1830s. Part II provides a detailed consideration of the industrial order through this same post-1810 time span: what I have called the first generation. The precise end points of the four chapters in Part II, however, do vary. Chapters 3 and 4 draw to a close around 1835. The discussion of employer–employee relations in Chapter 5 contains some material extending to 1840 and the beginning of large-scale immigration. The treatment of community responses to industrialization in Chapter 6 finds its natural boundary in the incorporation of Webster in 1832.

Part III is somewhat neater. Gathering up topics and themes raised in Part II, Chapters 7, 8, and 9 take the story up to the Civil War, covering what I have termed the second generation of local industrialization.

Chapter 10 (comprising Part IV) offers a summary glimpse of what befell the three towns after the period treated in this inquiry. It offers as well a concluding effort to underscore some of the more important themes involved in the coming of industrial order to Dudley, Oxford, and Webster, Massachusetts.

And finally a stylistic convention. I have used "factory" and "manufactory" interchangeably to mean textile mill.

This book has taken too long to complete, and the way has sometimes seemed arduous. It is pleasant, therefore, to offer thanks for the assistance I accepted over the years and the encouragement that lightened my efforts. Summer stipends from the National Endowment for the Humanities and the Emory University Research Committee opened up valuable research time. A grant-in-aid from the

Merrimack Valley Textile Museum and, at a later stage, a Daniels Fellowship from the American Antiquarian Society allowed me months of full-time writing. A number of students and friends helped with the dreary tasks of counting names on censuses and payrolls and checking citations: Mattie Anderson, Bill Glass, Stephen Henson, David Moore, Edward Shoemaker, and Patricia Sullivan all deserve special thanks in that context. Virtually every research facility I encountered proved cooperative, but specific acknowledgment is due the staffs at the American Antiquarian Society, Baker Library, Emory University, the Merrimack Valley Textile Museum, and Old Sturbridge Village. The town clerks of Dudley, Oxford, and Webster gave cheerfully of their time. So did the individuals I worked with at Cambridge University Press: my editors Steve Fraser and Frank Smith, and Leslie Deutsch. Jocelyn Shaw and Patsy Stockbridge uncomplainingly typed out more drafts than I care to recall.

I also wish to thank those upon whom I prevailed to read this manuscript. Stephen Bornstein, Thomas Dublin, Michael Ignatieff, and Robert Post provided helpful comments, as did my colleagues at Emory, Dan T. Carter and J. Harvey Young. Elements of Part II were initially distilled as a contribution to *Working Class America: Essays in Labor, Community, and American Society*, edited by Michael H. Frisch and Daniel J. Walkowitz, and numerous ideas in Chapters 3–6 of the present volume thus received the skilled scrutiny of those two historians. I am indebted also to the University of Illinois Press for permission to reprint certain passages. Gary Kulik made suggestions growing out of his own rich and extensive investigations into early American industrialization. Steven Hahn shared both his editorial expertise and his wide knowledge of themes running throughout the rural history of nineteenth-century America. Alexander Keyssar, whose research into unemployment in Massachusetts alerted me to the importance of antebellum labor markets, was a good friend: Unfailing in his encouragement, he asked hard questions and challenged my tendency toward imprecise and leisurely prose. Stephan Thernstrom offered sound advice on numerous occasions. Oscar Handlin, my thesis adviser, provided seasoned judgments rooted in his extraordinary grasp of the period and region. But he also, at every point, gave me the freedom to tell the story as I saw it. None of these individuals is responsible for all that I say here. They have my thanks for urging me to put down what I wanted to say as correctly and elegantly as I could.

My final acknowledgment is to my wife, Rosemary Eberiel. A scholar in her own right, and a most sensitive critic, she made countless valuable suggestions. She also, somehow, simply made it all possible.

PART I

Background and beginnings

To me there is something...delightful in contemplating the diffusion of enterprise and industry over an immense forest.

Timothy Dwight, *Travels in New England and New York*

There are places in New England where the custom [of commencing sabbath Saturday evening] is still observed in all its pristine strictness. They are not the manufacturing villages which are studded thickly along her wild and rapid streams...but they are the quiet old homes of the peasantry...the ancient farming towns of the commonwealth.

Nathaniel S. Dodge [John Carver], *Sketches of New England or Memories of the Country*

1   *The rural order:*
       Dudley and Oxford in 1810

I

In the first generation after 1810, in the adjacent rural townships of Dudley and Oxford, Massachusetts, men started building textile mills. The manufactories established in these communities during these years did not always last: Many of them succumbed to the treacherous economic currents of antebellum New England and dissolved rapidly into bankruptcy. But a good number did survive, and combined with the expanding array of commercial, handicraft, and nontextile manufacturing establishments springing up alongside the mills, local cotton and woolen factories ultimately brought profound change to Dudley and Oxford.

What happened in these towns was, of course, part of a broader story. The original implantation of textile mills into America, the earliest examples of their operation, their arrival and sustained presence in Dudley and Oxford – all this involved developments and individuals originating far beyond these communities. But it is equally true that changes overtaking Dudley and Oxford after 1810 were significantly conditioned by the towns themselves – and particularly by the social order informing these towns before the mills went up. On the one hand, this earlier pattern of life and labor paved the way for – indeed, critically stimulated – ensuing events. On the other hand, this same social pattern was, in many ways, deeply antagonistic to the coming transitions. Mores extant in 1810 and persisting well into the nineteenth century would, in fact, produce sharp conflicts between the townships and certain new enterprises – specifically the textile factories – that sprouted up in these communities. Indeed, the social order prevailing in 1810 would even provide raw materials for conflicts arising between managers and workers within these enterprises.

For all these reasons, exploring how it was before the mills arrived is a necessary first step in understanding both how the industrial order came to Dudley and Oxford and why its arrival proved so troubling.

3

II

In 1810, Dudley and Oxford still lived amid memories of the Revolution. Both communities had responded to the call for Committees of Correspondence in 1774 and 1775; and in 1776 both had "voted" (in the words of Dudley's town meeting) to "instruct our Representative[s]" to concur in the gathering enthusiasms of the Massachusetts General Court "Reletive to Independants." With considerably less eagerness, both towns had supplied materials and men to the ensuing military struggle with Britain; and both had joined in the voting necessary to establish new state and federal governments.[1] Taken as a whole, their contribution was neither more nor less than what most rural New England townships made to the revolutionary effort. But as in other northeastern townships – indeed, as in communities throughout the new nation – it was enough to permit events of the 1770s and 1780s to penetrate deeply into local culture.

Most obviously, there was the powerful impression made by returning veterans: Revolutionary soldiers from Dudley and Oxford who survived into the early nineteenth century were lionized by their neighbors, and the story of their martial careers was preserved as a precious community resource.[2] Then too, in subtle but important ways leading on to the 1820s and 1830s, the ideological debate that preceded the Revolution, and the comet trail of constitutional innovations that followed, deepened and extended notions of equality and independence. And finally, the War of Independence served residents of these towns – probably until the Civil War – as a reference point for public and private memories.

But the Revolution was scarcely the only link to the past. Equally significant was the continuing shadow cast by the earliest European pioneers of the area. Lying in the southernmost part of Worcester County, just north of the Connecticut border (Map 1.1), the land covered by Dudley and Oxford had first been settled in the late 1680s by French Huguenots fleeing their homeland after the revocation of the Edict of Nantes. Englishmen of the time were reluctant to push into the interior so soon after the devastating struggle with Indians known as King Philip's War, but the French were more daring. By 1688 they had secured the thirty families required for incorporation as a town, erected a sturdy fort, and even planted lavish gardens. But their gamble proved unlucky: In 1694 and again in 1696 Nipmucks attacked the settlement and, despite subsequent efforts to rebuild, effectively ended any organized Huguenot presence in the area. Several of the families lingered in the vicinity,

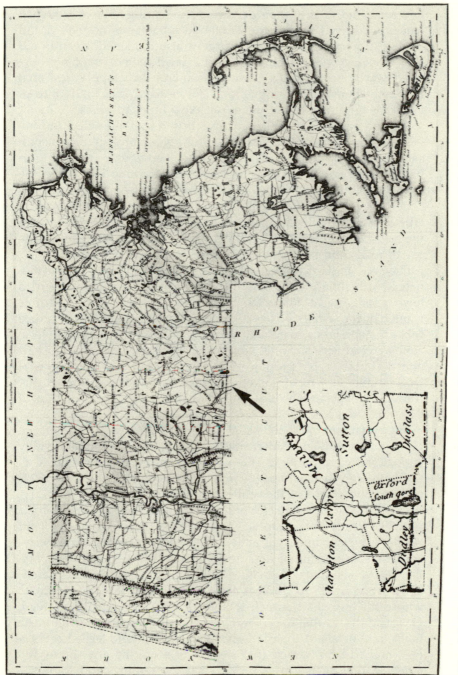

Map 1.1. Massachusetts, ca. 1822, with detail of Dudley and Oxford. (*A Complete Historical, Chronological, and Geographical Atlas;* Philadelphia, 1822; courtesy of the Map Collection, Harvard College Library.)

however, and in 1810 their descendants, bearing obviously French names, still lived among the 2,500-odd inhabitants of Oxford and Dudley. Traces of the fort and gardens also remained. Even in old age, Oliver Wendell Holmes retained vivid memories of his boyhood search for Oxford's "rose bushes and the grape vines" that revealed where French Huguenots had "rested...as a flight of tropical birds might alight on one of our New England pines."[3]

A more permanent settlement was begun by the English in May 1713. Suffering no Indian attacks, it quickly accumulated the necessary number of households and gained the status of township in July of the same year. This was Oxford. Abutting Oxford to the west, Dudley was settled by other Englishmen (including some from Oxford) soon thereafter and became a township in 1731. Like the Huguenots, early English settlers also left imprints: Descendants of the British pioneers inhabited the towns in 1810, and they still made use of roads and buildings established by their forefathers.[4]

Even the Indians among whom the Huguenot and English pioneers (with differing success) located their settlements proved to have a lasting role. Reduced in numbers, "their...lands taken as wanted by the settlers," a few members of the Nipmuck and Mashpee tribes nonetheless remained in the area, occasionally trading in local stores and at least for a while worshiping in local churches. Their ghostly but indelible presence was registered also in the names of local landmarks – most notably the huge lake in south Oxford that throughout the antebellum period retained its Nipmuck title of Chabanakongkomun.[5]

But by far the most pervasive link to the past was economic: In 1810, just as in 1750, Dudley and Oxford were both fundamentally agricultural communities. This does not mean, of course, that all residents were landholders. At any given moment in the early 1800s perhaps 30 percent of the adult male population lacked property. And several factors were at work during these years, most notably a slow but steady demographic growth pressing against limited land supplies, which almost certainly increased the number of propertyless residents and diminished the holdings of many property owners. But these constraints on owning real estate must not be overstated. Some who turned up landless between 1790 and 1810 were parents whose holdings had passed to the next generation. Others were young adults waiting upon their inheritances. Moreover, even those household heads in their twenties and thirties who lacked real estate, and had no immediate prospect of acquiring any, often still involved themselves in farming: some by renting land; others –

Table 1.1. *Nonagricultural establishments in Dudley and Oxford, 1791, 1801, and 1811*

	1791		1801		1811	
	Dudley	Oxford	Dudley	Oxford	Dudley	Oxford
Shops	1	1	7	6	5	13
Tanneries	1	1	4	1	3	2
Potash works	1	3	1	3		1
Gristmills	5	10	3	5	2	5
Fulling mills		1		1		1
Carding mills						1
Sawmills			4	4	2	8
Total	8	16	19	20	12	31
Combined total	24		39		43	

Source: AAS: Worcester County, Mass., Papers, 1675–ca. 1954, Tax Lists 1781, 1791, box 1, folder 2; Worcester County Valuation Records, oversize vol. 2.

though perhaps fewer than farmers might have wished – by serving as agricultural laborers.[6]

Even those who owned the commercial, processing, and handicraft businesses in these towns often engaged in agriculture. "There is scarcely a township in New England," runs a traveler's description from the early 1800s, "which has not a complete set of grist mills and saw mills."[7] As Table 1.1 indicates, Dudley and Oxford had sixteen such establishments by 1801, along with tanneries, potash works, fulling mills, and, under the rubric of "shops," a trip-hammer works and several stores and taverns, as well as nail-making and blacksmith establishments.[8] The increasing difficulty residents probably faced in securing property during these years helps explain why, taking both towns together, such enterprises increased even more during the next decade: Men unable to farm turned to milling or retailing. But often these ventures represented only partial detours from husbandry, for almost half the local craftsmen, millers, and merchants were also landholders – sometimes substantial landholders – seeking to augment their farming incomes. So, too, the three or four figures who served these towns as doctors and lawyers were actually farmer-lawyers, farmer-doctors, and sometimes farmer-doctor-shopkeepers.[9] In sum, nonagricultural occupations commonly existed as callings hyphenated to farming and were pursued as demands of husbandry permitted.

If agriculture remained the economic and vocational centerpiece of Dudley and Oxford, the centerpiece of agriculture was the family farm. Laboring on holdings averaging just under one hundred acres, the typical yeoman household contained between five and six people, occasionally including male and female servants but most often embracing simply a husbandman and his wife and children.[10] On this land, with these labor resources, farmers raised their crops: some fruit and garden vegetables, as well as rye, oats, barley, Indian corn, and (the most rapidly growing sector of their output) hay and dairy products. Besides cows, farmers kept pigs, horses, and oxen – the last two providing the work animals used in the fields of these communities.[11]

The crops and livestock they raised, coupled with a persisting jack-of-all-trades ability to fashion and repair at least some of their own tools, permitted yeomen to satisfy many of their own basic requirements.[12] Yet it would be misleading to view these residents as self-sufficient. Although voluntary societies were still almost entirely unknown in Dudley and Oxford,[13] family farms drew support from an array of extrahousehold connections. Kinship, for example, frequently linked noncohabiting Dudley and Oxford residents: Perhaps one-fifth of the local residents had relatives living elsewhere in the same township.[14] More generally, customary forms of cooperative labor brought town residents – both kin and nonkin – together in undertakings no single individual or household could accomplish. Rural Yankees of this period still collaborated in "berrying parties in the dull days of July...and...the long round of husking-bees" in the fall. They still "helped" each other during the busy harvest and planting seasons. And they still gathered for communal – and often highly raucous – house-raisings, singing as they heaved the timbers into place:

> Some oak and some pine,
> Some coarse and some fine,
> Some old and some new,
> Hand on the bottle – and that will do![15]

Finally, there were commercial transactions. As indicated by the presence of rented estates on the tax rolls, some inhabitants in these communities stood as landlords and mortgage holders to other townsmen. Far more pervasive, however, was the growing profusion of trade connections that crisscrossed these townships. One need go no further than the swelling list of mills, stores, and handicraft shops to realize that although husbandry continued to undergird life and labor, and although yeomen still needed little assistance in satisfying many needs, farmers had developed a solid reliance on "purchased" goods and services.

Storekeepers were pivotal in this developing commercial nexus. Often ranking among the more wealthy local citizens, usually building their trading careers atop substantial landholdings, merchants in Dudley and Oxford began importing items from coastal entrepôts at least as early as 1790. Through the next twenty years men like David Nichols of Dudley and James Butler, Andrew Sigourney, and Samuel Campbell of Oxford stocked such goods as tobacco, molasses, salt, rum, nails, snuff, shoes, books, and mirrors, and traded them for money or, as was more common, given the scarcity of currency in the postrevolutionary hinterland, crops and pledges of labor. These were the usual transactions. But it was not unknown for shopkeepers to rent out horses (by the trip), provide pasturage (by the month), and merge retailing with services like shoe repairing and sawmilling. Nor was it unknown for farmers in this period to run short of staples during the winter and so turn to stores for grain and meat as well as "city goods."[16]

On occasion, the exchange broadened into textiles. Because flax and wool were readily obtainable in the northern hinterland of the era, and because most Dudley and Oxford families owned flax and woolen spinning wheels as well as handlooms, a significant portion of local residents produced its own yarn and linsey-woolsey.[17] Indeed, using local carding facilities to help clean the raw fibers for spinning and local fulling mills to wash and shrink woven fabric, many households could turn out their own homespun clothing. Nonetheless, as early as the 1790s, families lacking spinning wheels and looms relied either on "store-bought" cloths produced by skilled urban weavers or on itinerant journeymen weavers passing through the countryside. And by 1810, even households that successfully clothed themselves by their own hand were turning to stores for some of the yarn they required or for supplementary products like ribbons and fancy stockings. Other families, discovering they could produce more yarn and cloth than they required for themselves, were trading the surplus for other enticing products filling local stores.[18]

There are seeds here for what happened later. The mounting frequency with which local residents were involving themselves in commercial and handicraft ventures, the increasing tendency of residents, including farmers, to rely on the marketplace for various goods and services – all this prefigures the role nonagricultural enterprises were to play in Dudley and Oxford after 1810. But all this also prefigures a critical tension that would arise between ensuing economic changes and entrenched community mores. After 1810 important elements of local economic developments – particularly the development of local textile mills – would be fueled by profit. But profit, although scarcely unknown among colonial and postrevolutionary Yankees, was not the polestar most Dudley and Oxford residents were accustomed to follow.

Certainly local yeomen demonstrated another perspective in the years before 1810. Like husbandmen throughout New England, farmers in these communities were undoubtedly familiar with the view that producing for a market (in the words of an early eighteenth century pamphlet) "animates the Farmer; keeps him to his Plough ...and makes him look Fat and Cheerful." But, however often they had begun "selling" foodstuffs and domestically fashioned dry goods to nearby storekeepers, Dudley and Oxford yeomen in the 1790s and early 1800s were by no means relying exclusively on "cash crops" or surplus cloth for their income. On the contrary, those involved in agriculture in this period retained the pattern – widespread in the Northeast throughout the colonial period – of orienting their labor as much around domestic consumption and production for use as around commercial gain.[19]

This posture, in turn, reflected two compelling pressures. There was, first, the continuing sensitivity of farming people to deeply rooted Anglo-American fears of "corrupt" dependency and to the attendant notion – voiced most compellingly by Thomas Jefferson but echoed by rural ideologues after him – that total reliance "on the casualties and caprice" of the market could rob even yeomen of their independence.[20] There was, second, the weight of practical factors. As they surveyed their hilly and decreasingly fertile fields, many Yankee husbandmen must have wondered whether they could ever produce sufficient marketable produce to support their families. Then too, in central and western Massachusetts, farmers could personally recall that grim moment in the mid-1780s when the whole fiscal and commercial structure of the Commonwealth seemed to conspire against them. An eastern-dominated legislature had simultaneously raised taxes and demanded payments in hard currency, thus presenting yeomen with imposts they could not pay. Authorities had pushed hundreds of foreclosures through the courts, the whole hinterland had crackled with resentment, and finally Daniel Shays had commenced his "Rebellion" – with Oxford as a center of his struggle in Worcester County.[21] Tempers had cooled considerably by 1810; in fact, by squeezing some yeomen off their farms and into commercial and handicraft ventures, the crisis had actually propelled local residents further into the market. But the economic terrain of Massachusetts still appeared precarious; and those who remained husbandmen were wary of viewing themselves entirely as businessmen. Scarcely self-sufficient in any literal sense, farmers nonetheless continued to labor as much to meet the "test of family need" as to maximize profit in the marketplace.[22]

Even residents whose interests extended into nonagricultural activities were not single-mindedly devoted to profit. Thus, throughout the colonial period and into the early 1800s, those who used local streams to power their grist-, saw-, fulling, and carding mills had by all indications succeeded in respecting the needs of their neighbors sufficiently to avoid extensive conflicts. It might well have been otherwise. Millers usually had to construct dams to generate the currents necessary to turn their waterwheels, and dams might have caused flooding upstream, blocked the flow of water downstream, and generally provoked community resentment over the violation of customary riparian usages. In practice, however, the situation was more calm. For one thing, the impact of any inconveniences caused by water-using artisans was softened by public awareness of the useful service the mills provided the community. Just as important, the mills did not turn so continuously, nor were the dams so substantial that significant hardships were likely.[23] The rivers were treated as a common good, and millers did not permit their desire for gain to outweigh their sense of riparian mutuality.

Comparable patterns had developed around credit. On the one hand, because cash was scarce and because more common currencies of labor and crops were subject to the seasonal rhythms of farming, owners of the stores and workshops that had sprung up in these communities had to place customers on accounts running on for months, years, even lifetimes. Indeed, by the early nineteenth century nearly one-quarter of the total assessed value of probated estates in Dudley and Oxford was tied up in debt, and at death nearly three-quarters of all local inhabitants had creditors.[24] There are even signs that within this system of extended borrowing shopkeepers served as informal bankers, by loaning out small amounts of cash they had managed to accumulate, for example, or "discounting" debts between neighbors by permitting creditors to purchase goods up to the amount they were owed and accepting pledges of payment from the debtors.[25]

On the other hand, it is significant that credit was extended readily and that legal action against delinquent debtors – although increasing through the early 1800s – was by no means as common or punitive as during the "great numbers of actions" preceding Shays' uprising.[26] Nor should it be overlooked that those providing credit and cash in these towns did so free of interest. Or that cash itself – when it was used – acquired value mainly in the context of specific transactions and hence served only fleetingly as an abstract medium to count up and hoard.

In sum, there were limits to what people could or would do for gain. This is not to suggest that prosperity was unimportant to local residents. Doing well was an ambition common among inhabitants who confined themselves to farming as well as those who were involved in nonagricultural activities. Indeed, the eagerness of some inhabitants to explore new ways to reach affluence would provide a further bridge to the business expansion soon to grip Dudley and Oxford. But the values and priorities that dominated before 1810 – and that continued in varying ways to color the life of these townships in succeeding decades – did not allow the balance sheet to rule. Under these norms, preserving an exchange of goods and services counted as much as accumulating wealth.

This ethos did not, of course, preclude stratification. More than half the residents of Dudley and Oxford had holdings worth less than the average per capita valuation in their community – and this does not include the ten to twenty elderly citizens, widowed mothers, and fatherless children each town annually supported as paupers. At the other end of the scale, both Dudley and Oxford contained a recognized economic elite of large landholders and landholder-merchants, of whom the richest 10 percent controlled nearly one-third of the total real and personal property in their townships. These were people like Aaron Tufts and Thomas Learned of Dudley or Abijah Davis, Jeremiah Kingsbury, Jonathan Davis, and the storekeeper-farmer Andrew Sigourney of Oxford – people who often owned several hundred acres of land, who had large houses and (a sure mark of early nineteenth century affluence) drove carriages. Such wealthy individuals stood out all the more sharply, moreover, because upward economic mobility was sluggish by the early 1800s. Nearly three-quarters of those inhabitants remaining in Dudley and Oxford between the 1798 and 1815 enumerations experienced either no economic improvement or outright decline.[27]

But what must be stressed are the limited consequences of this inequality. A salient characteristic of postrevolutionary Dudley and Oxford – and a cause of considerable friction amid the changing economic landscape of later years – was that affluent citizens enjoyed only limited leverage over the less wealthy. In the first decade of the nineteenth century, a rich man might well be creditor to residents less well off. But where borrowing was so common and defaults both rare and relatively painless, the rich did not fuse into a discrete, coercive class of creditors. Wealthy citizens commonly had debts as well as debtors; middling and poor yeomen held IOUs as well as mortgages;[28] and few creditors, whatever their economic position, were inclined to do more than badger recipients of their loans.

Nor did wealth typically yield the authority of an employer, for prior to 1810 no enterprise in either Dudley or Oxford required a large, full-time labor force. The more substantial landholders may have hired agricultural laborers to assist them. And some shopkeepers and millers may have used employees or (less often) apprentices. But the overall number of such helpers was probably fairly small; and if the pattern typical in rural New England was followed locally, such servants – whether or not formally indentured – were treated as part of their masters' families.[29] In brief, there was no way – no continuing, established institutional structure – through which wealth was translated into domineering economic power.

III

Describing this economy is easier than labeling it.[30] A setting in which commercial transactions were growing steadily more common but the imperatives of commercial capitalism were not yet entirely in the saddle – such a setting was neither "precommercial" nor "commercial." The compromise notion of "semicommercial" is perhaps more accurate but scarcely hints at the complex relationships spun out among residents of communities like Dudley and Oxford by the opening decades of the nineteenth century. In the end, however, specifying an optimal rubric is less important than identifying the situation prevailing by 1810: an advancing market economy still constrained by widely held, traditional community norms. Indeed, this pattern ramified far out into local society in the years before the coming of the mills, deeply conditioning habits and rhythms of daily life – and so, willy-nilly, shaping the milieu within which the industrial order would unfold.

Consider the clothing people wore. On the one hand, Dudley and Oxford inhabitants were using increasing numbers of store-bought ribbons, buckles, and shoes. On the other hand, the dress of early nineteenth century rural Yankees remained largely homemade and hence largely based on eighteenth-century precedents. Thus at work most men wore long, coarse linen shirts and homespun trousers or breeches; away from labor, their costume might include breeches, long frock coats, and, among the well-to-do perhaps a waistcoat. Women commonly dressed in corset-bodices, jackets, and skirts with linen, often brightly colored, aprons.[31]

And so with food. By 1811 the marketplace was providing access to spices, sweets, and rum; and it was also ensuring that bread and meat were eaten year round. But the essentials of rural diet still followed from colonial habits: milk, butter, cheese, rye bread, pork, beef (often served in stews), potatoes – a substantial but bland selection varied only by fruit, green vegetables, squash during summer and fall, and a good deal of hard liquor.[32]

Nor was the pattern absent from basic work processes. The spread of small milling operations throughout Dudley and Oxford inevitably exposed local inhabitants to a variety of waterpowered technologies. But except for Oxford's wool-carding shop (which went up in 1806), some examples of virtually all the handicraft, trading, and milling ventures extant in 1810 were present in the two towns by 1750. Their increasing number during the 1790s and early 1800s did not alter the kind of work they required:[33] In all these establishments, it was work performed alone or in small groups, with a minimal division of labor, not continuously but as the need arose.

As for agricultural labor, the late eighteenth and early nineteenth centuries, probably reflecting the increasing penetration of the market, witnessed a rising emphasis on productivity. To offset the smaller landholdings falling to many yeomen after 1750, for example, postrevolutionary farmers brought larger proportions of whatever fields and meadows they did own into active use.[34] And to offset the declining fertility of their long-used soil, they adopted certain reforms touted by agricultural pundits of the era: planting upland meadows with nitrogen-fixing English hay, for example. Because of these shifts, the overall agricultural output of Dudley and Oxford held fairly steady during the first decade of the nineteenth century.[35]

But the persisting themes of farm labor were more striking. Like husbandmen throughout New England, Dudley and Oxford farmers almost certainly continued to plant corn by the arduous hill technique, harvest hay with a scythe, and use the wooden plough familiar to their fathers. And by every indication, they ranked among yeomen still criticized by commentators for "insufficient manuring, the want of a good rotation of crops; and slovenliness in cleaning the ground." Equally important, the distribution of tasks within the farming household remained unaltered. For help outdoors, a husbandman still called on those of his sons strong enough for adult labor, joined (if the farmer was wealthy) by one or two servants hired for the year. Except possibly at the height of harvests, women rarely worked in the fields. In 1810, as in the very earliest years of these townships, wives joined daughters and young children in chores within and around the house: cooking, cleaning, sewing, and most of the spinning and weaving.[36]

But perhaps the most pervasive example of received mores' limiting the scope of change is found in the way these communities experienced time. Clearly there had been some change here: In 1717 Oxford was content to indicate that its town meeting would "continue...til one hour after sundown"; by the mid-eighteenth century both communities scheduled their meetings with more specific clock reckonings. "The Inhabetence of [Dudley] to meet and assembel...Wensday...at eight of the clock in the morning."[37] Just as significant, the increasingly dense quilting of commercial transactions, and the proclivity to pay for goods and services acquired in these transactions with labor, encouraged some effort to relate time with labor. Thus by the 1790s, local storekeepers accepted as "payments" labor by the day (pegging its value as a shilling and a sixpence in 1796); by the early 1800s they accepted "payments" of a third or even a quarter of a day's work time; and by 1810 both Dudley and Oxford were paying for some road work by the hour.[38]

But beneath this increasing precision, older, broader rhythms still controlled. The passing of seasons, for example, was crucial in communities that remained so heavily involved in agriculture. Spring still meant planting. It still meant beginnings of all kinds: A half century after calendar reforms had made January the first of the twelve months, New England townships persisted in commencing their fiscal and political years in March and April.[39] Summer called for steady, though generally unstrenuous, work – except in July when all available hands turned out to harvest hay. Other crops were gathered toward the end of September and into October, making these weeks perhaps the most hectic of the farming year.

Winter was more relaxed. This was the time when boys who worked alongside their fathers in other seasons might join their teen-age sisters in "winter school," or when they might be dispatched to live with a merchant or an artisan (not necessarily local) for training in a business or a craft – usually with the hope that they would return for spring planting. This was also the time when husbandmen were especially given to essaying nonagricultural ventures.[40] But, according to some contemporary observers, November-to-April was above all the period when yeomen did nothing but rest – a sharp criticism, given the persisting Protestant convention that idleness promoted bad habits. Indeed, it was probably nervousness about wintertime leisure that fostered a curious concern about joblessness in the region. Although few rural Yankees suffered outright unemployment, and although farmers of the region often complained of shortages among agricultural laborers, some postrevolutionary commentators worried that New England contained growing cadres of underemployed citizens: men who preferred "tavern-haunting, tippling, and gambling" to steady work.[41]

Within this progression of seasons, the yearly cycle was marked off by established holidays. Christmas was still not celebrated in Puritan New England. But there was no hesitancy in observing Thanksgiving as "the great festival" of the region, and by 1810 postrevolutionary celebrations of Independence Day and the battles of Lexington and Concord had joined the traditional autumn market and militia-training days to punctuate the calendar.[42]

But the most frequent hiatus in normal activities came on the sabbath. Following English Puritan tradition, this was a time, beginning Saturday evening and running through Sunday dusk, intended exclusively for meditation and churchgoing. The custom was evidently respected by most Yankees into the early nineteenth century: Timothy Dwight – surely the most pious of New England's many observers in this period – reported that in Providence "we saw a few carts entering the town [on Sunday] but were informed . . . that the inhabitants were strongly, as well as generally, opposed to this indecent intrusion." But there were exceptions. In Provincetown Dwight found weak souls using the sabbath for "visiting and sport," and occasional fines for sabbath-breaking in Dudley and Oxford indicate that the same phenomenon marred the hinterland. More significant, because more difficult to condemn, was that some Yankees found it absolutely necessary to labor on Sunday. "During the seasons of mowing and harvest," Dwight noted, the sabbath was "not unfrequently" given over to work.[43]

This last observation – that farmers occasionally worked through designated days of rest – deserves particular emphasis, for it signals more than moral deviation. It reveals that, despite some indications to the contrary, postrevolutionary New England communities like Dudley and Oxford generally avoided precisely defined, neatly calibrated notions of work time. In the first place, the time allotted to labor often expanded until tasks were completed. The busy planting and harvest seasons provide an obvious example of this, for during these weeks people simply stayed in the fields – into the evening, even into the sabbath – until the job was done. Such elasticity in work time also implied, of course, that little effort was made to govern the pace of labor. Farmers and farm laborers were responsible for setting their own speed; clerks in stores and craft shops may have had somewhat greater supervision, but they too proceeded at roughly their own pace. And even hours explicitly given over to work were interrupted with customary pauses for refreshment: Besides their midday meal, agricultural laborers expected three or four rum grogs every day along with (according to some reports) a "luncheon" before noon and another pause in the late afternoon for coffee with "bread, butter, fruit and fruit pie"; clerks in country stores counted at least on their late-morning rum toddy.[44]

So great, in fact, were the vagaries surrounding work time that in most instances time and work were left only loosely coordinated. Some labor might be purchased by the fraction of a day or the hour. But in communities like Dudley and Oxford, where in 1810 watches and clocks (even one-armed wooden shelf clocks) remained scarce,[45] workers were more often paid by the job than by the time it took to do the job. So Oxford in 1806 paid John Mackwell, a local farmer-carpenter, $1.58 "for repairing the old School House," and three years later it gave Nathaniel Stockwell $1.46 to chop and supply firewood for the same building. When wages were paid by the time spent working, moreover, the unit used was generally large and obvious. Thus teachers were paid by the month, most live-in servants by the year, and few outdoor laborers were employed for less than a "half day."[46]

IV

Grounded in economies expanding only slowly, laced with habits, attitudes, and rhythms still molded largely around customary patterns, everyday existence in Dudley and Oxford in 1810 contained much satisfying predictability. But more needs to be said about the kinds of communities these people believed they inhabited and their feelings toward these communities. Did residency in Dudley and Oxford yield a sustained sense of formal, corporate solidarity? To what degree did people feel loyal to the towns in which they had built their homes?

Probing such questions soon reveals shifts from earlier patterns that were sharper, deeper, and more consequential than changes in other areas of daily life. Dudley and Oxford probably never totally resembled the rigidly stable and unified communities scholars have occasionally tried to locate in colonial New England. But there are indications that three distinct pressures, all rooted in the early years of these towns but gathering momentum during the late eighteenth and early nineteenth centuries, significantly undercut whatever coherence these townships had initially possessed. As a result, even as they continued to share fundamental customs and values, local residents had grown increasingly uncertain about their communal identities. And by 1810 the hold that Dudley and Oxford had over their inhabitants had grown correspondingly uncertain.[47]

In some ways this trend encouraged a social flexibility that contributed directly to the coming economic transformation. But the diminished community coherence Dudley and Oxford evinced in 1810 would also stand in sharp – and ultimately troubling – contrast to the highly centralized, tightly administered, and closely organized social order spawned in some of the establishments soon to appear in these towns. Pointing simultaneously toward and away from what was about to happen, the factors weakening community solidarity are thus crucial features of the local milieu on the eve of industrial development.

One such divisive factor was the geographical separation of local residents. As danger of Indian attacks subsided, and as outlying acres came under cultivation, the initial inclination of inhabitants to live close together began to fade. Small new concentrations arose around the emerging stores and shops, but these establishments were themselves widely scattered. The overall trend – evident at least by 1750 and continuing into the early nineteenth century – was away from any single, obvious residential focus.

The consequences were inevitable. People in outlying areas found it increasingly difficult to comprehend their townships as unified social entities. Gradually acquiring more loyalty toward their immediate neighborhoods than toward their larger communities, some outlivers tried to separate themselves from the common enterprises, even the common citizenship, of their towns.[48] In most cases it was the location of local meetinghouses that fueled these efforts at disengagement,[49] for given the lack of residential concentration a site convenient for some was inevitably inconvenient for others. The problem was not trivial. Throughout the colonial era and well into the 1800s, the white and steepled meetinghouse was vital to rural

Yankee life as the gathering place for both sabbath services and town business. Those who found themselves "remot" from these buildings were thus seriously disadvantaged.

By 1810 Oxford had acquired lengthy experience with the problem. Declaring themselves unacceptably distant "from aney place of Publick worship" in their own town, various residents along Oxford's western boundary had requested the right to be "erected" into the newly formed community of Dudley in 1731, into Charlton in 1755, and into Ward in 1778. But even more corrosive to Oxford's unity was the running feud between residents north and south of the town's central "plain." Toward the middle of the eighteenth century, northerners managed to shift the meetinghouse to their part of town, but this only caused southern residents to grow restive and finally, in the early 1800s, to demand a change. In 1807 southerners – after three separate attempts – convinced a majority of the community's voters "to hold one half of the Town meetings in future" at another meetinghouse closer to their end of Oxford. The compromise eased tensions, but it also effectively prevented either meeting place from providing a continuing communal focus.[50]

Geographical cleavages in Dudley ran as deeply. Within fifteen months of the town's incorporation, its eastern and western contingents were hotly debating the "placeing [of] our meeting house." Calm was secured by locating the building roughly at the community's "senter" but, as in Oxford, disaffections continued. In the late 1790s, western residents joined with inhabitants of eastern Sturbridge and southwestern Charlton (the last group including families that had split from Oxford forty-two years earlier) in petitioning the general Court to be "set off [as]. . . a new Town." Fearing the loss of tax revenues and real estate if the westerners left, the rest of Dudley issued a strong remonstrance – passed "unanimously (Excepting 3)" – and defeated the secession movement. But the disgruntled minority continued their petitions, and eventually the General Court gave in. In 1816 the legislature voted that the township of Southbridge should be carved out of Charlton, Sturbridge, and westernmost Dudley – a decision demonstrating in the most graphic manner possible how geographical distance could undermine communal unity.[51]

But for some Dudley and Oxford residents, the divisive resonance of meetinghouses resulted from their sectarian connotations as well as their locations. In both townships the largest religious group, and for many decades the denomination most thoroughly entwined in local civic affairs, was the Standing Order of Congregationalists.

From the beginning of these towns and into the late eighteenth century, community taxes paid the salaries of Congregationalist ministers; and community meetinghouses were used for Congregationalist sabbath services. As time passed, however, competing religious loyalties began tugging at Dudley and Oxford, and the privileged place of Congregationalists became controversial.[52]

For Dudley, the initial expression of religious division came early. In 1744 nine community residents – probably responding to reverberations of the Great Awakening – declared themselves Baptists. Though lacking their own church building until 1814, the sect persisted and by the mid-1780s had been joined by other deviants from established Dissent: Quakers, for example, and also "several" persons who rejected orthodox Calvinist teachings on predestined saints and sinners in favor of the so-called Universalist faith in the eventual salvation of all men. Though evidently unaffected by the Awakening, Oxford also hosted Baptists and Universalists by the 1770s and 1780s – the latter group, drawn from "persons of wealth and influence," numbered forty-four by 1788 and had established its own church by 1791.[53]

As theological diversity expanded, non-Congregationalists grew resentful at the customary linkage of town government and the Standing Order. Massachusetts law did, to be sure, permit heterodox members of each community to request exemption from financing Congregationalist preachers, and at least by the early 1790s non-Congregationalists in Dudley and Oxford apparently had their ministerial taxes funneled to their own "societies." But because the town still imposed ministerial levies and because exemptions from funding Congregationalists were often still subject to approval by the Congregationalist majority in town meetings, it is scarcely surprising that local Universalists, Quakers, and Baptists remained dissatisfied. Indeed, even local Congregationalists sometimes fretted at paying taxes to support "the public gospel." Faced with such pressures, and undoubtedly sensitive also to the separation of church and state specified by the new federal Constitution, both townships saw concerted campaigns in the mid-1790s to sever religion from formal community authority.[54]

Dudley took the lead. In 1797 the town meeting of that community concluded that Congregationalists should choose and support their minister entirely through a private "society," like any other denomination. Sixteen years later, Oxford's Congregationalist preacher acknowledged that the "raising of my . . . salary by general taxation . . . seems to have been made the occasion of no small disturbance."

He resigned and in July 1813 – some twenty years before the state
constitution required separation of civil and religious affairs in the
Commonwealth – Oxford followed Dudley in awarding responsibility for the Standing Order to a Congregationalist "society."[55]

By 1815 this de facto disestablishment had soothed the "demon"
of denominational squabbling in both towns. Perhaps also encouraging religious calm was the common vocabulary of folk beliefs
shared by many New Englanders, at least as preliminary responses
to life's imponderables. Thus it was commonly supposed that "there
are 35 Unlucky Days in a Year." And a broad group of Yankees
would have echoed the yeoman who announced "I believe in ghosts,
only a little, just enuff to keep up an assortment." Yet there were
still occasional eruptions of sectarian suspicion. When a school built
by a Dudley Universalist burned in 1816, the proprietor publicly
declared his conviction that the fire had been set by townspeople
offended by his faith. And quite aside from overt antagonisms, the
boundaries between sects remained clear and deep, for some of
these boundaries evidently paralleled other cleavages. The apparent
clustering of wealthy residents among Oxford's Universalists helped
to distinguish this denomination. And there are hints that geography also underscored the line between sects: Oxford's Universalists
apparently lived mainly in the southern part of that town, and Dudley's Baptists were reportedly concentrated in that community's east-
ernmost areas.[56]

But the most powerfully divisive pressure acting upon Dudley and
Oxford was movement. The aggregate number of residents in these
two towns expanded only slowly in the decades after the Revolution: from 2,114 in 1790 to 2,503 in 1810, with each community
consistently contributing about half the total. But this sluggish growth
(which actually included a slight dip in Dudley's population between
1800 and 1810) encompassed levels of transiency that had almost
certainly increased since the mid-eighteenth century and had reached
quite remarkable dimensions by the early 1800s.[57]

To begin with, fully half the household heads living in Oxford in
1810, and 51.5 percent of those living in Dudley during that year,
were not born in these communities: At some point prior to the end
of the nineteenth century's first decade they had arrived from elsewhere.[58] But a more complete measure of local comings and goings
is revealed by comparing individuals listed in two consecutive manuscript federal censuses during this period. The results (Table 1.2) are
fully reliable only for the household heads actually listed in these

Table 1.2. Geographical mobility and persistence of household heads and individuals in Dudley and Oxford, 1800–10

| | Household heads | | | Aggregate arrivals plus departures, household heads | | Estimated aggregate arrivals, plus departures, individuals | |
	1800	1810	Persistence rate, 1800–10	1800–10	As % of household heads, 1800 (aggregate turnover)	1800–10[a]	As % of total population, 1800 (aggregate turnover)
Dudley	194	207	56.7	138	71.1	772.8	62.3
Oxford	218	251	61.9	127	58.3	711.2	57.5
Total	412	458	59.5	265	64.3	1484.0	59.9

[a] Household heads × 5.6 (average household size)
Source: MFCO, MFCD, 1800 and 1810; OVR, DVR.

enumerations. But because most coresiding family members appear to have moved with household heads, it is possible to estimate that roughly 1,500 people – nearly three-fifths of the 1800 aggregate population of both townships – passed through these communities between 1800 and 1810.[59]

And even these figures understate the situation. In the first place, comparing consecutive censuses bypasses the movement of families arriving in 1802, for example, and leaving in 1809. Equally important, the methodology masks the transiency of family members whose household heads remained in place: that children usually traveled with their parents does not mean they stayed put when their parents remained in Dudley and Oxford. Quite the contrary, before their final leave-taking from parental homesteads, New England children of this period commonly spent time away – serving as wintertime clerks or hired hands. As for their definitive exit, it can be estimated that of all sons born between 1780 and 1790 to parents remaining in Dudley and Oxford only about half of those living to maturity ultimately established local residences. The figure obviously ignores the transiency of daughters but offers at least a rough indication of the high rate of youthful movement.[60]

In sum, the early nineteenth century northern hinterland fairly hummed with Yankees passing across the landscape. Even as they railed against weekly treks to overly "remot" meetinghouses, New Englanders had evidently become thoroughly comfortable with less regular, but more extensive, travels. But the magnitude of this transiency makes it no easier to explain. Certainly adult household heads entering and leaving Dudley and Oxford reveal no clear-cut motivation. Newcomers were nearly all yeomen or farmer-craftsmen from nearby Worcester County communities and for the most part were neither rich nor poor. Departing household heads were similar: A few were wealthy, perhaps one-third were needy, but most were of the middling sort, often numbering among the residents with little or no land but typically possessing higher than average personal property valuations.[61]

It was thus dissatisfaction more than destitution propelling household heads to move. Still, the pressures undoubtedly appeared formidable. Amid the uncertain economic currents of postrevolutionary Massachusetts, many in the rural middle classes were easily persuaded to cast about for improved situations. Unhampered by sizable real-estate commitments, families leaving Dudley and Oxford may well have been seeking new, more fertile fields or – just as likely – an available water privilege for a mill or a busy road for a shop.

And so with the immigrants: Some may have arrived searching for more fruitful homesteads; but probably most were also drawn by opportunities – whether certain or suspected – to combine farming with some handicraft or commercial venture.[62]

Among children coming of age in the two communities, however, movement had a different complexion. With this group the central issue was land – or, more precisely, the lack of it. This problem, in turn, reflected two overlapping developments. First, the steady (albeit ultimately slow) population growth of these towns had by the end of the eighteenth century diminished the likelihood that children would inherit real estate. By the 1790s consecutive divisions of homesteads had so reduced family holdings that the average estate yielded property for one heir or at most two.[63]

The second development limiting access of young people to land related to the level of local indebtedness – and here is found the one disruptive consequence of the long-term credit on which Dudley and Oxford so heavily depended. Just over one-tenth (11.1 percent) of estates probated between 1790 and 1810 were insolvent. This meant that all property, both real and personal, was sold at public auction to pay off debts of the deceased. Of the remaining estates, 8.8 percent had so many debts outstanding that, although outright insolvency was avoided, it proved necessary to sell all the land listed in the inventory to satisfy creditors. Nor was this situation restricted to poor families. Ebenezer Learned, who was worth nearly $4,000 when he died in 1801, and William Dudley, whose estate was assessed at $1,123 in 1810, are just two examples of wealthy citizens found to be insolvent. Their children thus joined those of nearly every fifth (19.9 percent) household in Dudley and Oxford receiving absolutely no land from their families.[64]

All this – the shroud of debts covering many estates and the limited acreage of homesteads not engulfed by creditors – severely constrained the transfer of property from parents to children. Most households still found it possible to provide real estate to at least one son or daughter. But the majority of youngsters, and perhaps three-quarters of the sons, reaching maturity in these towns between 1790 and 1810 inherited no property. Of the landless daughters little is known. Of the landless sons, probably about one-third remained, finding work – though rarely much success or security – as agricultural laborers or clerks in one of the small craft or trading shops.[65] But the lack of property, or expectation of property, evidently inclined most young men to seek fortunes elsewhere. Having frequently spent earlier years oscillating between their parents' homes and distant jobs, they were ready upon coming of age to move again: to the frontier, to northeastern cities, or perhaps to just another township down the road. Indeed, for young men, at least, once the adhesive of landownership was removed, moving away became virtually the imprimatur of maturity.

Such, so far as can be determined, was the scope and logic of movement. But what were its effects? As the nineteenth century wore on, pressures on New Englanders to pass through communities like Dudley and Oxford would push some Yankees into entirely new forms of employment, including textile factory work. But more immediately, it seems likely that the exodus of sons from these townships helped raise the price of agricultural labor and produced both an older resident male population and an increasing – though not necessarily continuous – shortage of males of marriageable age. This skewed sex ratio, in turn, when combined with the difficulties nonmigrating young men often experienced in establishing themselves economically, raised the age of first marriage: from 24.4 and 21.6 years for men and women, respectively, between 1755 and 1775 to 26.3 and 22.6 years, respectively, in the twenty years after 1810.[66] More generally, patterns of movement among young people almost certainly loosened parental authority. Children obliged to make their way in the world with little or no economic help from mothers and fathers were bound to feel more independent – psychologically as well as economically – than youngsters receiving substantial inheritances.[67]

Yet such domestic corrosion was only relative. If Dudley and Oxford families had lost some power by 1810, they were still the most important emotional foci in the lives of local residents, the institution through which innumerable lessons, moral and practical, were transmitted across the generations.[68] On balance, transiency was thus probably more disruptive to links between households than to connections among coresidents. Certainly early nineteenth century commentators often fretted about Yankees whose wanderings removed them from the constraints and standards of settled life – and who thus seemingly provided further evidence of New Englanders' lacking steady, reliable jobs. Again Timothy Dwight provides the text. For despite his own wide travelings, this tireless commentator judged men like Connecticut's peripatetic tin peddlers to be "mere wanderers, accustomed to no order, control, or worship." And focusing on poor "labourers" generally, Dwight insisted that, far from demonstrating a purposeful search for better opportunity, the "shiftless" character of such Yankees both proved and explained their lack of wealth.[69]

In time, concern about lumpen "wanderers" would color the attitude of many Dudley and Oxford residents toward chronically unsettled factory employees in their midst. And even in 1810 some version of Dwight's suspicions probably circulated through the townships, making it difficult to form close attachments in a restless population. But transiency was so pervasive, so thoroughly ingrained in the social process, that it had other, even more corrosive implications. For where faces changed so quickly, and where local leaders were as likely as anyone else to have immigrated into these communities from elsewhere,[70] long-term residency ceased to be a compelling criterion for membership in town society. And this in turn, of course, made it more difficult for local inhabitants to regard shared residency in Dudley or Oxford as a distinct, unifying bond.[71] Except for local paupers, whose provenance was checked to ensure their qualification for support, local society was extraordinarily porous and hence devoid of sharp definition. Even the traditional equation between residency and local political participation had become uncertain. After 1805, residency requirements to vote and hold office were routinely reviewed before town meetings. But (except subsequently against millworkers) these rules were usually not enforced. By 1820 no one was particularly upset when Dudley blithely elected to various posts men later found ineligible because of "not having resided in the Town one year."[72]

V

In 1810 Dudley and Oxford still retained examples of community solidarity. The persisting convention of sharing certain jobs, the expanding rhythm of economic exchange, the links between kinsmen, friends, and inhabitants of the same outlying areas of these towns – all this clearly demonstrates the existence of ties among local residents. But it is equally clear that by the early nineteenth century such ties had grown increasingly narrow and fragile. Put simply: The cumulative impact of transiency, sectarianism, and residential dispersal made it harder in 1810 than in 1750 for people to experience Dudley and Oxford as compelling units of community life.

Two ramifications of this development require more detailed attention. The effect of diminished community solidarity on both the organization of public authority and the nature of local political and social hierarchies needs careful scrutiny. Because taken together, early nineteenth century notions of governance and hierarchy comprised another dimension of community life from which certain post-1810 businesses would deviate in noticeable and – to certain eyes – disturbing ways.

As suggested by Dudley's willingness to elect even ineligible residents to town office, the two communities had a broad political constituency. Although women could neither vote in town meetings nor hold positions in local government, most men could do both. The economic standard for participating in town affairs – payment of taxes "equal to two-thirds of a single Poll tax" above a regular "Poll or Polls"[73] was neither strict nor rigorously enforced. Local paupers were, to be sure, prohibited from voting in town meetings, as were, in some cases, residents of Oxford's North and South gores, two sparsely settled tracts under Oxford's jurisdiction but not part of the township proper.[74] The practice of denying South Gore inhabitants full town citizenship would ultimately play a role in a key controversy between Oxford and several local textile mills. In 1810, however, the exclusion appeared as a minor exception in a setting where the majority of adult men were also full-fledged town citizens.

The "Meetings" themselves – "regularly assembled" three or four times a year – undertook numerous activities. Through these civic convocations, townspeople reached out to participate in larger jurisdictions. Thus, they helped elect county officials (like county treasurer), participated in state legislative and gubernatorial elections (tilting heavily toward Federalist candidates), and voted in federal congressional and presidential elections.[75] Through their town meetings residents also levied taxes and organized communal supervision of local economies, annually electing a Sealer of Weights and Measures, for example, along with a Sealer of Leather, and a Sealer of Lumber. In all these ways Dudley and Oxford conformed to accepted notions of the "public interest." But against this activist spirit must be balanced the way the fissures penetrating local society by the early nineteenth century had caused local residents to limit the scope of centralized public authority. The basic bureaucratic mechanisms of community government – systematic maintenance of accurate records, for example – had never been highly developed.[76] But by the early nineteenth century there were clear indications of a weakening central administration. Thus, as already recounted, "support of the gospel" had by 1813 fallen to private societies in both communities. And there were other, equally telling, signs of the trend.

Schooling, for example. Dudley and Oxford had always funded education out of taxes levied on all local residents. By the 1760s, however, both communities had ceased employing a single school-master (passing him among schoolhouses scattered through the towns) and established a system of permanent schools, each in a different section of the community, with each section paying its own teacher from education taxes generated by that section's residents. Although by 1810 each community was electing a townwide committee to monitor its schools, the "district" system inevitably threatened to create wide disparities in the budgets of different local schools. None-theless, this decentralized structure was an entrenched element of civic administration by the end of the eighteenth century.[77]

And so with paupers. In a sense, the poor had always faced decentralized treatment: Nominally under the charge of "overseers" elected at large in the two communities, local indigents had in prac-tice received care from private families to whom the towns paid an annual fee. By 1810, however, this chronic lack of direct, centralized supervision had been accentuated by the towns' "efforts to reduce the cost of their necessary charges." Increasingly concerned only with the expense of poor relief, Dudley and Oxford began in the early nineteenth century to "auction the paupers off to the lowest bidder," which effectively reduced the role of overseers to compar-ing the bids.[78]

Finally, and perhaps most dramatically, the towns reduced their collective commitment to local highways. By 1802, for example, both communities had built upon the precedent of the balkanized school systems by creating self-supporting highway divisions.[79] But then they went further. Although public taxes – whether paid in cash or, as was more likely, in labor – continued to underwrite most road-work, the early and mid eighteenth century notion that taxes should support the whole cost of every road gradually fell away. In its place arose the view that because particular roads often helped particular residents more than others, the common good in no way required subsidizing each highway with public money, even public money raised in the road's own district. Or, to put the position more broadly: It was conventional wisdom by 1810 – in emphatic contrast to the stance several entrepreneurs would subsequently take – that it was not the common good for private individuals to equate their inter-ests with the common good.

Thus emerged a policy of requiring those who "more immediately benefitted" from a road to make larger contributions to its construc-tion and upkeep than other local residents. So Dudley agreed to build a road in 1794 but only "on condition that the persons owning the land where the road passes through promise to Give the Land

and fence the same free from any Expence to the Town." And so Oxford in 1810 voted "to give 50 Dollars to those individuals who are more particularly enterest in [a road] to enable them to fence [it]...the said individuals to be at the Remainder of the Expence."[80] At times none of these stratagems worked. When, for example, the county insisted – in the face of bitter protests from the towns – on the construction of a road that was of no advantage to any particular group of citizens, these communities were obliged to treat the project as a venture to be paid for by all residents.[81] But county roads were rare and by 1810 both Dudley and Oxford typically confronted the expense of highways by distinguishing between public and private interests so as to minimize the involvement of the towns. That done, the largest possible proportion of each project could be charged off to individuals benefiting most directly.

If gradual erosion of community solidarity limited the jurisdiction of formal, central community authority, it also blurred the calibrations of local hierarchies. Unlike the crisply etched rankings around which certain post-1810 enterprises would be organized, demarcations in postrevolutionary Dudley and Oxford had in many cases grown soft and unreliable.

The point of departure here is again town government, for traditionally the office a man held was a fairly clear index of his overall social standing. This was still the case to some degree as the nineteenth century opened, for just as in the early eighteenth century, the forty-odd posts Dudley and Oxford filled in 1810 still conformed to an obvious order. Except for the constables, who received small fees for collecting taxes, no office paid a salary. But those elected as selectmen (to govern between town meetings), as moderators (to chair these meetings), as assessors (to determine local taxes), or as deputies (to represent the towns in the General Court) – these were the men in important positions. The individuals taking these posts, moreover, were drawn from a remarkably narrow band of residents. Whatever its long-term impact on their political perspective, the Revolution did not cause townspeople to effect any sudden widening of their political leaders. Between 1800 and 1810, Dudley and Oxford filled 110 selectmanships with only twenty-eight men, and each town had several selectmen – four in Dudley and three in Oxford – elected six or more terms within this single decade.[82]

Finally, this leadership reflected the economic stratification of the two communities. It was a wealthy leadership. More than three-fifths of the selectmen in Dudley and Oxford between 1800 and 1810 (including all but one of the longest tenured) were in the top quartile of the 1798 tax list, and more than four-fifths were in the top two quartiles.[83] Not all rich men reached high office, of course, and interestingly those who did were almost always husbandmen. Farmers, not merchants or even farmer-merchants, led the towns in these years. But they were rich farmers. Again the names of Dudley's Aaron Tufts and Thomas Learned stand out, along with Oxford's Abijah Davis and Jeremiah Kingsbury, and their kin as well. Three-quarters of Oxford's selectmen between 1800 and 1810 were preceded into that office by an elder brother, a grandfather, or (most often) a father.[84] In sum, there existed a political elite. Along with their cadre of wealthy citizens, and largely coterminous with it, Dudley and Oxford in 1810 hosted a small circle of men for whom leadership in local affairs seemed appropriate.

And yet, in the final analysis, the significance of this elite may be questioned. For just as wealth did not lead to coercive economic power, so holding high civic office in the early 1800s yielded little real political power. The pressures that restricted community identity and the scope of community government, perhaps combined with a postrevolutionary reluctance to defer entirely to any political authority, all tempered obedience to local leaders. The decentralization of town government obviously contributed to this development by curtailing the influence of local officials elected at large. But other signs of diminished authority were also evident. After 1750 top officials found themselves increasingly challenged and criticized in town meetings; and in 1790 Dudley residents, judging it improper for even a leading citizen both to determine and collect community taxes, "voted not to allow" the wealthy and repeatedly elected moderator Jonathan Day "to serve as Constable and assessor." Moreover, in both towns by the late eighteenth century the brief for investigating particular problems went increasingly not to selectmen but to ad hoc committees. Comprised mainly of well-to-do citizens, such committees did not signal a democratization of local politics. However, they did prevent selectmen and other annually elected leaders from monopolizing policy-making responsibilities.[85]

The status of selectmen declined along with their power. Although the position was still honored, the distance separating this office from others in town government had diminished noticeably by 1810. In the 1750s local leaders had often filled other posts while serving as selectmen, but only rarely positions of lower status in the political hierarchy.[86] Between 1800 and 1810, however, more than half the selectmen holding another office – and 32.1 percent of all selectmen in these years – held posts considerably less distinguished than the selectmanship; two, in fact, served as hogreeves to monitor the wanderings of local swine. Nor did their status remain unalloyed after they departed office: More than 40 percent of local selectmen in the early nineteenth century were subsequently elected to an obviously lower position.[87] All told, political office had by 1810 become an unsatisfactory measure of social standing. Serving as selectman was still different from, and better than, serving as hogreeve. But when a man could be both at once, or could progress from leading the town to caring for its pigs, it was difficult to use either position as a barometer of status.

But town government was not the only institution showing signs of blurred rankings by 1810. In earlier years election as a lieutenant or captain in the town militia had represented an unmistakable announcement of overall community respect and confidence.[88] Militia companies still elected their leaders at the beginning of the nineteenth century and, like those commissioned during the Revolution, men thus promoted proudly prefixed their names with the ranks they had won. But unlike revolutionary veterans, militia officers in the early 1800s were undergoing a rapid fall in status.

As townwide commitments became less dense and certain, it grew increasingly difficult to determine collectively who deserved military honors. As a result, election of local captains and lieutenants devolved into the far simpler exercise of choosing men willing to provide drinks on Training Day. But – hardly a surprise – officers selected by this criterion were not always respected. Oxford's Lieutenant Reuben McKnight, for one, met persistent disobedience in 1815. He was later accused of "gross intoxication," which helps account for his troops' ragged performance. But his own view was that "it cost me two Cans [i.e., tankards] a year to treat my men" and that this investment should have brought him obedience. Confronted by men who plainly disagreed, McKnight achieved a magnificent rage: " 'By God if you do not dress [i.e., line up],' " he reportedly screamed at one unruly soldier, " 'I will cut your Horse's head off...By God I will cut your Head off...By the eternal God I will smite you.' " The record suggests that none of this had any effect.[89]

The configuration of church pews had also gone awry. As late as the 1780s, town meetings in Dudley and Oxford still assumed collective responsibility for "seating the Meeting House," and the distance between a resident's pew and the front of the church still expressed the community's conception of his standing. As the towns surrendered their formal involvement with religion, however, they also surrendered control over the churches and thus over the right to correlate seats and status. Since the private denominational societies did not pick up the responsibility, it was left for each individual to determine where he sat, and before long there had emerged an ongoing trade, even a speculation, in pews. Citizens bought these long wooden benches, or fractions of them, held them for a while, sold them for a profit, and used their gains to advance themselves by buying new pews nearer the front.[90] So Jonathan Harris styled himself "yeoman" when he bought Samuel Campbell's pew in 1807; Campbell, on the other hand, was a "gentleman," a term hitherto reserved for wealthy and prominent residents. By 1809, for no apparent reason other than his possession of a "gentleman's" pew, Harris also had adopted this title, in effect unilaterally announcing a social transition that formerly only the community as a whole could have certified.[91]

Where emblems of status changed so rapidly, however, their meaning inevitably grew less precise. Townspeople could not always keep pace with dignities claimed by their neighbors. Was a man a "yeoman" or a "gentleman"? The bills of sale for the pews reveal occasional outright bafflement – as in an 1802 transaction in which a certain Nathaniel Whitmore proudly labeled himself "gentleman" on his half of the agreement but was described more humbly as "blacksmith" by the man whose pew he was purchasing. The terms – and the rankings they denoted – evidently often held little more than idiosyncratic meaning.[92]

To some extent, wealth filled the vacuum created by this confusion. Prominent New Englanders had always been well off, but throughout most of the colonial period affluence was merely one of several attributes – education, for example, and piety – that leading citizens were expected to possess. By the late eighteenth century wealth had emerged as the mark of eminence outweighing all other considerations. Certainly it is clear that Abijah Davis, a frequently elected selectman and deputy in Oxford, owed his standing primarily to wealth. He was the town's eighteenth richest resident in 1798; he was also, if the scrawled "X" on his will is any proof, thoroughly illiterate.[93]

But in the end, the eminence wealth could bring was curiously inconclusive. The rich were visible, known, and respected. But the credentials of status following from money – a good pew or high rank in the militia – were of uncertain value. Unable to translate itself into direct, coercive economic power or potent political authority, wealth proved equally incapable of yielding definitive emblems of communal honor. And as the connections blurred between these key elements of the social order – wealth, status, economic and political power – the very notion of prominence grew problematic.

VI

New England townships were never static. By 1810 life in Dudley and Oxford had already shifted in important, often stressful ways from patterns evident during the first days of these communities. But after 1810, with the emergence of both new quantities and new kinds of nonagricultural enterprises, the story took a different turn.

Change continued. And all post-1810 change was to some degree linked to – indeed, built upon – structures and trends embedded in the earlier history of these townships. But as the nineteenth century wore on, there also emerged, scattered through the communities, examples of unprecedentedly rapid and profound innovation. Confronted by these new kinds of alterations, buffeted by their consequences, and struck by the greater *degree* of difference they revealed, residents of Dudley and Oxford gave greater attention to what seemed familiar. Fluid though it was, the social order as it existed in 1810 – and as it persisted into the antebellum period, shaping many areas of community life and work in counterpoint to the examples of heightened innovation – took on the gravity and coherence of custom.

Cotton and woolen mills contained the most dramatic instances of such novelty. For in the factory villages that began to appear during the second and third decades of the nineteenth century, the structure of social relationships, as well as the rhythm and content of daily labor, was fundamentally different from the social structure that existed in other, less rapidly changing local workplaces. And there was also in the mill villages a more centralized, dense, and extensive system of governance and a more firmly hierarchical linkage of wealth, status, and power than in the towns as a whole either in 1810 or in the generation that followed. It was the weight of these differences – these gaps between textile manufactories and customary forms of labor and community life that lingered outside these compounds – that would ultimately create problems. Exacerbated by broad cultural anxieties and specific personal hostilities, these differences would in time yield significant antagonisms and conflicts.

In 1810, of course, residents of Dudley and Oxford did not foresee the coming of the mills or the tensions these factories would generate. But neither did these people have long to wait before the drama began.

2   *Samuel Slater, textile mills, and a new economic landscape*

I

The first textile mill built in either Dudley or Oxford failed. In February 1812, after seven months of planning and construction, the Merino Wool Factory of Dudley began turning out broadcloth. The mill represented the investment of five local residents, including the wealthy and frequently elected selectman Aaron Tufts. Unfortunately for these men, it also represented an unlucky gamble. The factory was hit badly by the depression of 1816 and (according to local chronicles) "lost all its original capital."[1]

But the way had been opened. At one time or another in the two decades after 1810, some twenty textile mills went up in Dudley and Oxford. In 1832 alone the two townships contained more than a dozen manufactories, including one whose leading investor and administrator – undeterred by his earlier failure – was Aaron Tufts.[2] And with the coming of the mills – at once promoting and promoted by their arrival – local nontextile businesses also expanded. In the twenty years after the Merino Mill started operation, the economic landscape of these communities was deeply and irrevocably recast.

To consider how the transformation came about, it is necessary to look both inside and outside the two townships, for post–1810 economic changes were rooted in both the dynamics intrinsic to the social order of the communities and in factors beyond local, or even national, horizons.

Certainly any manufactory taking shape in these towns possessed an extensive provenance. The waterpowered textile factories that so profoundly altered local life drew upon and reflected a history of "perpetual" machine spinning that began in England in the mid-eighteenth century and opened its American chapter in the 1790s. More specifically, the mills of Dudley and Oxford drew upon and reflected the career of Samuel Slater. For Samuel Slater – the "Arkwright of America," the famous British immigrant who helped introduce waterpowered spinning into the United States – was also responsible for several of the largest, most successful, and most long-lasting cotton and woolen factories to appear in these townships.[3]

The textile industry would have achieved an enduring presence in Dudley and Oxford even if Slater had not appeared on the scene; such was the momentum toward economic expansion operating both throughout the region and within these communities. But Slater's arrival made a difference. It provided a direct, personal link between the rise of local manufactories and the overall growth of textile manufacturing in the United States – and so adds special luster to developments within these communities. And Slater's presence also contributed to the specific shape of post-1810 events in the two towns. With significant interests in both communities, Slater was a figure whose priorities, even whimsies, inevitably affected the face of local industrialization. It thus becomes important at the outset to establish who this man was – to identify his ambitions, his antipathies, his inclinations – by the time (very soon after Tufts and company began planning the Merino Mill) he began buying property in Oxford's South Gore.

II

Samuel Slater's career started twice. The first time was in England during the early 1780s when he joined the well-known cotton-mill owner Jedediah Strutt as a 15-year-old management apprentice. The berth was available because Strutt had befriended Samuel's father, William Slater, an Anglican yeoman of middling wealth and prospects residing in the Derbyshire town of Belper. As a result of this friendship, as well as his own need for administrative assistance, the wealthy factory master had offered to train one of Slater's sons at his mill in nearby Milford. Father William chose Samuel – and then precipitously died, obliging the boy to sign his own indenture papers when he presented himself to Strutt in January 1783.[4] The six-year apprenticeship that followed proved crucial to Slater, for it instilled the basic knowledge and attitudes that he would bring to the New World – attitudes that would become points of departure for all his American ventures.

His apprenticeship taught him, first of all, about the mechanics of waterpowered cotton spinning. The technology in Strutt's Milford cotton mills, where Slater spent his days, was organized around machines developed by Richard Arkwright, the itinerant Lancashire hair peddler-turned-inventor whose work Strutt had begun financing in the early 1770s. Consisting of waterpowered preparatory and spinning devices, the Arkwright machines distinguished the Strutt mills from establishments (both private homes and small "factories") still turning out yarn by hand-powered spinning wheels or by their successor, the spinning jenny. Appearing in the early 1760s, jennies were an elaboration of the spinning wheel that permitted the operation of several spindles simultaneously. But although jennies dramatically increased productivity, they were obliged to pause between different phases of their operation and thus could not be harnessed to continuous power sources like running water. Moreover, the jenny turned out a soft yarn suitable only for the weft (horizontal threads) in woven cloth. By contrast, Arkwright's "water frame", and the preparatory machines operated with it, ran continuously and produced yarn suitable for both weft and warp.[5] Weaving itself was still a hand process, and Strutt's only direct connection with cloth production was to distribute some "webs" of yarn to outlying hand-loom weavers scattered around his works.[6] Still, the broad utility of water-frame yarn was a significant selling point for the new machine.

When running correctly, Arkwright's technology required little strength to operate. Although men were needed as machinists and supervisors, women and children could "tend" virtually every apparatus used to produce cotton yarn by water. But if most factory berths were physically unstrenuous, they were still not easy to fill. On the contrary, acquiring an adequate labor supply was a continuously difficult task for early English mill masters, and observing how Strutt approached the problem was the second major lesson of Slater's apprenticeship.

The central issue here was that early cotton factories evoked deep suspicion and resentment. Most obviously, they represented a direct threat to "handworkers" still earning their livelihoods with spinning wheels and jennies. In 1779 such laborers had actually attacked a Lancashire mill owned by Strutt and Arkwright (among others), and there is evidence that handworker-fueled antipathies ran deeply in Derbyshire as well.[7] No less important, however, were concerns focusing on the novel disciplines imposed by early manufactories. The batteries of machines used by textile mills had to begin and end their daily operations simultaneously, which meant that employees tending the machines had to begin and end their daily labors in a punctually uniform manner. Thus, in sharp contrast to the natural rhythms and customary pauses that – in England as in southern Massachusetts – characterized preindustrial rural labor, textile managers stipulated from the outset that work in the mills would be organized strictly around the clock. Specifically, factories required a six-day week of twelve-hour days all year round, with each day embracing lengthy, continuous work periods.[8] "She went then at six o'clock in the morning" runs a report on a Strutt employee during the 1780s: "Breakfast was brought into the mill about seven o'clock; which she took standing. Worked till twelve o'clock, which was dinner time. Had dinner at home:...worked till seven in the evening and then went to home."[9] And finally, the techniques used by early mill masters to enforce discipline – including punctuality – in their factories were deemed particularly repugnant. The system of room overseers, fines, blacklists, and occasional beatings called to mind all too readily the loathed regimen of late eighteenth century parish poorhouses.[10]

So it was (as contemporary observers reported) that "the more respectable part of the surrounding inhabitants were at first averse to seeking employment in the [textile] works." And (as employers reported) those who did enter the "works" were commonly of such "loose and wandering habits" that they failed to fulfill the twelve-month engagements typically required by the mills.[11] Yet despite all this, Strutt's Milford and Belper mills – by all accounts "multi-storied buildings with 300 or 400 workers apiece"[12] – managed to secure the hands they needed.

Some recruits were probably pauper apprentices ("parish apprentices" as they were termed) delivered up by local officials. There were likely a few others, as Slater himself exemplified, who were taken on as nonindigent apprentices. Generally, however, Strutt preferred free wage laborers (whom he could hire and dismiss as need arose) over bound laborers (whom he could not). Of these wage-earning employees, a number arrived with no kin. But intrigued by the comparatively cheaper "price" of even well-paid child labor, Strutt also hired whole households, especially those with numerous youngsters. And all these workers – unattached and family, adult and child – he drew from far and near (from the poor nail-making neighborhoods of Belper and Milford, for example) by offering good wages and, even more significantly, an "enlarged benevolence and active philanthropy."[13]

Thus, inspired by the communities that eighteenth-century iron masters and coal owners had occasionally built for their workers, Strutt constructed "neat and comfortable cottages" for his operatives. Inspired more generally by the paternalistic sensibilities that had long conditioned relations between the powerful and less powerful in rural England, he organized fetes, during which he distributed food ("a sheep...roasted whole") and drink, all the while permitting "much Festivity." Following the example of his associate Arkwright, Strutt probably also arranged for fathers lacking berths inside the mills to be given outdoor jobs or have "Trades taught them." And finally Strutt took responsibility for the secular and divine education of his hands. By 1783 this dissenting Protestant mill master had equipped his Milford village (as well as his enclave in Belper) with a Unitarian chapel; several years later he invested the compound with a Sunday school. By introducing these latter institutions and insisting that his child workers attend them, Strutt effectively provided instruction for younger operatives without intruding into the six-day workweeks of his mills. Given their broad pedagogical responsibilities, it is not surprising that his Sunday schools taught reading and writing. No less significant, however, was their promulgation of the Protestant virtues of hard work, temperance, punctuality, and self-discipline, which thus permitted Strutt to link workplace discipline with Protestant notions of moral amelioration.[14]

Slater observed all this, and it became a vital part of the baggage he transported to the New World. But that baggage also contained the third lesson he had acquired from Strutt: the conviction that industrialists should exercise as much personal control as possible over their affairs. As Slater's own apprenticeship reveals, early manufacturers occasionally groomed nonrelatives as assistants. But deep suspicions persisted among late eighteenth century English businessmen regarding the reliability of managerial deputies, and factory masters thus typically retained direct supervisory authority or relied on close relatives. Consequently, even as he trained Slater, Strutt mobilized his sons, his wife, his brother-in-law, and at least one daughter to help run the family ventures. And he himself maintained almost uninterrupted daily contact with his establishments.[15]

Along with supervising their own mills, industrialists in a position to do so sought jurisdiction over the market by limiting competition. Richard Arkwright, almost certainly supported by Strutt, tried repeatedly until 1785 to retain monopoly rights over his machines. He failed, and the English textile industry was freed to spread through Derbyshire, Lancashire, and beyond. But given his master's attitude, Slater must have often heard assertions during his apprenticeship that factory spinning would only suffer if multitudes of mills had to battle for customers.[16]

Pressing in from different angles, quite possibly meshing with private temperamental needs to exert as much mastery as possible over his world, the young trainee was deeply affected by Strutt's strivings for control. Once in the United States, Slater would spend several years struggling to forestall the rise of competing mills, and he would never entirely surrender the fear that American manufactories could be ruined by overproduction. Moreover, after about 1800, the organization of his own ventures – including, in time, those in Dudley and Oxford – would reflect abiding efforts to protect his personal proprietary authority. Indeed, the theme of control – getting it, fearing the loss of it, finding ways to keep it – was pivotal during the second, New World phase of Slater's career.

It also explains why this second phase took place. Because, in the final analysis, the reason Slater left England was a desire to strike out on his own in an arena hitherto unexploited by waterpowered spinning. For eight months after his apprenticeship ended – from early January into the first days of September 1789 – the freshly trained young mill manager stayed with Strutt as a salaried supervisor in Milford. Sometime that summer, however, he saw an advertisement reprinted from a Philadelphia newspaper offering a reward to anyone introducing English textile technologies into the United States. This was inducement enough. It is true there were legal hurdles to overcome: Seeking to keep waterpowered spinning an exclusively British capability, Parliament had by this time passed laws prohibiting the export of perpetual machines or the emigration of trained operatives. But to Slater – 21 years old, single-minded, and amply ambitious – such strictures were neither morally compelling nor difficult to circumvent. Telling no one of his plans, disguising himself as a farm laborer, retaining only his apprenticeship papers as proof of his real identity (keeping these documents "concealed," so the story goes), Slater left London for New York in mid-September.[17]

He arrived two months later, as he hoped he would, in a Republic devoid of Arkwright technology. But he was perhaps less pleased to discover – as soon he must have – that many Americans were deeply antagonistic to the very notion of manufactories. New England merchants, for example, quite logically feared that introducing industry into America would reduce purchases of European manufactured goods and hence diminish the trade on which their prosperity rested. And to their objection was coupled the physiocratic outlook still saturating much of the land. The same concerns about "corrupt" dependency that led Dudley and Oxford yeomen to view the market warily led logically to a conviction that all industrial wage laborers, precisely because they depended on wages, were potentially "corrupt." Heightened by rumors of ghastly conditions in some British factories, this generalized anxiety created substantial resistance to textile mills in late eighteenth century America. "While we have land to labor then," ran Thomas Jefferson's famous pronouncement, "let us never wish to see our citizens occupied at a work-bench...For the general operations of manufacture, let our work-shops remain in Europe."[18]

Industry had its advocates, of course, and by the late 1780s and into the 1790s they began to be heard. Men like Alexander Hamilton and the Philadelphian Tench Coxe argued strenuously that industrialization would strengthen American society. Bypassing the Jeffersonian advocacy of minimally commercialized agriculture, such proindustrial ideologues embraced the argument – familiar, if not universally accepted, in colonial America – that yeomen actually needed markets to ensure their prosperity. By providing customers for foodstuffs, factory supporters maintained, manufacturing establishments would thus significantly aid farmers. As the defense of industrialization developed, it was also asserted that factories would aid merchants by generating goods for internal and (possibly) overseas trade. And finally, advocates of industry turned the central Jeffersonian objection on its head by insisting that the country as a whole would never achieve virtuous independence if it continued to depend on Europe for manufactured goods. "Not only the wealth," wrote Hamilton, "but the independence and security of a country appear to be materially connected with the prosperity of manufactures."[19]

This kind of reasoning helped foster the few attempts Americans had made by 1789 to organize textile factories. The net results of these various experiments, however, had been meager: a few jenny mills, usually dependent on local or state subsidies, saddled with indifferent machinery and, like their English counterparts, capable of spinning only weft yarn. Attempts to press further, and, specifically, attempts to reconstruct Arkwright's technologies, had failed completely,[20] which, of course, was why the Philadelphia advertisement offered to reward anyone capable of operating such machines.

Perhaps the American most thoroughly frustrated by this national inability to spin by waterpower was the wealthy Rhode Island merchant and manufacturer Moses Brown. Descended from a distinguished family of Providence Baptists, a convert to Quakerism, a man who had once withdrawn from business to seek "the Most True Peace of Mind," this complex, restless-souled figure had joined his son-in-law and co-Quaker William Almy in the late 1780s to organize jenny-spinning operations "in Different Sellers of Dwelling Houses" scattered throughout Providence. By using linen warps and having their yarn worked into cloth by handloom weavers, the two men produced a highly salable inventory of various fabrics, including corduroy, jeans, and fustians. But this was not enough. Moses Brown's ambition was to reproduce Arkwright's machines, and to that end he purchased several Yankee versions of water frames and tried to make them work. Like all Americans before him, however, Brown's efforts to spin "perpetually" were in vain. In the fall of 1789, convinced his struggle was leading nowhere, he sought outside assistance by initiating a search for someone "who had Wrought" water frames "or seen them wrought in Europe."[21]

He found Slater. The Englishman learned of Brown's quest soon after landing in New York. Letters were exchanged, and instead of heading for Philadelphia (as he had originally intended), Slater traveled north to Pawtucket, a small village just outside Providence, where Brown had gathered the nonfunctioning Yankee experiments. By April 1790 Slater had succeeded in fashioning the first two waterpowered spinning machines to run successfully on this side of the Atlantic.[22]

In view of the mythology that soon surrounded him, it is important to understand what Slater did *not* do. He did not invent. He did not even single-handedly reproduce, from unaided memory, the technology he had known in Strutt's mills. He drew from previous experience, of course, but he relied equally on the talents of local carpenters and ironworkers, as well as on "such parts" of Brown's failed machinery "as would Answer." It should be noted too that other Englishmen more or less familiar with Arkwright's inventions were slipping across the ocean. Sooner or later one of these figures would undoubtedly have built a functioning water frame even if Slater had never left Derbyshire.[23]

Still, it was Slater who did the job. By July 1791 his waterpowered engines were turning out yarn in sufficient volume and of sufficient quality to satisfy his Quaker associates.[24] By October he himself was sufficiently confident of his prospects to take a wife: Hannah Wilkinson, the 17-year-old daughter of a Quaker ironworker with whom he had been boarding.[25] And less than two years later, Slater moved into the Pawtucket Old Mill (as it was subsequently named), built along the rapidly flowing Blackstone River. A small factory by English standards (measuring only 26 by 40 feet and standing only two and a half stories high), the building nonetheless represented the first American structure designed from top to bottom as a "perpetual" textile establishment.[26] The opening of this factory in July 1793 marked the real inauguration of Samuel Slater's American career.

III

It took Slater nearly two decades to cross the thirty miles between the Old Mill and the site of his first factory in Oxford, South Gore, but these years are directly germane to what would later transpire in both Oxford and Dudley. For during this period Slater received what amounted to a second education. If his training under Strutt served as background to all his New World activities, what he experienced – and how he adapted – after 1793 represented the further schooling he would take with him into the Massachusetts hinterland. And because of his influence, his early American experiences would also condition the outlook and policies of many other New England mill masters, including his colleague factory proprietors in Dudley and Oxford.

His New World training began with the Old Mill. Slater shaped this factory. By the time it opened, Moses Brown had retreated into the role of friendly but distant *éminence grise* to the project. In his place stood Obadiah Brown, Moses' son, who joined with Almy and Slater to form the partnership of Almy, Brown, and Slater. The articles of agreement specified that Almy and Brown would supply logistical support to the mill – provide wages for the workers and cotton for the machines – and would retail the finished products. Slater was to bear half the expenses, receive half the profits, and – crucial to a man hungry to control his own shop – exercise full supervisory authority over daily operations of the manufactory.[27]

Not surprisingly, he used his authority to re-create production processes he had known under Strutt. In Rhode Island as in England, manufacturing cotton yarn began outside the mills, among outlying "pickers" who opened and picked clean the raw cotton. Next – again as in Derbyshire – the cleaned cotton was taken inside the factory and fed into carding engines whose water-driven, teeth-covered cylinders turned out strands of cotton called slivers. Slivers were then fed into the "drawing frames," which rendered their strands more even and parallel, and then into "roving" machines, which introduced a slight twist to the fibers. Finally, the bunched, attenuated slivers were attached to water frames, whose rapidly turning bobbins completed the process of twisting by turning the strands tightly around one another.[28] Throughout the Old Mill's early years – indeed, reaching back to 1790–91 – Almy and Brown employed Providence-based handloom weavers to transform some mechanically spun yarn into a variety of cloths. But to escape prohibitive competition with the inexpensive British fabrics that began pouring into American cities during the 1790s, the Old Mill soon relinquished most direct efforts to turn yarn into cloth. By 1796, Almy, Brown, and Slater were selling most of their yarn directly: to storekeepers, to households, and to journeymen weavers willing to battle the English imports.[29]

But as familiar as the machinery Slater used was the rhythm to which he set it running: twelve hours per day, six days per week, week in and week out.[30] So too, structural aspects of the Old Mill labor force followed the Strutt model: The great majority – and by 1796 virtually all – of the operatives in this factory were free wage laborers, many of them attached to families. And because Slater shared his English master's enthusiasm for comparatively cheap child workers, the family laborers were often youngsters.[31]

At the same time, however, the policies Slater implemented in his first American venture also revealed the constraints of its novel setting. They reflected, most notably, the fact that recruiting operatives in the New World was probably even more difficult than in the Old. This was due partly to the continuing pressure of America's comparative labor scarcity. Although late eighteenth century cities probably hosted more chronically underemployed workers than backcountry communities like Dudley and Oxford, prolonged joblessness was rare even in urban centers. Although Moses Brown had speculated that mills might provide work relief for distressed Rhode Islanders, and although Slater apparently hired down-and-out workers ("so many poor children," he would describe them in 1801),[32] the Old Mill could not fill its roster entirely with Yankees driven into industrial berths by long-term unemployment.

To the pressure of labor scarcity was added the active antipathy many New Englanders directed toward Slater's project. With only a few faltering jennies in operation, and with most New England spinning wheels (even those producing occasional marketable surpluses) operating less than full time – with all this as context, the Old Mill scarcely threatened an entrenched population of handworkers. Indeed, some residents of Pawtucket and Providence welcomed the promise of economic growth implied by the enterprise Almy, Brown, and Slater had initiated. But waterpowered cotton spinning also aroused opposition.

Antagonisms arose (as they had in England) because of the troubling novelty of the factory regimen. They emerged also as a logical extension of the physiocratic resistance some Yankees had mounted against building manufactories in the first place. And they arose in Pawtucket with particular ferocity in 1792 and 1793 when Slater and his partners started building a dam across the Blackstone River.

It was very "likely the largest dam yet built in America." In part this was because perpetual spinning technology required both larger and more continuous waterpower than previous New England milling establishments. But it was also because, from the outset, Slater and his mercantile associates set a healthy balance sheet as their principal goal. Unlike some proponents of industrialization who favored factories even if they lost money, the partners owning the Old Mill saw profits as crucial to their efforts – certainly more crucial than bending to received notions of sharing a river with neighbors up and down stream. Because their dam was so clearly intended for private gain, and because it was also linked to an Englishman and thus to connotations of harsh and degrading British industrial conditions, the disruption to established patterns of water usage that it threatened was deeply resented. In the end, the Old Mill proprietors overcame local objections. But this was not before Pawtucket artisans had physically attacked the dam and word had spread far into the countryside of a "war having broken out at Pawtucket."[33]

Taken together, the strands of suspicion and ill will winding through the community could only have hampered Slater's recruitment efforts. An equally serious obstacle, however, was the disruptive and restive spirit evinced even by those entering his factory. Not all Slater's early employees found industrial labor unattractive, of course. But many workers demonstrated an almost reflexive readiness to push back against conditions and pressures they found unpalatable.

Thus, it was widely rumored that the earliest operatives often supplemented their modest wages (27¢ to 80¢ per week for children, about $3.00 per week for men) by stealing raw materials and finished goods from the factory.[34] Also from the outset, and probably more directly disruptive to Slater's work rosters, was the refusal of operatives to stay put. In 1795, for example, workers protested the tendency of Almy and Brown to delay confirming contract agreements and settling wage payments by briefly absenting themselves and their children for a few days or hours – an early form of industrial job action. Others left more permanently – all through the 1790s – when breakdowns and delayed cotton shipments forced work stoppages or (especially among the men) when they found better paying jobs. And still others left because factory routines grated too heavily against preindustrial habits. Accustomed to quitting work at sundown, they resented laboring into wintertime evenings (their workrooms lit by candles) just so their factories could maintain consistent twelve-hour days. Accustomed to acknowledging seasonal changes, they left to harvest nearby hills during "whortleberry time." Accustomed to laboring at their own pace, they bridled at "machines...hurrying [them] up."[35]

All this – the simmering community hostility, the operatives' disaffection and restlessness – disclosed an important precedent. It was the original expression of antipathies New England factories would encounter repeatedly in the decades to come, from both workers within and townspeople outside their thick walls. Supplemented in time by new issues and emphases, swelling and fading according to regional developments and local conditions, such antagonisms would help define the environment in which Yankee manufactories – including those in Dudley and Oxford – took root. For the moment, however, it is enough to point out that one abiding consequence of northeastern unease with factories was to exacerbate the area's tight labor market, and thus to leave mill masters worried they would be "exceeding short of hands."[36]

Slater was the first New England textile entrepreneur to face the problem, and predictably he reached for familiar solutions. To calm his neighbors, he echoed the argument that mills would in due course help agricultural and commercial activities. To calm his employees, he drew upon his English training. Because Pawtucket already existed as a rudimentary village, there was no need to create a new factory community. But within a few years Slater brought stores and residences closer to his mill. And Sunday schools – though left optional and tilted more toward secular learning than in Derbyshire – had opened under Slater's direction, probably by 1792.[37]

But then he went further. Adapting his stance to the heightened skittishness of Yankee operatives, Slater solicited his laborers' loyalty by openly siding with their complaints to Almy and Brown over tardy deliveries of wages and supplies. He informed his partners he could not "bear to have" operatives ("my Children," he called the youngsters) lacking what was due them. And he claimed his two associates were wholly responsible when unpaid workers broke their agreements and left: "Probably the Common Law [enforcing contracts] is binding, but I think the Law of Equity and Justice is not."[38]

Beyond such verbal bristlings, Slater took precisely calculated steps to lighten factory discipline. On the one hand, he invoked British-style rules regarding punctuality and work procedures; and he reportedly "had no hesitation" in personally caning youngsters who "did not keep up their work."[39] On the other hand, he apparently put off introducing overseers at least through 1800, and (even more notably) he declined to adopt the panoply of fines and blacklists he had seen in Milford.[40] By avoiding such formally Draconian mechanisms, Slater evidently hoped to offset, at least partially, the grim reputation of textile manufactories.

The strategy is important because, to some degree, it worked; and because, having seen it work, Slater would use it again years later to attract employees for his Dudley and Oxford factories. In Pawtucket in the 1790s, community antagonisms toward the Old Mill remained sharp, and it is not clear that Slater's remonstrances ever pushed Almy and Brown into greater efficiency. But his efforts to curry favor among the workers brought results. Although they remained both rebellious and transient, employees generally turned up at his earliest Rhode Island factory in adequate numbers to keep the establishment running. Drawing on occasional widows but more often on laborers and artisans (along with their families) – both local and nonlocal, many of them sharing the Quaker faith of his partners, some of them well off, others down on their luck – recruiting from all these groups, Slater generally managed to marshal the work force needed to "tend" his machines.[41]

Once assured of an adequate labor force, the Old Mill quickly proved successful. By 1800 Almy and Brown had broadened their market to include shopkeepers throughout the northeastern hinterland (quite possibly including several in Dudley and Oxford), as well as merchants in coastal cities ranging from Boston in the North to New York, Philadelphia, and even Baltimore in the South.[42] The sales produced by this expanding retail network inevitably attracted the attention of other entrepreneurs, and by the time of Jefferson's embargo in 1807 at least seventeen new cotton-spinning factories – sponsored mainly by merchants and artisans from around Providence – had appeared in New England.[43] A momentum began building that would soon encourage Slater to build new mills of his own in the southern Massachusetts hinterland.

The embargo momentarily checked further growth. The prohibition of trade with England and France depressed the coastal markets on which many mills still depended, and the resulting sales contraction made new construction risky. As early as 1809, however, settlers in the trans-Allegheny West, finding themselves deprived of British fabrics, began demanding cheap cloths in quantities that more than offset the shrunken ranks of seacoast customers. Although after 1796 most Yankee factory masters had (like Slater) confined themselves to spinning, they moved quickly after 1807 to "put out" yarn to outlying handloom weavers who, laboring in their homes, could produce the shirtings westerners were demanding. Having responded to their new market, northern factory masters found sales and profits rising. Between 1808 and 1812, some thirty-six new mills – by this point deriving their capital as much from host communities as from coastal Yankees – were built in New England.[44]

Even woolen mills started going up. Waterpowered carding engines for wool had existed in America as early as 1793. (Oxford, it will be recalled, had such a machine by 1806.) But development of full-scale woolen mills was slowed by difficulties in fashioning a perpetual spinning technology for woolen fibers. By 1807 only six woolen factories – combining automatic carding machines with hand-powered jennies – had been built. Over the next five years, however, such establishments became far more common. Although probably not as responsive to western markets as cotton mills, and although only just beginning to acquire semiautomatic spinning "jacks," woolen mills turned out salable products and so emerged as attractive investments. Between 1807 and the end of 1812, forty-one new woolen mills were built in the United States, the majority standing along New England streams.[45]

All this construction ultimately provided both background and impetus for Slater's expansion into Dudley and Oxford. First, however, he had to reconcile himself to the notion of industrial growth – for initially the idea appalled him. He may have worried that some version of the antimanufactory spirit evinced in Pawtucket would erupt in other communities – and indeed he was right. In Woonsocket, Rhode Island, in 1808, for example, "residents...placed all the obstacles which they could" before the Blackstone Mill.[46] But with Derbyshire memories still clearly in mind, Slater undoubtedly also feared that unrestrained growth would proceed inevitably to overcrowding, and hence – disastrously – to "Scandelous men's" engaging in ruinous competition.[47] So, initially, he tried to stop the growth. He learned from himself: This purloiner of British mechanical designs swore early employees to secrecy about "the nature of the works"; he paid key operatives elevated rates to prevent their "aiding and assisting another Mill"; and he was "very cautious of admitting strangers to view" his technology. When perpetual spinning mills nonetheless sprang up (their construction often aided by his own former employees), Slater pressed his partners, and Moses Brown as well, to urge manufacturers not to "lower the price of Yarn" below profitable levels.[48]

Up to a point, the Quakers cooperated. They dispatched discouraging notes to men pondering the textile business ("You could not expect to rival those that had been so long acquainted with it"), and until 1814 they sought to persuade those who did build mills to follow rudimentary wage and price guidelines.[49] In the final analysis, however, expansion did not particularly concern Almy and the Browns. They proved this in 1799 by opening a mill of their own in Warwick, Rhode Island, and by giving every indication of having this establishment compete directly with the Old Mill.[50]

To Slater, of course, this was shocking. But it also convinced him that to maintain his preeminent role within the American textile industry he would have to augment his own holdings. By 1800, that is, Slater understood that the next phase in his adaptation to the New World involved personally undertaking new factories. As he embraced this perspective, however, he also, simultaneously, began recasting his managerial priorities. If he could not prevent expansion of the whole industry, then he would exercise increasingly firm control over at least some of the mills in which he had an interest. Henceforth, even the substantial authority awarded him by his contract with Almy and Brown would be inadequate. Henceforth, in certain manufactories with which he became involved, he would reserve for himself or his most trusted associates (usually kinsmen) dominant proprietary control.

So, assisted, but not dominated, by his wife's family, Slater set about building a new factory in Rehoboth, Massachusetts, just across the Blackstone River from Pawtucket.[51] A burst of local opposition – just the kind of reaction he feared industrial expansion might elicit – delayed the venture briefly. Rehoboth residents were angered by Slater's effort to acquire a tax exemption (and thus deprive their community of revenues), but by the end of 1801 the so-called White Mill was constructed, outfitted, and turning out cotton yarn.[52] Five years later, Slater built a mill in Smithfield, Rhode Island. Encompassing what was probably the first factory village constructed *ex nihilio* for an American manufactory and introducing the manually operated English spinning mule (which produced finer yarn than water frames), the Smithfield project was also supported by Almy and Brown. But Slater's preeminent influence over the project was obvious: The mill village soon bore the title Slatersville, and key supervisory responsibility quickly passed to John Slater, Samuel's younger brother, who had arrived from England in 1802.[53]

Five years after the Smithfield factory opened Slater again began considering new projects – so long, of course, as he could control them. He sold his share in the White Mill to his Wilkinson in-laws

and by the spring of 1811 began actively searching for sites suitable
for another factory. He was particularly interested in locations well
removed from Pawtucket, for the concentration of factories around
that community had created a shortage of households willing to
tackle the handloom weaving on which post-1807 spinning mills
depended so heavily. Thus Slater was intrigued when a young man
named Bela Tiffany, whom he had dispatched to investigate possible millsites, sent word of a spot he had found in Oxford, South
Gore.[54]

Tiffany's report was not entirely enthusiastic. Compared with the
bustle of coastal Rhode Island, the remote and sparsely populated
South Gore was, in his blunt estimation, "the most benighted part of
the globe." But he acknowledged that the location he had seen,
lying by a stream flowing from the huge Lake Chabanakongkomun,
offered compelling attractions. The available "water and fall" evidently already powered a gristmill, sawmill, and trip-hammer shop
with no difficulty and was "so situated that a mill may be erected
with as little expense as in any place I have seen." He needed to say
no more. Undeterred by his scout's caveat, buoyed by the promise
of abundant water supply, and apparently convinced that sufficient
weavers would be found in the vicinity, Slater moved ahead. By
May 1812 (three months after the Merino Mill had opened) he had
purchased the real estate necessary to build a new mill and to control the water flowing to it. A personal setback occurred in October
when Hannah, his wife of twenty-one years, died giving birth to her
seventh son and ninth child. But Slater pressed on, and in January
1813 the Green Mill started turning out cotton yarn.[55]

IV

In this way, at the age of 44, thirty years after starting his apprenticeship with Strutt and twenty years after his arrival in America,
Slater entered southern Massachusetts. Standing "fully six feet,"
weighing well over two hundred pounds, already wealthy and well
known, the "spinner" from England quickly emerged as a powerful
presence in both Dudley and Oxford.[56] The two townships made no
immediate objection to his arrival. By declining to petition for a tax
exemption, and by purchasing the other establishments using the
stream he needed, Slater initially forestalled concern about lost revenues and disrupted riparian privileges. A momentary flurry did
arise when Tiffany, realizing that some of the property he had acquired actually lay in Dudley, petitioned to have these Dudley acres

"set off" to Oxford. Dudley residents successfully defeated the proposal (electing Tiffany hogreeve to prove their pique and demonstrate his residency in their community), and the squabble quickly blew over.[57] Ultimately, other issues (including rivers and taxes) arose: The ambivalence toward manufactories in other townships would gradually take root in Dudley and Oxford. But by the time tempers boiled over, the "Arkwright of America" had significantly expanded his local holdings.

Thus, in 1815 he built a woolen mill alongside the Green Mill. This second South Gore enterprise burned down five years later, but its place was quickly taken by another cotton-spinning factory (the Union Mill), and the woolen manufacturing project was relocated on a site a mile to the west in Dudley. In 1824 Slater bought out an existing cotton-spinning establishment, also in Dudley and roughly a mile north of his woolen mill, and within a few years reorganized it into the Phoenix Thread Factory. Fifteen years after the Green Mill started up, Slater thus owned three distinct clusters of factories: one in Oxford and two in Dudley.[58]

But his holdings in Dudley and Oxford were not confined to factories. While somewhat more developed demographic concentrations emerged in the two towns shortly after 1810 (around Oxford's northern meetinghouse, for example, and at Dudley's "senter"),[59] both local populations remained quite scattered, and Slater's mills were in any case situated in relatively isolated areas. As a result, he had to construct extensive support facilities: stores and dyehouses, for example, and residences – separate houses for some of the managers, small boardinghouses for unattached workers, and cottages for households. Thus (as in Slatersville) his manufactories were really densely packed compounds. The Green Mill (and subsequently the Union Mill) stood in the East Village; the woolen factory was the centerpiece of the South Village; and around the Phoenix Mill soon blossomed the North Village.[60] And beyond each of these enclaves lay further holdings: the fields and meadows Slater purchased so that he could supply his hands at least partially from foodstuffs produced on his own land. By 1830 he possessed nearly two thousand acres of real estate in Dudley and Oxford, making him by all odds the largest single property owner in either township.[61]

In important respects, Slater's administration of this local domain reflected the route he had taken to reach the South Gore. To be sure, his managerial tactics and postures after 1813 would change in ways that would significantly affect relations within the North, South, and East villages and between these villages and the two townships.

But this does not lessen the persisting strength of ideas and attitudes Samuel Slater brought into "the most benighted part of the Globe." Up to his death in 1835, for example, and even into the 1840s, his factories, fitting English precedents to evolving American conditions, appear to have given continuing attention to the problem of attracting workers. Then too, through the 1850s, his three compounds followed the employment practices Slater had learned from Strutt and continued in America: of hiring mainly free wage laborers from a range of social and economic backgrounds and taking on both coresiding members of households and domestically unattached individuals. Moreover, until the late 1820s, he continued to distribute yarn to outlying handloom weavers, as Strutt had probably done to some extent and as Yankee mill masters had found advisable after 1807. And finally, throughout the antebellum era, with only partial and occasional exceptions, Slater and subsequently his heirs extended over their holdings in Dudley and Oxford the kind of personal control Strutt had exemplified and Slater had reemphasized in his affairs after 1800.

The continuity is the more striking because during much of this period another mode of organizing textile mills was gaining attention. Beginning in 1815, so-called Waltham-style factories started springing up along New England streams, especially in the northern part of the region. Large, heavily capitalized, and often owned by absentee merchant proprietors based in Boston, these mills were typically situated in towns that in time achieved substantial size: Manchester in New Hampshire and Lowell, Holyoke, and, of course, Waltham in Massachusetts. But such establishments stood out even more sharply because of two other characteristics. First, Waltham-style mills rapidly incorporated water-driven power looms (available in England by at least 1800) into an "integrated" spinning-weaving process carried out entirely within factory buildings. And second, until the influx of immigrants into New England mills during the 1840s and 1850s, it was the Waltham plan to recruit operatives almost entirely from unmarried daughters of middling Yankee yeomen and to billet them all together in large dormitorylike boarding-houses.[62]

Yet despite this countervailing model, the Slater villages in Dudley and Oxford retained their distinctive format. Indeed, more than just distinctive, the "family" (or "Rhode Island") style of these mills also proved influential. For Waltham-style mills were not typical. Until the 1850s, most Yankee manufactories were small country mills, probably concentrated in the southern half of New England and modeled to one degree or another on patterns the "Arkwright of America" had developed by the time he reached Oxford, South Gore.[63] It is thus scarcely surprising that all the non-Slater factories going up in Dudley and Oxford after 1810 closely followed his blueprint.

But it is time now to consider in more detail how these other non-Slater mills developed. Put more broadly, it is time to recall that Slater's arrival in Dudley and Oxford joined with certain propulsions toward economic change already gathering in the two communities. It is time to explore what it was besides the North, South, and East villages that sparked the transformations overtaking local society after 1810.

V

It was above all shifts in agriculture that prompted men outside Slater's compounds to make the investments necessary for a new economic landscape. The pressures shaping local husbandry in the second and third decades of the nineteenth century were not new. But their force increased substantially during these years, and the pace of change within local farming thus, inescapably, accelerated.

There were, first, demographic pressures. The population of the two towns jumped from 2,503 to 4,189 between 1810 and 1830[64] – an increase more than four times larger than the growth registered during the previous twenty years. Because local landholders generally declined to reduce homesteads below the hundred-acre average that repeated subdivisions had already produced by 1800, such population growth could only reduce the proportion of residents able to acquire the real estate necessary for husbandry.[65] Farming remained the largest single occupation in either community. But as early as 1820, only 70 percent of local residents willing to specify their occupation in the federal census cited "agriculture" as their principal labor[66] – almost certainly a substantial drop from previous decades. This, of course, meant that an increasing number of local residents looked with interest on the establishment of nonagricultural ventures. Indeed, there can be little doubt that it was precisely the expansion of stores, workshops, and manufactories that supported the growing local populations.

A second, more complex cluster of pressures derived from the increasing shadow of the market. It must be stressed that husbandry in Dudley and Oxford became only *more*, not fully, commercialized during the generation after 1810. Throughout this period, local yeomen were still cultivating an assortment of foodstuffs for their own consumption rather than concentrating exclusively on "cash crops" and profits. And, generally speaking, the practice of farming continued to knit comfortably with received notions of "family need" or what the *Old Farmer's Almanack* in 1837 called a "competency...for [husbandmen] and [their] families."[67] It was only within the context of this basic continuity that local farmers tilted more heavily toward market transactions.

The shift that did take place reflected the growing demand of regional urban populations for meat and dairy products. Thus, farmers in Dudley and Oxford increased their stock of cows by more than 50 percent – to a total of nearly three thousand – during the twenty years ending in 1831; and by the mid-1830s, despite a moderate decline in its swine population, Dudley alone was annually exporting to nonlocal markets some fifteen tons of beef and some sixty tons of butter, cheese, and pork. Responding to the growth of Yankee woolen mills, local husbandmen also tried their hand at sheep raising: They advanced from owning none of these animals as late as 1821 to possessing just under twenty-six hundred a decade later.[68] Nor did local yeomen approach the market only to sell. They also relied more than ever before on workshops and stores for services and goods. "Comparatively nothing," a Dudley resident reported in 1832, "is done in the household manufacturing."[69]

As it turned out, however, one consequence of this expanded commercial orientation in agriculture was to encourage investment in nonagricultural activities. In part, this was simply because deeper familiarity with the market made such investments seem more normal. But the augmented interest in nonfarming ventures also arose because post-1810 agricultural commercialization frequently left local yeomen in deep trouble.

The basic difficulty was the limited productivity of Yankee homesteads combined with sharp fluctuations in the market price of farm products. Beef, butter, cheese, pork, and (after 1820) wool all brought returns that varied widely from year to year[70] and not infrequently fell below the debits farms were running up with local artisans and storekeepers. Thus the dilemma facing many yeomen: Committed to raising more products for sale, increasingly preferring to buy services and goods, farmers were drawn deeper into the market but often simultaneously denied real hope of prosperity. Quite the opposite, for after 1810 local farmers generally received only a paltry return on their labors and commonly faced rising levels of indebtedness. Between 1790 and 1810 just under one-quarter of the value of probated property was tied up in debt. A sampling of comparable records from the next generation – the great majority of them evidently left by husbandmen – reveals debts totaling nearly one-third of the aggregate worth of probated estates.[71]

To be sure, after 1810 as before, most debts reflected the practical necessities of long-term credit arrangements. And it is also true that most debtors after 1810 continued to double as creditors. Still, the thickening haze of indebtedness was burdensome for farmers. As such, it helps account for the growing proclivity of local husbandmen – those who could marshal the resources – to combine farming with investments in nonagricultural enterprises. And, coupled with limited local land supplies, the increasing volume of debt also helps explain why residents were sometimes obliged to leave farming altogether, turning instead to some business enterprise. As had been true in previous years, children were particularly vulnerable to this pressure; indeed, their vulnerability grew. In the twenty years after 1810 the proportion of locally probated estates so enmeshed in debt that all property had to be auctioned off – leaving no land for expectant heirs – rose from the already high rate of 19.9 percent it had attained during the previous generation to the truly extraordinary level of 46.2 percent.[72]

All these constraints on farming also affected patterns of local transiency. Although there is reason to believe husbandmen were somewhat more rooted than other local residents after 1810, considerable numbers of yeomen found prospects unsatisfactory and decided to leave (at least some of them with families in tow). And their exit helped to depress overall persistence in Dudley and Oxford well below the roughly 60 percent level it had maintained earlier in the century (Table 2.1).[73] Children also left on their own with increasing frequency. Hitherto, despite all the comings and goings of youngsters, at least one child in most landholding farming households could count on receiving property, and hence at least one child had remained to run the family acres. Teen-age farming youngsters in the 1820s and 1830s continued the pattern of scouting other occupations (especially in wintertime) and then returning home. But with debt alone preventing nearly one household in two from distributing land to any child, it became more likely that a family's entire cluster of offspring would, in the end, exit permanently. At least thirteen farming households in Dudley and Oxford may have found themselves thus stripped of children by 1820.[74] And there is no question but that the emigration of sons picked up markedly: The proportion of young men who were born to parents living continu-

Table 2.1. *Geographical mobility and persistence of household heads in Dudley and Oxford, 1810–30*

	No. of household heads			Persistence rate household heads		Aggregate arrivals plus departures household heads		Aggregate turnover household heads	
	1810	1820	1830	1810–20	1820–30	1810–20	1820–30	1810–20[a]	1820–30[b]
Dudley	207	274	355	49.8	49.3	206	295	99.5	107.7
Oxford	251	294	351	48.6	48.6	220	294	87.6	100.0
Total	458	568	706	49.1	48.9	426	589	93.0	103.7

[a] Arrivals plus departures 1810–20 as percentage of household heads in 1810.
[b] Arrivals plus departures 1820–30 as percentage of household heads in 1820.
Source: MFCO, MFCD, 1810, 1820, 1830; DVR, OVR.

ously in these communities but who themselves declined to take up local residence grew from one-half to three-quarters in the generation after 1810.[75]

But it is important to realize that such heightened moving about characterized the entire rural Northeast: "It is said," wrote an English traveler during the antebellum period, that "if you ask a Connecticut Yankee in any part of the world how he is, he will, if not 'sick,' answer 'moving, Sir,' equivalent to saying 'well'; for if well, he is sure to be on the move."[76] This, in fact, is why residents leaving Dudley and Oxford could be more than replaced by newcomers. They were replaced by heads of whole households, for example, arriving from other communities and seeking better (or perhaps just different) opportunities in or out of agriculture or in some new blend of farming and nonfarming ventures. Or they were replaced by young adults choosing to leave their birthplaces, much as Dudley and Oxford youngsters were doing once inheritance expectations faded, but pausing, for the moment at least, to explore possibilities in these two towns.

The precise number of arriving inhabitants is unknown. It seems likely, however, that they accounted for most of the local population increase between 1810 and 1830.[77] And it is clear that, combined with household heads exiting between federal enumerations, incoming household heads cited in the censuses were sufficiently numerous to push the aggregate turnover of these individuals 29 to 39 percent above levels recorded during the first years of the nineteenth century.[78] But what is of particular importance in understanding post-1810 local economic change is that the new stores, handicraft workshops, and factories appearing in Dudley and Oxford were often undertaken by newcomers.

Can anything more be said about the expectations with which people entered this new generation of local business projects? The data here are at best imprecise and speculative, but looking ahead to the various ways nonagricultural undertakings would be structured in Dudley and Oxford, a few points may be ventured.

Among those backing the new workshops, stores, and mills were likely some who from the outset wished to "get ahead" as fast and as far as possible. In a sense this was a goal continuing directly from the long-standing ambition of many rural Yankees to do well. What happened after 1810, at least in Dudley and Oxford, was that those pursuing this goal expressed their aims more starkly and proved willing to challenge countervailing perspectives more openly than had earlier been the case. But other business proprietors in the post-1810 generation held to calmer ambitions. These were individuals who, like most local yeomen, wished to do well – but without embracing entirely the priority of maximizing profits. Indeed, there is reason to suppose that some young men entered local business ventures not as a way of forging beyond their parents economically but as part of parentally orchestrated efforts to help family members maintain their economic standing in an uncertain economy. Thus, a number of sons took up storekeeping, gristmilling, and blacksmithing in Dudley and Oxford with parental assistance – monetary assistance from yeoman parents unable to provide land bequests – and then tailored their own youthful business ambitions to the familiar dimensions of "family need."[79]

The division between these perspectives was by no means hard and fast. Amid the rapidly shifting post-1810 economic terrain of Dudley and Oxford, people moved back and forth between wanting to maximize gain and settling for "competencies." What does seem to have made a difference, however, was the kind of enterprise people supported. Like the Old Mill – which, for all its early compromises on discipline, never ceased its quest for profits – local cotton and woolen manufactories sought only a favorable balance sheet. It is true that textile investors removed from daily managerial responsibilities need not have been fullhearted entrepreneurs. But linked as they were to extra-local customers and the sweep of impersonal regional market pressures, textile mills in Dudley and Oxford were significantly insulated – detached – from the influence and logic of community custom. As a result, these institutions – and the proprietors most directly concerned in their management – were free to stress profits.

Nontextile ventures, by contrast, appear to have deviated from conventional priorities more gradually. Although rarely limited exclusively to local customers, these smaller businesses still catered mainly to nearby residents and hence still operated largely within the grid of customary economic practices and attitudes. As a result, although investors might oscillate between factories and nontextile projects, owning a workshop or store did not by itself push individuals toward qualitatively new outlooks.

The currents unleashed by different post-1810 businesses thus moved out across Dudley and Oxford at different speeds and different angles. Although the goals animating these establishments were all derived, to some degree, from preexisting attitudes, some ventures would impinge upon the entrenched rural ethos only gradually. Others would challenge that ethos almost immediately.

Table 2.2. *Nontextile enterprises in Dudley and Oxford, 1801, 1811, 1831*

	1801		1811		1831	
	Dudley	Oxford	Dudley	Oxford	Dudley	Oxford
Shops	7	6	5	13	51	51
Tanneries	4	1	3	2	2	1
Potash works	1	3		1		
Gristmills	3	5	2	5	4	6
Carding mills				1	1	
Fulling mills		1		1		
Sawmills	4	4	2	8	3	9
Total	19	20	12	31	61	67
Combined total	39		43		128	

Source: AAS: Worcester County Valuations.

VI

Who, then, were the local business builders, and precisely what did they do? Considering first the nontextile ventures, sources indicate a virtual explosion of activity. The number of such projects grew dramatically (Table 2.2), and by all indications a fairly sizable roster of individuals became involved in their establishment. In Oxford (where records are more complete), a sample of sixty-two nontextile businesses springing up at one point or another between 1810 and 1830 required the proprietary efforts of seventy-four men.[80]

There were, to be sure, exceptions to the general trend: Tanneries grew scarcer in these years; the last local potash works closed down; and here, as elsewhere in the Commonwealth, the need for fulling and carding mills was undercut by the mounting inclination of residents to purchase finished dry goods. Then too, in a development adding further fuel to local transiency, nontextile ventures that did appear after 1810 did not always endure.[81] But with all this acknowledged, the records still reveal these enterprises sprouting in extraordinary variety and mushroomlike profusion. The category of "shops" cited in Table 2.2, for example, embraced not only familiar ventures like stores, taverns, blacksmithies, and nail-making works but also unprecedented projects: two shoemaking shops, a bakery, a stove factory, chaise and bobbin-making manufactures, and a textile machine works.[82] As for the numerical increase of these undertakings, the figures in Table 2.2 specify that nontextile establishments nearly tripled between 1811 and 1831.

They multiplied so quickly because they were small, simple, and relatively cheap. It is true that some nail-making and blacksmith operations had grown larger since the 1790s and early 1800s; and ventures like the shoemaking shops and textile machine works were evidently fairly sizable. But compared to the cotton and woolen factories going up during the same period, all these enterprises were modest affairs. And (except possibly for the textile machine works and the post-1810 version of Oxford's nail-making shop) their technologies remained relatively simple and inexpensive.[83] Then too, individuals undertaking these ventures sometimes saved money by leasing existing buildings or (more often) by joining in small partnerships. Occasionally bolstered by kinship or by shared origins in other communities, such alliances made launching a new workshop or store both more attractive and more possible.[84]

The comparatively light financial burden of nontextile projects was particularly important given the limited resources of their proprietors. Although there would gradually emerge a significantly greater concentration of wealth in the two townships,[85] those backing smaller, nonagricultural businesses were far from uniformly wealthy. Usually newcomers (only 26 percent were residents of either community in 1800), they generally had access to little or no land (63 percent neither owned nor leased property beyond the plot on which their businesses stood) and their total assets appear moderate at best. Direct evidence on this point for the whole generation after 1810 is admittedly sketchy. But it is suggestive that, according to local tax enumerations, only one-third of those investing in shops, stores, and nontextile mills stood in the top quartile. Neither very rich nor very poor, most (57.4 percent) ranked in the broad middling strata of the two towns.[86]

Another characteristic of these men was their involvement in the daily operation of their properties. A number of these establishments, of course, were one-man operations. But even in undertakings boasting several proprietors and employing several workers, owners put in their hours. They might divide their time between several projects; and in some instances they continued to combine farming and nonfarming activities. Whatever the precise arrangement, however, each nontextile venture felt the presence of all its backers.[87]

But proprietary involvement did not connote permanent commitment. Some of the more skilled local businessmen probably did regard their enterprises as a vocation: Ezra and Elija Davis, for example, were two Oxford-born brothers who took up millwrighting and acquired sufficient expertise to found a "school," which became "widely known among the manufacturers in New England." And there was a recent arrival like Thomas W. Chatman who set up Oxford's machine-making shop. Such men were likely to remain in their trades for extended periods – whether or not they remained in Dudley and Oxford. But most proprietors of smaller local businesses did not regard their efforts as long-term occupations. Quite the opposite, for those owning and running projects tallied up in Table 2.2 moved from venture to venture – and those who left the two townships probably continued varied undertakings in other settings as well. Evidently finding it easy to acquire adequate technical knowledge, these investor-managers shifted unhesitatingly and repeatedly, probing new directions, discarding failed efforts: jumping (like Stephen and David Barton) from sawmilling to gristmilling or (like Seth Daniels) from chaisemaking to shoemaking.[88]

Then there were those who started manufactories: the individuals who, despite the controversial aura surrounding these enterprises, put up money for local cotton and woolen works. Records (again probably more reliable for Oxford) indicate that some ninety-three men besides Slater and his associates put up money for at least a dozen separate textile villages between 1810 and 1830.[89]

As already noted, the mills taking shape outside the North, South, and East villages followed the organizational format developed by the "Arkwright of America." Several owned farms and, until around 1830, quite a few distributed yarn to outlying handloom weavers. They too grappled with an endemically tight labor market and hired mainly free wage laborers (both attached and unattached to households) from a broad scattering of backgrounds.

One way non-Slater mills did *not* mimic his villages, however, was by failing. The 1816 depression that wiped out the original Merino effort also bankrupted two factories subsequently begun in Oxford, leaving some of their investors "ruined financially," others "arrested for debt and imprisoned," and still others "absent[ing] themselves to avoid arrest."[90] Still, despite the fatalities, enough local factories survived to bring the total list (including Slater's properties) to fifteen factories in 1831: six cotton mills and a woolen works spread through six separate villages in Oxford; three cotton and five woolen factories dispersed through six compounds in Dudley.[91]

Those who, for better or worse, sponsored the non-Slater factories occasionally had extensive local roots: Aaron Tufts in Dudley, for example, and Sylvanus Pratt in Oxford. But like the individuals backing smaller businesses in these communities and reflecting the rapid turnover of local residents generally, most men who invested in local factories were not long-term inhabitants. Although mills in Dudley and Oxford were never dominated by absentee owners, only one-fifth of their proprietors were born in the towns and only one-quarter were in residence by 1800.[92]

The occupational background of those sponsoring local mills was varied. Some who provided capital for cotton and woolen factories were farmers seeking to launch or extend interests in nonagricultural properties: Again Aaron Tufts may be cited. Just as often, however, mill proprietors were individuals who had been more or less squeezed out of husbandry and thus came to textile mills already experienced in commercial or artisanal activities. So Thaddeus Hall, who arrived in Oxford from Sutton, Massachusetts, some time between 1800 and 1810, was engaged in blacksmithing before backing the Oxford Cotton Manufacturing Company in 1814; and the DeWitt brothers, Alexander and Stearns, helped run a small store before taking a "prominent" part in founding the Oxford Woolen Company in 1826 and emerging as two of Oxford's leading industrialists.[93]

In most cases, investors maintained their assorted occupational commitments – as farmers, tradesmen, or farmer-tradesmen – throughout their involvement with mills. Because even more than owning nontextile enterprises, proprietorship of a manufactory rarely counted as a vocation. Each mill had a few investors (the DeWitt brothers and Aaron Tufts are examples) who possessed or acquired sufficient expertise to collaborate actively with the seasoned factory administrators that millowners usually hired; and each mill also had several other proprietors who kept close to the daily operations of their industrial properties. These were the true entrepreneurs, the true factory masters, behind local manufactories outside the North, South, and East villages. These were the men who reflected Samuel Slater's stress on personal proprietary control. But even these individuals generally viewed their time with textile mills as more an interlude than a definitive commitment. And most textile investors were far less involved. A majority of those backing local factories did little more than supply their money, place trust in their activist brother proprietors, and press on with other jobs.[94]

Certainly few of them could have lived off accumulated wealth – and here textile investors once more resembled their nontextile counterparts. The most active mill proprietors – the core of fully engaged factory masters – were often well off to start with and often got richer through their industrial activities: Again, Tufts and the De-Witt brothers are examples. But the majority of factory investors were far less affluent. Under one-third (28.9 percent) of the factory proprietors cited in local tax listings ranked in the top quartile, and other records suggest that perhaps three-quarters of Oxford's mill masters owned less than thirty acres of land. Once more it was the middle group of local inhabitants who were reaching out to new economic ventures.[95] More consistently than among proprietors of smaller projects, however, the limited resources of textile investors produced collaboration. Facilities for borrowing capital were still comparatively rare in the hinterland, and those backing local cotton and woolen factories had to group together to raise the needed funds.[96] Again kinsmen and newcomers from the same community joined with one another, but factory proprietors usually had to embrace more than a few relatives or friends. Up to twenty participants might be needed to find the $9,000 commonly required for a woolen mill or the $35,000 that even a small cotton factory could cost.[97]

Behind the parallels of, and differences between, textile and nontextile proprietors was, of course, the tendency of these two groups to overlap. On the one hand (as already noted), several millowners had previously dabbled in stores and workshops. On the other hand, millowners whose projects failed (and who survived the event) sometimes rebounded into nontextile projects. So Sylvester McIntire took up running a tavern after the Oxford Cotton Manufacturing Company went under.[98]

But the two types of enterprise were also linked because, in continuing and concrete ways, each supported the other. The rising number of stores in Dudley and Oxford, for example, aided local textile factories by providing retail outlets and a source of supplies. Of course, no textile mill confined its sale to these townships; and several mills opened their own stores to facilitate access to needed goods. Still, it was obviously useful for the mills to have some nearby customers, and Samuel Slater, for one, found it convenient to keep a running account at the Oxford General Store.[99]

On the other side of the ledger, manufactories provided powerful support for the explosive surge of post-1810 local economic growth. Indeed, it is just here that Samuel Slater's personal influence can be seen with particular clarity. For not only did he join with other industrialists in deciding – despite their common penchant for mill-owned farms – to use foodstuffs grown by nearby husbandmen to help feed the operatives; not only did he also join other mill masters in providing dry goods to local merchants and steady orders to handicraft enterprises – the millwright and blacksmith shops, for example, as well as the bobbin manufacturing and textile machine works – not only did he foster development in all these ways, he also promoted certain "improvements" helpful to all businesses in Dudley and Oxford. Throughout the post-1810 generation he pushed for better roads. And in 1823 he significantly enlarged local access to investment capital by taking a leading role – given his need for control, it was the only role possible – in founding the Oxford Bank.[100] Ironically, both the roads and the bank would in time contribute to friction between the mills and the two communities. But this scarcely diminishes the importance of these "improvements" in bolstering local business activities.

VII

This was how economic change came to Dudley and Oxford. It was a pattern of development in which Samuel Slater – animated by ambition, deeply conditioned by experiences in both England and America – made a fundamental contribution, but in which other entrepreneurs within the two communities also participated; a pattern in which textile mills were crucial factors, but in which smaller enterprises emerged concurrently and shifts in farming played an important role; a pattern in which both factories and nontextile ventures drew upon preexisting inclinations within these townships, but in which these post-1810 developments varied significantly in the degree to which they challenged received mores and structures. Such, in general terms, were the ways and reasons economic shifts took place in Dudley and Oxford during the second and third decades of the nineteenth century.

But this is only the starting point. To gain firm leverage on the changes rippling through the two townships, to understand how these changes fit into the entire social fabric of these communities, and especially how they related to – and conflicted with – values and institutions that changed more slowly or not at all – to understand all this necessitates probing further.

The following four chapters detail the new forms of life and labor emerging in the two towns and the consequences following from these innovations. As the largest and most complex of the post-1810 enterprises, textile mills necessarily provide much of the focus. But the extent – and limits – of change throughout the communities are considered: the shifting distribution of local populations through different occupations; the regimens people in these towns began encountering or, as managers, began developing; the new ways residents responded to these regimens both as workers and as local citizens. For only by considering the story from all these angles does its meaning become clear.

PART II

The first generation

Mr. Slater was not a man to be indebted for his success to midnight fancies and drowsy visions. His dreams were deep calculations and his calculations [were of] wealth.

Pawtucket Chronicle, May 1, 1835

Though the supply of our own great wants from our own farms might seem...a *pecuniary loss*, it is always in the end a *moral gain*, with which the pecuniary loss is not to be put in competition.

Henry Colman, *Second Report on Agriculture of Massachusetts* (1838)

3 People and work: the social structure of occupations

The character of local populations changed noticeably after 1810. The rapid demographic growth of Dudley and Oxford naturally played a key role in this transformation, as did the increased transiency of people through the two communities. The rising tide of emigrating sons, for example, contributed just by itself to a persisting shortage of marriageable males as well as to the continued overall aging of local residents.[1]

These developments were all important. But equally significant in shaping the human geography of these townships was the thorough restructuring of occupational patterns that occurred in this period. In a sense, this change has already been foreshadowed, for the reduced proportion of yeomen among local inhabitants obviously points to a fundamental transition in the way people were earning their keep.[2] And the rise of new nonagricultural establishments obviously signals where that transition was heading. But more needs to be said. Who filled the increasing variety of occupational openings? Who continued to labor on the farms? Were new kinds of jobs – jobs outside the agricultural household – opening up for females as well as males? For those handicraft, commercial, and manufacturing proprietors needing employees, whom did they hire? Who worked in the cotton and woolen factories? And where did millwork fit into their lives?

It is not possible to answer all these questions precisely or even with uniform imprecision. The data permit rough portraits at best and often no more than faint hints. But even hints are useful. Understanding who did what kind of work in Dudley and Oxford, and particularly gaining leverage on the distinctive features of factory employment, are crucial in understanding what happened in these communities during the first generation after 1810.

II

Those who continued to farm in these townships were bunched among the middling economic strata. It is true there were husbandmen among both the richest and poorest local inhabitants. But most farmers (including those who helped launch the spreading configuration of nonagricultural enterprises) were clustered into the second and third tax quartiles of Dudley and Oxford.[3]

And virtually all of them were probably beginning to feel short-handed, for local farmers were giving added emphasis to salable products in the same years that the persisting pressure of diminished soil fertility was pushing them to expand "improved" acreage on their homesteads more rapidly than ever before.[4] Naturally enough, yeomen continued to rely on horses and oxen for help. And they naturally also persisted in mobilizing anyone living in their households. Thus, older sons continued to shoulder some of the major outdoor work; and although some indoor tasks (making clothing for family members, for example) had given way to the convenience of store-bought goods, women and children still undertook numerous chores in and around farmhouses. But given the added acreage yeomen were trying to tend and given the occasional shrinkage of farming households resulting from the departure of children for new homes – given this burden, the job of farming may well have weighed heavily on the average husbandman.[5]

Like farmers throughout the Northeast, those in Dudley and Oxford probably sought to ease their labors by hiring nonfamily employees. Unfortunately, the accelerating expansion of New England's economy meant that other, often better paying jobs were starting to beckon. As a result, antebellum Yankee yeomen often found themselves as unsuccessful in retaining their servants as in retaining their children. "Mr. Thrifty," the apocryphal hero touted by the *Old Farmer's Almanack* during this period, often worried about the problem:

> And then there was old Patrick M'Coulter, he had lived with us for years, you know; I never thought of losing him. He was one of the best at the plough; he could swing a scythe as easy a lady waves her fan in dogy days; and then, with a cradle in the grain field, there was no one up to him; it was mere walking, walking, sir, for amusement! But Pat, too...has turned cobbler![6]

As in previous years, it is impossible to determine exactly how many servants labored for Dudley and Oxford farmers during the generation after 1810. There is evidence that the increased scarcity of agricultural laborers raised their wages (up to $10 to $12 per month plus board in Oxford by 1832),[7] which would have made it even more difficult for local husbandmen to hire extra hands. All told, the number of farm workers almost certainly did not grow and may well have slightly declined compared with previous decades.

The identity of these workers remains similarly uncertain. Probably they included both males and females, though the former almost certainly predominated. Probably too they were mainly youngsters and young adults, as often newcomers as locally born, who had been pushed off Yankee homesteads by economic pressures and who viewed their stints as temporary. Many of these people probably hoped someday to own their own homesteads (or to marry men who did) – perhaps out West, perhaps nearby.[8] But it is also possible that, as the occupational spectrum of the region widened and as opportunities in husbandry constricted, increasing numbers of these servants drifted permanently out of agriculture (or married men who did) – the way, in the end, even "old Patrick M'Coulter" had. But in the meantime they labored as they always had: by themselves or in small groups, supervised (if at all) by only the proprietor of the farm on which they were employed.

III

Some of the jobs pulling servants and youngsters off the farm were in cotton and woolen factories. But other kinds of work were also becoming available. At least to men. If patterns characterizing other Yankees can be applied locally, increasing numbers of women and girls from Dudley and Oxford were probably landing jobs connected neither with farms nor textile mills – even if only briefly – before marrying and returning to household responsibilities. For local females, however, such opportunities were restricted mainly to those willing to take positions as milliners, seamstresses, and domestics in the larger cities of the region.[9] Comparable situations inside Dudley and Oxford were rare. By 1830 both townships had begun replacing the young men they had customarily hired to teach "winter schools" with women. But the indications are that few of the small businesses emerging after 1810 employed either women or girls. Although similar ventures in other towns did occasionally use females, the labor force in local nonfactory establishments appears to have been largely restricted to males.[10]

It also appears to have been divided into small units. The total number of wage laborers employed by the stores, workshops, and nontextile mills of Dudley and Oxford may have approached 300 to 350 individuals by the early 1830s. And the evidence suggests that by this point a few enterprises – the boot and shoe shops, for example, and the textile machine works – probably had rosters of ten to twelve men apiece. But like farm laborers, most employees in local nontextile establishments worked in smaller groups. Thus, stores and taverns appear to have rarely had more than two clerks at a time, and the shops turning out bobbins, chaises, nails, and leather goods probably had two to five men on their payrolls.[11]

Another feature of the labor force in nontextile establishments was its lack of supervisory personnel. Since proprietors of these businesses, like proprietors of farms, held direct managerial responsibility, and since these businesses were relatively small, there was little need for intermediary overseers. To be sure, there may have been *some* need. It is not clear whether local boot and shoe works undertook all their work processes inside their shops or (as was becoming increasingly common) parceled out certain jobs to outlying families. But in either case labor undertaken in the workshops may have been sufficiently complex to warrant an "overlooker." Similarly, if Oxford's textile machine shop paralleled comparable establishments of the period, it probably used a foreman to synchronize the steps of production. At the same time, however, the local nail-making enterprise – which embraced some of the most elaborate technology outside textile factories – evidently did without overseers. And so with the other nontextile establishments: Only those owning these ventures had authority over those laboring inside them.[12]

Yet, despite their close contact, workers and proprietors in local stores and workshops were only occasionally linked as apprentices and masters. Indentured youngsters are mentioned as serving in Oxford's millwright "school" and chaise-making shop; and it is also true that forms of pseudoapprenticeship – lasting only three years and providing small wage payments – were common in the early nineteenth century and may have been scattered through nonfactory ventures in Dudley and Oxford. But the evidence suggests that most who worked in these establishments were free wage laborers, typically in their late teens or older. And as such, of course, they were entitled to men's wages: usually $1.00 per day – more than agricultural labor could get except during the busy harvest periods. Skilled labor in local workshops commonly received $1.25.[13]

So, totaling upwards of 350 individuals, divided into small groups, comprised mainly (if not exclusively) of adult, male, and nonsupervisory free wage laborers – this much seems clear about the labor force in the nontextile enterprises of Dudley and Oxford.

But several further characteristics may be at least hypothesized. Given the overall transiency of local populations, it seems likely that these employees, like farm laborers, included newcomers along with long-term town residents. Their goals undoubtedly also paralleled those of farm laborers: Some would have hoped to save enough to facilitate – sometime, somewhere – the purchase of a homestead; others would have judged nonagricultural work of some sort as their permanent lot. But in either case they were almost certainly restless. Generally engaged in enterprises lacking any developed apprenticeship structures, generally employed by proprietors who themselves felt little sense of vocation toward their ventures, workers in the small businesses of Dudley and Oxford appear to have rarely identified with their jobs. Except for the most skilled workers – the machinists, perhaps, or those employed by Oxford's proud band of millwrights or the "skilled bakers from Boston" – wage laborers in local nontextile enterprises rarely viewed their work as defining or permanent. This was why, despite the spread of local handicraft shops, there was no local flowering of artisanal culture between 1810 and the early 1830s. This was also why workers moved about. All but the most skilled appear to have repeatedly switched jobs. Even the most skilled commonly moved to other communities. Most of these workers did both.[14]

IV

Ultimately, of course, it was employment in local cotton and woolen mills that took pride of place as the largest genre of nonagricultural labor in post-1810 Dudley and Oxford. By the 1830s the aggregate full-time factory work force was nearly two and a half times the estimated total labor force in nontextile establishments.[15] Each individual mill, moreover, had a far larger roster and a far more extensive supervisory staff than any single workplace outside the mill villages.

But even these data substantially understate the situation. Because for some years the influence of the factories as employing institutions stretched far beyond the factory compounds. This was due to the mills' use of employees who worked only intermittently and resided, even during their stints, outside the mill enclaves.

Some ad hoc workers were Dudley and Oxford residents who labored, as need arose, at various outdoor jobs. They worked on the farms that local factories commonly operated; or they were hired (like F. Smith and "[?] Eldridge of Dudley") to "dig a canal" or (like G. Bacon) to cart goods to and from the mill compounds. But along with these employees, the factories also initially mobilized local residents – again as need arose – for more skilled undertakings. Thus,

Charles Brown was hired in 1813 "to frame and fit doors" for a new building put up by the Merino Mill; Slater's South Village employed Asa Wood in 1823 to "construct" a "dwelling house" ("in a good workman like manner. . . of the form of the one built by Orin Knight"); and all through the 1820s the East Village used Stephen Harwood to perform blacksmithing chores.[16]

As it turned out, such ad hoc laborers proved, for the most part, merely a temporary feature of factory life. By 1830 – for reasons best detailed in the following chapter – they had run afoul of the regimen instituted in local mills and had been supplanted by full-time operatives living inside the factory compounds. But so long as it lasted, this cluster of occasional, skilled and unskilled adult male employees was one way Dudley and Oxford manufactories went beyond the names carried on their daily rosters.

Another, more important way was the use these mills made of outworkers: pickers who labored in their homes outside the factory compounds to prepare raw materials for spinning; and handloom weavers, also laboring in outlying homes, who transformed mechanically spun yarn into cloth. Though virtually ignored in most scholarly treatments of antebellum textile establishments, outworkers cannot be passed over in the story at hand. They comprised a work force charged with tasks vital to the daily operation of family-style mills like those in Dudley and Oxford. And they were extraordinarily numerous.

Textile outwork was probably not the only form of "putting out" known to local residents: As already indicated, boot and shoe shops in these communities may have distributed certain tasks to outlying households.[17] And it also requires notice that not every local factory recruited outworkers: Woolen works evidently used pickers and handloom weavers (the latter often skilled men) billeted within the mill compounds. Moreover, the outworkers that were used ultimately went the way of occasional farm laborers and carpenters: At various points after 1810 – again for reasons best explored in the next chapter – cotton mills found outworkers unacceptable. But while it lasted, the scaffolding of weavers and pickers created by local manufactories was almost certainly the most widespread form of outwork in Dudley and Oxford.

From the outset Slater showed the way – and it is evidence from his records that particularly illuminates these outlying textile employees. Having entered the South Gore in part to secure adequate outworkers, his vanguard East Village quickly established an extensive system of pickers and weavers. Between 1813, when the Green

Mill opened, and 1818, when he switched to using full-time operatives to open and clean his cotton, Slater employed more than 150
pickers working outside his compounds. It was not until the late
1820s that he completely relinquished outlying weavers in favor of
the Waltham system of fulltime operatives (mainly young women)
tending waterpowered looms inside mill buildings. By the late 1820s
he had, in fact, even begun exchanging his skilled woolen handloom weavers for machine tenders. But by that time also the list of
outworking weavers carried at one time or another by Slater's East
Village had ballooned to more than seven hundred individuals, with
some three hundred working simultaneously.[18]

The geographical diffusion of outworkers was no less remarkable.
Even in the earliest years of the East Village, less than half its outworkers (48.2 percent) lived in Dudley and Oxford. The majority
were scattered through a system stretching south to Thompson,
Connecticut, north all the way to Athol, Massachusetts, and reaching across some fifteen townships in between (Map 3.1). Over time,
and probably because of increased competition for weavers among
mills in the area, Slater's outlying weavers and pickers began strad-
dling even more territory. Between 1825 and 1828, the last four years
that Slater used outworking weavers, less than one-quarter (23.8
percent) of these employees lived within Dudley and Oxford. The
rest spilled across twenty-nine townships lying in three states and
covering some eight hundred square miles (Map 3.2).[19]

But precisely who in these scattered communities agreed to weave
and pick? The data on this point are, unfortunately, very spotty, but
hints are provided by a sampling of Oxford outworkers successfully
traced back into local records.[20] The sample reveals, first, a majority
of weavers and pickers connected to families containing a husband,
wife, and several children. There were a few older women (widows
and spinsters) whose domestic affiliations are unclear; and it was
reported elsewhere that some weavers within households were women
"who have no other means of support except [domestic] service
(which is unpopular. . .) [and who] lodge with farmers and give half
the produce of their labor for their board and lodging."[21] But most of
the Oxford sample (82.5 percent) lived amid sizable groupings of
close relatives. Indeed, the actual labor of weaving and picking was
by all indications distributed across the membership of these families: Wives and older daughters wove; wives and children picked;
and husbands traveled to the mill to deposit the finished work and
collect new assignments. Occasionally, to be sure, older daughters
appear to have tackled outwork assignments on their own and re-

Map 3.1. Geographical distribution of outworkers serving the Slater mills, 1813–16. ("A Map of Massachusetts, Connecticut, and Rhode Island Humbly Submitted to the Citizens Thereof by Theirs Respectfully, E. Ruggles"; Walpole, New Hampshire, 1819; courtesy of the Map Collection, Harvard College Library.)

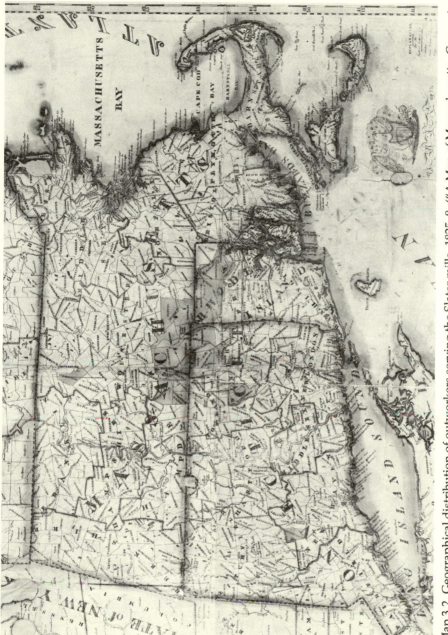

Map 3.2. Geographical distribution of outworkers serving the Slater mills, 1825–8. ("A Map of Massachusetts, Connecticut, and Rhode Island Humbly Submitted to the Citizens Thereof by Theirs Respectfully, E. Ruggles"; Walpole, New Hampshire, 1819; courtesy of the Map Collection, Harvard College Library.)

garded the resulting payments as their own private income. But for the most part both the duties and rewards of outwork were spread throughout the household.

A second characteristic of the Oxford sample is that most households taking on weaving and picking were not affluent. Nearly three-quarters of the outworkers turn up in the bottom half of the community's 1815 tax list, and just under 25 percent appear in the bottom quartile. And, finally, the sample's third characteristic: Oxford's outworking households did not depend entirely on picking or weaving for their livelihoods. The male household heads receiving cotton and "webs" of yarn were typically engaged in farming or some rural handicraft; and their households thus appear to have treated outwork as a supplementary, rather than a central, means of support.[22]

But a quick glance at the East Village records uncovers deviations from this portrait. Most obviously, there were exceptions to the characteristically part-time status of Oxford's outworkers, for increasingly after 1807 family factories like the East Village mills made use of journeymen weavers.[23] Often, like many of the artisans making up the famous Philadelphia handweaving trade, these were men who had migrated from England or Ireland. Often too, as the 1800s progressed, such migrants were impoverished and desperate figures: refugees from the savage dislocations in British handweaving during the 1830s and 1840s.[24] In general, however, there is no reason to suppose that journeymen weavers were all poor, any more than there is reason to suppose that they all followed the Oxford sample and divided their labor among household members. But what the Slater records do reveal is that these men worked full time. Some of them, in fact, evolved into employers in their own right, serving spinning mills – again including the East Village – as subcontracting "merchant weavers" who hired their own subsidiary system of outworkers.[25]

Still, to reiterate, these were exceptions: Most of the pickers and weavers Slater hired served part time. The East Village books indicate that outworkers typically took in jobs from the East Village in three or four stints per year and, judging from their output, did not labor continuously even on these occasions.[26] It follows that the earnings of Slater's nonjourneymen outworkers were not high. Paid in a mixed currency of cash, goods, and credit at the East Village factory store, their average recompense ranged from $7.79 a year (between 1813 and 1816) to $10.16 (during the 1820s), which, of course, simply confirms that this whole broad swath of Slater's outlying employees could not have lived exclusively on weaving and picking.[27]

Even if these people accepted work from other mills and even if their annual textile outwork earnings were thus two or three times the amounts posted in East Village ledgers, they would still have had to combine outworking wages with other sources of individual or household support.

This did not render outwork wages unimportant. Increasingly dependent upon the market for goods and services, but simultaneously engulfed in rising debt, many rural inhabitants turned to various forms of outwork not so much to get ahead as simply to hold their own. For weavers and pickers employed by the East Village, an extra $7.00 or $10.00 a year might provide the margin needed to purchase some sugar and extra meat or to replace worn shoes. Moreover, buried among Slater's "average" outworkers were numerous employees who were evidently so hard pressed – or belonged to families so hard pressed – that to maintain economic equilibrium they had to work substantially harder than most. Although still laboring only part time, fully 25 percent of nonjourneymen weavers carried by the East Village turned out a volume of cloth 50 percent above the norm.[28]

Part of the reason rural New Englanders used textile outwork to make ends meet was, of course, that the institution was in many ways built upon tradition. Immigrant journeymen weavers obviously looked back upon the heritage of an established craft. But nonjourneymen outworkers would also have found familiar the tasks distributed by the East Village. Even if they increasingly relied on store-bought goods, Yankees whose parents and grandparents had made linsey-woolsey would not have found picking and weaving cotton fundamentally alien. Nor did the division of labor common in outworking families mark a departure: Assigning indoor work like weaving and picking to women and children followed patterns long common in rural households. But what was perhaps most important, the characteristic role of outwork in the lives of these families paralleled familiar mores. Undertaking their labor not continuously but as they felt necessary, seeking more to preserve than to expand their economic horizons, nonjourneymen pickers and weavers effectively used outwork as a functional equivalent of the household manufacturing rural families had formerly performed to produce items needed in daily life. Youngsters and women would have found the neat fit of this transition particularly consequential. For it meant that just as these family members were losing indoor chores, like turning out homespun clothing, they could undertake at least somewhat comparable tasks for textile mills.[29]

But there was a key difference between the new and old arrangements. Outwork, unlike household manufacture, rested on a relationship between employees and employers. And (to forecast subsequent developments) it was tensions emerging between employees and employers – more specifically, between employees content simply to maintain themselves and employers who, more than any others in these communities, sought to maximize profits – that would critically undermine picking and weaving networks. Born of industrial needs, outwork would, in the end, fall prey to conflicts grafted deeply within the process of early industrialization.

V

Who worked inside the mill compounds? Who made up the full-time labor force of local textile factories? There was, first of all, the sizable staff of resident supervisors. Perhaps more than any other single cluster of employees in these townships during the generation after 1810, this was a group entirely given to using their jobs for personal economic advancement. It was a credential evidently typical of mill supervisors throughout antebellum New England: "Was any person to ask me, what recommends a man to the management of a cotton manufactory…in this country," the British immigrant Samuel Ogden pronounced in 1815, "I would answer, 'a desire to raise the interest of the person recommended'."[30]

Consider first the top echelon of resident supervisors. These were the "agents," the men responsible for determining production schedules, for maintaining adequate stocks of raw materials and adequate numbers of operatives, for supervising shipments of finished products, and for helping to shape and promulgate the "rules and regulations" of their establishments. It could make for busy days: "There are so many things to hear, see, settle, transact, digest, add, take off, increase and command," wrote a superintendent of this era, "all in and through the cotton dust that I can hardly tell what thing ought to come first."[31]

Beneath their specific tasks, however, agents found their role conditioned by a deep fear. Masters of family-style mills commonly shared the conviction – notable among early English industrialists – that entrepreneurs should if possible oversee their factories "in person" rather than rely on "agents, superintendents, and other servants, hired at large salaries, [but] having no interest in the ultimate prosperity of the concern."[32] The non-Slater mills of Dudley and Oxford reflected this viewpoint in two ways: first, unlike the absentee owners of Waltham establishments, at least a few proprietors of local mills kept in close touch with the daily operation of their industrial properties; and second, they chose agents from among these activist investors. Thus, although local textile mills, unlike smaller businesses, did not place every proprietor in direct managerial control, key factory managers *were* owners of these ventures – and thus supposedly possessed the requisite proprietary "interest" to discourage malfeasance. So the Merino Mill selected Aaron Tufts as its agent. And so, throughout its twenty-two-year career, the Dudley Woolen Manufacturing Company selected agents from a string of activist proprietors: John Brown, Nathaniel Lyon, Chester Clemons.[33]

For the North, South, and East villages the problem was more complex. As he had demonstrated even before arriving in the South Gore, Samuel Slater was committed to maintaining close personal contact with his industrial properties. There are indications, moreover, that over time he came to feel that he should hold his southern Massachusetts properties especially tightly, as though he had determined it was these enclaves that would most thoroughly exemplify his goal of direct proprietary control. However, it proved logistically impossible to remain constantly on station in Worcester County, for he was for many years still drawn to Pawtucket. He had remarried in 1817 and his new wife, Esther, was raising his six sons in this town.[34] Then too, Pawtucket remained the administrative headquarters for his various other investments. Besides the Old Mill and Smithfield interests that he held when the Green Mill opened, he joined with relations and friends in at least four other ventures (besides those in Dudley and Oxford) between 1813 and the late 1820s: the Amoskeag Mill in New Hampshire (1816); the Springfield Manufacturing Company in Ludlow, Massachusetts (1817); the Jewett City works outside New London (1823); and Rhode Island's first steam-powered cotton mill, the Providence Steam Cotton Company (1827).[35] Although less closely involved in these projects than in his Dudley and Oxford mills, Slater did monitor their affairs through his Pawtucket office, and he often insisted on personally viewing their operations. All this drew time and attention away from the North, South, and East villages.

The solution he implemented up through the late 1820s was pragmatic and shrewd. Since his sons were still too young to assume managerial responsibilities, and since the adult males he most trusted at this point (his brother, John, and the various Wilkinson men) were fully occupied elsewhere, he accepted the need for agents. But he took precautions. He bolstered the commitment of his superintendents by selling them proprietary shares in the works they governed and simultaneously preserved his own dominant role by retaining majority interest, demanding a barrage of detailed reports from his resident agents, and touring the southern Massachusetts villages – more often than his other mills – to inspect their daily progress. By these means he injected himself into the running order of the three enclaves: He evaluated the work turned out; he stipulated requirements for "steady," punctual, "industrious and temperate" workers and then helped select them; he fixed wage levels, provided his favorite hands with cash gifts, and chided the less favored for their "unfaithfulness"; and he even stayed abreast of gossip – "the bobbin turner has run away with a certain woman...," was his breezy report after one visit, "no doubt she is a *likely* woman."[36]

Despite its overall efficacy, however, this managerial format did not last. Slater made one exception in implementing the strategy, and it proved so spectacularly disastrous that as the 1820s wound to an end he moved abruptly to recast his administrative structure. The exception arose in 1822 when Edward Howard, a "rotund, rosy, and jolly" Englishman, formerly engaged by the Merino Mill and active in Slater's initial East Village woolen works, became both agent and equal partner in the newly constructed South Village. Unfortunately, it was discovered sometime between 1826 and 1829 that "the big Yorkshireman" was stealing merchandise from the South Village store.[37] Slater's response was, first, to buy out Howard's one-half share in the woolen works, and then (reckoning that three of his sons were by now sufficiently mature to administer factories) to place his southern Massachusetts properties under the co-ownership and revolving supervision of John, George, and H. Nelson Slater. By the end of 1829 these three young men – aged 24, 25, and 21, respectively – had joined their father as co-proprietors of the South and North villages; by 1833 the East Village too was entirely owned and managed by the Slater family. The three enclaves continued to use officials called agents. But henceforth such figures lacked any proprietary "interest" in the mills and worked under the careful scrutiny of a Slater heir – as well as under the frequent scrutiny of Samuel. For the "Arkwright of America" continued to make his flying visits, living during these sojourns in the "fine brick home" he had built in Oxford.[38]

Taken together, Slater and non-Slater agents in Dudley and Oxford displayed a range of credentials. The non-Slater mills took on both newcomers and long-term local residents, but in either case the men had little direct training in textile manufacturing: Again, Aaron

Tufts is a leading example. Slater, on the other hand, considered only candidates well versed in the business. Bela Tiffany, for example, who served as agent and co-partner of the East Village until 1816, had previously worked for Slater in Pawtucket. Another agent, John Tyson, was an experienced dyer from the Providence area. And even the notorious Edward Howard came to Slater seasoned from his Merino stint and equipped with "a general knowledge of the process of wool manufacture."[39]

Whether veterans or novitiates, agents serving local mills had some direct contact with the hands. Even in the North, South, and East villages, where they always had to consult with one or another Slater, superintendents usually personally hired and paid operatives in their factory. Yet there also existed abiding distinctions between these figures and their employees. Agents might prowl extensively about their mills – even "in and through the cotton dust" – but most of their daily labor was performed in isolated counting rooms. There are indications, moreover, that their living quarters were separate from, and considerably plusher than, the tenements and cottages reserved for operatives.[40] And, finally, agents received higher recompense than anyone else working for the factories. Owners of family mills did not join their Waltham counterparts in requiring superintendents to be "gentlemen" of high "social standing"; and agents in Dudley and Oxford were probably only moderately well off at the outset of their stints. Once at work, however, superintendents had handsome incomes. Nathaniel Lyon, for example, had an annual salary of $500 from the Dudley Woolen Manufacturing Company in the early 1820s; and the combination of wages and his "interest" in the East Village dyehouse helped John Tyson amass an estate worth $20,000 by the time he died in 1821. Nor did Slater's agents fail to do well after they were reduced to straight salary. In 1835 the annual pay of the East Village resident superintendent was pegged at $840.[41]

Earnings like these made the position of factory agent attractive to economically ambitious men. Mill superintendents were not necessarily bound permanently to factory careers, and some used their incomes to underwrite nontextile projects. On the other hand, those who lingered in manufactories and who (like Slater's post-1829 agents) did not hold proprietary interests may well have hoped one day to purchase (or at least lease) their own factories.[42] Although direct elevations from salaried agent to mill master did not occur in Dudley and Oxford mills in this period, they took place just often enough elsewhere to emerge as a credible goal for superintendents.

Below the agents were the room overseers. Although Slater had avoided these intermediary officials in his earliest Pawtucket works, they represented one form of heightened managerial supervision that he in fact did come round to introducing into his factories. His Old Mill and the Rehoboth factory both probably housed "overlookers" by at least 1802,[43] and his Smithfield property almost certainly had them from its inception. It is thus hardly surprising – though it clearly distinguished his ventures from most local nontextile establishments – that Slater used overseers in Dudley and Oxford. Nor is it surprising that every other entrepreneur organizing mills in these townships did likewise.

Overseers were always adult males and were typically stationed in every important factory workroom. Perhaps sitting at a "small desk, near the door," but more likely "walking to and fro in the room, or else standing in a place where he can see the greatest part of the hands that are at work," overseers were to "attend to the business of [their] Room[s]." Specifically, they were charged with training new operatives, monitoring the attendance and overall performance of hands under their charge, and (their central duty) enforcing rules and regulations laid down by agents and proprietors.[44]

In return for these duties, overseers (according to data from the Slater mills) received an average of $1.25 per day or roughly the going rate for skilled adult male workers in Dudley and Oxford. Although far below an agent's income, such wages could also appeal to ambitious men, whether or not they remained in the mills. Like superintendents, overseers were by no means rooted in manufactories and often invested their earnings in quite different endeavors. But also like superintendents, some overseers lingered within the industry, usually motivated by hopes of rising into higher posts – of becoming agents and proprietors themselves one day. And once again, although such advancements were evidently unknown in Dudley and Oxford in these years, they occurred often enough in antebellum Yankee mills to create credible expectations.[45]

But there were also significant differences between agents and overseers. There are hints, for example, that overseers generally came from less affluent backgrounds than superintendents. And it is certain that overlookers were selected far more consistently for their direct knowledge of factory life and work. Alfred Kingsbury, who supervised the weaving room of the Oxford Woolen Company in these years, had proven technical qualifications when he was hired; and James Millar, overseer of finishing in the same mill, came to this post after years of training and work in Middlefield and

Bellingham, Massachusetts.[46] Given his preference for experienced superintendents, it is hardly surprising that Slater also chose veteran overseers: "Wanted at Samuel Slater's factory in Oxford," announced the Green Mill in 1821, ". . . an Overseer for a carding room who has a *thorough* knowledge of the business." And in 1824 the same mill advertised for "a person to take charge of a Spinning Room that has had experience in that business." Indeed, Slater often did not even look beyond his own work force: Fully one-third of the men known to have acted as overlooker in Slater's Dudley and Oxford factories during the twenty years after 1813 had begun as operatives in these very establishments.[47]

Overseers also distinguished themselves from agents through their proximity to operatives. Laboring, and perhaps even boarding, alongside workers, room overlookers were inevitably drawn into more continuous contact with employees than either agents or nonagent proprietors – no matter how often the former left their counting rooms and no matter how intensely some of the latter (like Slater) involved themselves in mill operations.

Proximity, of course, could breed familiarity: "Deacon Howland," Slater disclosed after one of his visits to the East Village, "has married the young girl whom he had some difficulty with in the Card room some time since."[48] More generally, their close interaction with hands could promote conflicting loyalties. Striving to serve agents and proprietors, antebellum Yankee overseers were nonetheless often known to be sympathetic to employees serving under them; finding themselves sympathetic toward employees, overseers occasionally overcompensated, asserting their allegiance to factory policies with what (from the operatives' perspective) seemed excessive harshness.[49]

But whatever crosscurrents tugged at their emotions, overseers were, in the final analysis, members of the managerial elite ruling the factory villages. As such they shared important attributes with the agents and the mill masters of Dudley and Oxford – especially the owners, usually affluent, who took an active interest in factory affairs. In different ways and degrees, these men stood indisputably atop the social order of the mill compounds. As subsequent chapters will reveal, the authority they wielded over their enclaves was neither pervasive nor irresistible: It was bounded both by management's own priorities and by the operatives' developing opposition. Nonetheless, inside the industrial enclaves, proprietors, agents, and overseers represented an extraordinarily concentrated form of eminence. To an extent greater than had existed anywhere in Dudley and Oxford in 1810 or (as will become clear) anywhere outside the manufactories during the succeeding generation, these figures combined wealth, power, and prestige. It was, in fact, precisely the contrast between the position such men enjoyed within their industrial compounds and patterns prevailing elsewhere in Dudley and Oxford that would contribute to the frictions slowly emerging between the two townships and their manufactories.

VI

And, finally, the operatives, the largest single population of wage laborers to emerge in Dudley and Oxford in the generation following 1810. These were the full-time factory workers who labored inside the mill buildings, who were for the most part billeted inside the mill villages, and who always received – never gave – supervision. In 1832 the dozen-odd textile factories in Dudley and Oxford were using 816 such employees, of whom more than one-third (37.9 percent) worked in the three Slater enclaves. And by the same date the total population of his small North Village – including operatives and nonworking members of operative families – probably approached 70 individuals, and the East Village likely contained more than 550 residents. This kind of density, this number of people living and working close together, did not exist in the two townships in 1810 – and did not exist in succeeding decades except within factory compounds. A new scale was involved. Almost certainly the largest structures to appear in antebellum Dudley and Oxford (even Slater's small North Village Phoenix Mill stood three stories high and measured 81 by 34 feet), textile factories contained bigger concentrations of laboring individuals than any other local workplaces. And despite the somewhat increased clustering of residences across the two townships as time went on, factory enclaves clearly comprised the most densely populated villages to emerge in either Dudley or Oxford between the Revolution and the Civil War.[50]

Table 3.1 offers a glimpse into the evolving dimensions of Slater's East Village labor force, the most thoroughly documented group of local operatives. As these data reveal, the overall size of this work force was sensitive to economic turnabouts. Through its first three years, the East Village encountered steadily increasing demands for its products and reacted by expanding its payroll – and hence its output – substantially. The depression of 1816 reversed this trend by necessitating sizable layoffs. And although the shift from outworkers to residential pickers helped augment East Village rosters after 1818, the buffetings Yankee mill masters like Slater received from the 1819 panic significantly slowed recovery from the earlier slump.

Table 3.1. *Average annual work force, East Village, 1813–35*

Year	Average annual work force	Year	Average annual work force
1813	54.5	1825	130.8
1814	78.3	1826	130.0
1815	100.5	1827	131.0
1816	51.0	1828	136.5
1817	55.5	1829	132.5
1818	53.8	1830	132.0
1819	71.8	1831	186.0
1820	76.0	1832	180.8
1821	87.3	1833	177.3
1822	95.0	1834	116.3
1823	89.5	1835	139.3
1824	121.5		

Note: The size of each year's work force is an average of rosters posted in April, July, October, and January.
Source: SC: Slater and Tiffany, vols. 84, 88–91.

The big jump between 1823 and 1824 – from an average annual labor force of 89.5 to one of 121.5 – is somewhat mysterious. It may reflect the temporary inclusion on East Village payrolls of workers from the Phoenix Mill (which Slater had just purchased); or it may reflect Slater's initial experiments in hiring operatives to "tend" power looms. Generally, however, it is evident that, after 1820 as before, shifts in the number of East Village operatives were due mainly to managerial efforts to match changing demand with changes in over-all production. Thus the limits on growth through the late 1820s and into the early 1830s almost certainly reflected the series of bank and business failures (especially pronounced in 1829) that ruined many textile entrepreneurs and induced caution among survivors. (The abrupt expansion in 1831 is misleading, for it merely signals the availability, beginning in that year, of payroll figures for the Union Mill, which had actually started operation nine years earlier.) And the figures for 1834 and 1835 bear the imprint of further discourag-ing pressures: the rising cost of cotton and the shipping price of goods sold by these manufacturers. Again Slater weathered the storm, but as Table 3.1 indicates, he did so in part by reducing his East Village roster.[51]

Along with its shifting size, another salient structural feature of this labor force was its division by age and sex. Building on patterns set in England and generally preserved in early Yankee mills, jobs for men, women, and children inside Slater's East Village were more or less distinct. Boys "pieced" (tied up loose threads) for the mule spinners, and both boys and girls (their overall number evidently roughly equal) worked the carding engines and "doffed" (changed) spindles in the spinning room. Older girls and women ran roving and drawing frames and operated spinning machines and (after their introduction) power looms as well. The older brothers and fathers of operatives often joined locally recruited workers on the farms operated by these mills. Adult males who held berths inside the factories served as mule spinners, machinists, skilled handloom weavers in the woolen villages (until around 1830), and also as dressers, dyers, and other kinds of "finishers." And some men, of course, were supervisors.[52]

By 1832, when reliable quantitative data on the entire population of local operatives first became available, men comprised just under one-quarter of the East Village mill workers. This was roughly equivalent to figures for other local cotton factories, but it contrasts sharply to ratios in local woolen manufactories. Persistently less automated than cotton mills, and hence more dependent on skilled and physically strong employees, woolen works in these communities (again in 1832) listed payrolls in which adult males ranged from somewhat over one-third (the Tufts Woolen Mill) to nearly one-half (the Oxford Woolen Company) of all operatives employed.[53]

Comparably exact statistics are not available for women. Because power looms were almost always tended by older girls and women, shifts to this technology in the late 1820s and early 1830s strongly suggest that older females formed a larger proportion of local operatives in 1832 than in 1813. At the same time, however, the sources tend to blend "women and girls" so that precise counts of either group are difficult. At a rough guess women by the early 1830s were more numerous than men in cotton mills, less numerous in woolen mills, and comprised 40 percent of the labor force of all Dudley and Oxford factories – about 5 percent more than the total number of men. Combined with available figures for "boys" in these factories, this estimate, in turn, throws light on the number of child operatives. Specifically, it appears that children from 8 to 16 years old were (like women) more common in cotton mills than in woolen mills and represented around 25 percent of the total population of full-time textile workers.[54]

Since the East Village was not a Waltham-style enterprise, a third structural characteristic of its labor force involved the presence of family groups. It must be emphasized that only very rarely were *all* members of families simultaneously working inside a given mill or even simultaneously living inside a given mill village. Moreover, as will become apparent in subsequent probings of the factory regimen,[55] the precise proportion of family workers shifted significantly under different economic conditions. Still, by 1831 two or more members of thirty-two separate family groups were living and laboring in the East Village; and throughout this period at least two-thirds of this compound's work force had a parent, sibling, or child toiling in *some* room of the Green or Union mills. Something close to this ratio probably existed in other Dudley and Oxford cotton factories, but woolen mills once more reveal a different pattern. Employing comparatively fewer children and women, the latter enterprises also appear to have hired comparatively fewer workers linked by close kinship. Only one-third of the operatives in the Dudley Woolen Manufacturing Company, for example, ever shared the payroll with family members.[56]

But whether male or female, adult or child, attached or unattached to family groups, most operatives in all the local factory villages were free wage laborers. Indentured hands were not unknown among northern textile factories of this era; and some of the woolen hand-loom weavers kept on tap within the Merino village initially included short-term apprentices seeking to learn "the business of weaving in all its branches," in twelve months.[57] But this arrangement did not last beyond 1815 and in any case affected only a few workers. Following the policy of Slater's early mills, and paralleling the pattern typical of nontextile enterprises in these communities, cotton and woolen manufactories in Dudley and Oxford filled most of their berths with wage-earning employees.

VII

Such was the structure of the mill labor force. But obvious questions remain: Where did these operatives come from? Why did they come to the mills? Who were they?

Like the majority of millworkers in early antebellum New England, most employees of Dudley and Oxford factories were native Yankees. But for local operatives, at least, the predominance of ethnic Americans scarcely translated into a pattern of uniform geographical origin. Although there are indications (derived mainly from letters sent by millworkers) that manufactories in Dudley and Oxford recruited principally from southern New England, they clearly did *not* take employees from a few nearby communities. Of the the fifty-two households known to have worked in the East Village between 1813 and 1819, only seven (13.5 percent) lived in either Dudley or Oxford in 1810 and only two (3.8 percent) show up in the 1810 federal enumerations of the seven Massachusetts townships bordering on Dudley and Oxford. A comparable sample between 1821 and 1830 reveals 33.3 percent resident in Dudley or Oxford in 1820 but only 7.9 percent dwelling in contiguous communities. The proportion of operatives living in the vicinity of the East Village at least briefly before entering this enclave was thus growing. But even between 1820 and 1830 nearly three-fifths (58.7 percent) of the household heads Slater hired began the decade more than thirty miles away. Data from other local mills were scantier, but there are signs that these establishments, too, included on their rosters workers who had crossed considerable distances to secure their positions.[58] Recruited occasionally by agents but more often by advertisements ("Wanted at Samuel Slater's Factory...one or two large Families of Children"; "Wanted Immediately – A First-rate [wool] Jenny Spinner...at the Stone Factory – Dudley") or by word of mouth ("I have heard you was in want of someone"),[59] operatives entered these factories from communities scattered across Massachusetts, Connecticut, and Rhode Island and occasionally New York, New Jersey, and even Delaware.

To some degree, the nonlocal origins of Dudley and Oxford operatives simply reflect the geographic flux characteristic of all New Englanders in this era; millworkers, after all, were scarcely the only persons entering these townships between 1810 and 1830. But the extensive territory from which local mill employees were drawn also points to the difficulty small country mills of the period faced in finding laborers. The general shift toward nonagricultural work did, it is true, produce sufficient recruits that manufactories (as in both Dudley and Oxford) often emerged as a community's largest employer of nonfarm labor. On the other hand, antipathy to factory work – a sensibility building upon concerns already evident in the 1790s – remained sufficiently pervasive in the hinterland that country mill masters commonly found it impossible to fill their payrolls from a few nearby townships. It was different for Waltham-style manufactories: The wider reputation of these larger ventures attracted more regular streams of job applicants and permitted recruitment from, if not nearby communities, at least a comparatively small number of locations. But for family mills the task was rarely so easy. In Dudley and Oxford, at least, managers had to draw from a wide assortment of townships to drum up the hands they required.[60]

Yet hostility to millwork was only part of the reason staffing proved difficult. Other factors also contributed to the problem – even when (as detailed shortly) mills began recruiting employees thoroughly experienced in factory work. Again continuing from the 1790s, but aggravated by the competition for operatives among New England's increasing number of textile factories, the region's overall labor scarcity played a role. So did the fact – yet again developing from patterns in the late eighteenth century – that operatives lingered only briefly in any given mill. Although factory employees in Dudley and Oxford rarely limited their stints to a single season, managerial efforts to balance reduced sales with reduced payrolls, combined with the continuing restlessness of the operatives themselves, produced average East Village engagements ranging from 1.1 years (for those employed in 1813) to 1.4 years (for those on the payroll in 1830), with at least 6 percent (10 percent in the Dudley Woolen Manufacturing Company) remaining less than half of any month and a persisting majority (60 percent in 1813 and 51 percent in 1830) staying nine months or less.[61] It followed that, except during economic downturns when payrolls shrank and operatives clung to jobs in hand, managers faced an almost endless chore of filling slots vacated by departing workers.

Yet there was obviously another side to the story. Despite all the indications of reluctance among Yankees to become operatives, enough men, women, and children did show up to permit local factories to function. The precise balancing of pressures and inducements played out between particular managers and workers before rosters could be filled turns out to have been an exceedingly complex process and may thus be left for the full-dress analysis undertaken in Chapter 5. What is relevant at this point is the more general question of why early nineteenth century Americans even considered entering factories like those in Dudley and Oxford.

Not surprisingly, there were many reasons. Some people, it seems, were simply not put off by the poor reputation of manufactories. Others came because of friendship or kinship with hands already in place: "My sister is coming to work there this week," announced a prospective employee of the Dudley Woolen Manufacturing Company in the 1830s, "and I will come in two weeks."[62] And, of course, money also played a large role.

Like other country mills, local factories appear to have initially paid employees in a mixture of goods (usually from stores run by the mills) and cash. But although operatives continued to run up credit at factory retail outlets throughout the post-1810 generation, cash payments grew more common as time passed.[63] By 1832 wage payments appear to have been entirely in currency, and averaged out – for every man, woman, and child operative in Dudley and Oxford – to 54.1¢ per day. If each mill had kept to its optimal 310-day working schedule (6 days per week each week of the year) and if all workers had labored all day every day, the average annual factory wage would have come to $167.71.[64]

To be meaningful, however, these data need to be broken down to reflect divisions within the local textile work force. Thus, men with berths inside the mills averaged daily wages of 87.9¢ and projected annual wages of $272.49; boys and girls received 25.2¢ daily with $78.12 projected annually; and women got 42.6¢ each day and $132.06 for a full working year. These distinctions produced another: Because woolen mills employed comparatively more men, average daily wages in these factories ran 18.4 percent above those in the cotton mills. And, finally, the difference between workers attached to families and those unattached: In Slater's North Village in 1832 earnings of the latter group ran nearly 25 percent ahead of the former contingent (which included children), and families as units earned just over twice what unattached employees received.[65]

But even these figures need refining. In the first place, mills did not run 310 days per year: Machines broke down, shipments of raw materials were delayed, and water supplies were occasionally disrupted. Nor did every operative turn up every hour the mills did run. Workers got sick or stayed away for a few hours or days or picked up and left completely. As a result, *actual* earnings of Dudley and Oxford operatives virtually always fell at least 10 percent below levels estimated for always-punctual, never-absent employees of always-running factories.[66]

In the second place, the wage data cited thus far refer to *gross* earnings. But part of this money had to be spent immediately to cover living costs. Workers occasionally rented cows (at $1.00 per month) from their employers. More often they rented housing: A majority of all operatives and a wide majority of family workers lived in the mill villages, paying from $1.00 to $7.00 per month for space in company lodgings.[67] Those in the boardinghouses probably believed they received good worth for their money. Certainly the meals were ample:

> For breakfast and supper Coffee or Tea with sugar and cream
> Brown and White bread or Cakes or pies and butter and cheese

and meat, Ham fresh meat or a substitute which shall be acceptable to the boarders. Dinners for each week one day baked pork
and beans with pudding 2 days fresh meat roasted 2 days a variety boiled Saturday a good Fish dinner.[68]

But the expenses still mounted. In Slater's North Village Phoenix
Mill in the early 1830s the cost of cows and boarding reduced average annual earnings by one-sixth for unattached workers and by
more than one-quarter for families.[69]

And then there were debits run up (usually in factory stores) for
clothing and other staples. Although such charges can only be estimated, they probably represented the stiffest economic drain of all.
Unattached workers may have escaped fairly lightly, but data stitched
together from several Slater records indicate that families could easily spend several hundred dollars – often from 50 percent to more
than 70 percent of their gross earnings – on purchased necessaries.
Because mills usually subtracted a worker's outstanding expenses
before distributing wages, the economics of factory village life effectively reduced the amount of currency managers had to keep on
hand. But by the same token, these economics also drastically undercut the net income operatives could derive from factory stints.
After covering all their bills, workers may well have found much of
their earnings – perhaps 65 to 95 percent among some family employees – entirely used up. Indeed, a few local millworkers seem to
have actually ended their stints in debt. "I am owing the . . . [mill],"
Joseph Collier admitted to the South Village in the late 1820s, "and
have not the money to pay."[70]

But if payments offered by manufactories were so extensively
whittled down, how could wages quoted by mill masters like those
in Dudley and Oxford have helped pull Yankees into millwork? Part
of the reason was that some operatives did win substantial net earnings. Skilled adult male machinists and mule spinners, especially if
they had no families, could make $400 or $500 a year over and above
their expenses.[71] A second reason was that the wages of factory labor
received far greater publicity than the operatives' net incomes, and
for many prospective employees factory wages were higher than the
going rate in other available jobs. The wages of most men and older
boys in local mills, for example, at least equaled, and often surpassed, what agricultural laborers could expect through most of the
year. Women too often discovered that wages in small country factories were an improvement over pay scales in other occupational
niches they were exploring in this period. And even children –
whose comparatively low rates helped pull the average factory wage

in Dudley and Oxford some 20 percent below average daily payments to the all-adult labor force of a contemporary Lowell manufactory – even children could earn more in millwork than in other undertakings open to them.[72]

VIII

In the final analysis, however, the motivations drawing Yankees into manufactories reflected the variety of the operatives themselves. Perhaps more than any other group of local wage laborers, textile operatives were a mixed lot. There was no "typical" factory employee. On the contrary, what remains to be said about the identity and goals of local millworkers reveals the presence of several social types.

Some operatives (exact numbers are not possible) took up millwork not out of pressing need but from choice: Because they believed factory stints would provide helpful, even exciting, interludes in their lives. Comprised principally of single, young adults of middling economic standing, this contingent included ambitious men – like a certain Calvin Phipps in the East Village – who hoped (probably naïvely) that factory earnings would provide capital to expand their estates. It included a few – like Oxford's Hollis Witt – who were simply waiting upon inheritances of farms or businesses they knew would come their way. And, perhaps most frequently, it included people from relatively comfortable farming backgrounds who were unable or unwilling to proceed directly into lives of husbandry. They were men like Nathan Hall and Jonathan Day, sons of wealthy landowners whose patrimony, though substantial, included little or no real estate.[73] And, especially after family mills began needing young women to tend power looms, there were at least a few recruits like those the mills of Lowell and Waltham sought to employ in this era: "respectable" women who wanted their own money (because they were "in need of clothes" or wished larger dowries); or who wanted to find husbands; or who wanted simply a change from the treadmill of chores on small Yankee farms.[74]

Unlike Waltham-style proprietors, however, family mill masters like those in Dudley and Oxford did not try to limit their payrolls to operatives from "proper" economic and social backgrounds. Following the precedent set by Slater's Old Mill, they also hired "destitute and very poor" people who used factory berths as temporary refuge from pressing want. Often they were unmarried sons and daughters shifting out of farm life with the particular further credential of needing to find work quickly. A few were younger children of hard-pressed Yankee parents (both rural and urban) dispatched to the mills in custody of other households. Needy widows also turned to local factory villages: So Mrs. Samuel Ammidown found berths for herself (as boardinghousekeeper) and her children (as operatives) when her cordwainer husband died leaving only $80.[75]

But probably a larger number of poor operatives arrived as members of households led by two living parents. The impressions that can be teased from letters and genealogies suggest most such households came from rural areas: They were headed by landless laborers or by yeomen whose "small and poor farms" no longer provided adequate support. Other hard-pressed households were led by men seeking relief from sudden setbacks in artisanal or commercial ventures: William Googins, for example, who brought his household to the East Village after losing his ship and fortune to a French privateer during the War of 1812.[76] Indeed, moving beyond specific cases, the data suggest that a considerable number of millworking families may have undertaken factory engagements precisely during periods of maximum economic strain: during phases of their life cycles when the "greatest number of children" were born but a large proportion remained too young to earn wages in any labor besides millwork.[77]

The presence of such households offers the final explanation for why operatives entered millwork despite the threat of low net incomes. Workers suffering the most sharply diminished net earnings in factory villages were almost always attached to families, and often, it seems, to families who arrived in local mill compounds already poor. Even in a period of general labor shortages, families in economic extremis probably had limited options, and a stint in a textile factory could thus seem attractive by default. Using all their earnings for food and lodgings would not have appeared a critical drawback to people who might otherwise have had difficulty feeding or sheltering themselves.[78]

A final group of operatives were veterans: workers who arrived at local manufactories already well versed in millwork and who, by all indications, passed on to other factories when they left. Deriving originally from a mix of farming, commercial, and artisanal backgrounds, ranging economically from the needy to the quite well off, veterans overlapped the two contingents already discussed. Nor did they sharpen their identity by remaining permanently in industrial labor. Few veterans ended their laboring days in textile mills, and many seem to have moved back and forth between mills and various nonfactory jobs. Nonetheless, veterans deserve notice as operatives

who devoted appreciable fractions of their working lives to manufactories and who probably possessed greater allegiance to their
trade than most wage laborers passing through Dudley and Oxford.

The earliest veterans had been Irish and English operatives who
had found work in the American mills of the 1790s. A few "Old
Country men" continued to hold factory berths throughout the antebellum period, but native-born New Englanders were soon also
billing themselves as experienced textile workers. Often they were
adult males and highly skilled. Thus in 1823 a Yankee fully expert in
wool finishing wrote the Dudley Woolen Manufacturing Company
asking "if you are in want of one of my trade." By the mid and late
1820s, however, and increasingly during the 1830s, less skilled jobs,
including positions reserved for women, fell to candidates with millwork already under their belts: A certain Miss Lamb, for example,
knew enough about factory employment in 1827 to stipulate before
her arrival at the Dudley Woolen Mill that "she would like a broad
loom." Indeed, even children could achieve veteran status: "I can
spin or weave," claimed John Brierly in a note sent to the South
Village from a Framingham, Massachusetts, mill village in 1829.
Then he added – in the breathless, run-on style and spelling of a
man living just at the juncture of written and oral expression – that
he had "one boy that can spin one gerl that can wave on a pour loom
another his large enough and one boy that has ben feeding the
breaker in the carding room."[79]

Why veterans remained involved in factories as long as they did
has no simple answer. Undoubtedly there were young men and
women who saw prolonged millwork as simply a readily available
way of enjoying the advantages of a wage-earning job. For the boys,
of course, there was also the lure of advancement: from unskilled
child labor to skilled men's work or to an overseer's post and thence,
possibly, to posts of agent and proprietor. To some degree, the
laddered vocational expectations of agents and overseers thus penetrated lower male positions in a manufactory as well. Again it bears
emphasis that few in New England, and no one in Dudley and
Oxford, climbed all the rungs. Yet the steps of advancement were
palpable and occasionally some were taken: Piecers did become mule
spinners, and (as indicated by Slater's recruitment of overseers) young
men could climb into "overlooking" jobs.[80] All this was sufficient to
keep ambitious individuals in the mills for a while. But there were
other, less striving employees with different reasons for staying on.
Operatives trapped on treadmills of low or nonexistent net earnings, for example, may well have concluded that seeking new kinds

of employment without savings was not an option to be seized quickly. And probably some employees – like professional soldiers of every age – found institutional discipline a positive comfort.

These were the hopes and rationales leading veterans to linger in textile manufactories. Indeed, these hopes and rationales were evidently sufficiently compelling that veterans became increasingly numerous in Dudley and Oxford factories between 1810 and the early 1830s. Local managers, for their part, began stipulating as early as 1818 that (like overseers) workers who had previously "worked in a mill would be preferred."[81] More significant is the fact that between 1810 and the 1830s a mounting proportion of operatives arriving at local factories had actually put in previous stints in these very establishments. In 1820, 4.5 percent of East Village employees of all skill levels had logged earlier stints in this compound; in 1830 the figure was just under 33 percent. Together with increasingly frequent claims of experience from other mills ("I have worked for the Pocasset Co. over 16 years and I think I should be able to suit you"), these figures point to an expanding presence in local mills of operatives thoroughly familiar with manufactories.[82]

Since much the same was happening in mills all over New England, there occasionally arose a curious anomaly in the labor market of millworkers. By the 1820s some veteran operatives were so enmeshed in their round of factory berths that they resisted shifting into other occupations even during "hard times" when factory jobs were scarce. Amid the general pattern of mills having to search widely for operatives, there were thus moments when experienced workers found themselves pleading for positions. Foreigners probably faced the greatest duress, for when jobs grew scarce, Yankee mill masters generally favored Americans over immigrants. "It's Really Discouraging in the Extreme," an English wool finisher told Slater during a slump in the woolen trade in the late 1820s: "I have tryed all the country from New York to this port [Boston] and its neighborhood without being able to meet with employ . . . surely this is not the case through all America if it is give me Old England with all its Disadvantages."[83] But Yankees too sometimes had difficulty finding work. William Shaw from South Brimfield, Massachusetts, wrote the South Village during the same slump, cautiously suggesting a previous stint in this factory should strengthen his application: "In memory of past times I again refresh my mind by writing to you my situation that I am not employed." And another woolen worker wrote after "a absence of 3 years" in the hope "you will *if possible* give me a suitable birth." Sometimes workers simply stated their need: "I have a large family," the letter (quoted earlier) from John Brierly concluded:

> and as had no settled place since the factory was
> burnt here if you would like me to work for you
> please writ by the first and state how you pay...
>
> No more from Yours –
> John Brierly[84]

But unemployment among veteran millworkers was exceptional, and the main consequence of their increasing ranks was not poignant job applications. In Dudley and Oxford, at least, the principal consequence of the veterans' growing numbers was a slowly strengthening sense of unity among the operatives.

Because at the outset factory workers in Dudley and Oxford had been deeply fragmented. Most of the divisions followed directly from characteristics already attributed to these employees. Thus, they often arrived in the mill villages as strangers from widely scattered communities, and they typically remained only briefly; their experiences within the compounds varied tremendously according to age, sex, and income; and their broader loyalties to co-workers were often undercut by more immediate commitments to family members and by the divergent backgrounds and expectations implicit in the presence of middling, poor, and veteran employees.

And there were other corrosive pressures as well. Inside the mill buildings workers were separated by the distribution of different departments across several floors (for no mill had fewer than two stories) and between different rooms. And even inside the same room workers had to contend with the deafening roar – "like frogs and Jewsharps all mixed together" – thrown out by the machines.[85] Containing very likely the largest and most thickly populated interior work spaces existing in the early nineteenth century New England hinterland, textile mills thus, paradoxically, also introduced unprecedentedly numerous and emphatic separations among employees gathered inside their walls.

Then too, within the mill villages, a key factor inhibiting unity was the absence of facilities permitting sizable numbers of operatives to meet easily and comfortably. Divided between boardinghouses and separate family cottages, local factory workers (unlike the Waltham-style employees with their large common dormitories) found even their lodgings conspired against significant gatherings. As indicated by Map 3.3 of the South Village, operatives bedded down in more than a dozen separate dwellings. Besides the small

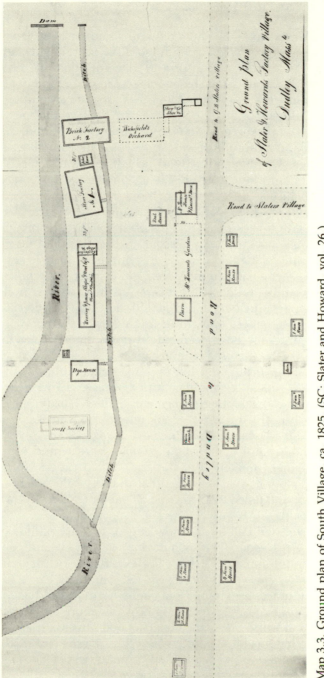

Map 3.3. Ground plan of South Village, ca. 1825. (SC: Slater and Howard, vol. 26.)

store (leased to "Day and Co." and standing next to "Wakefield's Orchard"), there was evidently no place to hold substantial indoor meetings; indeed, a plan of a Merino Mill boardinghouse reveals that not even the larger tenements contained communal rooms.[86]

Nor did workers often join together outside the compounds. There is no evidence of broad operative participation in the two Masonic lodges that flickered up in Oxford during this period. And there is certainly no indication of widespread operative involvement in town meetings. The demanding work schedule of the factories, an apparent inclination to enforce residency and property requirements for the franchise at least somewhat more strictly among operatives than among other local inhabitants, the particular obstacles faced by East Village employees as inhabitants of the politically ambiguous South Gore – all this effectively discouraged widespread participation in local politics. The few workers living outside factory enclaves may, it is true, have enjoyed more frequent contact with community civic and social institutions. But except for three or four mule spinners who managed to join Oxford's militia and some involvement in local religious activities, operatives in Dudley and Oxford during this period appear to have been cut off from opportunities to meet and mingle within the broader currents of town life.[87]

Persisting throughout the post-1810 generation, such factors by no means precluded social contact among millworkers. It is significant in this regard that 65 percent of East Village operatives who married during their stints took another village resident as mate. But the steady constraint of divisive pressures and obstacles meant that among local operatives generally there would never develop more than a "limited" camaraderie, a camaraderie that was most intense among small groups, that did not rule out broader collaborations but failed to encourage a "habit of solidarity" among non-relatives.[88]

And yet, with all this acknowledged, an important evolution still took place. Despite their own intrinsic variety, veteran operatives at the very minimum did share the experience of previous bouts of millwork. And within the confines of "limited" camaraderie, common references springing from earlier berths would have promoted at least *greater* unity. Larger and probably more heterogeneous than other local work forces, the rosters of operatives carried by manufactories in Dudley and Oxford would thus, by the late 1820s, also drift toward a measure of worker unity unknown in the fields, stores, and workshops of these communities.[89]

IX

This was the social organization of occupations in Dudley and Oxford during the first generation after 1810. It was not a simple pattern. Involving different kinds of people laboring in a steadily
expanding assortment of jobs, reflecting broad regional trends toward transiency and away from agriculture – encompassing this
whole evolving arrangement of individuals and work, the structure
outlined here was unavoidably complex.

But it does identify important protagonists in the social history of
the two towns. Coupled with the proprietors of new ventures, the
farmers, small-business employees, artisans, outworkers, agents,
overseers, and operatives working in Dudley and Oxford in this
period embraced a large fraction of the two local populations, a
pivotal constituency among those facing the transitions pressing
upon these communities.

But precisely what did these people face? And how did they respond? These questions have no single answer. The very heterogeneity of the occupational social structure in Dudley and Oxford
underscores that what happened in these townships during this
period cannot be treated as the unified experience of a single undif-
ferentiated population. The specific changes, or lack of changes, and
the specific new pressures or persisting traditional conventions that
different local residents felt in their daily lives or saw around them –
this is what has to be considered. Because this was what industrialization meant.

4 *The industrial order*

I

The economic structure of Dudley and Oxford during the generation after 1810 had three broad characteristics. First, the increased, but still significantly limited, commercial involvement of agriculture. Second, the dramatic expansion of small-business establishments; and third, the appearance of manufactories along the streams of the two communities. Together with the emergence of investors to sponsor the new shops, stores, and textile mills, and the alterations in local occupational patterns produced by post-1810 ventures, it was farming, small-business activities, and textile manufacturing that determined the basic economic format of Dudley and Oxford between 1810 and the early 1830s.

In a sense, the three strands were complementary. Local agricultural patterns, for example, both reflected and supported the spread of nonagricultural enterprises to at least some degree; and shops and factories, for their part, often provided mutual technical and commercial encouragement. But there were significant distinctions among the organizational regimens – the basic internal orderings – of the three economic sectors. And to understand what local residents faced in this period, it becomes important to identify these distinctions: to specify precisely how yeomen governed – or, as it turned out, failed to govern – their daily affairs; how nontextile businesses were administered; and how cotton and woolen manufactories orchestrated their machines and workers.

The ordering of life and labor inside the mill villages requires particularly detailed treatment. It was by far the most complex disciplinary structure – involving dense, sometimes conflicting interweavings of new ideologies and practices – and it impinged directly upon the largest single group of local wage laborers. But taken as a whole, the populations of Dudley and Oxford confronted the order of agricultural and nontextile labor as well. And in the final analysis, it was the blend – and contrast – of regimens ramifying through all three economic spheres that shaped the experience of local residents in the decades after 1810.

100

II

A key factor conditioning farm life in these years was the lack of adequate labor. As already remarked, the average yeoman's effort to improve a larger proportion of his homestead with a fixed, or even diminishing, roster of children and servants represented a wearisome burden. The pressures behind this burden – the reasons that youngsters permanently quit their farming homes and that agricultural laborers required increasingly high wages – have already been explored.[1] But how did the shortage – or expense – of farming labor affect those remaining on the homestead?

In the first place, it added new shadows to relations between parents and their offspring, for the rising number of permanent youthful departures had cultural as well as economic dimensions. On the one hand, these departures almost certainly strengthened the belief among sons and daughters (even while they remained on the farm) that they could and should ultimately seek independence. Even if (as was probably often the case) departing children launched into ventures with their parents' blessing and assistance, the children themselves may well have experienced an unprecedentedly vivid sense of autonomy. "The weight," observes one student of youthful culture in this era, "was increasingly on the side of independence."[2]

For their part, parents seem to have responded to the wave of departures with growing frustration and worry. Anxiety about the integrity of domestic life had been part of American discourse, both public and private, since the earliest colonial days. But beginning in the 1820s, mounting steadily in the 1830s and 1840s, pressures on the family seem to have become sufficiently disruptive to generate a new structure of feeling about rural life: a sustained wondering among rural parents – by turns nostalgic and angry – about whether they could get the job of farming done and whether, even if they could, farming as they had known it was not in serious jeopardy. For even if it was economically rational for a given yeoman's children to leave, was not the basic continuity of husbandry threatened by the flight of "every farmer's son and daughter"?[3] And even if children turned to nonagricultural ventures with the approval of their parents, could not these same parents still accuse their sons of turning into "dandies" (into "Tom, my Twattle") when these young men decided that "it was ungentlemanly to know how to handle a hoe or a pitchfork"? Could not these parents complain that, with so few daughters willing to "join the mother in her domestic duties," young women were growing up "so little informed..., they can hardly cook a potato"?[4] And could not these parents also fear for the viability of their own farming ventures? "Why thus alone at your ploughing, Mr. Thrifty?" asked the *Old Farmer's Almanack* in one of its famous cautionary dialogues:

> O, sir, my boys have all left me and turned shoe-peggers. I was in hopes to keep at least one of them to help carry on the farm; but they have all five gone... If this is the way things are going on, our farms must soon run up to bushes.[5]

Yeomen in Dudley and Oxford could not have avoided this mounting sense of vulnerability. Nor could they have offset their concern with hired laborers. It was not only that such workers were scarce and thus expensive but also that relations between farmers and servants showed increased strain. If trends evident in other communities held up in Dudley and Oxford, local farmers using agricultural workers could afford to hire them only by the season rather than by the year as formerly.[6] And this, in turn, meant that such workers were less frequently treated as full members of the farming household. Contemporary reports held that even skilled reapers were refused permission "to sit at table with the family." And testimony was growing that farm laborers, for their part, no longer felt any shared interest with their yeoman-employers. Instead, laborers were said to display a "plebian envy of those above them"; and they "do not consider themselves bound for any length of time, and occasionally absent themselves for a day or two without giving notice of their intention."[7] With employers, as with children, there was the sense of a domestic chemistry turning increasingly sour: "So you see," intoned the Almanack's bitter-sad summary in the early 1840s,

> that it will not do to trust altogether to servants, though you may think them all trustworthy. Slam! Slam! go the green blinds, amidst the storm, in the absence of the owner; but what care servants about this?... Was the master at home, eyes ears, and feet would all be in full employment. But, suppose now, in these modern times, so famous for *quid pro quo*, your servant has as many eyes as Argus, sleeping with two only at once – would he heed or care for this rattle and ruin? Not unless there is a special provision for it in the bargain; for good old fashions are done away.[8]

But in the end, any shifts in social relationships on local homesteads were more than offset by the continuities of farming life. To balance scarce labor, for example, yeoman households throughout the region retained the custom of aiding one another during busy planting and harvest seasons. Despite the rapid transiency through these two communities, nearly one-fifth of all farming households in Dudley and Oxford may still have had relatives of some sort living in the vicinity; and together with neighboring friends and acquaintances, those kinsmen would have provided a safety net of willing workers.[9] Nor should the altered dynamics between parents and children be exaggerated, for the fact remains that children often *did* move on with parental advice and consent. And there exist, in any case, too many examples of widely scattered relatives maintaining contact with one another to assume that family bonds crumbled beneath the comings and goings of rural Yankees.[10]

But the most concrete continuities lay in the actual processes of husbandry, in the ordering of daily agricultural work. The evidence here must again be culled from across the region. But the indications are that agricultural commercialization had by no means proceeded far enough in the early nineteenth century to force wholesale revision in the routines of Yankee farming. On the contrary, yeomen like those in Dudley and Oxford evinced almost glacial reluctance to alter the substance of their daily labors.

Their inertia is the more notable because the period witnessed repeated efforts to alter farming technology and technique. New machines – cast-iron ploughs, horse-drawn cultivators (for corn), and hay rakes – were introduced,[11] and a deluge of new agricultural journals advised an entire curriculum of new methods. The basic seasonal rhythms of Yankee farming were not challenged. But yeomen were called upon to use more manure, to adopt soil-saving crop rotations, to confine homesteads to the acreage they could entirely cultivate every year, and generally to adopt rigidly systematic methods of "general management." "A farmer needs more drilling in this business," announced *The Young Farmer's Manual* in a passage that neatly captured the zeal of antebellum farming reformers, "than a general does in military tactics to be able to manage an army of soldiers."[12]

But even the most enthusiastic missionaries of change found Yankee husbandmen to be slow converts. New tools were not totally ignored, and fertilizer and English hay evidently did gain broader favor. But the revised hardware never won more than spotty acceptance, and apart from a trend toward eliminating summer fallows, there was little systematic crop rotation. Moreover, judging from the steady complaints of reformers and data from Dudley and Oxford, most New England farmers maintained or raised productivity by "improving" more acres within their homesteads rather than by limiting homesteads to just those fields and meadows they could continuously exploit.[13]

Why this resistance to change? In part it was probably simply an intuitive hostility toward the unfamiliar. But a recent analysis concludes that Yankee stolidness in the early antebellum era also arose because innovations "intruded upon a system of production which represented a rough balance between the various resources applied within each farm unit." New England farmers might shift more heavily toward the market, might cultivate more land per farm, might demonstrate more concern over soil fertility, and might even (as they did in Oxford in 1812) organize agricultural societies to promote these trends. But to go further would have disrupted the "form of balanced operations" yeomen had achieved.[14] New technologies were thus rejected, not out of "rural idiocy," but because using them would have produced surpluses beyond levels they could sell or consume, or because (especially in the case of hay rakes) they would have required unreasonable allocations of scarce labor resources to smooth out rocky New England fields. And so with crop rotations: The investment of capital and labor called for was frequently beyond Yankee husbandmen or involved an expanded production of crops (like wheat) that were already produced in large and cheap supply beyond the Hudson River.[15]

In sum, reforms were often impractical. But it was also the case that even feasible innovations implied an outlay of resources that made sense only if farmers were committed to the market and only if they were willing to adopt the long-term perspective of businessmen. In fact, farmers had by no means wholeheartedly adopted this position.[16]

It was, to reiterate, a question of balance. If New England yeomen placed greater stress on marketable goods during the 1820s and 1830s, and if they were drifting increasingly into nonagricultural enterprises, the tilt to commerce still did not necessitate a thorough acceptance of market priorities. Most farmers still mixed their quest for gain with a commitment to immediate "family needs." In Dudley and Oxford (as already noted) it was probably often to satisfy such "needs" that farmers undertook business ventures or helped sons and daughters move in this direction. Within the context of farming itself, the persisting stress on household priorities was demonstrated in the continued cultivation of foodstuffs for domestic consumption. And it may even explain why local husbandmen resisted smaller landholdings: For it might have been believed that preserving farms of some size would increase the possibility of passing on land to heirs. That debts and youthful migrations often eviscerated this hope would not have weakened its fervor. Indeed, considering northeastern farmers generally, the abiding importance of family priorities underlay antipathy toward many elements of the reform program. Unwilling to accept gain as their exclusive goal, farmers saw little reason to reject "the customary practices of an area."[17]

Not surprisingly, such recalcitrance met strong criticism from agricultural writers of the period. The stubborn Yankee husbandman was reduced virtually to a stock character and ridiculed repeatedly as a man "who condemns new things because they are new; who dislikes to see them attempted, and likes to see them fail."[18] In communities like Dudley and Oxford attacks on yeoman conservatism often also led to observations that farms represented the cultural antithesis of textile mills. Factories, after all, were easily taken to represent the very culmination of "general management" and commercialization. Pursuing an argument initiated by profactory writers in the late eighteenth century, agricultural reformers hailed antebellum manufactories as crucial instruments in forwarding the market's leavening influence on the hinterland. The capacity of mills to provide a "ready home market" for farm goods, it was said, was the "impelling and most efficient cause of Agricultural employment"[19] in New England. If, therefore, farmers were seen as consistently rejecting an innovative and profit-hungry outlook on life, they could scarcely avoid also being viewed as rejecting the entire influence of textile factories. Thus the stereotyped contrast: "For within the hum of a single textile mill," a Connecticut pamphlet concluded as late as 1850, "there is more...skill and science applied to practical art and labor than in a township of farms."[20]

But this was to put the matter pejoratively. Husbandmen who resisted full-tilt commercialization, and the scattering of writers sympathetic to them, could describe their stance very differently: as evidence that farming yielded a prosperity "money cannot purchase, and money cannot measure...[,] a competency for the evening of life,...a mind unencumbered from the vexatious caprices of trade and speculation."[21]

Indeed, judging from the town–factory controversies that would ultimately erupt in Dudley and Oxford, yeomen in these communities may well have taken a further step. Precisely because manufactories were so frequently linked to "bookfarming," there is reason to suppose yeomen who resisted the latter may have come to regard the former with particular alarm. Surveying what was befalling them as the nineteenth century advanced, farmers of this stripe would have found little difficulty in judging factories as the source of several long-term, profound, and painful dislocations. Such husbandmen, after all, would hardly have failed to notice that their children were not simply leaving but frequently "posting off" to mills, or that the commercialization encouraged by mills often yielded more debt than prosperity. It was credible, in brief, for Yankee farmers to hold textile factories in some measure responsible for the changes pounding their lives. Sharpened and rendered more immediate by other challenges the mills would in time appear to pose – in particular, challenges to community notions of governance and social hierarchy – a general, brooding sense of grievance among yeomen of Dudley and Oxford could easily have contributed to the friction slowly emerging between the two townships and their mills.[22]

III

The daily operations of small, nonagricultural enterprises in these communities are, if anything, even more difficult to uncover than labor routines on local homesteads. But sufficient clues do exist to suggest that, like farms, many nontextile businesses clung to established conventions.

In their work rhythms, for example, rural stores apparently still permitted late morning breaks for toddies, and many handicraft enterprises evidently retained similarly discontinuous schedules. Thus it is certain that Oxford's scythe-making shop shut down completely five months every year. It is not certain, but it is likely, that employees in local boot and shoe shops also cut down work in certain seasons and (following patterns persisting in this trade) may well have taken off occasional days throughout the year to undertake other jobs or just to fish.[23] And if examples from other communities provide any example, much the same irregularity probably obtained in the smaller one- and two-man workshops. Even the region's mythically reliable blacksmith "Seth Steady," whose "hammer is heard at the dawn of the day, and [whose] fire blazes in his shop during the evenings," worked at his trade only from September to March. The entirely unmythical Nailer Tom outside Providence labored year round and even aimed toward six-day weeks; but he still frequently took to the road on many afternoons to settle accounts or to fetch supplies or (in the summer) to work "a mong the Hay."[24]

The most continuous and rigorously specified labor schedule outside local textile manufactories was probably found in Thomas Chatman's textile machine works. There, if comparable enterprises of the period are indicative, employees faced twelve- and fourteen-hour days and may even have found their attendance checked by "timekeepers."[25] But such arrangements were exceptional in Dudley and Oxford in this period, for work outside factory villages generally proceeded far more sporadically. Indeed, after 1810 as before, payments for labor were typically not linked to time at all but continued to be doled out by the task.[26]

Nor, for the most part, had the division of labor advanced very far. Again there were exceptions. It has already been suggested that local boot and shoe works may well have embraced enough division of labor to cast some employees as overseers and distribute certain jobs to outlying households. Chatman's machine works also may have used overseers and (again drawing on nonlocal data) may have divided its shop operations into several departments: a blacksmithy, possibly a foundry, pattern and drafting rooms, the machine room for tooling parts of each apparatus the shop produced, and an assembly area. It is likely too that within the machine room labor was broken into further discrete steps, each distributed to different clusters of employees.[27]

But this was not the overall pattern. The relatively small size of most nontextile operations meant that jobs were commonly undertaken entirely by a single individual or shared equally among a few people. In fact, even Chatman's enterprise probably embraced practices that blunted the impact of divided work processes. Machine shops during the 1820s and 1830s typically used the "inside contracting" system under which individual skilled machinists "contracted" for specific jobs, hired whatever help they needed, signed for appropriate tools and materials, and were paid (either by the piece or the day) at the job's completion. By permitting substantial autonomy to each contracting machinist, the arrangement tended to curtail the overseers' authority and prevent machine making from collapsing into a progression of minutely defined rote jobs performed entirely by unskilled operatives.[28] In important ways, the machines Thomas Chatman produced thus likely stood as handicrafted creations.

But what of machinery used in nontextile establishments; how far had the technology of their daily activities advanced? It would appear not very far: It was the general absence of mechanically elaborate hardware, it may be recalled, that helped reduce the cost (and thus facilitated the growth) of these ventures.

Once more the exceptions deserve notice. At least three triphammers, one of them waterpowered, were used in Oxford (in one instance to manufacture scythes) during this period. By 1814, moreover, Rufus Moore had purchased for his small nail-making shop a rather extraordinary machine that automatically "*cut* and *headed* [nails]

at the same time."[29] Some dexterity was needed to run this apparatus, but a contemporary description of a similar mechanism in Newark
reveals that the "machine's feeder" had little control over either the
pace or substance of his labors:

> The human portion of the machine holds in his hands a staff or
> stick, one end of which rests in a prop behind him for the sake of
> steadiness, and upon the other end is a clamp with which the
> plate is held. As the action of the cutter is not reciprocal, it is
> necessary that the plate should be turned at each cut; and as the
> machine moves rather rapidly, this is a delicate operation which
> the feeder only acquires after considerable practice...
>
> When the plate is cut up the feeder throws his clamp over a
> spur which projects from the side of the machine, pries it open,
> throws the remnant aside to be reheated with the rest of the
> scraps, seizes another plate with a pair of pincers, fixes it in his
> clamp, and goes on as before.
>
> The machines are gauged to cut different-sized nails, and their
> speed decreases in the same ratio as the size of the nail increases.
> Thus the machine which cuts a "twenty-penny" moves at about
> one-eighth the speed of another which is cutting "eight-pennies."[30]

But such machines were scarcely the norm outside local mill compounds. Despite their probable divisions of labor, the boot and shoe
shops of Dudley and Oxford would have possessed only hand-powered
tools. And Chatman's machine shop was probably equipped with
no more than "very primitive" technologies: treadle-run lathes, cold
chisels, hammers, and files.[31]

Work schedules, division of labor, technologies – these are all
obvious aspects of the regimen informing nontextile businesses after
1810. But equally important is the way motivations of nonfactory
proprietors (already touched on briefly)[32] were confirmed and reflected in the actual ordering of local stores and workshops.

With at least some involvement in nonlocal market dealings, a few
of these establishments were evidently touched, to at least some
degree, by desire for financial success pure and simple. There are
indications that after 1810 businesses increasingly began suing to
collect debts rather than permitting credit to extend indefinitely.[33]
Then too, the steps probably taken by the cordwaining and textile
machine shops to introduce supervision, division of labor, and (in
the machine shop) timekeeping suggest that proprietors of these
ventures were intent on increasing productivity and reducing costs.
The owners and managers of these particular enterprises may have
ranked, in fact, among the most profit-conscious local businessmen

outside those involved in the daily operation of cotton and woolen manufactories.

Even storekeepers occasionally tilted in this direction, with several managing to link themselves directly to the energies and ambitions of waterpowered textile operations. The General Store Craggins and Andrews ran in Oxford was not a factory store in the sense of standing in a mill village. But their account books (laid out in the latest double-entry bookkeeping style) indicate that, besides selling goods and "sundries," the two proprietors were by the early 1820s running a power-weaving shed employing a dozen women. And although William Law's store in Dudley did not trade only with millworkers, it was the conduit (again by the early 1820s) through which operatives of a local manufactory received their wages.

Yet this increased emphasis on profit proceeded only to a point. If debts more frequently led to judicial wrangles, it was equally true that credit remained widespread and interest-free. Moreover, the apparent absence of organizational and technological innovations in most nontextile ventures – indeed, the apparent limits to changes even in shoe and machine shops – suggests that individuals connected to these enterprises (employees if not always employers) had not entirely forsaken customary notions of how and why work should be done. Nor had barter disappeared. Although money was used more frequently after 1810, most purchases (even in stores associated with textile production) were paid with labor or in kind: currencies that promoted exchanges of goods and services more easily than systematic calculations and accumulations of gain.[34] And finally, the way proprietors exploited local resources signaled the persisting strength of customary attitudes. Nontextile millers and trip-hammer operators, for example, clung to notions of communal good, at least to the extent of sharing local streams with minimal fuss or friction.

The core rationale of nonmanufactory ventures thus embraced considerable variety. Indeed, some enterprises actually may have simultaneously retained and rejected earlier mores. On balance, however, the routines of most small businesses in this period expressed the same restrained commercial ambitions characterizing local stores and workshops before 1810. This hesitancy to adopt new motivations would not as easily or as necessarily have connoted the antifactory animus attributable to agricultural conservatism. For in the debates that swirled about in these years, farmers found it easier – and judged it more necessary – than merchants or blacksmiths to perceive mills as threatening. Yet, in the final analysis, the policies and practices typical of most local nontextile projects during the second and third decades of the nineteenth century confirmed a perspective closer to the yeoman's quest for success that "money cannot measure" than to the sustained profit seeking that fueled local manufactories.

IV

Profit, of course, had always been the goal of New England textile factories. From the 1790s up through later antebellum decades, manufactories operated to make money. Not all of them succeeded, of course. Slater's ventures (both before and after his arrival in southern Massachusetts) demonstrably did well; and the large works at Waltham reportedly registered returns of more than 20 percent during the 1820s. But many country establishments brought no more than 5 or 6 percent on investments, and numerous bankruptcies followed every economic downturn.[35] Whatever fortune actually fell its way, however, each mill at least sought a favorable balance of trade.

Thus factories like those in Dudley and Oxford diverged from prevailing rural conventions. It was not just that these enterprises boasted payrolls larger than other local businesses, or that they routinely used machines matched in complexity only by Rufus Moore's nail-making apparatus, or that they employed a division of labor that certainly equaled, and probably surpassed, the most thoroughly subdivided work arrangements outside factory walls – it was not just all this but also that local manufactories pursued market priorities with a single-minded enthusiasm unmatched by most nontextile businesses. If, for example, factories in Dudley and Oxford occasionally paid wages and accepted payments in goods and if they constantly complained about the scarcity of money, they also tended to stipulate. "no barter" as soon as possible. And although these mills (like others throughout the region) routinely extended six to eight months' credit to customers, they also frequently awarded discounts of up to 4 percent for prompt payments – an arrangement that effectively levied interest on postponed reimbursements.[36] Of all local businesses, moreover, manufactories were perhaps the readiest to sue over debts. They were certainly the readiest to build unprecedentedly large dams across local waterways, even though (unlike the stream harnessed by the Green Mill) the brooks and rivers thus blocked off were often needed by other Dudley and Oxford residents.[37] And if, despite all such efforts, smaller Yankee mills on the average still earned little more than farms, this fact produced unrelieved concern among factory masters. There was no effort to celebrate mills as havens from "vexatious caprices of trade and speculation." Low profit margins in manufactories yielded only complaints about the price of technology or demands for governmental subsidies and tariffs or calls for improved efficiency.[38]

And yet, despite its obvious centrality, profit did not dominate the way owners and enthusiasts of textile factories justified the construction of cotton and woolen mills in the generation after 1810. Now it is true (in ways detailed presently) that these men implicitly intended their rhetoric to encourage attitudes and performances compatible with business success. But it is the explicit, formal message of their slogans that must first be examined, and here a rather different brief for manufactories emerges. Exploring the order of life and labor in antebellum textile factories – including factories in Dudley and Oxford – starts with this different brief, this ideology, generated in the early nineteenth century to explain and defend these new institutions.

To some degree, it was an ideology built upon the effort defenders of Yankee mills had always made to describe factories as more than self-serving. The early arguments that manufactories could fuel overall American economic prosperity – arguments initiated by Alexander Hamilton and Tench Coxe and invoked by Slater in the 1790s – did not disappear. Factory ideologues continued to insist (increasingly in chorus with agricultural reformers) that mills provided useful markets for farmers; and such propositions offered continuing points of departure for profactory statements. But as the 1800s wore on, economic defenses of mills were increasingly alloyed with themes of social reform.

There were precursors of the trend. As early as 1785 profactory writers in England had praised Jedediah Strutt's factories, and particularly his Sunday schools, as effective weapons against the "Tide of Immorality" supposedly washing through England's working poor. "In that first generation of industrialization," a recent student of English institutional discipline has concluded, "factories could still be justified not simply as technical achievements, but as moral ones as well."[39] Even across the Atlantic, the United Company of Philadelphia had maintained in 1785 that waterpowered mills would bring "a general and laudable spirit of industry" to their employees; and of course Hamilton had spoken early on of factories providing Americans with "independence."[40] But in the United States such rationales appear at first only sporadically. It was during the years after 1810, and continuing up through roughly the mid-1840s, that supporters of Yankee manufactories began consistently suggesting that mills showed "regard to the welfare of their operatives" and that consequently "Hundreds" of mill employees were being "reclaimed, civilized, Christianized."[41]

How did mills perform this ethical magic? First, it was said, by providing employment that was more "regular" – and thus more conducive to anchored, responsible social interaction – than seasonal or occasional labor. "A steady employer," Harriet Martineau pronounced approvingly during her tour of American mills, "has it in his power to do more for the morals of the society about him than the clergy themselves."[42] But factories supplemented their uplifting efficacy by also imposing particular disciplines on their hands: "prudent and effectual regulations against disorderly and immoral behaviour." "Rules and regulations" varied from mill to mill. But, generally speaking, Yankee factories of this period – including family mills like those in Dudley and Oxford – demanded that during working hours operatives display the traits of punctuality, temperance, "industriousness," "steadiness," and obedience to mill authorities. Adopting (though probably few realized it) the materialist psychology advanced originally by John Locke and later by (among others) David Hartley and Benjamin Rush, antebellum factory spokesmen maintained that people were malleable and hence that steady applications of mill discipline would "improve" employees.[43]

It can scarcely be ignored that the notion of effecting reform through discipline linked manufactories to several other institutions emerging in this period. It created similarities between factories and the new schools spreading throughout the North, for example, as well as with the penitentiaries, poorhouses, and insane asylums that began appearing in antebellum America. Like mills, these expanded facilities for students and deviants were frequently described by advocates as efforts to "correct" social ills through "regular" routines. The endemic transiency of postrevolutionary America, the restless lurching from job to job, the fissures opening up in families – all this (the argument ran) had eroded "external restraints" that had once "repressed the passions of men"; lacking such "restraints," citizens of the young Republic were sinking beneath rising tides of crime, insanity, and poverty. If America was to survive, "internal and moral restraints" had to be substituted. Thus, along with their other instructional duties, schools were commonly charged with using institutional regimens to implant the values – indeed, the compulsions – of good behavior. For students who failed to heed the lesson and subsequently – inevitably, it was supposed – succumbed to social pathology, the new asylums were to employ tireless routines to reintroduce stability into their inmates' psyches and so instill habits requisite for life on the outside.[44]

This was the context within which mill masters implemented factory discipline in the years after 1810. Of course, other employers of the era administered their ventures amid the same cultural clues and anxieties. But because of their complexity and because of their need to synchronize large labor forces, manufactories were particularly likely to adopt regimens paralleling strictures in schools and asylums. And they were thus particularly likely to find themselves described in terms of such institutions. The British immigrant Samuel Ogden was using a figure of speech soon to become commonplace when he announced in 1815 that "a cotton factory is a school for the improvement of ingenuity and industry."[45]

This is not to suggest that all operatives accepted the factory order as educational or therapeutic, for they assuredly did not. Many millworkers in the generation after 1810 found reasons and methods to resist their employers' regimen. Indeed, the tugs back and forth between managers and operatives over work discipline, and the compromises that consequently developed, represent a crucial unfolding motif in the antebellum history of textile factories. Nor would it be correct to suppose that mill masters modeled all their policies around contemporary reform programs. Aiming primarily toward business success, daily practices of manufactories like those in Dudley and Oxford were actually becoming steadily less compatible with the ameliorative project proclaimed by their ideology. The point is rather that mill masters, managers, operatives, and northerners generally were all familiar with the idea of the factory-as-asylum. It was an important part of the meaning that mills had begun trailing across Yankee society by the second and third decades of the nineteenth century. And it was thus an important element in the way these establishments came to be experienced in New England.

But a distinction has to be made between the ideologies of Waltham-style and family mills. Although proprietors of both genres adopted the rhetoric of uplift, those supporting the larger ventures could also drift into more conservative formulations. Because these factories aimed to hire mainly "well-educated" young women from middling and "virtuous rural homes," the Waltham regimen was often depicted more as *maintaining* than improving their operatives' moral character. It was to *protect* their workers that these factories imposed tight supervision over the girls' boardinghouses, implemented curfews, and made church attendance mandatory. And it was their putative success in returning their employees to the countryside with "unsullied reputation" that permitted boardinghouse mills to boast that they would never harbor the degradation rumored to fill England's factory centers.[46]

Some family-mill owners took issue with this vision, claiming that "mammoth Waltham establishment[s]" replicated, by their very size, the worst features of Old World industrialization.[47] But there was a more pervasive and important ideological distinction: Small rural mills consistently clung to their claim of effecting improvement. Even though their operatives were by no means uniformly poor, factories such as those in Dudley and Oxford never wavered from the claim that they "combatted...vice, ignorance, and poverty."[48] In fact, they dared not waver. For given the close connection between "vice, ignorance, and poverty," once masters of family mills acknowledged hiring any poor workers, they willy-nilly faced charges of fostering "contagion." Grafted deeply into Anglo-American social thought of the eighteenth and early nineteenth centuries, the notion of contagion linked moral decay and physical disease as aspects of a common deformity and concluded that immorality, like sickness, could spread rapidly among tightly clustered gatherings of the "vicious, improvident, and indigent." Country-mill owners who recruited poor employees into their closed workplaces might thus be guilty of serious "abuse" unless they used discipline to "change the current of vice from its filthy and offensive channel."[49] An obvious implication was that only "prudent and effectual regulations" separated family mills from pesthouses.

And there were further implications as well. If poor people required institutional tutelage, and if poor operatives often came from the countryside, was not rural life itself flawed? The answer was inescapably affirmative – and here country mill proprietors and their supporters extended the distinction agricultural reformers posited between backward farms and efficient factories. Here, in fact, was the entrepreneurs' ideological counterattack against antifactory suspicions likely circulating among husbandmen. Without factories to buy goods, provide employment, and organize "moral and religious instruction," it was suggested, the hinterland would descend into "wretchedness." Samuel Slater himself described a rural landscape devoid of mills as characterized by "universal bankruptcy and poverty; the utter extinction of the arts of civilized life; in fine, a retrograde movement of the whole community to ignorance, weakness, and barbarism."[50] By the 1820s and 1830s, the order of country mills was thus moored to a rationale that dismissed the basic worth of country life.

Such were the rather stern conclusions following from an ideological commitment to uplift. Against this grim tone, however, must be set the more friendly, or at least more familiar, connotations of the rubric commonly invoked to summarize the order of rural factories. Striving to specify both the authority and responsibility of this regimen, aiming to emphasize its ameliorative and altruistic impulse, owners and supporters of country mills took to calling these factories "paternalistic." It was a powerfully evocative term, an efficient and effective label for the perspective industrial ideologues sought to advance. Domestic concepts and themes were much in mind during antebellum decades, after all, for the family was widely perceived as a frontline social mechanism in the battle for good behavior, a structure whose supposed unraveling was a key reason asylums had become necessary.[51] Waltham-style factories and specifically their minutely monitored boardinghouses occasionally carried the label. But because smaller rural mills could claim the direct personal involvement of "fatherly" proprietors, paternalism seems to have achieved particular currency in early nineteenth century discussions of New England's smaller textile ventures.

Thus Dexter Ballow of Mendon "with his sleeves rolled up, and his working suit on...watched over the welfare of his help with parental solicitude."[52] And thus Samuel Slater maintained "a strict, though mild and paternal scrutiny of the conduct of the workpeople" and "a kindly and paternal interest" in their "welfare." Indeed, it was just this "interest" (so the celebratory commentaries continued) that permitted small Yankee mills to remain just as distinct as Waltham-style establishments from England's "corrupt" factory communities. Certainly the example Slater set in his "care and efforts, extending through forty years," went far to explain "the superior condition of the manufacturing villages of Rhode Island and the adjoining districts in moral and social respects as compared with that of most manufacturing villages of Great Britain."[53]

Paternalism, of course, also inserted an obvious paradox into the ideology of factory order. For here were manufactories – establishments far larger than the shops and stores still typical of the Yankee hinterland – emerging as the only ventures self-consciously wrapping themselves in a rhetoric of personal, managerial involvement with each employee's "welfare." Here were business ventures that flatly contradicted the conventional rural emphasis on "family need," calmly describing themselves as households writ-large and brimming with fatherly concern.

None of this, however, has prevented paternalism from achieving a permanent place in discussions of New England textile factories. As late as 1874, long after Samuel Slater's death, a local historian described the North, South, and East villages as resembling "one large and well-conducted family, where the head is not only respected, but regarded with attachment and pride, as the patriarch and father." Even more significantly, modern scholars looking back to Yankee mills of the early nineteenth century have commonly employed the notion of paternalism. They have used the term both pejoratively (to describe an overly intrusive managerial presence) and approvingly. But in either case the concept itself is entrenched within the historiography of early antebellum New England manufactories.[54]

V

Probing the ideology of factory order is the point of departure for understanding that order. But the way Yankees experienced textile mills in this period was also shaped by how management used this ideology for its own ends. If the formal apologias surrounding manufactories help identify an important cultural resonance of antebellum cotton and woolen factories, equally important are the self-serving advantages mill masters implicitly sought to win through their apologias.

Put simply, factory masters intended their ideology to promote behavior leading to profit as well as reform. Claims of concerned "interest" and "parental solicitude," for example, were aimed toward calming suspicions stirred up within and around antebellum manufactories. Then too, the diligence, sobriety, and punctuality employers sought to instill in their "reclaimed" workers were obviously also the traits of a highly productive labor force. But perhaps the clearest expression of this pragmatic manipulation of ideology lies in the way managers justified their dealings with families inside the mill villages. Because, ironically enough, arguments pivoting around assertions of paternalism were used to legitimize the intrusions factories made into the households under their jurisdiction.

The relationship between family mills and the families they hired was complex. On the one hand, these factories took steps to preserve – even bolster – customary domestic patterns among their hands. Thus (judging from East Village and Dudley Woolen Manufacturing Company data) local factories not only provided cottages so that family members could live together; they also went out of their way to retain family workers during economic depressions.[55] In both good and bad times, moreover, the bookkeeping iconography of these mills reveals further efforts to acknowledge conventional household relationships and hierarchies: by listing coresiding operatives together, whatever their job assignments, in the Time Books; by transferring wages earned by younger children directly to their parents; and by always paying fathers at higher rates than any of their operative offspring.[56]

Such policies helped assure the viability of families inside local factory compounds. But it would be fundamentally incorrect to construe the operatives' domestic life as entirely determined by factory priorities. However strongly antebellum reformers may have *wished* families would instill "internal restraints," disaffections emerging among local operatives in the years after 1810 make it highly unlikely that parents of Dudley and Oxford factory workers systematically cooperated with management to produce "steady" young laborers. There are, in fact, reasons to suppose that millworking families maintained their strength *despite* the factory order. Factory policies supporting the integrity of operative families were only part of the picture.

In the first place, mills did not prevent children above 14 from receiving their own wages or occasionally even taking up lodgings separate from their parents and siblings. Nor did managers prevent operatives in later teen years from mimicking nonfactory youths of comparable age in leaving to seek employment opportunities – for both extended and brief periods – many miles from their parents.[57] But of greater significance was willingness of local mills to intrude directly on operative families. Occasionally managers specified precise billeting arrangements: In 1829, for example, the East Village permitted Mary Kingsbury to live in the compound "on condition" that her unemployed father "does not remain."[58] Much more regularly, and hence much more consequentially, factory administrators took pains to prevent families from working together. Siblings might tend adjacent machines. But a close scrutiny of job assignments inside four local factories suggests that at least until the late 1830s managers systematically separated parents and children during the working day.

Probably the mills feared that adults placed near their offspring would challenge the overseers, or if overseers themselves, that they would cause friction by favoring their own youngsters. Coupled with contemporary prejudices against wage-earning mothers, such concerns would explain the exclusion of married women from local factory payrolls during the generation after 1810. Fathers were never totally barred, but those with berths inside the mills were segregated from their children. Even the relationship between mule spinners and their young piecers was purged of kinship: Despite sporadic references to spinners "find[ing their] own piecers," most local mule operators evidently let management select these assistants before 1840, and most boys serving as piecers thus ended up tying threads for nonrelatives.[59] As time passed, moreover, it became increasingly difficult for children to find their fathers anywhere inside the mills. An emerging pattern of awarding skilled "male" jobs to unmarried men (promoted from below or recruited from outside) forced growing numbers of male household heads to remain idle, accept outdoor jobs, or leave the factory villages to seek work elsewhere. In the East Village, the proportion of families with fathers working somewhere inside the Green or Union mills fell from nearly three-quarters in 1817 to just over one-third in 1830.[60]

The work-time separation of children and parents must have affected domestic relations. Far more than the broad, gradually accumulating pressures acting on parent–child relations of farming families, management's intrusions forcefully and directly challenged received notions of parental authority and responsibility. The operatives preserved their families. But in settings where parents controlled neither the work nor the discipline their children faced during working hours, where both parents and children were subjected to the same overriding managerial control – in such settings parental prestige could only suffer. And this is where claims of paternalism proved so useful. Owners and admirers of country mills like those in Dudley and Oxford asserted that factories could legitimately undermine patriarchy among operatives because they themselves were acting in loco parentis. When pressed to defend their stance more precisely, factory masters sometimes pointed to schools, arguing that mill families "delegated" parental authority to managers just as Yankee households surrendered authority to teachers.[61] More often mills simply stressed their "regard" for workers. But in either case, it seems clear that rather than signaling continuity between operative families and the factory regimen, managerial assertions of "interest" and paternalism were invoked to justify managerial interventions between parents and youngsters.

Did any of this work? Did self-interested protestations that factories "showed regard" soften antagonisms toward these establishments? Did grounding labor discipline in moral uplift produce industrious operatives? Did stressing paternalism reduce concern about the domestic disruptions attending factory employment? To some extent, the ideology probably did all this. In Dudley and Oxford the halo of arguments surrounding manufactories by the 1820s and 1830s almost certainly provided at least some counterweight to the suspicions stirred up by factory villages. It quite possibly helped draw some Yankees into millwork (those entering factory jobs out of choice, for example), and it may well have encouraged these recruits to work diligently and without complaint during their stints.

But the suspicions were at most modified, not eradicated. Despite the mill masters' ideology, local operatives and townspeople still felt a strong – even growing – ambivalence toward the mills. Indeed, what requires notice at this point is that the ideology itself could generate alarm. A vision of paternalistic factory villages might strike sympathetic commentators as idyllic, as a conception underscoring the progressive potential of textile mills. But to those who viewed factory villages less as arenas for social therapy and more as merely places to live and work, the notion could have different implications.

It could, for example, make mill villages appear curiously anachronistic. Even while factory enclaves were introducing an architectural scale, social order, and demographic density that stood out dramatically in the postrevolutionary Yankee countryside, there is a sense in which their description as a "large and well-conducted family" could provoke nostalgic memories. By emphasizing the close-knit quality of mill life, by stressing how factory hands operated under the authority of a few officials, the paternalistic motif signaled ways in which manufactories more closely paralleled the more centralized and consistently hierarchical society of seventeenth and early eighteenth century rural New England than the fluid, physically dispersed, and lightly governed townships of the late eighteenth and early nineteenth centuries. Invoking paternalism, in other words, could make mill villages seem like throwbacks to an earlier age.

But the ideology could also make mills seem dangerous – and here was the final paradox of paternalistic rhetoric. Yankees might express concern about rising social instability and weakened family bonds. But Yankees who heard mill managers repeatedly stress their "paternal scrutiny" of textile hands could also worry that manufactories harbored conflations of executive power inappropriate in a nation dedicated to "liberty." This latter concern arose because, in the final analysis, paternalistic slogans surrounding factory order collided head on with another perspective: the widespread desire

for a society peopled by citizens living in rough equality and independence and the correspondingly widespread fear of overweaning
authority. They confronted, in sum, the "republican" ideology that
had fueled the Revolution and that remained deeply influential during the early antebellum era. From a republican viewpoint, fatherly
mill masters could seem like "monarch[s]," and to all the other
complaints about manufactories could be added the charge that they
were run like "tyrannies."[62]

So it was that the immigrant industrial apologist Samuel Ogden
had acknowledged as early as 1815 that Americans often opposed
textile factories because they believed operatives were "subjected to
tyrannical rule." So too, by the late 1820s a Providence newspaper
assumed that managers ruled "their mills with a rod of iron" and
then raised the portentous suspicion that mill masters might "step
out into the community with the same air...What is this but tyranny[?]"[63] And a few years later, also in Providence, there appeared
an extraordinary poem by "Sui Generis: Alias Thomas Man." Of
thin literary merit, the work is nonetheless notable for its unflagging
catalogue of factory-induced ills. Among them:

> For liberty our fathers fought
> Which with their blood they dearly bought,
> The Fact'ry system sets at nought. . . .
> Great Britain's curse is now our own,
> Enough to damn a King and Throne.[64]

By the late 1820s and through the 1830s, concern about "tyranny"
penetrated criticisms issued against both Waltham- and family-style
factories.[65] Because of their more obviously personal proprietary approach, however, owners of country mills were especially vulnerable to the charge, often (as it turned out) from people living in
townships surrounding or lying near manufactories. In Dudley and
Oxford specifically, "tyranny" – raised in various forms and contexts
– would prove a highly explosive issue.

VI

Such was the character – and uncertain efficacy – of attempts to use
ideology to aid rural mills. But there is a final perspective on claims
of proprietary "regard" and "paternal interest" that needs to be
considered. Management's slogans have to be placed within the
context of routine mill operations. For it turns out, at least in the
manufactories of Dudley and Oxford, that notions of factory paternalism were not simply used by self-interested mill masters; pater-

nalism was also *limited* by structural constraints and long-term policies
that dictated the flow of daily factory life. Understanding the regimen of local manufactories requires specifying these constraints and
policies. And it requires exploring how they imposed limits on the
ideology antebellum factory supporters so loudly proclaimed.

The fundamental constraint was the market. The iron pressure to
maintain profit margins and stave off losses cut across any pledge of
"regard" or "interest." Despite management's commitment to provide "steady" employment, for example, full-time operatives (especially those unattached to families) were, as noted earlier, routinely
laid off during slumps. Moreover, as the number of Yankee mills
continued to increase during the 1820s and 1830s and as competition
among them intensified, factories moved to confine their pay scales
– in both good and bad times – under formal guidelines designed to
control production costs. Although mill masters in Dudley and Oxford might occasionally act out proprietary largesse with cash "presents" to favorite workers, the East Village had determined by 1837
that the "average price of all the labor of every description should
not be more than 35 to 37 1/2 cents per yard."[66]

It was this same growing competitiveness, and the effort it produced to increase efficiency, that explains why local mills (as forecast in Chapter 3) revised their use of ad hoc hands. Several tasks,
for example, became more seasonal. Up through the 1830s men
were still hired from surrounding townships to join with the brothers
and fathers of operatives in tending crops, driving wagons, and
digging ditches for the mills. But to cut costs, local factories began
reducing such hands. By the late 1820s, Slater, for one, was mimicking Yankee farmers and jettisoning his agricultural laborers as quickly
as possible in the fall. "As soon as Captain Starr [supervisor of
outdoor labor] can spare some of those high priced farmers," Slater
wrote to his East Village agent in August 1828, "do have some of
them dismissed." And again a month later: "I hope Capt. Starr has
before this dismissed Mr. Kemp and several others off the Farm."[67]

Skilled ad hoc workers faced a different kind of pruning. Rather
than continuing to distribute occasional jobs among several local
artisans, factories found it more efficient to recruit a single carpenter
or blacksmith into the mill compound, employ him full time, place
him under close supervision and a regimen of precise instructions,
and pay him by the month or year (instead of by the job). Thus the
Dudley Woolen Manufacturing Company had its own blacksmith
shop as early as 1824. For its part, Slater's South Village shifted Asa
Wood from sporadic to full-time carpentry in 1828, and the East

Village orchestrated the same change for blacksmith Stephen Harwood in 1832.[68]

But the most dramatic transformation, affecting the largest group of employees, occurred among outworkers. Again, the basic issue was management's desire, fueled by market pressures, to increase efficiency. Proprietors of cotton mills, it is true, had vented impatience with outlying pickers and weavers even before perpetual textile production had reached southern Massachusetts. Working for the most part whenever and for as long as they wished, aiming to supplement, rather than maintain, household incomes, such employees had never labored as reliably or as carefully as some proprietors had wished. "A part of this day's cotton," Slater had moaned as early as 1791, "appear as if the mice had been in it as it is picked all to pieces." Indeed, even outworking journeymen weavers had faced criticisms for being tardy or careless or for following the "almost traditional" practice among English weavers of stealing portions of the cloth they produced.[69] But it was after 1810, against the background of rising competition, that rural cotton factories began consistently pushing for greater efficiency. And they pushed especially hard after 1814, for at that point cloths produced by outwork began meeting stiff rivalry from cheap, coarse fabrics turned out by the power looms of Waltham-style factories.[70]

Judging from East Village records, local mills responded to all these pressures promptly and forcefully. Beginning virtually with the opening of the Green Mill, Slater ordered "poor picking" returned "to Pick Over." Beginning around 1816, he cut the piece rates of his weavers (to reduce costs) and limited their output exclusively to the plaids and checked goods that were beyond the capacity of early power looms. What was equally important, he sought to impose tighter discipline. After 1816, outlying weavers who took more than eight weeks to work up a web or who turned in faulty cloth faced probation or even expulsion from the network: "In future . . . examine closely as to weaving, and have good weaving or none from S. Sears and family"; "No more weaving [for E. Sprague's family] . . . under any conditions."[71]

These goadings had effect. Slater's outworking weavers were returning their cloth far more promptly by the mid-1820s than ten years earlier; and (undoubtedly motivated in part by the lower piece rates) they also, as a group, turned out 10 to 15 percent more cloth per work stint.[72] Yet it was not enough. For even after the new standards and schedules were implemented, all outworkers continued to set their own daily work pace; and most of them – all but journeymen – continued to view their employment as simply a stop-gap. So long as it retained these basic structural features, outwork could never achieve the efficient productivity mill masters demanded.

So outwork was replaced. In 1818 the East Village exchanged its outlying pickers for picking machines (probably available since 1807) operated by full-time factory employees.[73] In 1823, impressed by the experiments in power-loom "weave shops" already running in Oxford, and evidently possessing the necessary liquid capital, Slater began introducing waterpowered looms into the Green Mill. His discovery that unit production costs were lower with the new technology, combined with a sudden infusion of inexpensive British handwoven cloths in 1825–6, hardened his resolve. In 1828 Slater summarily dismissed the several hundred handloom weavers then on his books and bequeathed his production of cotton cloth entirely to young women tending power looms inside the East Village.[74] Because they labored only part time, the majority of outworkers thus laid off probably did not suffer too seriously from their dismissals – certainly they did not experience the catastrophic immiserization of contemporary British handloom weavers.[75] But journeymen weavers must have faced considerable economic disruption, and all outworkers had regarded their East Village wages as at least useful supplementary income. Slater's decision to terminate his picking and weaving networks was thus scarcely congruent with his putative "regard" for employees.

Non-Slater cotton manufactories in Dudley and Oxford probably eliminated outworkers at about the same time as the East Village. But significantly, several local proprietors, including Slater, also went further. The same logic leading them to dismiss outlying pickers and cotton weavers also led owners of woolen mills to dismiss the skilled handloom weavers living and working inside these enclaves. Although less sharply buffeted by competing Waltham and British cloths than cotton establishments, woolen factories felt sufficient pressure to cut weaving piece rates in the 1820s. Then too, because of their skill, woolen weavers occasionally evinced an independence – and once, amid a protest over falling piece rates, even a militancy[76] – that must have worried local factory managers. Attracted by the greater control implicit in hiring semiskilled operatives to tend power looms, and (again) finding that machine weaving offered substantial savings in unit labor costs, Slater had shifted much of his cloth production in the South Village to water-driven looms by 1830.[77] And so with other factories: The Dudley Woolen Manufacturing Company had begun considering these machines in 1824 (because "it will make the weaving come [i.e., cost] very low indeed"), and by the end of the decade this mill too was depending largely on power looms.[78]

Woolen handloom weavers, in sum, discovered they were not exceptional. In the context of uncertain sales and rising competition, these skilled employees found that for them, as for other hands, management's "regard" was constrained by management's need to get and keep profits.

But the limits of management's "regard" were also revealed by steps not taken. Unlike Waltham-style mills – with their scrupulously monitored boardinghouses and tight supervision of operatives' leisure time – local mills made little consistent effort to extend their order into the operatives' nonworking hours.

Consider, for example, the relatively laissez-faire attitude taken toward the period of each day in which workers were in their quarters or went shopping. Judging from the Slater mills and the Dudley Woolen Manufacturing Company, the relative isolation of the factory villages encouraged most full-time operatives to use company residences and company stores. But it was never required that employees live within the mill villages, and it was only sporadically required (in the South Village, for example) that they buy provisions from company retail facilities.[79] Mills did appoint individuals (often widows) to administer their boardinghouses, but if Dudley and Oxford factories followed the pattern typical of other rural mills in this period, such officials exerted little control over employee behavior. "Trouble at the boardinghouse," complained the agent at a small Exeter, Massachusetts, factory in 1831, because "the girls in one chamber frightened the girls in the other at 12 o'clock at night."[80] As for family cottages, except for occasional – and undoubtedly disturbing – interventions to stop particular kinsmen from coresiding, these residences apparently received no supervision at all.

Given the received wisdom that factory life would improve operatives, it is perhaps even more noteworthy that local mills failed to initiate strenuous campaigns to educate their hands. It is true that several proprietors did attempt to establish schools within their compounds: Their motivation appears to have been largely financial, and (as detailed in Chapter 6) their efforts in any case met heated resistance in Dudley and Oxford town meetings.[81] But what needs to be stressed here is that no matter where schools were located, factory masters (again judging from the Slater mills and the Dudley Woolen Manufacturing Company) never required children to attend classes. Quite the opposite: Eager to retain youngsters on their pay-rolls, factory masters obliged parents to petition for the "privelege" of dispatching millworking offspring to school. So Abel Dudley's two daughters received the "privelege of going to school 2 months each – one at a time – and [their brother] Amos is to work at 4/wk when they are out." But Abel Dudley was exceptional. Most opera-tive households needed the wages their children earned, and most local mill children were thus innocent of formal education. In the East Village, only six families requested schooling (for a total of ten children) between 1827 and 1836.[82]

Upon close examination, even the millowners' commitment to "devine instruction" appears tempered. Dudley and Oxford as a whole during this period witnessed abundant religious interest: At least four revivals crackled across the two communities between 1810 and the mid-1830s. Moreover, Congregationalists, Baptists, and Universalists in one or the other of the two townships had all gath-ered sufficient support in these years to build new meetinghouses, as did a new group, the Methodists, who began meeting in Dudley during the 1820s.[83] Now, there is evidence that millowners sympa-thized with all these developments. In a general sense, after all, entrepreneurs and philosophes of the textile industry had always sought to link characteristics of good hands – punctuality, sobriety, "industriousness," "steadiness" – with received Protestant morality. This had been Strutt's goal in fashioning Sunday schools in Derbyshire, and the theme had persisted in America, providing useful theologi-cal ballast to arguments highlighting factory uplift. Dudley and Ox-ford factory masters were thus entirely in character when (as local chronicles reveal) they supported local churches and (in part through Slater's efforts) helped introduce the Sunday school to southern Massachusetts.[84]

But the nature of their support needs careful definition. In the first place, the contribution in time and money made by millowners was no greater than investments made by proprietors of nontextile en-terprises. Gristmillers, blacksmiths, and (above all) storekeepers were equally generous to local religious institutions and campaigns.[85]

In the second place, the religious bequests made by millowners were remarkably diffuse. As a group, local textile proprietors sup-ported Congregationalists, Baptists, Universalists, and Methodists.[86] Indeed, such ecumenicalism was displayed even by individual millowners: by members of the Slater family, for example. Born an Anglican, married to a Quaker, Slater's religious activities in Paw-tucket soon moved beyond his early Sunday school to include participation in Baptist, Episcopal, and Catholic churches; in southern Massachusetts, his son George supported (at one time or another during his career) Baptists, Methodists, and Congregationalists.[87] It followed from their scattered theological involvement that, although some local churches received substantial backing from millowners, no church was supported exclusively by factory proprietors. It followed too that factory proprietors did not regard any one sect as the exclusive vehicle of their religious ambitions.

But equally significant was the restraint of their ambitions, particularly as they related to operatives. Local mill masters do not appear to have systematically planted churches inside their villages: The Methodist chapel in which George Slater took interest, for example, went up "near" the East Village and even then only in 1833. The evidence also suggests that factory masters urged, rather than required, employees to attend church (or Sunday school). The Slaters – both father and sons – were undoubtedly pleased that some employees (including overseers) did attend the Methodist chapel, just as proprietors of Dudley's village factory (later Slater's North Village) were undoubtedly pleased to see a Baptist society start meeting in a loft of their mill in 1814.[88] But the indications are that only a fraction of the textile labor force in either Dudley and Oxford ever committed itself to regular churchgoing.[89]

And it is likely that those who did attend went as much to please themselves as their employers. In the fellowship of church meetings and revivals, in the harsh but clear message (especially available from Baptists and Methodists) that sin was always present in life and could only be overcome through effort and discipline – in all this, operatives may have found solace. But churchgoing did not offer only anesthesia. Scattered through the records are hints that, in the end, workers would use religion to galvanize their mounting, restless grievances against management. Rather than something received passively from patriarchal employers, religion should be understood as something operatives took for themselves – when they wished and largely for their own purposes.[90]

Taken together, the force of economic pressures and the limited involvement in nonworking hours comprised two significant limits on management's protestations of "paternal interest." The automatic, impersonal discipline imposed by "perpetual" technology comprised another.

The machines in Dudley and Oxford mills up through the early 1830s bore close resemblance to those constructed in the earliest

American manufactories. The waterpowered picking and weaving technologies that local cotton factories adopted along the way were, of course, new. And the spinning mule that Samuel Slater's brother John had helped introduce into Smithfield was employed in local enterprises at least by 1820. But overall, despite some modifications, the carding, roving, and throstle (water-frame) spinning machines used in the cotton factories of Dudley and Oxford were not qualitatively different from technologies used in the first Yankee textile manufactories. Nor did local woolen works vary appreciably from their prototypes. Again, there was the shift to power looms; and although they apparently always used residential pickers, woolen manufactories may also have started performing this process mechanically by the 1830s. But carding engines remained essentially unaltered, and the only shift in woolen spinning was to place more semiautomatic "jacks" alongside the jennies.[91]

The relatively fixed inventory of machines did not mean that all operatives inside mill buildings tended waterpowered mechanisms. Work in factory machine shops was probably performed with hand tools; mule spinning and (in the woolen mills) jenny spinning both remained hand-powered throughout the period; and roughly half the operation of woolen jacks continued under the spinners' manual control. Moreover, certain preparatory processes necessary for power-loom weaving remained largely or wholly free of mechanization. The application (dressing) of a starch solution (sizing) to harden warp threads was accomplished with warping and dressing frames, but preparation of the sizing was a difficult, hand-operated procedure, and the dressing operation as a whole ranked among the most highly skilled – and well-paid – jobs in local factories. "Drawing-in" threads through the tackle and harness of power looms was a semiskilled job (usually reserved for women), which was also performed entirely without mechanical aid. Finally, although the gigging (raising the nap) and shearing of woolen cloths may have benefited from water-driven machines, key finishing processes like dying and bleaching persisted as tasks performed mainly by hand in both cotton and woolen mills.[92]

Yet all this was exceptional. Most operatives – perhaps 60 to 70 percent – laboring within the mills worked on machines powered by the energy of falling water. And the mechanically dictated work rhythms of such "perpetual" machines represented an inescapable, continuous, and anonymous pressure that intervened between workers and any human supervisors – even the watchful, circulating room overseers.

In some cases the work pace thus dictated was steady, as in the task of feeding "laps" of cotton to the carding engines. More often, tending machines involved irregular bursts of activity. This might take the form of collecting processed material from a machine: "doffing" full bobbins on spinning frames and replacing them with empty ones. Or it might involve the kind of work performed by power-loom weavers and throstle spinners: gazing at spindles and shuttles pounding before them in order to be ready – at any moment – to reach in and tie off (piece) threads broken during the weaving and spinning processes.[93] This latter task is also what "piecing" for mule spinners entailed. The young boys assigned this job had to attach threads broken during "the few instants" when the mule, having advanced forward along its tracks, was pushed back to its frame. As a result, although mules were not waterpowered in this period, the "lively little piecers" were, effectively, another group subjected to mechanically governed work rhythms. Indeed, because of the distribution of jobs by age and sex in the local mills, most operatives under machine discipline were either children, like piecers, or young women, like weavers and spinners,[94] which in turn created a curious irony deep in the daily chemistry of mill operations. Given the assumptions of adult male dominance implicit in management's paternalistic rhetoric, factory supervisors undoubtedly assumed that women and youngsters would be particularly receptive to claims of patriarchal authority; but women and youngsters were precisely the operatives at least partially buffered from such claims by the more immediate drumbeat of demands issuing from their machines.

This does not mean that machine discipline was necessarily experienced as harsh. Child operatives (the doffers for example) were often able to play between chores. And the fact that operating machines like power looms and water frames required little physical strength often led contemporaries – even workers themselves – to conclude that machine tending was easy. Labor requiring constant attention and repetitive motion (instead of obvious exertion) was so novel that the strain it produced was not immediately understood. So it was that millworkers complained of swollen feet from standing so many hours and of listlessness from (they supposed) overeating and insufficient exercise. But even into the late 1840s the work itself was judged "not laborious"; "not half so hard," wrote one woman, "as...attending the dairy, washing, cleaning house, and cooking."[95]

Nonetheless, machine discipline did intervene between employees and management's supposedly personal and paternal authority – and it intervened more emphatically as years went by. Because another consequence of increasing competition among Yankee mills was a decision by factory masters to increase output by expanding the number and speed of machines assigned to operatives. In the East Village between 1817 and 1835, the number of water frames per spinner doubled (from two to four). In the same village between the mid-1820s and the mid-1830s, the output per power loom jumped two and a half times, and the output per spinning mule climbed by just under 40 percent.[96]

The final limitation on management's relationship with the hands, and particularly on the personal proprietary relationship conjured up by invocations of "paternalistic interest," was the bureaucratic dimension of early antebellum mills.

This took three forms. There was, first, the hierarchical chain of command already remarked: the division of authority under which the most frequent and direct dealings with employees was in practice left mainly to officials below owners and agents. There was, second, the complex bookkeeping apparatus common even among smaller family mills. Monitoring the operation of such enterprises – recording and balancing out sales, costs, orders, production levels, and shipments of raw materials and finished goods – required an interlocking array of Time Books, Day Books, Ledgers, and Blotters far more elaborate than records typically generated in Dudley and Oxford by either the town governments or nontextile business ventures. One result of factory paper work, however, was that information shaping management's outlook – and particularly data disclosing the growing competitive necessity for increased efficiency – was unavailable to mill operatives. The arrival and implications of a major market downturn were obvious. But beyond such dramatic episodes, proprietors were motivated by pressures that remained largely opaque to their hands. And the hands, consequentially, may well have felt distanced from their employers, may well have found it difficult to believe that they labored in common cause with those paying their wages.

The most significant bureaucratic aspect of the factory order, however, was its webbing of established bylaws and procedures. No full listing of "rules and regulations" has survived from Dudley and Oxford mills. But drawing on comparable manufactories of the period, local prescriptions were probably both written and unwritten, probably focused mainly on work-time activities, and probably ranged from stipulations concerning how work was to be done (how, as opposed to when, threads should be pieced) to specifying that operatives evince a punctual, respectful, and sober demeanor on the job.[97]

Not all directives were always enforced. It was, in fact, precisely amid these "rules and regulations" that managers and employees would develop many significant compromises in the regimens of local factories. Still, the rules in principle dictated the norms of mill labor. What is just as significant, they dictated norms that, again in principle, were fixed – and hence impervious to nuances of personal relationships. Even the nonmachine discipline of factory rooms – even the discipline implemented by overseers – was more likely to derive from established codes of behavior than from personal understandings between supervisors and hands. As a result, although certain strictures (like prohibitions against tardiness) were freighted with moral "interest," management's rules inevitably introduced an element of formality between employers and employees.

"Rules and regulations" ran like stiff girders all through the order of local mills, but they are especially obvious in management's treatment of time. It was not, after all, the number of working hours that was novel in early manufactures: It was customary for rural Yankees during harvest seasons to labor as long as operatives. Nor, as demonstrated by their willingness to yoke factory ideology to received religious values, did millowners break new moral ground by emphasizing punctuality. What was striking about textile factories – from Strutt's establishment up through the mills of antebellum New England – was the metronomic inflexibility of their work schedule.

After 1810, as before, Yankee factories aimed to run seventy-two hours per week. They generally operated "from the time it is light enough to work," which meant their precise starting-up times changed with the seasons. Moreover, because clocks were still rare in the hinterland, and because "boys [who] rung the Bell" to wake mill-village residents rose themselves at slightly different hours from day to day, the moment of starting up could vary even within a single week.[98] But once under way, rural factories planned to run twelve hours a day (continuously except for breaks at seven o'clock for breakfast and twelve-thirty for "dinner") six days a week every week of the year. The only days off management accepted were Sundays and whichever of the two or three regionally celebrated annual holidays happened to fall on week days in a given year. Work by candlelight during winter months thus continued to be the norm, and during such periods the New England custom of commencing sabbath observances Saturday at dusk obviously went by the board. Logistical and mechanical difficulties might force unexpected pauses, of course, but only the conventional postrevolutionary holidays of Thanksgiving, the Fourth of July, and April's Fast Day were accepted as scheduled interruptions.[99] In Dudley and Oxford it is likely that the only nontextile venture to essay the rigid operating timetable typically sought by local manufactories was Thomas Chatman's machine shop.

The inflexibility of factory schedules pressed all the more heavily on operatives because mills made strenuous efforts to evaluate (though again not necessarily to require) their workers' obedience. Like pre-1810 factories, New England mills in the second and third decades of the nineteenth century generally measured labor by time. In Dudley and Oxford most millworkers from the outset received wages calculated by the number of days or, more exactly, the fraction of days they put in. Even wages designated at weekly or monthly rates were actually tallied up in units of twelve-hour working days. As a result, supervisors naturally desired to reckon their employees' attendance with great care. Indeed, even workers paid by the piece (mule spinners and after 1830 many power-loom weavers as well) had their daily presence noted down in minute units. Transcribed (in coded shorthand) into Time Books, attendance in the Dudley Woolen Manufacturing Company was recorded to the nearest three hours in the 1820s – almost certainly a more accurate standard than that used for nontextile employees (save for some highway workers and, again, possibly the men in Chatman's employ). The Slater books were equally precise before 1817. Thereafter – as yet one more emblem of Slater's mounting stringency – the unit became the nearest ninety minutes.[100]

VII

Thus the different faces presented by the regimen of local textile mills: On the one hand, the factory order put forward a credo of personal managerial "regard"; on the other hand, it was, in practice, a self-serving regimen, limited in scope and bounded – in some respects increasingly bounded – by technology, bureaucracy, and the vicissitudes of the market.

For all its internal divisions, however, the factory order was clearly distinct from organizational patterns informing most other economic activities. Indeed, it is tempting to see a linear progression among the different regimens operating in Dudley and Oxford. From the altered but still essentially semicommercial outlook and traditional organization of local farms and most small businesses, to the more intensely commercial ambitions and more elaborate administrative structure and technology that likely characterized a few of the larger nontextile enterprises, to the waterpowered machines, complex divisions of authority and labor, and (in practice) the thoroughly profit-centered goals of cotton and woolen mills – all this might seem to suggest a straight line of development.

But it must be remembered that these regimens coexisted. In many ways the changes emerging during the second and third decades of the nineteenth century – even the dramatic novelties introduced by manufactories – developed out of mores and pressures already extant in 1810. Yet there was no consistent, pervasive evolution of local economic institutions. If custom could lead to entirely new kinds of ventures, it could also encourage the retention of patterns in agricultural and business activities that were distinct from – even hostile to – innovations embraced by textile mills. The coming of industrial order in Dudley and Oxford between 1810 and the early 1830s represented not an irresistible advance down a single track but the pressing forward of several institutional structures and strategies.

It was within this complex pattern, this milieu embracing both change and hesitancy to change, that local residents – in different ways, for different reasons, and according to their own varying perspectives and goals – would fashion their responses.

5   *How the operatives responded*

The industrial order brought conflict. As the consequences of post-1810 developments pressed through their communities, inhabitants of Dudley and Oxford found themselves responding amid rising waves of tension and friction. Two distinct sets of controversies developed. The first was between the mills (and their supporters) and groups of local townspeople who were not employed by local manufactories. The other cluster of controversies – and the one requiring consideration first – arose between the operatives and managers within the mill compounds.

By all indications, local employers not involved with manufactories had generally calm relations with their laborers. Some farms undoubtedly witnessed momentary tensions between yeomen and their restless children or servants; and some workshops probably saw occasional irritations flare up between proprietors and their laborers. But there is no evidence of employer–employee frictions persisting as a continuing theme outside the mills. Generally more relaxed, holding closer to customary patterns, and (assertions of factory paternalism notwithstanding) also more intimate than manufactories, nontextile workplaces in Dudley and Oxford offered comparatively little occasion for laborers to protest their situation. Unsupported by the props of urban artisanal culture, even craftsmen – even those facing what may have been fairly stringent conditions within local machine and cordwaining shops – seem to have been quiet between 1810 and the early 1830s.

Textile operatives were demonstrably not quiet. Indeed, far beyond the gestures of resistance sometimes evident among the more stubbornly recalcitrant outworkers, the resistance demonstrated by full-time hands inside the mill villages profoundly affected the social chemistry of these enclaves. Encompassing goals and strategies that never changed and others that evolved slowly over time, reflecting both aspirations of individual employees and the gradually increasing unity of millworkers, the opposition mounted by textile opera-

133

tives was a basic theme in local manufactories throughout the generation after 1810.

II

But it should be emphasized at the outset that millworkers neither all nor always resisted. Unraveling the ways factory employees coped with their situation makes clear that one strategy was simply obedience. And this, of course, was largely a consequence of the personal and "kindly" aura in which mill managers clothed themselves. Slater, for one, loomed large in the experience of his hands and not infrequently excited their admiration: Two operatives actually named sons after him.[1]

Overseers and agents were honored less vividly, but they too could attract enthusiastic followings among the operatives. Youngsters separated from their parents during working hours could grow strongly attached to their in loco parentis room supervisors. Indeed, the loyalty demonstrated by both youngsters and women operatives to one North Village official in the late 1830s caused his successor to fear "that some of the hands will rebel and refuse to do duty under me."[2] Then too, young men promoted or appointed into skilled jobs occasionally felt a pressing need to confirm their worthiness in the eyes of the agents who had hired them. An extraordinary letter sent by a woolen sorter named James Carter to the South Village in the 1830s reveals how distressing the loss of such approval could be. The immediate pretext for the note was a wage dispute. It quickly emerges, however, that Carter was troubled less by the possibility of reduced earnings than by the implied criticism that such a reduction signified. First the prelude:

> When the Mariner is tost too and frow by gales and storms he takes the first opportunity for to see what Latitude he is in and if more brakers he poots about but if his corse is right he raises more sails and goes a head in my case I think the helmsman ought to luff a little, nevertheless I shall have him to Judge after finding what Latitude we are in.

Then to the matter at hand:

> You say you have considered the worth of my Services by the pay from year to year, if that is the way you Judge of my Services there is others that think more of my Services than you do, for I can prove that three years of my time I have worked for you I could have made from 100 to 150 [dollars] more than you paid me...and I further say when a man does not work for the inter-

est of his employer it is high time that his days be shortened [and] another take his place, if my endevours have not met your expectation I will now say I think wool assorting the most important branch of Manufacturing and since I have ben heare my endevors has been for to give perfect Satisfaction if I have failed it is my inability if I have not given satisfaction I am shure I will not give dissatisfaction.[3]

But workers also acceded to the more formal bureaucratic strictures of the regimen: time discipline, for example. It will be recalled that during Slater's first years in Rhode Island operatives had sometimes left the Old Mill because they disliked working long hours year round. "The first night I lit Candles," Slater had acknowledged to Almy and Brown during that period, Benchley "sent for his Children to come home" and "it took a considerable and warm debate" to retrieve them.[4] By the second and third decades of the nineteeth century, however, a cultural accommodation of some magnitude had taken place. Attendance continued to dip slightly in autumn, probably because operatives were spending a few hours on scattered days helping to harvest nearby fields. But it no longer sparked a "considerable and warm debate" when mill managers made clear that in principle they expected employees to work full days twelve months a year. By 1830 the average operative in the Dudley Woolen Manufacturing Company registered 77.9 percent attendance. The comparable figure for the East Village was 91.3 percent, which included a steady 20 to 21 percent with no absenteeism at all.[5]

Such pliability and loyalty obviously imply that some factory workers in Dudley and Oxford accepted industrial rhythms and strictures. But docility turns out to be only part of the overall operatives' response. Despite the soothing rhetoric management invoked, despite the workers' broadening accommodation to elements of industrial discipline, employees in local manufactories persistently blended obedience and deference with efforts to push back against the men and rules governing them.

They did so in large measure because the industrial order penetrating Dudley and Oxford encompassed such varied patterns. Like other rural New Englanders, millworkers knew – often from direct experience – that the farms, stores, and small workshops scattered across the countryside ran to rhythms and purposes very different from those evinced by textile factories. In Dudley and Oxford the contrast left many operatives discontent. It left them, for all their adaptation to twelve-hour days, often still viewing demands imposed by manufactories as unprecedentedly stringent. It left them keenly sensitive to the way changing market conditions and management's unflagging desire for profit combined to make factories more demanding as time went on. And it left them sensitive as well to the political barbs that – partly in direct response to management's paternalistic slogans – were often directed at textile mills: If two operatives named sons after Slater, another named his heirs Liberty and Independence.[6]

It was such considerations – often deepened and focused by specific disaffections over particular managerial policies – that lay behind the resistance developing in local cotton and woolen factories during the generation after 1810.

III

At times the opposition was individualistic: The numerous divisive pressures separating factory employees tended to channel resistance into actions essayed alone or in small groups. At times it also involved operatives' denying the legitimacy of the factory order. And at times the two themes intersected. This had happened during the 1790s (in Benchley's defiant gesture "the first night" candles were lit) and it continued up through the 1830s. Thus some parents – despite the ideology of managerial "regard" and "concern" – would not accept the daily separation from their children. Peter Mayo – acting alone, refusing to compromise, almost certainly knowing that his resistance precluded continued employment with Slater – was dismissed from the East Village in 1827 for trying "to controul his family whilst [it was] under charge of the Overseers."[7]

And thus management's fear of arson. Beginning in the early 1800s and on through the 1830s, rumors abounded in New England that some of the many fires suffered by textile factories were the "incendiary" work of disgruntled Yankees, including disgruntled operatives. So Slater acknowledged, "Many are of the opinion" that an 1811 mill fire in Pawtucket "was set . . . willfully."[8] In Dudley and Oxford, at least five factories burned before 1840. Two of these were woolen mills belonging to Slater, who seems never to have been certain about the cause of the conflagrations.[9] His suspicions of foul play were never proved, nor were the precise issues that might have prompted such attacks ever explained. But if any local factory fires did represent arson, the episodes would clearly suggest the presence of employees so offended by the factory regimen, and so marginally committed to factory berths, that they willingly destroyed their source of employment.

Given the variety of people laboring in manufactories, however, it is not surprising to find confrontational gestures mixed with quite different forms of opposition. Thus, from the earliest days of New England mills and on through the post-1810 generation in Dudley and Oxford, factory workers also resisted in ways that assumed the continued existence of mills and their own continuing employment as operatives. Here was accommodation that avoided docility. Here workers resisted to bolster their earnings or to assert their autonomy or perhaps both at once – but in cautious ways. And, unlike the more aggressive styles of opposition for which men were generally responsible, here was resistance that women and older teen-agers of both sexes frequently undertook.

It is, of course, conventional scholarly wisdom that the women and youngsters employed in antebellum factories took up labor resistance only slowly and with some difficulty.[10] But there is a sense in which the adult females and older youngsters inside manufactories actually may have been ripe for disaffection. Since mill berths often represented their first paying jobs, such operatives might well have experienced an especially vivid tension between, on the one hand, novel feelings of independence born of their wage payments and, on the other hand, disciplines imposed on their daily labors. Indeed, this tension was very likely the final factor offsetting the supposed susceptibility of these workers to patriarchal authority: Not only did women and youngsters frequently confront the anonymous demands of waterpowered machines; they also faced the disconcerting way factory regimens undercut the autonomy that factory wages seemed to promise.[11] The result was not pervasive militancy; obviously, these employees often did feel loyal to their managers. But it was also possible for them to feel disappointed and impatient – which was probably why many of them participated in certain measured forms of resistance throughout the early decades of New England's textile industry.

Absenteeism was one example. Even though punctuality demonstrably increased, staying away from the mill rooms for a few hours or days remained for many Yankee operatives – women and youngsters as often as men – a satisfying, relatively nondisruptive way to assert autonomy from industrial pressures. Punctuality "improved," in other words, but only up to a point. Even with the high attendance rates they demonstrated by 1830, it was still true that employees in the East Village and the Dudley Woolen Manufacturing Company were collectively absenting themselves about 15 percent of working hours.[12]

There are also hints that these workers stole. Continuing the thievery apparently common among Old Mill operatives (and commonly charged to journeymen handloom weavers as well), local factory workers – again acting alone, again including women and youngsters – were accused of supplementing their incomes by taking manufactured yarn and cloth along with raw cotton and wool. As with absenteeism, stealing did not threaten the existence of local factories. But officials conceded that they had "to rise sometime before the sun" each day if they wished to preserve mill property.[13]

This inventory of certain and probable resistance – seeking "controul" over children, arson, absenteeism, stealing – persisted throughout the generation following 1810. As time passed, however, and as conditions changed, this continuity was bracketed by important shifts in the complexion of resistance.

It is evident, for example, that management's mounting stringency prompted new and more varied opposition. At the same time, the growing realization that textile mills would not soon fade away, and the growing number of workers prepared to invest many years in factory employment, meant that tactics aimed at rejecting or destroying mills received less emphasis than efforts to achieve a modus vivendi within the factory order. Veterans whose personal economies precluded easy exits from millwork or whose ambitions included advancing up mill hierarchies were not without critical feelings toward factory regimens. But the expanding cadre of experienced operatives preferred to retaliate in ways that would neither elicit dismissals nor threaten the continued solvency of their employers.

Thus, if local operatives followed trends common in other rural mills of the era, they soon began secretly sabotaging their machines – not to destroy the technology but simply to provide themselves with temporary respite. In 1829 the agent at a small Yankee woolen mill discovered his "back Piecer Lewis Kingman, throwing... off [bands on his mule] and at last cuting the spindle and one of the main bands." He concluded that "for Boldness and Cunning the above tricks surpasses all description," but they were probably no more than what many factory superintendents were encountering.[14]

Less destructive but probably equally satisfying, East Village power-loom weavers by the end of the 1820s appear to have synchronized their piecing of broken threads so that, despite their looms' steady speed, they were able to vary the speed of their work across the days of the week. Judging from Green Mill records in 1832, these women generally adopted a slow-to-fast rhythm: Beginning low on Monday, weaving output rose as the week progressed, with Thursday through Saturday emerging as the most productive days two-thirds of the time, and with Monday and Saturday linked as the days of lowest and highest cloth output, respectively, in nearly one-quarter of the fifty-three weeks examined. In effect, the East Village weavers were taking as their unit of labor time not the workday but the workweek. And, as was often the case among employees who received – or took – the privilege of distributing labor over several days, these operatives found it subjectively more restful to begin slowly and finish up quickly.[15]

In a sense, even clothing served to express the workers' needs and priorities. Adult male operatives and children dressed unremarkably. But by the 1820s and 1830s observers almost always mentioned that factory girls were (to quote Harriet Martineau) "well-dressed...[with] their hair...arranged according to the latest fashions." Charles Dickens reported that women working in Lowell were "well-dressed" (though "not," he was pleased to add, "above their condition").[16] Various motives undoubtedly encouraged women in this direction, including a desire to appear attractive to available men. But dressing up may also have enclosed a resistance of sorts: a prideful assertion of femininity upon entering the largely male arena of wage-paying jobs, a declaration of independence against the "drudgery of the mill and its drab vicinity."[17]

Although rooted (like all resistance) in attitudes shared by operatives, the emerging responses to machine discipline and "drab" industrial villages noted thus far were still essentially individualistic gestures. But here the increasing presence of veterans brought further changes. For with their expanding numbers, and with the resulting development of at least greater fellowship in the labor force, there emerge hints of a more dense and self-conscious occupational culture slowly taking root in the mills – and of operatives gradually building on this culture to organize forms of collaborative resistance.

It is significant, for example, that by the 1820s local workers routinely manipulated a specialized jargon of "slubbing billey[s]" and "dresser-warper[s]."[18] Moreover, despite the absence of meeting places inside the villages, there is reason to believe that local operatives had by this point also adopted the custom – shared among factory hands on both sides of the Atlantic – of punctuating the beginning and end of the candlelight work seasons with "lighting up" and "blowing out" parties.[19] Then too, it is possible to tease from the records hints that workers inside the mill rooms were becoming increasingly likely to help one another or to cover for one another during brief absences. And it is likely they also learned how to communicate within the factory rooms despite the racket of the machines. Judging from modern mills, they may have developed systems of hand signs. Judging from other antebellum factories, they almost certainly learned that by "speaking close to the ear of an operative, and quite loud, we could make the inquiries we wished."[20]

None of this, to reiterate, produced a "habit of solidarity." All this added up to no more than "limited" camaraderie. But the shift does seem to have produced a measure of coordinated opposition. Once again the clues are elusive. Yet there are traces of whispering campaigns and slowdowns aimed at discrediting excessively demanding supervisors: "And above all things you do," Slater wrote in 1820 to his son John then on duty in the East Village, "be constantly on your guard to not take an active part with anyone against Mr. Porter because he has found fault with him for Indolence, etc."[21] There are hints too of a strange choreography of funeral attendance, by which operatives took off half days to bury their friends and relatives but made no effort to attend services for managers.[22] And it is possible to surmise – if only after the fact, from the shifts in factory routine they induced – the goals and efficacy of such tactics.

In effect, operatives collaborated to fill a vacuum. Lacking established traditions specifying "normal" demands in factory work, operatives sought to create these norms. Time discipline was once more a focus, for if workers balanced punctuality with certain levels of persisting absenteeism, they also collectively appropriated management's seventy-two-hour week and turned it to their own purposes. Thus, whereas in 1814 Slater's Slatersville employees were "willing to work as long as they do to [i.e., in] Pawtucket," even if that meant a few minutes longer, by the 1830s in the Dudley Woolen Manufacturing Company and as early as 1817 in the East Village, work beyond seventy-two hours, even five minutes' worth, was regarded by the hands as "extra," to be purchased with "extra" pay.[23] The stringency with which the mills calculated punctuality was thus paralleled by the workers' invention of overtime.

Comparable boundaries appeared around production. In the years before machine-made cloth undercut their position, handloom woolen weavers in the Merino Mill set output ceilings and demanded bonuses for added work. Similarly, Slater's mule spinners and powerloom weavers did not reject assignments of more and faster machines during the 1820s, but they insisted that the added output be accompanied by higher gross earnings. And women throstle spinners, who operated twice as many machines in 1835 as in 1817, received both more pay *and* pay at higher rates for "tending extra sides."[24]

Thus developed a kind of balance. The increased stress on forms of opposition that permitted continued employment in the mills, and especially the emergence of collaborative efforts to distinguish normal from "extra" demands, suggest that many operatives were coming to accept the factory order but simultaneously modifying the regimen with their own requirements. Accepting factory life on these terms – this giving and taking between employers and employees, this tugging back and forth in ways both sides could more or less accept but which also underscored the differences between them – this was an established pattern in local mill villages by 1820.

Once, however, in the late 1820s, the balance collapsed. The result was the single expression of overt militancy experienced by these villages during the first generation after 1810.

IV

The incident arose because the South Village imposed a wage cut on its cassimere handloom weavers. The competitive pressures that forced general piece-rate reductions among handloom weavers during the 1820s led finally, in the spring of 1827, to a cut that the skilled weavers working inside Slater's woolen compound found intolerable. The precise size of the reduction is not known. But it was evidently too large to be either accepted or offset by managerial compromise in other areas of factory life. The affected weavers (as Slater reported to the Dudley Woolen Manufacturing Company) announced their "determination not to weave unless at the old prices": in other words, to strike.[25]

The South Village "turnout" in 1827 should be viewed in two ways. First, as the consequence of pressures playing across life and work in Slater's woolen village, the strike did not arise *ex nihilo* or even merely as a response to a wage cut. The weavers' "determination" derived in part from their position as skilled workers who had not been promoted from below and so felt no particular debt to management. More than most millworkers, they had a sense of customary worth and status; and thus, more than most, they were prepared to protest sharp economic demotions. Doubtless too, the South Village weavers drew inspiration from the general rise of labor militancy in antebellum northern cities like Philadelphia, New York, and Boston. Indeed, the operatives' transiency makes it likely that South Village weavers had learned from events in other mills: the 1824 strike in Pawtucket, for example, which marked the first full-scale American textile turnout.[26] But most of all, the 1827 confrontation arose from the long-building momentum of resistance – the tradition of individual gestures, the collaborative insistence on "extra" pay for "extra" work – brewing within the mill villages of Dudley and Oxford. Despite the short stints of local operatives, the heritage of defiant gestures, and the boundaries that had been established around acceptable managerial demands and acceptable employee performances – all this was preserved from year to year and communicated to any employee entering the manufactories. This heritage and these boundaries were the points of departure for the 1827 strike.

In this sense the South Village incident illuminates a pattern common in the labor confrontations of America's early industrial era. For throughout the opening decades of the nineteenth century, strikes typically emerged out of lengthy struggles between employees and employers to establish the lines and limits of their relationship. As in the South Village, so in other workplaces experiencing turnouts, strikes were usually conservative efforts to forestall changes – whether wage cuts or changes in working hours or (sometimes seemingly trivial) amendments in work rules – that employees felt went too far too fast: as though a threshold had been reached that laborers were unwilling to cross without a struggle. But as in the South Village also, such eruptions of militancy were usually shaped by – indeed, are comprehensible only in light of – lengthy prior histories of fencing between workers and their employers.[27]

The second way the South Village turnout should be viewed, however, is very different. It must be seen as a failure: Local operatives could mount a strike by 1827, but they could not win one. Despite advancing bonds of common experience among these workers, countervailing factors – the wide acceptance of some forms of discipline, the personal loyalty to managers evinced by some workers, and above all the obstacles to unity recounted earlier – all remained too strong. The weavers stood alone, and Slater triumphed simply by pressing ahead with his already contemplated decision to replace hand-powered woolen looms with water-driven weaving engines.[28]

Nor did the strike provide a helpful precedent to operatives. There was no further turnout among local millworkers until 1858, and the second strike was as fruitless as the first. Nor, interestingly enough, did the political energies of operatives undergo any sudden increase. This last point must be made cautiously, for it is true that southern Worcester County did deviate from voting patterns characterizing the Commonwealth as a whole. Although most Massachusetts citizens after 1810 shifted their support from Federalists to National

Republicans (and subsequently Whigs), both Dudley and Oxford provided occasional majorities to Jacksonian Democrats in the late 1820s and early 1830s. But given the difficulty operatives likely faced in qualifying for the franchise, employees in local mills probably did not play a leading role here. Judging from regional patterns, the best guess is that support for Jackson's party in these townships depended more on the "anti-aristocratic" resentments of hard-pressed yeomen than on the disaffections of factory hands. Then too, there is no evidence of local millworkers in subsequent years sending representatives to conventions of Massachusetts laborers or rushing to support the movement to implement the ten-hour workday. In sum, although not necessarily politically inert, operatives in these communities were scarcely galvanized into sustained, forceful activism by the strike of 1827.[29]

Yet none of this is really surprising. For if textile turnouts followed patterns typical of antebellum labor disputes, textile operatives remained for the most part less militant than other laborers of the era. Certainly they were less likely to mount strikes than skilled urban workers, among whom craft traditions were typical rather than exceptional and who consequently possessed clearer standards to defend and greater unity with which to wage the defense. The strikes and public protests antebellum millworkers did organize, moreover, were concentrated in urban factories. City operatives, after all, could draw support from craftsmen and various nearby social organizations. And operatives in Waltham-style urban factories had even further inducements. By hiring mainly adult, single, middle-class women and housing them in a few large dormitories, Waltham factories ironically produced a labor force more homogeneous and unified, more uniformly quick to treat wage reductions and tighter disciplines as challenges to their status – in short, more prone to organized militancy than employees of the more numerous, small, rural mills of the New England countryside.[30] Yet it is just these hundreds of family factories that require attention. For their record implies that turnouts and other large, overt protests, although scarcely unknown, were not the notation in which most antebellum operatives registered resistance.

Other notations obviously existed. The sweep of individual and joint opposition winding through local mill villages is surely sufficient demonstration that the absence of frequent turnouts does not mean operatives were quiescent. It makes no sense to measure the resistance of millworkers like those in post-1810 Dudley and Oxford solely in a calculus of large public confrontations.

But at the same time it seems fair to question the effectiveness of the opposition that such operatives did use. Did their resistance significantly lighten the burden of working within the factory order? After all, managerial vigilance must have limited, even if it did not prevent, whatever stealing, arson, and machine breaking transpired in local manufactories. And there are indications that other gestures of resistance had only limited impact on the gradually tightening stringency of mill operations. Even after securing their "extra" rewards, for example, the output of mule spinners and weavers in the Slater villages increased more than their gross wages in this period by 33.9 and 49.2 percent, respectively.[31] In an important sense the operatives' responses considered to this point, though far from inconsequential, seem to have left mill masters with the upper hand.

Yet there is more to say. A close reading of local factory records reveals one response that did force significant compromises from management. It is a response thus far glimpsed only in passing: leaving.

V

In itself, the restlessness of Dudley and Oxford millworkers is not remarkable. These working people lived amid communities – amid a whole region – in which moving about was commonplace. But factory workers may have been the most restless of a restless people.

Data derived from the Slater records, and depicted in Figure 5.1, reveal that aggregate arrivals and departures of operatives passing through the East and (after 1827) North villages dipped below 100 percent of the average annual labor force of these enclaves only twice between 1813 and the mid-1830s, whereas the mean aggregate turnover stood at 162.7 percent. Nor did this movement merely register passage through the payrolls: Just as most employees traveled substantial distances to reach these compounds, so most – around 80 percent – moved beyond nearby townships after leaving the Slater roster.[32] Since information on millworker mobility is far more precise than information on local mobility outside manufactories, it is possible that the transiency of Slater employees seems remarkable only because the precise turnover of other local residents is unknown. At a rough guess, however, Slater's operatives were probably twice as mobile as nonfactory inhabitants (including nonfactory wage laborers) of Dudley and Oxford.[33]

As the graph also demonstrates, rates of overall operative mobility could alter substantially from year to year. Most of the larger

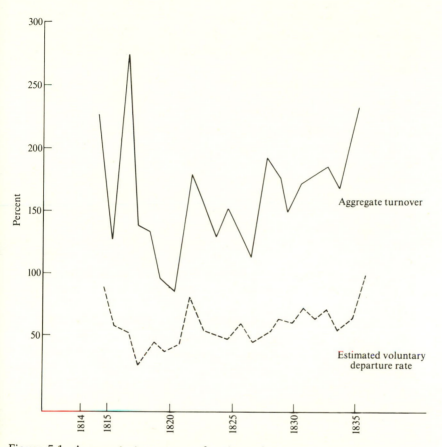

Figure 5.1. Aggregate turnover and estimated voluntary departure rates, Slater employees, 1814-35. Data cover East Village, 1814–27; East and North villages, 1828–35. Consistent data not available for the South Village. (SC: Slater and Tiffany, vols. 84, 88–91; Phoenix, vol. 24.)

shifts probably arose directly from the changing economic conditions manufactories confronted in this period. Thus, turnover climbed sharply in 1816 because management responded to the depression of that year by dismissing approximately half the Green Mill labor force (see Table A.1). The decline in overall mobility during the next several years reflects a general stability in the size of the East Village work force, as well as the inclination of workers, sensitive to the continuing impact of "slow times," to retain those jobs they had. By 1821, however, and continuing through the mid-1820s, conditions had improved sufficiently to permit employees to move about freely;

indeed, the half decade of enforced stability seems to have encouraged a particularly sharp burst of movement in 1821, as though a pressure valve had been suddenly released. The next significant increase in aggregate turnover, during 1827, reflects Slater's decision to weave cotton cloth entirely by power looms and his related decision to recruit women operatives to run these machines. The economic uncertainties of 1829 and 1834–5 subsequently constricted movement, but generally through the late 1820s and early 1830s rates of overall arrivals and departures remained high.[34]

All this, however, reflects mobility arising from decisions made by both managers and workers. To gain firmer leverage on transiency resting on choices made by operatives alone, a voluntary departure rate (also shown in Figure 5.1) was computed for Slater's employees.[35] Although again varying from year to year (again generally falling during downturns and rising during prosperity), this rate – admittedly only an estimate – strongly suggests that large numbers of workers annually left Slater's factories because they wanted to. The indications are that, except for the depression years between 1816 and 1820, at least 45 percent, and usually well over half, of his average annual labor force *chose* to depart (see Table A.1).[36]

Along with its volume, other structural aspects of this willful mobility warrant attention. First, it varied somewhat with skill level and sex. Both mule spinners and power-loom weavers had below average voluntary departure rates, suggesting that workers who were better paid (and often promoted from below) or who were female were comparatively slow to take to the open road. But the differences between rates registered by these two groups and the norm for all Slater employees were not systematic and never exceeded 20 percent.[37] A further, more significant feature of transiency was that it ranked among the operatives' more private responses to the factory order. It has already been suggested that movement undercut social ties within the village; what requires attention here is that workers appear to have usually left by themselves or with just a few others.

Even families rarely departed as a unit. This is perhaps not surprising when it is recalled that local mills did not prevent older children from leaving the compounds and may even have forced fathers to move on by reducing the number of berths open to male household heads. But the statistics are still dramatic: Exactly half the departing youngsters and well over half (56 percent) the departing fathers sampled from the East Village payroll left kin behind when they quit this enclave.[38] And it is likely that comparable numbers of workers arriving at local manufactories had left close relatives at

other mills when they set off for Dudley and Oxford: "My family,"
announced a father entering the Dudley Woolen Manufacturing Company in 1831, "will remain at Millbury for the present."[39]

The geographical dispersal of operative households did not signal
the collapse of domestic relations any more than did the daily separation of coresiding parents and children within the mill villages. On
the contrary, a further important variable affecting mobility rates
among Slater employees was precisely domestic attachment: Workers
with kin in the factory compounds remained 50 percent longer and
were 30 percent more likely to return than unattached operatives.[40]
Nor should it be overlooked that throughout this period and all
across the region *some* Yankee kinsmen – both millworkers and non-
millworkers – traveled together and that those who were separated
often remained in contact with one another.

Still, the fact remains that movement among operative family members was largely a private act. And – as was also true throughout the
period and all across the region – this undoubtedly caused distress.
For although it was not anomalous in antebellum Yankee households, the departure of youngsters always carried at least the threat
of terminal separation. Even young children could disappear: "My
daughter...about 12...left the service of the Cotton Factory at Wa-
tertown," reads an advertisement in the *Massachusetts Spy* of 1816.
"Since that time no intelligence whatever has been received respecting her."[41]

But why did family members leave? Indeed, why did any operative leave? There was no single answer. Those using millwork as a
temporary expediency departed when their expectations matured:
Their inheritances came through; or their dowries grew sufficient.
Others left simply because, like many New Englanders, they were
accustomed to movement. Or, in rare instances, they left because
they had saved enough to buy a business or a farm. Or (especially
among fathers lacking regular berths and perhaps feeling ineffectual
in the villages) they left because they found better situations elsewhere. Or (especially among children who could expect neither training nor bequests from their parents if they stayed) they left because
factory labor was intolerably tedious: "Picker boy sick of the mill,"
wrote the agent of a small rural mill in this period, "paid him 8¢ and
sent him home."[42]

Operatives had left factories for such reasons beginning in the
1790s, and local millworkers reflected these promptings through the
1830s. Gradually, however, another motive emerged. As mills grew
more numerous across New England, as there emerged among employees cadres of operatives committed to long stretches of factory

work, and as these operatives were subjected to increasingly stiff demands, some workers began using movement not to leave textile work but to improve their situation within it.

This was obviously a strategy for prosperous times. Depressions, as already noted, reduced the mobility of operatives; and those who did move during slumps sometimes accepted any available opening and even angled for multiyear contracts.[43] Yet against this must be contrasted a mounting inclination of veterans to use good years as hunting seasons for better positions. Again there were precedents: Slater had lost skilled men to another mill as early as 1802. But by the 1820s and 1830s the pattern was commonplace and had broadened out to include women and youngsters. In the East Village in 1834: "More [power-loom weavers] have given their notice to Leave to go to...where they can do better"; in the Dudley Woolen Manufacturing Company in 1841: Workers are "leaving our employ [because] more wages wanted." But maximizing income was not the operatives' only priority. They moved to secure more compatible overseers or more flexible "rules and regulations" or better working facilities: "I am not satisfied with my [finishing] shop here and intends leaving here"; "I am not very well pleased with the Business here there is not Water to Scour the Wool and Probably never will be."[44] Indeed, among workers who rarely voted and whose other forms of resistance had only limited effect, mobility may well have emerged as the principal means of avoiding "corrupt" dependency on their employers – of asserting independence.

But operatives did more than merely seize existing opportunities. They also used movement, or the threat of movement, to bid up the value of their services and so *create* better jobs for themselves. They could do this because mobility presented difficulties for factory managers. Ideologues – ignoring the fact that often the same workers were passing from mill to mill – occasionally tried to paint high turnover as a valuable feature of New World manufactories: It proved (they said) that America, unlike England, had "no permanent factory population."[45] To those actually running the mills, however, the rapid comings and goings of workers meant trouble. The task of assigning incoming workers to suitable jobs, preparing lodgings, and keeping records up-to-date taxed administrative capacities. Then too, the stream of demands for terminal wage payments could create severe cash shortages.[46] Most serious, however, was the way in which transiency aggravated the tight labor market that New England mills often confronted. Recruiting hands was inevitably made more difficult when managers had to replenish their rosters not once every so often but repeatedly – in some cases almost continuously.

All early manufactories faced this challenge. But the greater fame of Waltham-style factories, and the somewhat higher overall wage rate they could quote for their all-adult work force, appear to have given these establishments an edge over family mills in securing recruits at short notice. Thus, although rarely left "short of help" for long, factories in Dudley and Oxford frequently had to scramble to fill empty positions.[47] So great was the pressure that the news in August 1834 that the "Salmon Falls factory was wholly destroyed by fire yesterday" led a local mill official visiting near the conflagration to consider only the operatives suddenly available for hire: "The hands are all of course out of employ," he wrote to Dudley, so "if any hands are by us wanted you will inform me."[48] It is likely hands were wanted, for in the same month, the East Village agent reported that

> the prospect for the four weeks to come is not...good...as I am all ready short of weavers...I have sent out in all directions after weavers but have not as yet had the good Luck to get any – weavers are very scarce in this vicinity I do not know of a Mill in this vicinity that have a full supply etc.[49]

Here was the workers' leverage. At least by the late 1820s and all through the 1830s prosperous times saw operatives with jobs already in hand routinely (though often secretly) soliciting offers from other mills – mills rumored to need hands and desirous of hiring veterans – to win better "bargains" for themselves. The trick was to indicate availability without suggesting that a new job was absolutely necessary. Thus George Hanson's letter to the South Village in the mid-1830s:

> I am informed that you are in want of a giger...I shold be hapy to receve the job as I do not expect to stop hear an other year altho I cold if I wanted to my reasons for not stoping hear proberly I will give som other time ples not to communicate this to any one as you now [i.e., know] storyes curculates very fast.[50]

Or another letter to this manufactory around the same time from an operative in Fall River, Massachusetts:

> The purpose of this is to enquire if thou would have a board for me in the course of a short time as I partely expect to need one, though I am not yet decided.[51]

But in all cases the goal was to win a better situation: "I am [given] fair pay...where I am now," a prospective Slater employee wrote in 1827, "[and it] would not be an object for me to change places unless I can receive as pay one dollar pr. day and board."[52]

Not infrequently, factories needing workers and wishing to recruit experienced hands were actually maneuvered into bidding against each other. So Anne Smith – with a commendably straight face – admitted to the South village agent that after agreeing to work for him she had received a better offer from: "Mr. Dennys or rather I set my price. . . so high that I did not suppose he would send for me but he has taken me at my price and for this reason I am obliged to say I cannot work for you."[53] Or consider a certain Mr. Richards who, early in 1831, as his Southbridge, Massachusetts, employer subsequently reconstructed events, "said he should like to stay but said he should want a little more wages, and I immediately made him an offer of more wages, and he wanted to consider of it – and did so some time." As it turned out, however, Richards was simultaneously wooing an offer of $1.50 per day from the Dudley Woolen Manufacturing Company, which he kept in mind when he finally informed the Southbridge mill that "he wanted so much – a fifth [?] more" from that mill. "And [he] gave me," concluded the Southbridge manufacturer, "till the next day to decide – as I understood it – and the next day I agreed to pay him his price."[54]

VI

There were, of course, limits to what workers could win this way. Mills needed operatives. But the continued presence of workers with low net incomes reveals that managers were too protective of profit margins to give all employees what (as Slater had once put it) "their unlimited consciences. . . dictate them to ask."[55] Similarly, the tendency of the factory regimen to grow more demanding suggests that officials declined to dismantle disciplines they believed promoted productivity. Concessions gained through movement were thus confined to the margin, where proprietors thought compromise was at least potentially affordable. Yet even here the stakes were sufficiently high to create fierce struggles – the most dense and protracted to develop within these villages – as management sought to control the mobility of millworkers and as operatives sought to retain freedom of movement.

So it was that local mills implemented contracts. Agreements putatively binding operatives to fixed employment periods had occasionally been used by mills as early as the 1790s. But the Merino mill and Dudley Woolen Manufacturing Company throughout their careers, and Slater's Dudley and Oxford villages after 1824, used twelve-month – April to April – work contracts consistently.[56] Until around

1830 most of these agreements stipulated that final wage settlements would be deferred until the conclusion of the contracted period. The contracts might provide that all wages should be withheld "until expiration of yr"; or they might permit "expenses through the year" and the balance in April; or they might provide "15% of the wages outstanding on demand and the rest at the beginning of April next."[57] But whatever the precise formulation, the basic intent was clear: to "pay off the hands" only once every twelve months. In effect, management was trying to create an industrial work year beginning and ending (ironically enough) during the same springtime weeks that rural town meetings had customarily closed and opened their annual calendars.

Such an arrangement helped management in several ways at once. By delaying payments, the mills effectively granted themselves interest-free loans. Moreover, although year-end payments required elaborate preparations ("we shall want for paying off the help and other needs by 1st of April next about $6,000"), postponing wage settlements probably also eased the liquidity problems often faced by rural manufactories.[58] But the basic aim of the contracts was to affect the operatives' transiency. The goals were, first, to reduce movement (if workers traveled only in April aggregate turnover could not exceed 100 percent) and, second, to funnel such movement into predictable, brief periods each spring.

But the effort failed, partly because employers proved more interested in obliging workers to honor yearlong engagements than in honoring such engagements themselves. The East Village did, to be sure, increase springtime hirings: Between 1814 and 1824, 39 percent of operatives taken on by this compound were recruited in April; between 1825 and 1835 the proportion taken on in April rose to 45 percent. Layoffs, on the other hand, continued to occur as market conditions warranted, and in the twenty years after 1814 most payroll reductions took place during the summer or fall. The numbers do not reflect a firm pattern: There was no drift toward consistently letting hands go between May and October. But the statistics are sufficient to demonstrate that East Village supervisors were not prepared to respect the twelve-month industrial work years they sought to impose on their hands.[59]

The most critical obstacle to holding operatives in place, however, was the stance taken by the operatives themselves. Now it is true that as the nineteenth century wore on Yankee millworkers increasingly peppered their letters with references to yearlong factory "seasons" ("my situation [is] that I am not yet employed for this Season").[60]

And it is true too that in the years immediately following the introduction of contracts the proportion of Slater's southern Massachusetts workers choosing to leave in April picked up noticeably. But among local operatives at least, the overall trend in the post-1810 generation was actually away from voluntary April departures and toward a fairly even distribution of exits throughout the year. Thus, between 1814 and 1824, 34.1 percent of voluntary departures from the East Village were undertaken in the spring; between 1831 and 1835 the figure for both the East and North villages was 28.9 percent, and for the 1825–35 decade as a whole it stood at 31.2 percent. (In the Dudley Woolen Manufacturing Company during the early 1830s the proportion of springtime voluntary departures was higher – 34.1 percent – but this was exactly matched by the percentage of summertime voluntary exits.)[61] As these statistics suggest, management's threat to restrict "final settlements" to the "expiration of yr" was easily circumscribed. Operatives owing money to the mills simply took "French leave...in the night." Those with net wages due them blithely denied the legitimacy of their contracts ("I made no engagement...for any particular time I should not think any one could have any objections [to] my leaving") and not infrequently managed to persuade their next employers to help secure the money – and in one instance even the clothes – that their "unexpected" departures had caused them to leave behind.[62]

Faced with such recalcitrance, local mills could only retreat. The evidence on this point is admittedly contradictory, suggesting that different factories proceeded at different speeds and with some inconsistency to reconcile themselves to defiantly mobile hands. In the Slater villages, however, the basic trend seems clear. Despite lingering declamations that agents would not pay employees until their "time is up," wage settlements in the North and East compounds by the early 1830s, and perhaps even by the late 1820s, appear to have generally slipped into quarterly, monthly, and, in one instance, even bimonthly rhythms. Moreover, although some operatives continued to sign on for extended stints and although a few dutifully honored the full periods to which they had pledged themselves ("This will serve to inform you that I am under a contract...for a nother year...I find my Self Bound to them"), most post-1830 agreements in the Slater villages covered fewer than twelve months and contained clauses permitting "either party [to] be released" by giving four weeks' notice.[63]

But contracts remained only one front of the battle. Local managers sought other ways to attract and retain operatives. They tried, for example, to lure employees with inflated "bargains" and then "cut down" after filling their rosters – to which operatives responded by demanding guarantees of good faith with all offers.[64] More defensively, managers tried to protect their payrolls against other mills by establishing guidelines for wages and by threatening to sue any factories "enticing" employees already under contract. But this too proved useless. The difficulties that had forced Almy and Brown to give up trying to regulate "prices" for labor in 1814 persisted into the 1820s and 1830s: Mill masters were simply too numerous and too often desperate for hands to stop their "inveigling." Slater himself was accused of improperly approaching employees of another manufactory.[65] And in the 1820s the Dudley Woolen Manufacturing Company blundered into a battle royal with mills in Woodstock, Connecticut, and Southbridge, Massachusetts: "It is certain," reads the enraged letter addressed to the Dudley agent,

> that when we commenced work at Woodstock... you engaged at once in hiring our help, that you sent up time and again for our help, and in fact took away most of it; that you Sent up men with Horse Chaise, and Waggons for their conveyance. That you have indirectly at different times at this place [Southbridge] Sent up horses and Chaises etc. for our Spinners, . . . [that you are] sending to my neighbors to have our girls meet them for the purpose of hiring them away.[66]

Once again, however, it was the workers' own resistance that proved most significant. Civil actions against "enticements" required sworn statements by employees; but because employees had often directly or indirectly invited overtures from another mill and because these overtures typically meant better "bargains," operatives called on to testify would, as Slater's lawyer glumly acknowledged, as soon "cut our throats" as tell the truth.[67]

The final managerial ploy was to stress the ethical importance of staying put. Along with punctuality, rootedness was, in fact, what factory masters always had in mind when they set "steadiness" among the principal desiderata of early textile employees. As already noted, local millworkers – at least those employed by the Slater mills and the Dudley Woolen Manufacturing Company – did become quite punctual, even hoisting management on its own clocks with overtime. But their extraordinary transiency makes clear that operatives never accepted the moral necessity of remaining in a manufactory a moment longer than they wished. Indeed, it was through mobility that millworkers demonstrated their capacity to blend piety with resistance.

The blend is demonstrated, first, in the fact that signs of religious interest among local operatives were not accompanied by any consistent or significant drop in the workers' total annual movement. Millworkers might join religious groups (especially those "near" the mills), and they might participate in revivals, but neither development definitively reduced their determination to move on.[68]

Focusing further on the revivals, however, raises a second possibility. Four bursts of religious "enthusiasm" erupted in Dudley and Oxford between 1810 and the mid-1830s: in 1813, 1822, 1831, and 1835. Community histories indicate that these spiritual upswings were scattered across the calendar year, emerging any time from late spring through July to late fall and into December.[69] But whenever they occurred, the immediate period of all four revivals – not the whole year, which showed no persistent net variation, but the months surrounding the episodes – saw changes in the mobility of Slater operatives. Specifically, during the revivals voluntary departures were always low (reaching either their smallest or second smallest volume of the revival year); following the revival, however, voluntary departures always increased. The significance of the variation should not be exaggerated. The specific months witnessing low to high shifts in exit rates during revival years were in every case involved in similar shifts during the years bracketing enthusiasms. On the other hand, three postrevival departure surges (in 1813, 1831, and 1835) were more substantial than comparable increments during the years lacking revivals.[70]

Religious enthusiasm thus takes on a curious coloration. Millworkers – at least those inclined to religous concerns – evidently paused to participate in revivals. But whatever factory managers may have hoped or expected, these spiritual awakenings merely caused the operatives to postpone their departures – caused them often, in fact, to express their pent-up restlessness with accelerated transiency once the religious dust had settled. Indeed, the link between revivals and subsequent increases in mobility may have been even more direct. It may be speculated, but not proved, that, so far from inducing consistent docility, enthusiasms actually strengthened the operatives' psychological capacity to push toward their goals. It is possible, that is, that the salvation these laboring people experienced gave them the confidence, determination, and perhaps even the discipline to press their familiar strategy of mobility all the more firmly.[71]

VII

Thus, management could not prevent operatives from leaving. Contracts, threats to other millowners, the underscoring of the morality of stability – none of these strategies was effective. But even as these approaches faltered, local mills began pursuing a different tack. Once again the records are only suggestive. But what they imply is a campaign by managers to give their villages a good reputation – not to stop hands from departing but to make it easier to find replacements. Part of this program, of course, involved the "kindly and paternal interest" already considered. But these factories also went further. Unlike Waltham-style administrators, who used fines, firings, and blacklists to enforce discipline,[72] factory officials in Dudley and Oxford reacted to their more severe staffing difficulties by offering what amounted to a hidden contract: a tacit agreement to avoid such Draconian measures.

Every social institution implicitly specifies which formal regulations will be stressed and which ignored.[73] It will be recalled, in fact, that the pressure of a tight labor market led Slater to avoid mobilizing harsh disciplinary techniques as early as the 1790s. But given the rising pressure for increased efficiency in the decades after 1810, it is surely remarkable – and indicative of more than just personal inertia on Slater's part – that this pattern of restraint both persisted and broadened out, emerging as a characteristic of many small antebellum family factories.

It was not, to be sure, characteristic of all these mills to the same degree. Rhode Island's Peace Dale factory, for example, evidently fined tardy workers. And strictures against liquor were apparently backed up rigorously in the Manville mills, also in Rhode Island. On the other hand, it was a common complaint during the early 1830s that operatives in most rural manufactories of southern New England spent their Sundays "consuming rum, even in some villages...in which the sale of rum was forbidden."[74] In the southern Massachusetts factories under review, sobriety was also required; but drinking was tolerated outside working hours (Slater's store sold "drams"), and an agent for the Dudley Woolen Manufacturing Company had no qualms about recommending an operative who had been "the worse for liquor but once during 12 months." Punctuality in these mills was stressed and measured meticulously; but tardiness was not fined. Obedience to mill officials was mandated; but records of five local factory villages suggest that by 1835 only three workers had been dismissed for "misconduct" and that "work badly done" met only sporadic sanctions.[75] The way these mills treated their employees' nonworking lives also becomes more explicable in this context: Local factories may have shied away from tightly supervised residences and recreational hours in a calculated effort to avoid irritating their hands. And finally, for all the fuss made about workers leaving "untimely," operatives who quit before "their time was up" were never pursued or sued and (again unlike Waltham practices) their names were not "sen[t] around": "I shall make some inquiry after them [two runaways]," Slater informed son John in 1825, "tho I shall not make much trouble to find them."[76]

It is important not to exaggerate this administrative slack. It did not raise wage levels or countermand increased work loads or alleviate the mounting precision with which work time was calibrated (nor did it even offset Slater's earlier decision to impose overseers) – in short, it did not offset the increasing burden of the factory order. Nor, as already seen, did it remove the need many operatives felt to resist that order. Yet this pattern of informal leniency may well have represented the greatest victory local workers wrung from their employers, for it guaranteed a small but valuable addition in daily freedom. This, in turn, is perhaps the final reason strikes were rare in mills like those in southern Massachusetts. It is also why, from management's perspective, leniency was a successful policy: Despite their constant worry about labor shortages, manufactories like the Slater and Merino mills could usually rely on their "good" reputation to attract sufficient employees.

Here, then, was the final compromise: a "bargain" benefiting both managers and workers. But the question remains how operatives discovered that certain mills tacitly voided strict enforcements of "rules and regulations." The answer can only be that they informed one another. Circulating through smaller factories, especially in southern New England, veteran millworkers learned "the customs of all the villages roundabout."[77] And at least by the 1830s the same informal networks that communicated news of openings were also ranking the mills. Thus a woman (with "a family five in numbers") told the South Village agent in the late 1830s that "Mr. Bigelow recommended your factory to me if you think there is a prospect. . .I would come. . .and see you." And around this time a young man informed the same factory: "You may think [it] rather strange why I keep writing to you the reason is that your place has been recommended to me as a good one."[78] This could have been hypocrisy. But it is equally likely that such statements disclose that transiency among experienced operatives was coming to rest on shared evaluations – and hence was providing further reason for separated friends and relatives to remain in contact. Although continuing to reflect and effect divisions within the labor force, movement may thus have grown gradually less atomizing, may have reflected to some degree the increased unity of textile workers. Even movement, that is, ultimately may have involved a kind of community.

VIII

But what, finally, did the operatives' resistance signify? Or, to place the issue within the context in which it was experienced at the time: What was the meaning of the whole, complex, back-and-forth tugging between these working people and the men and rules they faced. No single characterization is entirely adequate. But considering the operatives' reactions together with the regimen pressing upon them, it is difficult to ignore signs that what occurred in local mills during the generation after 1810 – and what the workers' opposition both reflected and helped create – was class.

For at least by the 1830s the net result of all the conflicts and compromises was a clear demarcation between the priorities of employees and employers. One side wished to maximize output and minimize labor costs; the other side sought a regimen permitting the best "price" and the greatest independence possible. When every allowance is made for concern and "kindly regard," on the one hand, and deference and obedience, on the other, this opposition is the axis around which local mills came to revolve.

There was, to be sure, an imbalance in the consciousness of the competing groups. Managers acted with consistent forcefulness to achieve their goals. Operatives, by contrast, should be seen as a class in itself that acted overtly for itself only to a limited extent. Yet millworkers quite obviously did find ways to resist, and at least "limited" forms of cooperation, of community, increasingly underlay their opposition.

In sum, the manufactories of Dudley and Oxford – emerging as social institutions with new technologies, new disciplines, and new, more emphatic commercial ambitions – engendered a new kind of relationship between employers and employees. The enterprises that claimed parallels to "large and well-conducted" households were in fact arenas in which new kinds of conflicts and compromises were worked out, in which people learned to decipher – or more accurately to create – the new "rules of the game" for the unprecedented experience of factory labor. It was by contributing to this new relationship, these new rules of the game, that the operatives' resistance revealed its full significance.

6   *How the towns responded*

In one respect, resistance to manufactories in Dudley and Oxford was the same inside and outside the factory compounds. Like operatives, local residents not employed by textile mills felt that these establishments were imposing – with increasing force as time went on – novel and unpleasant pressures on their lives.

Once again it is significant that manufactories stood out so distinctively. The tendency of local mills to reach into town life in ways contrary to conventional community practices was felt the more keenly throughout Dudley and Oxford because nonfactory business enterprises rarely essayed such invasions. As for operatives, so for townspeople, it was impossible to ignore the differences – indeed, the contradictions – between the factory order and abiding patterns of life and work outside the mill compounds.

There was, to be sure, one critically important distinction between tensions arising inside manufactories and the slowly emerging bundle of town–factory disagreements. Tussles between operatives and managers found immediate expression in workplace issues: work loads, wages, and – the most heated controversy – the volume and timing of employees' transiency. Controversies between the mills and the two townships, on the other hand, pivoted around community-wide issues. Here the mills confronted not their own employees but a varied constituency of people drawn from numerous occupations and strata: people who experienced their grievances not as industrial workers edging toward a sense of class but as citizens of New England townships.

The community opposition that thus developed had limits. It was expressed most often in town meetings, gatherings in which probably most adult male inhabitants (though relatively few textile operatives and no women of any occupation) could participate. But the town-meeting minutes from this period, even when supplemented by other, more private announcements of concern from individual residents, all indicate that the hostility factory masters met from local inhabitants not in their employ arose sporadically, never fo-

158

cused on all the mills existing at a given moment, and rarely signaled anything approaching unanimous community antipathy. Indeed,
some of the irritation mill masters faced actually came from owners
of other local mills. Town–factory controversies, in sum, developed
against a broad background of town ambivalence.

Yet the controversies did take place, and they played a critical role
in the post-1810 history of Dudley and Oxford. For gradually, despite all the limitations, the friction grew more intense. And ultimately, exacerbated by Samuel Slater's personal ambitions and
intransigence, the rising curve of community–mill antagonism produced irreconcilable conflicts, heated confrontations, and finally the
incorporation of an entirely new township.

II

When it arose, trouble between mills and nonoperative residents
emerged out of specific incidents and reflected concrete concerns.
The basic pressures shaping these incidents and concerns, however,
become clear only within the overall context of town life. More
specifically, they become clear only after understanding that both
the organization of local government and the general organization –
in fact, the general meaning – of social hierarchy in the two townships resisted wholesale transformation during the first generation
after 1810. For as the story unfolded, a significant part of the reason
nonoperative residents found manufactories distressing was that
the nature of community governance and hierarchy in Dudley and
Oxford remained qualitatively different from the more innovative
order of local factories.

Local government, for example, continued as a relatively unintrusive
and decentralized institution. Certainly it was less intrusive and less
centralized than the administrative structure mill managers – both in
theory and to a large extent even in practice – exercised over hands
during working hours.

After 1810 as before, the limited scope of public authority in these
communities reflected the limited sense of solidarity town residents
felt toward one another. As already remarked, notions of common
good were still woven into the routines of local residents. After all,
many yeomen still shared labor; substantial numbers of residents still
cooperated in using streams and providing credit; and many separate
households were still linked by friendship and kinship. But pressures
curtailing mutuality among local inhabitants also persisted. In the
1820s and 1830s, just as in 1810, residents were divided by sectarian

allegiances, by geographical separation within the townships, and above all by transiency, which, if less pronounced than among full-time millworkers, had still reached significant levels by the second and third decades of the nineteenth century.[1] Taken together, the persisting effect of all these constraints on community coherence was to restrain the jurisdiction and structure of local government.

Thus the business undertaken in local town meetings broke no new ground. Roads, for example, continued to be launched only if those particularly benefiting by their construction consented to make extra contributions. So Dudley in 1821 "voted to accept" a road but only "on condition" that residents whose property bordered the new thoroughfare agreed to give the land and undertake all fencing at "no expense to the Town."[2]

Religion too remained a private concern. In 1823 Oxford momentarily reverted to eighteenth-century patterns and voted town funds "for preaching." And in 1822 Dudley's town meeting did help build the "basement story" it began using in the community's new Congregationalist meetinghouse.[3] But these were anomalies. What went on in local churches, most (if not quite all) responsibility for building any new churches, and even the nurturing of revivals was all left to the "societies" of each denomination. As with roads, so with churches, for it was still understood that the common good – and the common treasury – required residents whenever possible to avoid equating their private interests with the common good.

The same reluctance to expand governmental activities is reflected in the treatment of local paupers. Although the number of people receiving public support in Dudley and Oxford grew steadily after 1810 (reaching twenty to thirty-five individuals per year in each community by the early 1830s),[4] both townships resisted implementing more elaborate institutional responses to indigency. By 1821 in Oxford and by 1828 in Dudley, the practice of selling "the Poor at Auction" to "the lowest Bidder" had been refined to selling them "all at one lot" to a single "Superintendent of the Poor."[5] But this still left paupers in private hands. Reluctance to accept more direct public involvement led both townships time and again to reject the notion of collecting indigents into community-run work farms. Despite the widespread contemporary conviction (duly reported by an ad hoc committee in Oxford) that poor farms enjoyed "abundant success and in some instances has proved a source of revenue rather than an expense," Oxford did not adopt the reform until 1832. Dudley waited until 1839.[6]

Nor did the structure of local government reflect greater innovation. The bookkeeping of town officials was as primitive in the early 1830s as it had been in 1810; town offices were still filled gratis and hence part time; and the central administrative apparatus of these communities continued to share authority with semiautonomous and financially unequal highway and school districts. Once, in 1827, Dudley tried to centralize supervisory and fiscal control over its highway divisions.[7] And the same town made three separate efforts to equalize the financial resources of its school districts, the last time in 1822 when a group of residents suggested that "one half of all the money raised in Town for Schooling...be divided equally among the nine districts, without regard to numbers of Scholars or Taxes." But the Dudley town meeting voted down each attempt. Oxford, for its part, did not even try to resolve its governmental balkanization until 1832.[8]

The nature of hierarchy within the overall social order of these townships was not quite so impervious to change. Wealth, for example, became even more exclusively the measure of rank after 1810, and, equally significant, the distribution of wealth altered noticeably. Although mills continued to find investors from a broad range of social and economic backgrounds, the appearance of a few large and persistently successful factories in Dudley and Oxford produced a substantial bunching up of community resources. The latter town's more detailed records reveal that the share of community wealth controlled by the richest 10 percent increased nearly 25 percent during the twelve to fourteen years after 1815, edging up to 53.7 percent of the community's total assessed valuations.[9]

But in the end, continuities again seem to outweigh new developments. However concentrated it became, wealth in 1830 was linked only slightly more firmly than in 1810 to townwide emblems of high status and power. Indeed, after 1810 as before, it is not at all clear such emblems existed.

The affluent factory proprietors who took an active interest in their properties, the well-paid supervisors who worked with and for them, such men enjoyed substantial authority and eminence within their mill villages. But in the first generation of local manufactories, these men had no way to replicate throughout the two communities the economic power they exercised over their employees. The tax revenues such individuals provided the towns generated a certain broad influence, of course, and those who helped start the Oxford Bank in 1823 acquired some leverage over the direction of local economic development.[10] But in practice the bank disappointed factory owners as often as it deferred to them, and the pressure of taxation could be used on, as well as by, millowners.[11] And so with the common markers of community-wide prestige: Rich men – whether or not they were involved in mills – continued to regard good church pews and officer's rank in the local militia as their perquisites. But because they were purchased, such badges remained of dubious value.

Not surprisingly, rich men also found their way into high political office. Indeed, data from Oxford suggest that this township may have grown more inclined to pick its selectmen from a narrow clutch of wealthy residents during the post-1810 generation. By the end of the 1820s, the proportion of Oxford selectmen drawn from the top tax quartile had moved from around three-fifths to four-fifths, and the fraction selected from the top two quartiles had shifted from 87 to more than 90 percent.[12] At the same time, however, the average tenure of selectmen was diminishing, and the concrete significance of this office was at least as problematic in 1830 as it had been twenty years earlier.[13] Its power was still circumscribed by the decentralized character of town government, the persistent tradition of ad hoc committees, and the continuing – even increasing – tendency of residents to challenge their elected leaders in open meeting. And the status of the office remained limited as well. Although the proportion of selectmen subsequently or simultaneously holding lower posts declined after 1810, neither trend disappeared. Between 1820 and 1830, just under half the men tackling another office with their selectmanships, which was close to one-fifth of all selectmen, took on a less important job; and just under one-quarter of all selectmen filled a lower position later on. It was still better to be a selectman than a hogreeve in the early 1830s. But it was also still difficult to use either position as a precise barometer of social standing.[14]

Another indication that high political offices failed to express social standing accurately was the remarkable failure of certain men to fill these positions. Although it had become fairly common by the 1820s for local selectmen to have interests in business as well as farming, both Dudley and Oxford showed notable reluctance to choose anyone connected to manufactories. Aaron Tufts (and his son George) held important offices in Dudley after 1810; and one of Oxford's leading factory masters, Alexander DeWitt, was elected selectman three times and representative to the General Court twice during the late 1820s and early 1830s. But these were exceptions. Of the more than one hundred individuals known to have direct involvement – managerial or proprietary – in local factories, only eight became selectmen between 1820 and 1830. Among Slater's supervisors, moreover, the lack of political participation extended to virtually all town offices. Only three resident agents were chosen for *any* position: one (in Dudley) for the school committee, the other two (one in each town) for hogreeve. As for the Slater family itself, Samuel's son John served a term as hogreeve and another as school committeeman, both in Oxford. His brother George did achieve the office of selectman in Dudley in 1830, the only representative of the Slater villages to reach that office in either township during this period. But it was just for one term.[15]

The electoral unpopularity of millowners and managers is not difficult to explain. These men were likely often passed over because it was supposed that the nonlocal connections of their enterprises would draw their attention far beyond the boundaries of Dudley and Oxford. Samuel Slater, for one, was even insisting by the mid-1820s that his legal residence was North Providence, Rhode Island.[16] Then too, the slowly maturing friction between the two townships and their manufactories may have led residents to ignore their more industrially committed neighbors when springtime elections came around.

But whatever the cause, the result was that those responsible for establishing and administering the largest local business enterprises did not carry their importance over into town government. The men who played major roles in shaping the new economic landscape of Dudley and Oxford were only rarely the formal political leaders of the two communities.

This obviously does not mean that such individuals were unimportant in local civic life. After 1810, as before, an elite existed in Dudley and Oxford: Rich, respected, and familiar to any resident, it was a group whose views had to be at least acknowledged. Whether or not they were politically active, wealthy residents instrumental in establishing local factories were inescapably members of this elite. At the same time, however, it is evident that no group, no elite, had more than limited leverage over the two townships. As had been true before 1810, so it continued to be true: There was no way, on a community-wide basis, to consistently synchronize wealth, power, and prestige. What this meant after the mills appeared, of course, was that a significant difference existed between the nature of leadership in the towns taken as a whole and the kind of leadership mill masters and their deputies imposed – or at least tried to impose – over their factory villages. The contrast would prove pivotal as tensions rose between the two communities and the manufactories they contained.

III

Such was the context within which factories and nonoperative residents played out their skirmishes. But now: what were the specific incidents and concerns that produced these controversies? What were the precise issues that came between townspeople and their mills?

They varied. Some reflected themes persisting from the first days of manufactories in and around Pawtucket. Controversies over water, for example. Like Rhode Islanders in the 1790s, Dudley and Oxford residents became angry when factories started violating riparian customs. As was true elsewhere in New England, local manufactories built dams that made damage and disruption inevitable; and for all their rhetoric of aiding the rural economy, cotton and woolen factories were too obviously profit seeking to hide riparian trespasses behind claims of public service. Indeed, despite court rulings increasingly favorable to textile mills,[17] even other factory owners could feel aggrieved: Thus, proprietors of a small cotton factory in Dudley sued the South Village in the early 1820s for flooding their French River privilege. But other constituencies could also become aggravated. It was the majority view of all residents participating in Dudley's April 1824 town meeting, for example, that Aaron Tufts should spend his own money to repair a town road that was damaged when his dam broke.[18] And Mr. Corbin, who threatened "another action" in 1834 because the all too solid dam built by the Dudley Woolen Manufacturing Company did not "let the water down," had no apparent proprietary involvement with textile factories.[19]

Another issue dating from the early years of textile factories was the vexed question of taxation. No local factory applied to the state for an exemption from local levies. But in the same breath that he specified his legal home as Rhode Island, Samuel Slater also asserted that his nonresident status in Dudley and Oxford made certain local taxes inappropriate. Thus, in 1825 when Oxford sought to tax the Oxford Bank stock he held as personal property, he grew incensed, arguing that the assessors evidently viewed him as "an Inhabitant of Oxford" when in fact "I am considered an inhabitant of N. Providence and pay a tax on personal property there." So he sought relief: "If there is any hole in the law," he told son John, "that I can *run in* or *creep* into I wish to do it."[20] Nor did Dudley escape his anger. The reasons are less clear, but he was sufficiently irritated by taxes that this town imposed in 1829 and 1830 to flatly refuse all payments.[21]

The Oxford episode flared briefly into an ugly wrangle, with local assessors ordering "the collectors to attach [Slater's bank] property and...have the same sold at public Auction." But because the Slater family retained at least sufficient bank stock to engage in direct disputes with this institution several years later, it seems likely that Oxford's assessors and the "Arkwright of America" ultimately found a compromise.[22] The argument with Dudley, on the other hand, reached no solution. In late 1832 the town agreed to abate some levies "on machinery."[23] But by that time the situation had been radically transformed by the carving off of all three Slater villages into an entirely new township, and the indications are that Samuel Slater and sons never paid the contested taxes.

Community irritation over riparian usage and taxation was obviously heightened by the novelty of what textile factory masters were doing and saying. After all, proprietors of local gristmills were not flooding roads. And no one argued with local assessors as strenuously as did Samuel Slater. But the novelty was itself related to the political and social setting in which these disputes took place. Factory masters who built dams so extensive that they caused hardship whether they stood or collapsed were in effect violating the received understanding that local residents should avoid claiming special prerogatives for their private interests. The anger over factory dams, that is, arose in part because millowners seemed to be asserting that their riparian interests were paramount. Similarly, Slater's refusal to cooperate with local assessors went considerably beyond accepted disagreements with elected leaders. By protesting the Oxford levy, by defiantly refusing to pay the Dudley tax, he was asserting unprecedented unilateral authority. In effect, he was trying to exercise over the towns the kind of leadership that he enjoyed in his factory compounds.

The same pattern applied to another cluster of issues that began emerging. At first glance, these further disagreements appear centered on subjects curiously distant from town–factory disputes: the management of the Oxford Bank, the organization of certain school districts, the construction of certain roads. Indeed, the growing concern over such topics – the tendency as time went on for schools, roads, and the bank to generate even deeper alarm than taxes and river privileges – implies a curious evolution. It was as though the two townships were progressing toward increasingly subtle, even abstract frictions. But the arcane disagreements cutting across post-1810 Dudley and Oxford with increasing frequency were in fact highly explosive. They were inflamed, first by the various free-floating concerns residents of communities like Dudley and Oxford came to feel about manufactories as time moved on. The threat to customary agricultural life, which Yankee yeomen seem to have perceived in textile mills by the early nineteenth century, and, more directly, the conviction shared by many New Englanders by at least the 1820s that cotton and woolen factories connoted "tyranny" – such broad concerns fed into debates on school districts, roads, and the bank. Yet part of the reason this infusion occurred, and thus a second reason these debates grew so heated, was again the overall political and social configuration of Dudley and Oxford. Because in jousting with townspeople over school districts, roads, and the bank, mill masters seemed to be challenging prevailing notions of local governance and leadership.

The resulting divisions were not always clear-cut. Residents with no direct connection to manufactories sometimes sided with these establishments. And when it was not their own personal policies that were being challenged, individual factory masters often sympathized with antifactory postures of their fellow townsmen. On balance, however, it was the pervasive communal sense of violated norms that explains why school districts, roads, and the Oxford Bank led to differences between the two townships and their factories.

IV

Consider first the Oxford Bank. The facility was incorporated in 1823 to provide "public utility and convenience to the inhabitants" of Oxford and surrounding communities. Residents from seven townships petitioned for the bank, and a slate of forty-two individuals (probably identical to the list of petitioners) bought stock in the new venture. In Oxford, the enterprise drew considerable support from merchants like Andrew Sigourney, as well as from both Abijah and Jonathan Davis. But those involved in textile factories were no less enthusiastic. A man like Aaron Tufts, for example, invested more than $1,000 in the project because he knew such an institution would tremendously ease the logistical burden of providing cash payments to his employees. The bank's most important enthusiast, however, was Samuel Slater. Together with his wife, his son John, and his deputy Andrew W. Porter, Slater immediately bought a plurality of stock in the bank, and he made broad use of its services. In 1827 alone he funneled more than $25,000 through his local account.[24]

The problem, from the perspective of at least some millowners, was that the bank was too independent. Factory proprietors might own stock, and Tufts and Andrew Porter did hold two of the bank's nine directorships. But no Slater reached the governing board, and millowners as a group soon learned that the bank would not always do their bidding.[25] Thus, in the early 1830s, managers of the Dudley Woolen Manufacturing Company were turned down cold for a loan: "The Board thought it would not be safe at this time to [increase] our loans beyond our present engagements."[26] And thus Samuel Slater found himself increasingly disturbed over "engagements" the bank did make. The "scarcity" of money in the spring of 1828, for example, led him to hope that the Oxford Bank "will not be over liberal in her loans"; and later that same year he announced that "if that Company wishes to retain my name in the firm they must see that payments are punctually met at maturity."[27]

From the perspective of those who did control the bank, however, and very likely from the perspective of other townspeople watching from the sidelines, the disaffected millowners and managers were being unreasonable. Once again, certain men connected to factories were acting as though their priorities and judgments, however unwise for others, should be accepted unquestioningly.

So the two sides continued to spar – until finally Samuel Slater acted. After first delegating son John to support an 1830 petition asking the General Court for a twenty-year extension of the bank's charter, Slater reversed field and early the following year headed up a petition of fifteen long-term and recent stockholders (including sons John, George, and Nelson), arguing against "the renewal of said Charter."[28] Some local mill masters – Tufts and the DeWitt brothers, for example – did not join Slater's remonstrance. And the ploy in any case failed to convince the Massachusetts legislature.[29] But the spectacle of Oxford's leading industrialist orchestrating an effort to sabotage a valued local institution could scarcely have created favorable impressions among town residents.

The controversy surrounding school districts was more extended, but the core disagreement was evident from the outset. On one side, several factory villages wished to "draw off" from the school district in which they were situated to form independent districts and "school their children at their Factor[ies.]"[30] On the other side, the townships were reluctant to let this happen.

Those requesting separate factory schools had purely practical motives. Given the notably relaxed attitude local mills took toward education, management's goal in having their own districts was less to promulgate instruction than to ease financial and logistical burdens. Since town school taxes were assessed on both "numbers and property,"[31] it was likely that taxes on the improved real estate of a factory compound would run higher than the outlay a mill village would have to make to provide its own facilities for the small number of children (judging from the East Village) desiring schooling. Then too, maintaining their own school districts would permit factories to exchange the often haphazard schedule followed by local authorities for a fixed academic calendar, which in turn would permit managers to know in advance when youngsters bent on becoming "scholars" would have to be replaced.

The objections raised by Dudley and Oxford were in part also practical. If factories hoped to save money by running their own schools, town school districts from which mills wished to withdraw were deeply concerned about losing sizable portions of their tax revenues.

But looking ahead to positions revealed in a subsequent struggle with Slater, there is reason to believe that the towns also had other concerns. Specifically, it is likely they were worried about the new phenomenon that factory villages with educational responsibilities would represent in these communities. Permitting mill compounds to become self-contained educational districts would create zones in which civil administration would be harnessed to the authority of factory management, and factory management would acquire the added legitimacy of serving as an arm of civil administration. Such a hybrid was worrisome. By melding private business and public governance – "corporate rights" and "municipal authority," as Dudley inhabitants would later put it – factory villages would achieve power far more dense than that characteristic of decentralized town administrative structures.[32] By taking on a function hitherto reserved to the towns, the mills – despite all their claims to be aiding the rural economy, despite all their assertions of "kindly" paternalism – were again threatening to loom larger than most Dudley and Oxford residents felt appropriate for private interests.

Thus the townships resisted – and again Samuel Slater emerged as a principal antagonist. As early as April 1815, Slater's young supervisor Bela Tiffany had asked the Dudley town meeting for permission to "draw off" school taxes raised on the small portion of East Village property in that township. Because the village lay mainly in Oxford's South Gore, Dudley chose not to object.[33] But this got Slater nowhere, for Oxford's town meeting was simultaneously refusing to let him "draw his school money for those under his care."

The East Village remained firmly grafted to Oxford township's School District No. 2.[34]

Eight years later Slater tried again. In the March meeting of 1823 Oxford was asked to decide whether "the Town will set off Samuel Slater and others...into a School District by themselves." This time the community chose an ad hoc committee to study the question and report back at the next meeting. The membership of this committee is not known. Evidently, however, it included figures sympathetic to Slater's position, for the recommendation that emerged was to let the East Village have its school district. This proposal, however, was quickly rebuffed by a majority of the April town meeting: "Voted not to accept the report of the committee chosen at March meeting last past on the petition of Samuel Slater." And the town voted the same way when Slater tried once more a month later. This time acting without advice from any advisory committee, Oxford's assembled residents decided "not to accept...Samuel Slater's petition in setting him off into a school district by himself."[35]

Frustrated by the dogged resistance he was meeting from Oxford, Slater turned to Dudley. In 1824, just after he had purchased the so-called Village Factory (and set out to transform it into the North Village), he petitioned Dudley for the right to organize a separate school district for this manufactory. Dudley, whose opposition to Slater on this issue was generally less confrontational, acceded to the request but then added that the new school district would be kept closely "under the inspection of the Town's examining School committee."[36] In itself this was not unusual: Every school district nominally operated under the community's central school committee. But it was uncommon to call attention to the fact, and in doing so Dudley may have been attempting to check the augmented authority Slater and his deputies were about to acquire.

At best, however, Dudley's strategy only partially salvaged the town's prerogatives. A more successful tactic surfaced the following year when the community placed the South Village at the center of a sparsely populated new educational district. By permitting this compound to thoroughly dominate a town district, the tactic effectively undercut any potential request from Slater to implement a separate school for this manufactory and still avoided a formal conflation of civil and corporate authority. The compromise evidently worked, for the South Village never petitioned for an independent school district.

The issue of education emerged a final time in March 1829 when

Oxford received yet another petition from "Samuel Slater and others in South Oxford Village [i.e., the East Village] to draw their school money to be expended in supporting a school in Said Village." Once again convening an ad hoc committee, the town selected Richard Olney, Stearns DeWitt, and Learned Davis. As those who elected them must have known, all these men were at that very moment involved in the recently established Oxford Woolen Company. Given its membership, it is scarcely surprising that the committee approved Slater's request. Nor is it surprising that immediately after submitting its report this committee suggested that the Oxford Woolen Company receive similar permission.[37]

This time the town meeting gave in: In April 1829 both the East Village and the Oxford Woolen Company were permitted to organize their own school districts. And with this precedent established, other local manufactories soon pressed their cases. In November 1831 both the Perry Mill in Dudley and another mill in Oxford received permission to "draw their school money and expend the same" within their compounds.[38] The resolution of the issue, however, did not expunge the hostility it had caused.

As it turned out, Oxford accepted the East Village school district just as the final issue between the towns and their mills came to a boil: roads.

Textile factories needed roads. To succeed, a manufactory required year-round access to markets and supplies, which meant year-round access to transportation routes. Slater, for one, took an active hand in promoting improved roadways throughout southern New England (and by his death was even lending support to the Norwich and Worcester Railroad).[39] Once again, however, difficulties arose because local mills tried to get what they wanted in ways that struck townspeople as inappropriate.

At first there were no problems. If a manufactory wanted a particular road constructed, it submitted the route to the town meeting and agreed to make special contributions toward its construction and upkeep. Thus Oxford in 1814 "voted to accept...a road from the factory near Lieut. Joseph Stores...free of all expense to the Town." And in 1812 Dudley agreed to put a road by the Merino Mill with the understanding that "the M[erino] Factory Company are to give the land and fence the Same."[40] This pattern did not disappear, but factory proprietors and managers slowly began advancing the idea that the cost of roads helpful to their enterprises should nonetheless be borne by the entire community. In 1816, for example,

Slater was able to persuade Dudley to alter a road leading to the East Village ("and near there") at town expense. And by 1819 Oxford agreed to carry the full cost of a "Road from Mr. Joseph Eliot's Factory."[41]

Yet some mill masters were not satisfied. After all, so long as town meetings retained final authority over new roads, voting residents of Dudley and Oxford were potentially still capable – and occasionally still willing – to insist that textile mills, like other private ventures, make extra payments for the improvements they wanted. The prospect was unsettling to those closely involved in local manufactories, and several of these men launched efforts to place control of certain new roads entirely beyond community authority.

Once more Samuel Slater had a pivotal role. In 1824 he supervised the creation of the Central Turnpike Corporation and supported plans by that organization to build a "turnpike road" through Oxford and Dudley "to the Connecticut line." Turnpikes in antebellum Massachusetts were not, of course, the exclusive project of mill proprietors. These toll highways were generally regarded as attractive investments, and the local turnpike counted several yeomen and merchants (including Oxford's Jonathan Davis) among its thirty-nine stockholders. It should also be noted that even investors involved in manufactories were not necessarily committed to aiding only their own enterprises. Although his invocation of the common good was somewhat more broad and formal than was usually heard from local residents, Slater was undoubtedly sincere when he suggested that the new thoroughfare would "be of great Public convenience not only to [inhabitants] of Massachusetts but [also] to those of Connecticut."[42]

At the same time, however, there was scarcely any mystery about who would benefit most from a road that, from its inception, was intended to pass directly by "Samuel Slater's [East] Factory Village in Oxford and Dudley." And it was at least an even bet that whatever money investors – including the largest investor, Samuel Slater[43] – put into the venture would soon be returned in tolls paid by all those – including all those residents of Dudley and Oxford – who used the new highway.

Oxford's citizens did not object to the situation, perhaps because the turnpike lay largely in Dudley. But Dudley residents grew increasingly angry. They must have known that early nineteenth century turnpikes generally permitted free passage to citizens of townships traversed by these highways.[44] And they must have realized that the Central Turnpike Corporation's failure to grant this courtesy meant that the whole community was gradually paying for a road that so heavily benefited Samuel Slater. By the fall of 1828 Dudley's town meeting finally acted:

> Voted that a Committee of three be chosen to confer with a Committee which may be chosen by the Central Turnpike Corporation in regard to the conditions upon which the inhabitants of the town of Dudley may travel upon the Turnpike road from the house of Captain William Larned to the Village of Samuel Slater Esq. in Oxford provided that the Town shall discontinue the whole, or part of the Town road leading from said Larned's to the said Slater's Village.

The town, in other words, agreed to give the corporation a full monopoly on roads across southeastern Dudley in return for favored treatment on tolls. The corporation evidently accepted the compromise, and for a while the controversy subsided. But it was another decade before the issue was definitively put to rest, and there is scarcely any doubt that Dudley was deeply dissatisfied with Samuel Slater's turnpike.[45]

Oxford was even more dissatisfied in 1828 when Slater petitioned Worcester County to change "the Sutton road" running through Oxford to the East Village.[46] In effect, Slater "and others" (not identified) were asking for a county road; and county roads – because they had to be supported equally by the whole community – had always met firm opposition. A little more than a decade before Slater's petition, Oxford had spent months in a furious rearguard action against a county-ordered highway before finally bowing to the Court of Sessions.[47]

But Slater's county road was even more objectionable than most, for here was a project, which the whole town would have to shoulder, that demonstrably helped but a single man. Here was another direct attack on the belief that no single private interest within the community should claim equivalence with the common good. Here was another direct challenge to the restrained leadership characteristic of both Dudley and Oxford. Here, in brief, was the dark side of paternalism, a clear example of a mill master trying to "step out into the community" to control his neighbors the same way he tried to control his employees. Slater's county road gave pungent immediacy to the query the *Pawtucket Chronicle* would pose a year later: When mills intrude into town affairs, "What is this but tyranny?"[48]

So Oxford protested. Instead of simply voting a resolution rejecting the projected highway – the normal response to county roads – the town meeting passed a strong remonstrance and selected three men (none of them involved in any manufactory) to deliver it personally to the county commissioners:

> Voted [reads the remonstrance] that the principal alterations in the Road prayed for by Samuel Slater and Others are deemed by the inhabitants of the town of Oxford as unnecessary and inexpedient and should any inconsiderable alterations be deemed of public convenience and necessity by the Honorable County Commissioners, that such alteration be made with reference to the Interests and wishes of said inhabitants as of said petitioners.[49]

The remonstrance had little effect. The county insisted, and Oxford bent its collective energies to amending the Sutton Road the way Slater wanted. By 1830 the highway was finished and the controversy was moot.[50] But once again local residents had vented sharp dissatisfaction with the "Arkwright of America."

V

Toward the end of 1830 there was a brief lull in the friction between the two towns and their factories. Slater's tax dispute with Dudley remained outstanding, but there were no arguments over water rights going on, and disagreements over roads, schools, and the bank had, for the moment, all subsided. Yet tensions and antipathies spawned by these controversies remained, and it was not long before hostilities recommenced, kindled into the most tumultuous confrontation of all by a final potent factor in the local environment: Samuel Slater's temperament.

It is important to keep Slater's impact in perspective. Town–factory conflicts ultimately derived from deep incompatibilities between the priorities of mill villages on the one hand, and the conventions and values of the communities surrounding mills, on the other. Such incompatibilities could arise quite aside from Samuel Slater: in Woonsocket in 1808, for example, and in Seekonk in the 1820s.[51] What happened in Dudley and Oxford was actually part of an extensive trajectory of comparable episodes scattered across New England. And even in these two communities, tangles between nonoperative residents and local factories did not always or exclusively involve the North, South, and East villages. Still, within these two townships, Slater obviously cast a long shadow. He was the millowner who pressed the hardest against community norms, and the one who drew the sharpest protests. And ultimately it was his decision, reflecting the tilt of his personality, to precipitate the climactic collision with Dudley and Oxford.

There was, in the first place, Slater's need to feel independent. His whole biography reveals a drive to exercise as much control as possible over his own affairs. He had left England to escape the hindrance of an "overcrowded" industry; and he had ventured into southern Massachusetts to enjoy fuller, more direct authority over at least some of his holdings. Given the obviously high premium he placed on autonomy, it is hardly surprising that Slater was frustrated by the obstacles Dudley and Oxford continually placed in his path. It did not matter that the towns only partially deflected his plans; that they interfered at all was a nuisance Slater was unwilling to tolerate. Indeed, by the mid and late 1820s, his impatience had expanded into a generalized irritation with community decisions even on issues bearing only tangentially on his factories. Thus, although he supported Andrew Jackson at least until 1832, Slater was vexed in 1828 when a majority of Oxford voters opposed a National Republican candidate for governor whom he admired. The town's refusal to support a poor farm also struck him as foolish; and once, in 1826, blithely overlooking the problematic voting rights of all South Gore residents, he even considered swaying a community vote on this issue by stacking a town meeting "with more or less of the hands" from the East Village.[52] He evidently never followed through on this last plan. The mere fact that he entertained the notion, however, indicates the level of his impatience and his contempt for the dignity of New England town meetings.

But Slater's irritation with Dudley and Oxford also reflected a shift in his attitude toward the North, South, and East villages. Never a man of wide intellectual curiosity, always a figure whose "devotion to business prevented much attention to literature or politics,"[53] Slater appears to have become *more* absorbed in his mills and more worried about their continued prosperity as competitive pressures mounted during the 1820s. Much of his anxiety, of course, found expression in the stiffening regimen of his three local compounds. But there are also hints that Slater grew personally more preoccupied – indeed, obsessed – with business problems. By the late 1820s, even news that his son John's infant daughter had died could not entirely distract Slater's thoughts. His letter of condolence did acknowledge dreaming of the child: "I dreamt that her Nurse presented her to me and that she was a little perfect beauty." But then, after the briefest nod to his daughter-in-law, he rushed back to the central theme of virtually all his letters in these years: "Do let me hear how you all do, and how business is getting along in each and every department (frequently)."[54]

The concern Slater felt about his mills, and the attendant intolerance he felt for community opposition, rose significantly after 1829. The long-building and embarrassing confrontation with Edward Howard came in that year. But more significantly, so did the most serious wave of failures to pummel the southern New England textile industry since 1819. Slater's North, South, and East villages were not directly threatened. But several factories whose notes he had endorsed did go under, and the indebtedness Slater thus incurred approached $300,000.[55]

He managed to raise the funds. Indeed, Slater used the occasion to affect a consolidation of his personal holdings that ultimately proved quite profitable. He sold his interests in the Old Mill, the Amoskeag Mill (in New Hampshire), and the mills he had co-owned (with his brother) in Jewett City and (with Almy and Brown) in Smithfield. He simultaneously took full control of the Providence Steam Cotton Company, as well as factories at Central Falls, Rhode Island, and Fitchburg and Wilkinsonville, Massachusetts.[56] But all this scrambling about cost Slater a good deal of time and worry, and the final consequence of the Panic of 1829 was to underscore in his mind the cost of vulnerability. During the remaining six years of his life he was frequently riven with fear for his mills' survival.[57] And within two years he was implementing plans to protect himself definitively from all the burdensome interference of Dudley and Oxford residents.

VI

He made his move on June 3, 1831. On that day the General Court received a petition "praying for the incorporation" of a new township "to be formed of Oxford South Gore and a part of the towns of Oxford and Dudley."[58] The new community was to be called Webster, a tribute to the staunch defender of New England's textile industry then representing Massachusetts in the United States Senate.

Because the petition purported to come from local inhabitants, Samuel Slater – who had so recently and loudly claimed residency in North Providence – did not sign it. But there could be little doubt who was behind the document. The names of Slater's sons George and John (then living in the North and East villages, respectively) figured among the signatures; and of the 172 other names, most – perhaps 85 percent – belonged to people working in Slater factories.[59] Nor was there much mystery over the basic reason for the petition. Along with a cotton mill owned by one Zera Preston and a few unrelated stores and workshops, the boundaries proposed for the new community neatly encircled the North, South, and East villages. Tired of wrestling with Dudley and Oxford, Slater had decided to create a new town for his mills.[60]

The rationale put forward by the petition was shrewd. There was no mention of past disagreement with local residents, not a word about troublesome votes in town meetings. Instead, Webster was justified because its inhabitants were "remot," precisely the argument New Englanders had always used in seeking the incorporation of a new township. "Most of said population is distant from [the center of] Dudley from three to four miles – from Oxford from four to five miles," read the petition, "[and] it is burdensome and inconvenient to travel so great a distance to attend town meetings and for other town purposes." Noting also that "nearly one half" of the projected township (i.e., the territory lying within the South Gore) "has hitherto been denied" full town citizenship, the petition concluded that "it would greatly promote the prosperity and happiness and convenience of said population to be admitted to separate municipal privileges."[61] Most of this, of course, was thoroughly disingenuous. Except for his brief thought of trooping hands into Oxford's town meeting in 1826, Slater had demonstrated little concern over his employees' ability to leave the factory villages "to attend town meetings" or "for other town purposes." But he realized that Webster's incorporation would appear more logical if it was presented in terms the Commonwealth had often previously sanctioned: the isolation of "the premises petitioned for."

To some, however, Webster never seemed logical. Town meetings in Dudley and Oxford had always resisted requests by inhabitants to be "set off" into other townships. And the same response greeted Slater's petition: In the fall of 1831 a majority of town voters in both communities agreed to dispatch strong remonstrances to Boston opposing the incorporation of Webster. The exact number and identity of people joining these anti-Webster majorities have unfortunately not survived. But several characteristics of Slater's opponents stand out plainly enough.

In the first place, they were generally confined to areas outside Webster's projected boundaries.[62] This, of course, was largely because many of those "within the territory petitioned for" worked for Samuel Slater. Just as a large proportion of signatures on his petition turned out to belong to operatives in the North, South, and East villages, so most – at least two-thirds – of the 1,068 people slated to inhabit the new township "were either [directly] employed by Messrs.

Slater" or lived with those who were.[63] And such employees, although they willingly sparred with management during working hours, evidently did not share the towns' particular sense of jeopardy when "Messrs. Slater" launched efforts to establish a new community. The few nonoperatives living within this territory were similarly disinclined to resist, probably because they hoped for lighter tax loads. Undoubtedly aware that the prospective township had the double advantage of containing few paupers and embracing several good roads,[64] potential nonfactory residents of Webster probably assumed that public expenses, and hence personal tax assessments, would be lower in Webster.

In sections of Dudley and Oxford not sought by Slater, however, resistance was, if not unanimous, at least widespread. Certainly there was no occupational division over the question, no sense of class demarcations. The few details that can be teased from documents indicate that both farmers and merchants took a stand against Webster, as did proprietors and managers of several mill villages. Thus, Oxford appointed both the merchant Jonathan Day and one of the Oxford Woolen Company's principal investors, Alexander DeWitt, to carry its remonstrance to Boston. Dudley elected Aaron Tufts as moderator of the meeting in which that town adopted its remonstrance, and then chose their moderator's son, George, to argue their case personally before the General Court.[65]

Not surprisingly, the arguments produced by this wide-ranging opposition included a fair measure of economic self-interest. Rejecting Slater's claim of isolation as total fantasy ("the petitioners [face] far less [inconvenience] than falls to the lot of a large portion of inhabitants of other towns"), both Dudley and Oxford stressed the losses they would suffer through Webster's incorporation. Oxford worried about losing "about one-sixth part of its taxable property" along with control over a "considerable portion of the water power" upon which many of its manufacturing establishments – both Slater and non-Slater – depended. Dudley was similarly disturbed, indicating that Webster would encompass "more than one-third of the population and more than one-quarter of the ratable property of the whole town [i.e., Dudley before the division]."[66]

But both communities also pressed on to more abstract questions. It is not possible to know precisely how intensely local residents felt about these broader, less obviously self-serving objections to Webster. It is surely significant, however, that the arguments these people produced reflected the same concern local inhabitants had expressed as citizens of New England townships during earlier community–

factory controversies: That a millowner was demanding too much; that he was asserting himself so forcefully and extensively as to threaten accepted patterns of governance and leadership. Indeed, transposed into a factory master's campaign for an entirely new township, such entrepreneurial ambition seemed so dangerous that an entrepreneur such as Alexander DeWitt could promote factory schools but still oppose Slater's petition. In sum: Despite past fights, the towns (as shown by their wish to keep Slater's villages) were, in 1832 as always, resisting not mills as such, but their effect on local life.

Thus DeWitt (for one) could agree that the new township would not permit the balancing of constituencies customary in Yankee communities. Distorting the statistics somewhat in its excitement, Oxford's town meeting pointed out that "in a large town various interests balance each other. But in the proposed town, there will be one interest – three-fourths of the property and one-half of the population will be under one interest."[67] Dudley's residents pursued the same theme, using what were probably more accurate figures to drive the argument home:

> Nearly two thirds of the real and personal estate, within the limits of the town prayed for by your petitioners, are in the possession and under the control of one individual; and two thirds of the population are in the service and employment, and in a great measure dependent on him.

Because of its peculiar economic structure, Dudley's remonstrance continued, Webster would witness a peculiar centralization of government and a peculiar conflation of authority. Like a factory-run school district, the new town would be unprecedentedly dense, immune to the balancing, "watchful influence of a large agricultural community." In fact, Webster would emerge, inevitably, as an extreme example of a millowner trying to "step out into the community":

> To incorporate the town prayed for under circumstances like these, your remonstrants believe, would be impolitick, and contrary to the spirit of our free institutions and republican principles. It would be investing an individual, not merely with corporate rights, but with municipal authority – a power too great, your remonstrants apprehend, to be wielded by one man under a free government.[68]

Finally, the character of Slater's employees, the people who would constitute the majority of Webster's population, had to be considered. The evaluation local townspeople offered was not flattering. Ignoring, or perhaps simply unaware of, the complex fencing that went on between workers and managers inside the North, South, and East villages, Dudley and Oxford town meetings seemed to view Slater's employees as essentially passive. And more: Remarkably rootless even for New Englanders, virtually always lacking landed property, factory workers appeared to nonoperative townspeople in 1832 as distressingly unstable. Said Dudley:

> Of the whole population now residing within the limits of the town prayed for, a vast proportion are transient and floating, men laborers from month to month, or year to year. Of the 115 of your petitioners within the limits of Dudley no more than 17 are freeholders.[69]

The failure of local residents to be more sympathetic toward Slater's employees had several important ramifications. In the first place, it could only have contributed to the belief among these workers that they were different, and hence it could only have clarified and strengthened their emergent sense of class. In the second place, it sharpened the distinction between town and operative antagonisms toward the mills. In an important sense, community residents and millworkers were both concerned fundamentally about the novel power factory masters were claiming and the novel pressures they were exerting. But just as operatives did not view the incorporation of Webster as a significant new threat, so townspeople did not regard North, South, and East village employees as potential allies in a broad struggle to limit Slater's ambitions. Quite the contrary: The most immediate consequence of the towns' posture toward the operatives was to deepen their anxiety about Slater's potential domination of Webster. For it hardly seemed likely that the landless, aimlessly restless workers whom townspeople perceived wandering through the factory villages would be able to withstand the overwhelming "one interest" in the new township.

But all the protests and concerns came to nothing. By January 1832 the Committee on Towns of the Massachusetts General Court had bowed to Slater's petition (and very probably his influence in the legislature) and granted permission to the "petitioners" to incorporate Webster.

Yet there had been one hesitation. The complaints raised by Dudley and Oxford about the economic losses they faced were dismissed out of hand. But the further issue underscored by the remonstrances – the potential control of Webster by "one individual or . . . one family" – this, committee members conceded, required "serious consideration." In the end, they eased their minds by evoking the democratic mechanisms of New England town government. The logic and language of their position are murky. But what the legislators appear to suggest is that the capacity of Webster's residents – presumably including factory operatives – to elect their community leaders would "operate as a salutary check to any power which [the Slater family's] present situation might give rise to in the hands of a few." Ignoring the constraints that long hours and rapid turnover would almost certainly place on the participation of factory workers in Webster's town meetings, ignoring the peculiar blend of public and private authority that Dudley had warned would fall into Slater's hands – ignoring all this, the committee declared its faith that "the subordinate employments of a part of the population in [the Slater] business transactions" would be offset by a "permanent equality in municipal concerns."[70]

VII

In this way, for these reasons, and propelled by this slender hope of democracy, Webster was created. The first town meeting of the new community in March 1832 signaled a major triumph for Samuel Slater. At one stroke he had freed himself from the obstructionism of Dudley and Oxford and opened up a whole new instrument through which to promote his interests. But just how directly he would be able to govern the new town, and how free it would remain from internal rifts – none of this was clear in 1832. It would be several years before the nature of Webster became apparent and before it could be determined just how far Slater's community actually diverged from the practices and institutions of Dudley and Oxford.

PART III

The second generation

Then [in the 1820s] our people engaged in manufactures. The streams were dammed, and the mighty powers of nature were set to spinning and weaving.... Those of you who have arrived at my age, and are therefore acquainted with the condition of things throughout our country towns thirty years ago, know that the change is almost magical.

Horace Mann, "Speech, Delivered at Dedham, November 6, 1850"

Consider the girls in a factory, – never alone, hardly in their dreams.

Henry David Thoreau, *Walden*

7   *Society and economy in three towns*

The issue "of the hour," announced a post–Civil War observer of the New England countryside, is "not how many bushels of corn or potatoes to the acre, but how many yards of cloth to the loom." Quickly piling on details and adjectives, the commentator developed the point that in the 1870s rural Yankees were intrigued not by the "value of the smiling meadow and the fertile field" but by "swift running" streams capable of powering factories and "the barren ledge" on which such factories might be located.[1]

Much the same sensibility could have been found in southern Worcester County during the 1840s and 1850s. For economic change in the New England countryside grew substantially more rapid and pervasive in the late antebellum period, and hinterland townships like Dudley, Oxford, and Webster found themselves drifting increasingly far and fast from the social order that had characterized rural communities when the nineteenth century opened.

It was also true, however, that in Dudley, Oxford, and Webster – as elsewhere in the rural Northeast – old ways had not vanished. Quite the opposite: Although less sharp and disruptive than in previous years, and although varying considerably between the new town of Webster and the two older communities of Dudley and Oxford, the gaps – and tensions – between innovation and custom continued to shape the way local residents responded to conditions around them. To one degree or another, it remained the case that economic growth was not of a piece and that it touched different areas of life and work at different rates and with different intensities.

But it is best to tackle the late antebellum ramifications of local industrialization in logical sequence. Chapters 8 and 9 will explore the reaction of Dudley, Oxford, and Webster inhabitants to their second generation of industrialization. The present chapter prepares the way for that discussion by considering the nature – and limits – of those social and economic changes that determined what local industrialization meant in the years leading up to the Civil War.

183

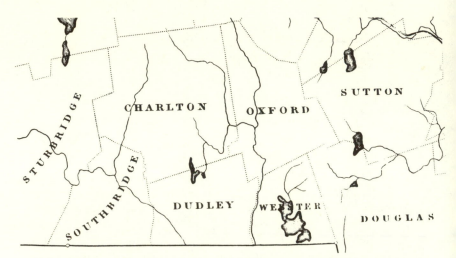

Map 7.1. Detail of south-central Massachusetts, ca. 1842, showing the new township of Webster. ("A Map Showing the Congressional Districts of Massachusetts as Established by the Act of September 16, 1842[184?]"; courtesy of the Map Collection, Harvard College Library.)

II

Consider, first, an area of the local social order in which change was both clear-cut and significant: the populations of Dudley, Oxford, and Webster.

Certainly there is no question that the number of residents in the territory controlled by these three townships increased sharply during the second generation after 1810 (see Appendix: A note on transiency). In the immediate aftermath of Webster's incorporation, Dudley and Oxford naturally suffered demographic declines, as some 1,100 of their inhabitants were precipitously "set off" to the "new town prayed for." Between 1840 and 1860, however, Dudley's population grew by more than a quarter (28.4 percent), reaching 1,736 in 1860. During that same period, Oxford's population jumped to 3,034, an increase of nearly three-quarters (74.2 percent) since 1840 and a population 1,000 larger than the town had registered before Webster's creation. But it was Webster itself that expanded most quickly: The new town's population more than doubled – surging from 1,403 to 2,912 – in the two decades ending in 1860. The net consequence was that the total number of residents in this part of southern Worcester County increased by more than four-fifths – from 4,189 to 7,682 – between 1830 and 1860. None of the three communities reached the

Table 7.1. *Age distribution of antebellum Dudley, Oxford, and Webster populations, in percentages*

Year	Proportion of aggregate populations		
	Under 16	16–45	Over 45
1810[a]	43.5	39.3	17.2
1820[a]	43.3	42.0	14.7
1850	35.2	48.5	16.3
1860	34.7	46.9	18.4

[a]Dudley and Oxford only.
Source: MFCD, MFCO, 1810, 1820, 1850, 1860; MFCW, 1850, 1860.

12,000 inhabitants needed to meet the Commonwealth's formal standard for municipal status. But by the time the Civil War began, Dudley, Oxford, and Webster were clearly all townships that had experienced substantial population growth.[2]

As significant as their growth, however, was the shifting structure of local populations. Average age, for example, continued spiraling upward. Whereas the ratio of males and females remained largely unaltered,[3] the proportion of older residents of both sexes expanded. Indeed, as Table 7.1 indicates, it is now possible to see the full dimensions of a shift that began well back in the nineteenth century. Between 1810 and 1860, the proportion of local inhabitants under 16 fell from 43.5 percent to just over one-third, with the remaining inhabitants first bunching into the 16-to-45 age bracket and then gradually also spilling into later years.

Age structure was in turn conditioned by another structural shift: the arrival of foreign immigrants. Although precise local data on ethnicity are unavailable before 1850, there can be little doubt that until the 1850s all but a handful of Dudley and Oxford residents (most of them skilled textile employees) were both native-born themselves and the offspring of native-born parents. By the late antebellum era, however, the picture had changed dramatically. The proportion of Dudley, Oxford, and Webster residents who were either first- or second-generation foreign immigrants had reached 22.6 percent by midcentury and 36.5 percent by 1860. And because inhabitants of foreign descent tended to be relatively young, this new ethnic configuration colored the distribution of age among local residents. Overall, the people of these towns were growing older; but overall too, the older a resident was, the more likely he or she would be of native, rather than foreign, background.[4]

A full inventory of the foreign backgrounds playing across these communities involves a lengthy list. Occasional Poles, Italians, Scots, and Swiss were living in these towns during the 1850s, as were larger numbers of Germans and Englishmen. As Table 7.2 makes evident, however, most residents of foreign birth or extraction claimed either Irish or Canadian backgrounds.

The Irish passage to America is by now a familiar story. Forced into exile by the accumulating erosion of their agricultural economy and ultimately, between 1845 and 1850, by the potato famine, thousands of impoverished Catholic Irish peasants entered northeastern coastal cities during the fifth and sixth decades of the nineteenth century. By the 1850s some of them had begun penetrating the hinterland, traversing the countryside with gangs building canals and railroads or securing jobs, usually as semiskilled or unskilled workers, in expanding communities like Dudley, Oxford, and Webster. For their part, Canadians were occasionally escaping from the political upheavals that shook America's northern neighbor during the late 1830s. More typically, they were propertyless refugees from the declining husbandry of French-speaking Quebec, individuals and young families – again Catholic and poor – pressured from their communities by the familiar conundrum of a growing population pressing against limited land supplies. Preferring the United States to the frequently expensive and utterly isolated homesteads of Canada's own interior, French Canadians drifted down through Maine, Vermont, and Massachusetts – for a season or a year or longer – again ending up most often in unskilled or semiskilled jobs.[5]

As a group, Irish and Canadian newcomers thus added to the ranks of lower-income residents. And hence one of their most immediate effects on local society was to widen the gap between rich and poor. Although the records are not entirely comparable for the three townships, the richest 10 percent living in Dudley and Oxford by 1860 appear to have controlled proportions of community wealth (46.8 and 55.6 percent, respectively) unprecedented in the nineteenth century. And in Webster, the same upper stratum possessed 63.2 percent of that town's resources by the time the Civil War started.[6]

But the arrival of immigrants from foreign lands coincided – and ultimately intersected – with yet another structural change in local populations: an altered distribution through major occupational categories.

Table 7.2. Ethnic composition of Dudley, Oxford, and Webster populations, 1850 and 1860, in percentages

	1850				1860			
	Dudley[a]	Oxford	Webster	Aggregate	Dudley[b]	Oxford[c]	Webster	Aggregate
American[d]	78.7	83.5	70.1	77.4	62.2	73.3	54.7	63.5
Irish	11.7	10.3	9.7	10.6	22.8	15.3	18.7	18.5
Canadian	2.7	2.4	10.6	5.7	11.4	5.9	17.8	11.6
English	3.4	1.9	5.3	3.5	1.2	3.8	3.7	3.2
German	1.2	1.0	3.1	1.5	1.2	0.9	4.6	2.4
Scots	2.3	0.9	0.9	1.2	1.2	0.8	0.2	0.7
Other[e]			0.3	0.1			0.3	0.1
Total	100.0	100.0	100.0	100.0	100.0	100.0	100.0	100.0

Note: Ethnicity is here determined by father's nativity or, if that is unknown, by the individual's own nativity. See n. 4, this chapter.
[a]Twenty-one residents of uncertain ethnicity. [b]Thirty-seven residents of uncertain ethnicity.
[c]Eight residents of uncertain ethnicity. [d]Includes free black residents. In 1850: fifteen in Dudley, twenty-six in Oxford, and five in Webster.
in 1860: fifteen in Dudley, twenty-six in Oxford, and five in Webster.
[e]Swiss, French, Polish, Italian.
Source: MFCD, MFCO, MFCW, 1850, 1860.

This followed from a trend in all three townships toward increased business activity. A few enterprises – the Oxford bakery and distillery and the shops turning out bobbins, textile machines, and carriages – appear to have fallen away. But their disappearance was hardly noticed. Between 1838 and 1840 the Norwich and Worcester Railroad established depots in both Oxford and Webster,[7] and the strengthened access to markets and supplies that this provided quickly encouraged a broad increase in business ventures. By 1840, the aggregate number of nontextile projects in the area covered by the three townships was nearly two-thirds greater than in 1831. And by the 1850s there was a host of new businesses: an establishment producing firearms in Dudley; forges and works manufacturing cordage, tinware, and (briefly) "spectacles and philosophical instruments" in Oxford; and in Webster, shops producing soap and tallow candles, "chair and cabinet manufactures," another tinware works, and (probably as a substitute for the vanished distillery) a brewery. There were also businesses that persisted and (as often as not) became more extensive: brickmaking facilities, for example, as well as tanneries, taverns, and retail stores.[8]

Considering all the three townships, however, the key developments were unquestionably in shoemaking and textiles. The former branch of manufacturing fairly exploded. Its aggregate local labor force climbed from twenty-five individuals in 1832 to forty times that number as the antebellum period closed. By the mid-1850s there were more than five hundred male shoemakers in these communities, some of them working in shops and others at home, with another four hundred and eighty odd female "binders" organized into a local outwork system, which thus took up where outlying weaving and picking had left off some twenty years earlier.[9] Textile operatives multiplied less dramatically, largely because the number of local mills increased only from fifteen to eighteen between 1831 and 1860. Nonetheless, the roster of millworkers in Dudley, Oxford, and Webster probably approached twelve hundred individuals by 1855, more than one-third above the operative labor force in the two older townships twenty-five years earlier.[10]

A detailed examination of this broadening business activity will be undertaken presently. For the moment what matters is how the trend affected the number of people committed to key occupations within the three communities – and the answer is quite straightforward. In 1820 it was still possible for some 70 percent of Dudley and Oxford men with known vocational commitments to describe themselves as farmers. Husbandry continued to rank as a leading job designation through the 1850s, but then the ratio fell off. At midcentury,

Table 7.3. *Percentage of Dudley, Oxford, and Webster labor forces in the four leading occupations, 1860*

	1860			
	Dudley	Oxford	Webster	Aggregate
Farmers	27.6	14.6	5.9	13.2
Shoemakers[a]	14.8	26.2	12.6	18.0
Laborers[b]	18.1	15.1	12.3	14.2
Operatives[c]	22.0	27.4	50.6	36.2

Note: Local labor forces calculated from all males and females whose occupation is cited in the 1860 census. Since female shoe binders were evidently not counted in this enumeration, the proportion of shoemakers indicated here is probably low. See n. 9, this chapter.
[a]Shoemakers, cutters, binders, shoe manufacturers.
[b]Laborers, farm laborers, railroad workers, teamsters, servants, housekeepers, washerwomen.
[c]Operatives, watchmen, overseers, mule spinners, piecers, wool sorters, spoolers, speeder-tenders, picker-tenders, carders, weavers, dresser-tenders, dyers, giggers, finishers, spinners, warpers, drawers-in, machinists.
Sources: MFCD, MFCO, MFCW, 1860.

it stood at just over one man in four. By 1860, when female occupational listings (except for binders) began to appear in federal censuses, farmers were not only less numerous than laborers (most of whom admittedly did agricultural work, though only as hired employees); as Table 7.3 indicates, they also ranked behind shoemakers and textile operatives. The last named contingent had by this point, in fact, emerged as the single largest occupational group in the aggregate labor force of the three communities.[11]

This was the general trend. But what Table 7.3 also makes clear is that this line of development was not pursued to the same degree in each township. The proportion of laborers attributed to the three townships probably reflects their varying need for agricultural hands, as well as construction workers for a somewhat anomalous surge of construction work that happened to be under way in Dudley as the antebellum period closed. The other major occupations, however, display an obvious pattern. Within the context of an overall shift from agricultural to nonagricultural pursuits, Dudley and Oxford remained the most anchored to farming, and Oxford proved the most receptive to boot and shoe manufacture. Webster, by contrast, took the lead in textile employment. Containing more textile mills (seven in 1855) than either of the other two townships, including among its factories the three Slater villages, which alone employed at least 50 percent of all local operatives – encompassing all this, Webster was by 1860 providing berths to about three-fifths of the millworkers living in these three communities. In sum, Dudley and Oxford still contained mills, but Webster had emerged as far more the authentic New England mill town.

Which in turn provides an explanation for the fact – emerging as a final implication of the data assembled in Table 7.2 – that the three communities did not contain an equal number of foreigners. Commonly poor and often unskilled, first and second generation immigrants tended to concentrate in a few jobs. There were occasional English merchants and tailors and at least one German painter and stonecutter. But most residents of non-American ethnicity, and particularly most residents of Irish and Canadian heritage, were not spread evenly across local occupations or even across the four largest local occupations. Only a tiny number became farmers, and relatively few took up shoemaking. Instead, the great majority of these newcomers (86.0 percent in 1860) were laborers or – their other major occupational niche – textile operatives. By the 1850s, three-quarters of all workers inside local mills were first- and second-generation immigrants from another country; just under 70 percent were recent arrivals from Ireland or Canada.[12] Thus Webster, with its dense aggregation of mills and comparatively small farming sector, persistently registered the largest contingent of non-American inhabitants. By the same token, the relative homogeneity evident in Oxford's ethnic composition reflected that town's large population of shoemakers and (by 1860) its comparatively small number of laborers. Certain details remain mysterious: Why the Irish so vastly outnumbered Canadians in Dudley and Oxford, for example. But the broad shape of local ethnic patterns, and specifically the differences between Webster, on the one hand, and the two older communities, on the other, are obviously tied to variations in the economic structure developing in these townships.

Growing steadily larger, displaying new patterns of age, ethnicity, and occupations – these were fundamental characteristics of local populations during the later antebellum era. So was unprecedented restlessness. The far from insignificant transiency rates chalked up by local residents in earlier decades were far outdistanced after Webster's incorporation. Movement had been common; it became endemic.

In part, the heightened transiency reflected larger numbers of newcomers. The new languages and accents that began to be heard on local roads during the 1840s and 1850s obviously signified a substantial influx of residents from beyond local boundaries. But not all newcomers were foreigners. Seeking jobs – most often as operatives or casual laborers but sometimes also in stores and various workshops – people entering Dudley, Oxford, and Webster included those of native as well as foreign ethnicity. In Webster in 1860, for example, just under one-half (48.6 percent) of all residents arriving since 1850 were ethnic Americans.[13]

Departures also contributed to local transiency rates, of course. To an important extent, the decision to leave these communities in this period reflected the growing landlessness of local inhabitants. As the number of farmers declined and as the limited supply of land (much of it probably still encumbered by debt) continued to block many farming children from inheriting real estate, the number of residents tied to Dudley, Oxford, and Webster by property ownership fell off to about one-third the aggregate population of the three townships.[14]

But the drift from farming to commerce and manufacturing tended to limit not only acquisition of property but upward economic mobility of all kinds. The data here are far from exhaustive. What clues there are, however, suggest that of the residents who lingered for any length of time and shifted into new jobs, only a small fraction – certainly no more than a quarter – achieved meaningful occupational or economic advancement. This relative lack of opportunity naturally encouraged restlessness: The towns could attract newcomers, but the absence of broad and reliable patterns of upward mobility led many residents to move on before too long.[15] Between 1850 and 1860, the persistence rate of inhabitants in all three townships was 22.5 percent, less than half the rate estimated for Dudley and Oxford household heads between 1820 and 1830.[16]

Once again, however, the situation was not identical in all three communities. Occupationally, the most transient people were operatives and laborers; the most rooted were farmers and (despite the pronounced restlessness of some shoemakers) handicraft and workshop employees. Ethnically, the largest number of residents persisting a decade or more were American; the quickest to move on were of Canadian background, followed closely by those of Irish descent.[17] The net result, of course, was that Webster stood out from its two neighbors. In the factory town Slater had created, persistence during the 1850s ran 7 to 10 percent lower than in the two older communities.[18]

A final aspect of local populations that needs consideration is the residential configuration of Dudley, Oxford, and Webster inhabitants. Where did these people live? And with whom?

In some respects, little had changed on this front. A majority of inhabitants still lived in single-family dwellings, with the remainder divided between multiple-family houses and (especially among highly transient operatives and laborers) the boardinghouses that stood inside factory compounds and (in a few cases by the 1850s) elsewhere in these towns as well.[19]

Patterns of coresidency within these lodgings continued to reflect earlier choices. Late antebellum censuses provide firm evidence of households hosting nonkin boarders,[20] and boardinghouse residents still typically arrived and departed free of domestic attachments. Then too, weaning processes already in evidence during earlier decades persisted into the 1840s and 1850s: Thus there are scattered signs of older children establishing separate local residences or moving away altogether; and there are hints of fathers in wage-laboring households continuing to leave their families behind when they sought new jobs in new communities. Still, conflating the three local populations, the family was still the basic unit of habitation. Well over 90 percent of all residents shared housing with a spouse, child, sibling, or parent. And even when it did not produce coresidency, kinship probably still encouraged a certain clustering within the same community. Indeed, the proportion of households with relatives living nearby may actually have increased between 1830 and the end of the 1850s.[21]

All this is pretty much as it had been in previous decades. But there were also signs of significant modification in local residential arrangements. In the first place each community had by this point developed what amounted to a town center. There was still substantial demographic dispersion; and the thickest human concentrations that did exist almost certainly still gathered around the manufactories – themselves still dispersed – of these townships. But notable new concentrations of houses and shops had emerged near the Oxford and Webster railroad depots, as well as around Dudley's Congregationalist meetinghouse.[22]

In the second place, residential patterns began to reflect ethnic predilections. Although the phenomenon did not affect all groups equally or any group with total consistency, there is evidence that families of Canadian, American, and (to a lesser degree) Irish background only took in boarders of their own lineage; that residents of multiple-family dwellings and boardinghouses chose to live in build-

ings in which their ethnicity was heavily, if not exclusively, represented; and that buildings thus dominated by a particular ethnic
group lay close together, forming small subzones (even within the
mill compounds) of houses tilting toward one or another ethnic
group.[23] In this sense, and to this extent, the cultural components of
local society turned in upon themselves – and so generated new
kinds of divisions among residents of Dudley, Oxford, and Webster.

III

Such were the salient, and demonstrably changing, features of Dudley, Oxford, and Webster populations during the second generation
after 1810. But other features of life and labor in this period also
merit attention. The first newspaper published in any of these communities, *The Webster Weekly Times*, made its appearance in 1859.
And religious activities also require notice. At least four more "enthusiasms" penetrated this area of southern Massachusetts during
the 1840s and 1850s. And once again there was institutional growth:
In the years after Webster's incorporation, Methodist societies in all
three townships put up new chapels, Baptist and Congregationalist
groups constructed meetinghouses in Oxford and Webster, and during the 1850s Catholics in these same two communities built churches
for their services.[24]

But probably a more important determinant of the daily social
order was the nature of daily labor. Certainly it is impossible to
understand what was happening without, for example, looking more
closely at farming. This is partly because, despite its reduced presence, husbandry remained an important occupation in each township; but it is also because farming – again in all three townships –
remained comparatively immune to evolution. Although agriculture
did not escape the late antebellum era completely unmodified, the
alterations were few, and those that occurred generally only deepened trends long in process. Against the background of dramatic
demographic shifts sweeping these communities, farming in southern Worcester County evinced many of the same characteristics it
had in 1830 and in some cases even 1810. The impact of such agrarian conservatism naturally varied with the size of the farming interest in each community. But in all three townships yeomen represented
a link to the past, an anchor against change.

Two persisting characteristics of the yeomen themselves have already received notice: that they were usually American born and
bred, and that they were typically less transient than other resi-

dents. But the economic ranking of husbandmen also remained largely unaltered. Whereas the arrival of poor, nonfarming immigrants tended to elevate yeomen into higher income brackets, most husbandmen appear to have still clustered within middling strata.[25]

Nor had the labor resources available to these men altered appreciably. Children were certainly no more inclined to linger on family farms in the 1840s and 1850s than they had been during the 1820s and early 1830s. Throughout New England, rural observers continued to lament the logistical difficulties and domestic frictions arising when sons "go and come as they please, leaving their fathers to solitary employment in their . . . fields."[26] Precise local data on youthful departures are unfortunately not available for these later years. But it is plausible that young emigrants from parental farms grew steadily more common as the antebellum period wound down. After all, the possibility of inheriting real estate (as already suggested) remained unlikely at best, and the continuing pressure of high costs and uncertain incomes weighing upon farmers could easily render husbandry unattractive even to those in line to receive homesteads. So it was that the number of local farming families with no children at all remaining as coresidents almost doubled between 1820 and 1860; and the number of youngsters living with farming parents but pursuing nonagricultural work appears to have increased as well.[27] But the most poignant indication of children turning away from parental homesteads is that by the late 1850s farmers in Dudley, Oxford, and Webster were almost exclusively middle-aged and elderly residents. During the forty years after 1820, the proportion of local yeomen over 45 jumped from just under one-half to more than two-thirds, a far more rapid rate of aging than that experienced by local populations as a whole. In 1860 the average farmer in these townships was 53.2 years old.[28]

If children increasingly declined to help in the fields, a few local yeomen undoubtedly still found it possible to drum up friends and neighbors to lend a hand. A more certain, and probably a more extensive, source of assistance came from hired hands. By the 1850s, yeomen in Dudley and Webster were sharing the services of fifty to sixty farm laborers, most of them newcomers to the towns and about a third of them immigrants from Ireland or Canada.[29]

But this squadron of hired recruits did not alter the basic complexion of the local agricultural work force. In the first place, farm workers were not very much younger than the farmers hiring them. Generally in their late thirties or early forties, these laborers only strengthened the general sense that ploughing, planting, and reaping were no longer tasks appropriate for those commencing their working lives. In the second place, there were not enough to go around. Whether the total contingent of agricultural workers had grown or diminished since the 1830s is not clear, but by 1860 there were nearly four farmers in Dudley and Webster for every available employee. It follows from this ratio, of course, that the wages of agricultural employees probably stayed high – perhaps even rose – during the 1840s and 1850s. And this in turn would have encouraged the same social and emotional distance already evident between yeomen and their servants in earlier years. Confronted by high labor costs, local husbandmen almost certainly continued the practice of taking on hired workers only in months of planting and harvesting. And the indications are that by 1860 many farmers in Dudley and Webster declined to board laborers in their own homes even during these seasons.[30]

None of this diminished productivity. Neither manpower shortages nor the tensions that likely crisscrossed relations among farmers, youngsters, and servants reduced the output of local fields and meadows. On the contrary, the amount of grain and hay raised within the area covered by these communities increased 51.1 and 45.1 percent, respectively, between the early 1830s and the mid-1850s. The more complete data on grain cultivation even reveals increased yields per acre.[31] As their output expanded, moreover, local farmers also appear to have passed further into the market. This was a trend shared by other rural New England communities of the period and enthusiastically endorsed by agricultural reform journals. "Let our farmers study their true interests," commanded the *Plough, Loom, and Anvil* in 1852:

> Let them not stand while others are getting ahead. Let them be up and doing something to supply the wants of the towns and cities in their vicinity; and not the necessities only, but the tastes also. Let them raise flowers, even, if it will pay a profit. Why not?[32]

Why not, indeed – but in practice southern Massachusetts husbandmen did not go quite this far. They may have sold some of the potatoes they were raising by midcentury; and by 1855 the "preparation" of lumber and firewood "for market" had become a $69,000 business (centered in Oxford) that provided occasional employment to 235 men. But the deepening commercial orientation of local yeomen found its major expression in more dairy products: After suffering a decline following Webster's incorporation, the combined cow population of the three towns climbed 28.8 percent between 1840 and 1855, and by the latter date the three communities were collectively turning out some forty-seven tons of butter and cheese.[33]

In the end, however, these shifts were all shaped and limited by the conservatism still lying deep in the heart of Yankee agriculture. In all three townships, as in many other rural northern communities of these years, the actual work processes of farming – the practical, daily meaning of husbandry – remained remarkably unchanged.

Certainly there was no widespread recourse to new tools or techniques. The farms that textile mills continued to operate through this period may have occasionally experimented in new technologies: a "mowing machine" evidently passed across some Slater-owned meadows in 1855, and in 1854 the South Village was offered use of "2 too horse Power machines... that thrash and winow..." grain.[34] Then too, yeomen throughout Dudley, Oxford, and Webster were clearly making greater use of nitrogen-fixing hay in this period; and judging from regional developments they were probably also relying more heavily on cast-iron ploughs and fertilizer:

> Ply, ply men! No stopping now to see the pigeons fly. Our Yankee soil has grown old, and needs working and enriching. Down, down with the beam, Jonas.

But this was all. Despite various mechanical devices available by the 1850s, Indian corn (still the most important grain in local fields) was in all likelihood still planted by the time-consuming hill method. Threshing, harvesting, and reaping machines were at best exotic exceptions in these communities, and the hay rake (which had been around from the 1820s) still lacked a significant following anywhere in the Northeast. And for all the widening acceptance of fertilizer, there was still little systematic effort to use crop rotation to maintain or restore soil fertility.[35]

How, then, could harvests grow larger in Dudley, Oxford, and Webster? Despite their limited manpower, local husbandmen probably continued to "improve" ever larger portions of their holdings. It seems clear, moreover, that any acres they brought under cultivation were worked with relentless intensity. Indeed, one of the reasons so many youngsters rejected farming in this era may have been that late antebellum yeomen were laboring as hard as any farmers in New England history.

The basic reason husbandmen clung to familiar methods was itself familiar. Most of the changes advocated by reformers continued to seem impractical, or unnecessary, or both – especially to farmers still reluctant to plunge headlong into the race for financial gain – for this was the final continuity in local agriculture. Once again the evidence is only suggestive. But there is reason to believe that even as farmers proceeded further into commercialization, they remained sensitive to older, nonmonetary priorities. To some degree, their orthodoxy merely rationalized the economic stringencies they faced: With cost and income curves operating against even the most thoroughly market-oriented yeomen, it was soothing for farmers to claim that profit was not what they were after anyway. Yet most Yankee husbandmen, including those in southern Massachusetts, seemed genuinely reluctant to jettison traditional perspectives. In fact, the gap between those few farmers eager to embrace reform and the recalcitrant majority seems to have become sharper and more rigid as time went on.[36]

So it was that the *Old Farmer's Almanack* retained its broad popularity by continuing to insist that profit was not the chief aim of northeastern agriculture. Unlike the "merchant and manufacturer" and their risky quests for affluence, the magazine asserted in 1855, the farmer should remember his proper reward was secure "independence":

> What has the industrious farmer to fear? His capital is invested in the solid ground. He draws on a fund which, from time immemorial, has never failed to honor all just demands.[37]

Considering Dudley, Oxford, and Webster specifically, "independence" evidently still involved meeting family requirements. Thus, although directing increased efforts toward marketable products, local husbandmen persisted in raising crops of sufficient variety to satisfy most of their own food needs. And for a while at least, the agricultural surplus that did develop was so small that it failed to meet both regional urban demands and the requirements of local manufactories. "The inhabitants of [the mill villages]," reported a Slater official during this period, "are in danger of starving to death (which of all kinds is the most dreadful). The Town [i.e., Webster] does not affort 1 [barrel] of flour or 1 Bush[el] corn or 1 of cheese or 1 leg of bacon." It also bears notice that the size of local homesteads, though gradually falling off, remained sufficiently large to suggest a continuing – if by now commonly frustrated – hope that perhaps some children would remain on the land.[38]

The stress farmers seem to have placed on domestic needs scarcely rendered their work any easier. But it enclosed a final demonstration of the inertia at the center of local agriculture: an important expression of the lack of change that made husbandry stand out – against more rapidly shifting components of the social order in Dudley, Oxford, and Webster.

IV

The stores and workshops building up in these communities present obvious claim as one such rapidly shifting component. Penetrating unevenly but broadly into the three townships, nontextile businesses of this period demonstrably strengthened the commercial and manufacturing sectors of local economies and helped recast local occupational structures. Yet even here, even within the structure and operation of these ventures, evidence of change alternated with patterns persisting from earlier decades.

Just as in the first post-1810 generation, for example, proprietors of local nontextile businesses during the 1840s and 1850s demonstrated an ability to shift into new projects as need and opportunity arose. (Thus Wilson Olney ran a retail store in 1835 and a shoe shop in 1854, and Erastus Ormsbee exchanged a tavern for a store in 1846.) Similarly, investors generally continued to be newcomers: In Oxford (where data are most complete) just over three-fifths of those backing stores and workshops by the 1850s were not present in this community when the decade opened.[39]

The economic standing of these figures, on the other hand, did change. Nontextile investors (again judging from Oxford evidence) were slotted more evenly through community income strata – were less bunched toward the middle – than during previous decades. Of thirty-nine backers of nonmanufactory projects who could be traced into local records, one-third ranged toward the top of their local economic pyramids, one-third toward the bottom, with the remaining third scattered through intervening brackets.[40] Combined with frequently rising capitalization costs, the lack of extensive personal wealth among small business proprietors led to changes in the way these individuals financed their enterprises. Leasing (rather than building or purchasing) facilities was still a frequent solution. But there were evidently new strategies. Local investors may have looked increasingly to the Oxford Bank for venture capital; and, probably of broader financial utility, the percentage of undertakings commanding the resources of two or three individuals had about doubled by 1860. By the time the Civil War started, small partnerships had emerged as virtually the standard proprietary unit of nontextile enterprises in Dudley, Oxford, and Webster.[41]

The labor force hired by these establishments also embraced novel features. Certainly it was larger. The especially rapid increase of shoemakers has already received notice. But the overall expansion of nontextile ventures meant that the number of wage laborers employed by other trades must have multiplied as well. The best guess is that by 1860 this whole roster of workers in local shops and stores approached eight hundred individuals – more than twice as large as it had been at any time between 1810 and the early 1830s.[42] Then too, the average age of these employees – early to mid-thirties in 1860 – may have represented an increase from earlier years. Their net incomes probably shifted too, but in the opposite direction. The position of clerks and workshop laborers on local tax lists (all but the most skilled were in the bottom quartile), combined with data on workers from other communities, all suggest that these employees enjoyed little, if any, improvement in economic standing and may often have suffered outright decline in real wages.[43]

The ethnicity of this labor force, by contrast, remained essentially unaltered. Because most foreign immigrants and their youngsters worked as casual laborers or operatives, employees recruited by stores and workshops continued by and large to be the offspring of native Americans. They also continued to be male. Local jobs outside manufactories for women and girls unquestionably expanded during the late antebellum era. Most of the increase, however, resulted from the growing roster of outworking female shoe binders, who labored in their own homes, and the swelling list (especially among Webster's young Irishwomen) of domestic servants, who worked in someone else's house. The 1860 enumerations reveal more women schoolteachers, as well as a few milliners and dressmakers who may have worked outside domestic settings; and there is reason to suppose that bonnet making in Webster took place in an enterprise with some thirty female employees. But through the 1840s and 1850s, just as in earlier decades, the great majority of wage laborers taken on by stores and workshops were men.[44]

With proprietors and employees reflecting such cross hatchings of change and persistence, nontextile businesses disclosed their most complete and dramatic innovations in other areas: in their technology, organization, and underlying rationale.

To start with – and part of the reason these enterprises were probably becoming costlier to build – it is likely that more local workshops were using more sophisticated machinery. Rufus Moore's curious and complicated apparatus for cutting and heading nails ("at the same time") was by now almost certainly matched elsewhere in these communities. In Dudley's firearms manufacture, for example: If patterns documented in other midcentury Massachusetts townships found local expression, this establishment was using turret lathes, drop and tilt hammers, as well as rifling, stocking, and milling machines. Such technologies (some of them driven by water) did not necessarily abrogate the inside-contract system or the need for a few highly proficient machinists.[45] But they inevitably reduced the average skill level of workers hired to manufacture guns.

A more pervasive change – and probably a more compelling reason these ventures were becoming costlier – was a shift toward bigger payrolls. Although a few enterprises retained the two- to four-man rosters typical earlier in the century,[46] the general trend was toward more extensive operations. Thus by the mid-1850s Dudley's firearms shop and tannery employed ten and six workers, respectively; Oxford's two cordage works together hired twenty-seven workers; the (mainly female) labor force in Webster's straw-bonnet shop totaled thirty-two; and the rapidly multiplying shoe undertakings seemingly averaged – quite aside from their retinue of outworkers – around fifteen laborers each.[47]

As the size and (in some cases) mechanical complexity of local workshops increased, so also in all likelihood did the stringency of their work rules. Certain trades, like shoemaking, retained seasonal labor rhythms. But when they did operate, most nontextile establishments of the 1840s and 1850s (perhaps even retail stores) probably evinced disciplines hitherto seen only occasionally outside cotton and woolen factories. Again judging from other communities, the odds are that "drams" and customary pauses gave way to a firmer insistence on sobriety, clock-regulated punctuality, and more careful monitorings of each employee's output.[48]

So too divisions of authority and labor became more pronounced. The number of agents and overseers almost certainly increased; and there is no doubt but that specific work processes were more frequently whittled down to mere parts of jobs. Thus, coupled with its strong technological base, the small-arms industry was by this point broadly – if not universally – committed to the "American system": a manufacturing method that confined most employees to the narrowly defined task of turning out constituent (and interchangeable) parts of guns.[49]

But specialization also grew apace in shoemaking, where no new machinery appeared. Divisions only just evident in the two local cordwaining shops of the early 1830s had by the end of the 1850s clarified into a production system. There were a small number of manufacturers ("shoe-bosses") who supplied the raw leather and (sometimes aided by merchants) marketed the finished product; a slightly larger contingent of cutters ("clickers") employed by manufacturers to carve the leather into appropriate shapes; a sizable cluster of journeymen shoemakers who worked either in shops (sometimes alongside clickers) or at home to attach upper and lower parts of shoes; and finally, an equally large but entirely female and exclusively outworking roster of binders who assembled the "uppers." This pattern was naturally not ironclad. Some cutters probably ran their own businesses; and in at least one instance a local manufacturer undertook only bottoming and binding, returning his work to cutters in another township. But as the antebellum period ended, most of the half million pairs of boots and shoes produced annually in Dudley, Oxford, and Webster were turned out through this four-tiered structure.[50]

The collective impact of new machines, larger payrolls, stiffer discipline, and more tightly specified work assignments must have significantly altered the character of nontextile ventures. Certainly employees inside these establishments would have felt the change: The new organization and technology required them to work harder and produce more during the very period they were receiving little, if any, improvement in wages. From the perspective of their employers, however, the innovations were only reflections of another and more fundamental shift in the motivation behind nontextile businesses. By the 1840s and 1850s, far more than in earlier antebellum decades, the "drive for profits" had emerged as a dominant inspiration.

Older perspectives did not disappear. There were still store owners and workshop proprietors (especially among those who continued to combine business with husbandry) for whom nonagricultural investments were intended more to maintain than advance economic standing.[51] But by all indications, people with interests outside farming were no longer content with "competencies." Indeed, drawing on both local and regional sources, it appears that beyond the zone of tradition generated by husbandry, customary economic ambitions and styles of exchange were fading throughout rural New England by the 1840s and 1850s. Thus there emerged the accelerating inclination among rural tradesmen to demand payment in cash rather than in goods or labor. Less concrete, but equally persuasive, signs are found in the premonition voiced by many hinterland Yankees of the period that "love of wealth" was advancing steadily around them; that theirs (in the words of a Northampton editor) was a "gambling, speculating age for money making." And finally it is surely significant that the growth of stores and workshops in southern Worcester County coincided with improved railroad access to nonlocal markets, and that many of these multiplying ventures (like shoe shops) were particularly known for their broad trade connections and their intense emphasis on commercial success.[52]

A balance had altered. A desire for profit was scarcely novel among local residents; it was present in the eighteenth century, and (it will be recalled) several workshops may well have pursued the goal intensely in the 1820s and early 1830s. But over the next twenty or thirty years what had been exceptional among small nonagricultural projects became commonplace. The change was sufficient to tilt the fundamental character of these businesses away from the norms of husbandry and closer to those of cotton and woolen manufactories.

V

Manufactories remained thoroughly committed to profit. Maintaining perspectives and priorities that consistently characterized early waterpowered factories, textile mills scattered through this area of southern Worcester County during the 1840s and 1850s continued to measure success entirely by the balance sheet.

That this was no longer remarkable – that local stores and workshops were by now also prone to stress profit margins – inevitably meant that manufactories stood out somewhat less sharply in 1860 than in 1820 or 1830. Indeed, many of the shifts – in technology, size, and administration – affecting nontextile businesses served to blunt at least partially the vivid distinctiveness that had once marked cotton and woolen factories. And the mills themselves bolstered this trend by undertaking relatively few fundamental innovations. Although textile factories were by no means static during these later years, there is a sense in which their slowed evolutionary pace permitted other businesses to catch up.

But only to a point. Manufactories may have blended more smoothly into the surrounding social landscape, but they still remained distinctive enough. In 1860, as in 1830, textile mills generated the most revenues; they still deployed the most consistently intricate array of sophisticated machines; they still displayed the most intricate divisions of labor and administration; and they still evoked (though again still without consistent enforcement) what was probably the most thoroughly formalized and widely remarked codicil of time and work discipline. In sum, it was still textile factories that contrasted most vividly with the customary values and procedures that, here and there (in farming, for example), continued to pattern daily life.

Like nontextile ventures, but probably to an even greater degree, cotton and woolen mills had become more expensive by the end of the antebellum era. In part this was because manufactories grew larger. In 1855 local factories averaged seventy-three operatives laboring inside their walls, making them not only by far the largest employers in Dudley, Oxford, and Webster but also about 16 percent larger than the Dudley and Oxford factories of the early 1830s. Then too, the few mechanical innovations mills did introduce in this era almost certainly made it more expensive to establish a manufactory. Local cotton mills had likely adopted the self-acting (and completely waterpowered) spinning mule by this point, and the shift from throstle frames to faster (and more productive) ring-spinning machines was probably well under way. Wool spinning witnessed less change (semiautomatic jacks remained the machine of choice in most mills), but weaving received a substantial mechanical boost from the spread of Crompton power looms. Throughout the Northeast generally, and in at least a few local factories specifically, these looms were used during the late antebellum period to turn out fancy cassimere cloths.[53]

None of these technical advances – nor the several minor improvements in preparatory and finishing technologies that probably also found acceptance in local mills – even remotely approached the burst of ingenuity marking the opening stages of America's textile industry. But combined with the mills' increased size, the likely presence of a few new machines helped peg the average initial cost of local factories – both cotton and woolen projects – at about $40,000. Precisely how far this departed from capitalization figures for earlier manufactories is not certain. But it is surely suggestive that in Rhode Island the price for constructing and equipping family-style cotton factories was often at a higher level in 1860 than in 1830, and the cost of woolen mills jumped nearly sevenfold during the same period.[54]

In late antebellum Dudley, Oxford, and Webster the individuals who underwrote the larger and almost certainly costlier manufactories included a number of familiar faces. The DeWitt brothers continued as major investors in several Oxford mills (including the Oxford Woolen Company) at least until the mid-1840s; and Aaron Tufts remained a central figure in at least one Dudley factory until his death in 1843. During this later period, however, just as during earlier decades, most of those organizing local mills were recent arrivals. Certainly Dudley's leading mill master of this era, Henry H. Stevens, did not have a long local residency behind him when he commenced his activities in the late 1840s. And nine of Oxford's ten known factory proprietors during the 1850s entered the town after the decade had opened.[55]

What is surprising, however, is that the practice of co-ownership among local factory owners fell off sharply. Most mills were still backed by partnerships. But despite the probable rising cost of initiating textile manufacturing, several establishments evidently operated under a single proprietor. And the partnerships that existed contained at most three or four members – far fewer than the fifteen to twenty participants usual in the first generation after 1810.[56]

How were these men – acting alone or in such restricted clusters – able to fund cotton and woolen mills? In some cases they succeeded simply because (unlike nontextile entrepreneurs) they were rich. The data do not permit systematic distinctions between wealth accumulated before involvement in textile projects and wealth resulting from these ventures. But it seems plausible that there were mill masters who had used their own resources to inaugurate manufactories, for by 1860 nearly two-thirds of mill proprietors linked to Dudley, Oxford, and Webster income records stood among the richest tenth of community populations and more than four-fifths (85.7 percent) ranked among the richest two-tenths. Late antebellum factory owners, in sum, were roughly three times more likely to occupy the top rungs of community economic hierarchies than during the first generation after 1810. This was a salient characteristic of town society in this era – and another factor contributing to the widening gap between rich and poor.[57]

For mill masters who were, or at any rate started out, in less flush circumstances, other solutions could have beckoned. By seeking capital from Boston or Providence mercantile circles or from New England's expanding banking facilities, less wealthy factory owners could have managed to set up business alone or with just a few associates.

Or, whatever their income level, these entrepreneurs could choose an altogether different solution. Far more often than during the first post-1810 generation, late antebellum textile ventures were lodged in rented quarters. Many local factory "proprietors" were thus actually tenants of millowners whose own textile efforts had failed or whose other interests made it more convenient to lease their space and machines. So, in the 1850s, Waterman Fisher (from Connecticut) rented the upper stories of his Oxford mill as a knit and stockinet works and the basement to a twine manufacturer – all before taking over the property himself in 1852 to produce cotton goods.[58]

But there is also the particular proprietary structure of the Slater villages to consider. The critical event here was Samuel Slater's death. The founding father of the North, South, and East villages suffered from chronic rheumatism and frequent stomach distress from 1829 on. Though maintaining careful – often compulsive – scrutiny over his mills during the next several years, he was rarely entirely fit. He fell ill for the last time in the spring of 1835, and on April 20th of that year, in his "fine brick home" in the East Village, he died.[59]

He left behind a personal estate estimated variously at between $1 million and $2 million, and a string of obituaries that neatly reflected the ambivalence often surrounding Yankee mill masters in the mid-1830s. "Mr. Slater," announced the Whiggish *Providence Journal* on April 22, "had long been one of our most enterprising and respected citizens...In all the relations of life he maintained a character for probity and integrity seldom equalled." On the other hand, the *Pawtucket Chronicle*, a newspaper given to venting concern about the "tyranny" of factory masters, bid farewell to the "Arkwright of America" by noting that he was

> not exactly a generous man...His object was gold. No man was more indefatigable. Bonaparte never pursued schemes of conquest, never followed the phantom of ambition more constantly, than did Samuel Slater his business. With him there was no second object to divide his thoughts.[60]

For his family, however, the problem lay less in settling Slater's reputation than in deciding how to manage the holdings he had accumulated. The basic structure remained that of partnership, but ultimate administrative authority rested at first on a triumvirate of sons. George and Nelson (aged 31 and 27, respectively, when their father died) took up station in Webster. John (30 years old in 1835) assumed control of the Providence office and the various non-Webster properties with which the Slater name was involved: the Providence Steam Cotton Company, the Wilkinsonville works (by now renamed the Sutton Manufacturing Company), and the Smithfield mills at Slatersville in which Samuel Slater had reinvested after selling his shares in 1829.[61]

But this arrangement did not last. Sometime in 1837 John fell ill with tuberculosis. Seeking relief, he sailed to St. Croix, but without result. He died on that island in early 1838 – and then, in an almost excessively bizarre coda, was packed tightly in a rum barrel and shipped back to Providence for burial. Five years later, George died suddenly, leaving Nelson, then 35, steward of his family's scattered interests.[62]

Nelson endured. Basing himself initially in Providence but ultimately moving his household to Webster, this youngest of the sons Samuel Slater had involved in his mills continued as chief managing officer during the remainder of the 1840s, through the 1850s, and on into the post-Civil War period. It was Nelson who introduced steam (though apparently mainly for finishing and heating purposes)[63] as well as new machines into the local Slater factories. It was Nelson (probably using earlier profits for capital) who built new mill buildings in the South and North villages. And it was Nelson who oversaw a general expansion in the local Slater work force that left him by far the largest industrial employer in Dudley, Oxford, or Webster.

Ranging below the proprietors of virtually all local factories – both Slater and non-Slater – were subordinate managerial figures. Here the format had changed only slightly.

There were agents. In non-Slater mills, they were usually, but in these later years not always, one of the proprietors; the Slater mills continued to rely exclusively on salaried superintendents with no claim of ownership. But whatever their precise interest in their mills, the duties of such men remained wide: "We hope you will not ask of us anything that you do not strictly need," a Webster agent wrote to the Slater office in Providence during the late 1830s, "as we have sufficient business of importance to keep our hands, head, and eyes actively engaged from before sunrise to eight o'clock at night." In the Slater compounds, at least, the reward for performing these duties continued to place agents atop the rest of the payroll. Thus, an agent is cited in 1858 as having received sufficient earnings to purchase $23,000 worth of Webster real estate. And at roughly the same moment, the onetime South Village agent James Robinson – effecting a kind of advance unknown in the first generation of local factories – actually emerged as co-proprietor of his own Webster manufactory.[64]

Below the agents were again the overseers. Still receiving higher wages than operatives (but not agents), still occasionally promoted from among skilled adult male factory workers (though now frequently passing through an intermediary rank of "second hand") – still reflecting all these characteristics, overseers persisted as a crucial element in factory administration. In 1860, as in 1830, they were responsible for synchronizing the carefully specified divisions of production from picking and carding through spinning and weaving and on to finishing and dyeing. They, more than anyone else, had to monitor the "good order" among the operatives of each factory room: the punctuality, sobriety, and overall "steadiness," which, despite some shifts in mill regimens, still comprised the heart of local factory discipline. In the daily relations between manufactories and their hands, overseers still occupied management's front lines.[65]

VI

But who were the hands? Who provided the labor needed by late antebellum mills in Dudley, Oxford, and Webster? Once again it needs to be recognized that not all factory employees worked inside factory buildings or even labored full time for manufactories. Outlying weavers and pickers no longer existed, of course; and (preserving policies already in place by the 1820s and early 1830s) whatever skilled artisans the mills needed were kept close at hand and employed throughout the year. But local factories still hired laborers on an ad hoc basis for occasional, unskilled outdoor jobs.

They worked on the farms the mills continued to operate. Or they drove wagons or fetched firewood or (more often) put up new buildings or dams. They were always male. Those assigned to farm labor (like their counterparts employed by local yeomen) averaged around 40 years of age and were mostly American. Those charged with nonagricultural tasks shared the same age but were more apt to be Irish or Canadian. The size of this labor force is impossible to pin down, but at a guess just under half of all local farm workers – roughly 170 individuals – and a sizable majority of all those specifically designated "laborers" (as distinct from farm laborers) in local censuses drew wages from the mills.[66]

The outstanding characteristic of these employees was their marginality. It did not matter that one in five lived inside the mill villages as brother or father of full-time operatives. Just as cost-conscious mills of the late 1820s had followed farmers and "dismissed" their outdoor help immediately after fall harvests, so cost-conscious mills in the 1840s and 1850s paralleled yeomen of their era and hired outdoor workers only when – and so long as – they were required. A few employees managed to alternate between farming tasks and factory positions;[67] but most outdoor hands had to search elsewhere in the community once their jobs were done – or (just as likely given their transiency) take their search to entirely new communities. "I approve of your suggestion that 3 yoke of Oxen...be sold," Nelson Slater wrote his North Village agent in 1845 as winter weather ended the year's outdoor work. The corollary followed: "and [that] the number of hands be reduced to correspond with remaining Teams."[68]

Table 7.4. *Average annual work force of North, South, and East villages in Webster, 1836–59*

Year	East Village	North Village	South Village	Aggregate
1836	65.3	25.3	81.5	172.1
1837	109.5	26.0		135.5
1838	97.1	44.5		141.6
1839	106.5	70.3		176.8
1840	121.6	69.8		191.4
1841	119.3	66.3		185.6
1842	115.0	63.0		178.0
1843	116.5	74.8		191.3
1844	104.3	81.3		185.6
1845	104.8	149.5		254.3
1846	120.5	214.5		335.0
1847	115.0	221.3	122.3	458.6
1848	115.3	233.3	108.0	456.6
1849	113.8	246.8	103.8	464.4
1850	122.3	233.3	158.7	514.3
1851	136.0	254.8	213.3	604.1
1852	146.3	242.8	235.8	624.9
1853	141.8	251.3	232.8	625.9
1854	148.0	260.8	199.3	608.1
1855	157.8	286.5	191.0	635.3
1856	162.5	311.1	204.8	678.4
1857	149.5	262.8	166.5	578.8
1858	168.8	332.0	202.5	703.3
1859	206.5	384.8		591.3

Note: The size of the annual work force is an average of rosters posted in April, July, October, and January. Consistent data unavailable for South Village.
Source: SC: Slater and Tiffany, vols. 84, 89–91; Union, Mills, vols. 144–51, 155–6; Phoenix, vols. 24–30; Webster Woolen, vols. 66–9.

Operatives presented a different story. As was true of millworkers in the very earliest local factories, those who daily entered the rooms of late antebellum mills in Dudley, Oxford, and Webster were needed every hour these establishments were running.

But as had also been true in earlier factories, this did not preclude variations in the number of operatives from year to year. The data on the Slater villages assembled in Table 7.4 display the choppy progression of payrolls undoubtedly characteristic of all local factories and are clearly reflective of the period's uneven economic conditions. Although the first surge in the number of East Village employees (between 1836 and 1837) simply reflects the addition of listings for weavers, the decline shown in 1838 is a fair measure of layoffs stemming from the 1837 depression. And the gradual expansion of the East Village roster during the years that followed was clearly a response to the generally prosperous – though highly competitive – conditions visiting Yankee mills from the late 1830s through the 1850s.[69] But amid this overall trend lay frequent deviations, one of the largest being the contraction resulting from the 1857 panic.

Much the same pattern of general but discontinuous net growth obviously characterized the North and South villages. In these enclaves, however, the reason behind the sharpest increments – and in fact the basic reason that the total Slater work force expanded faster than the 16 percent net growth typical of most local mills between the 1830s and the 1850s – was Nelson's construction program. As Table 7.4 implies, new buildings went up in the North Village between 1844 and 1846, and the South Village witnessed its expansion about six years later.

Needed continuously but in varying numbers – this was the experience of local operatives throughout the entire pre–Civil War era. Also in keeping with earlier years was the fact that few operatives came from communities immediately surrounding the mills. Indeed, there are signs the proportion had dwindled: Whereas 24.1 percent of male household heads hired by the Slater compounds between 1813 and 1830 are known to have previously resided in either Dudley or Oxford, only 5.1 percent of employees sampled from operatives entering the East Village during the 1850s were living in Webster when that decade started.[70] In large measure, of course, the figures reflect the gathering presence on mill payrolls of foreign immigrants and their families. But even native operatives had dispersed origins: Fewer than half (48.0 percent) of the ethnic Americans living inside Webster's factory enclaves in 1860 had been born in Massachusetts. Still learning about available jobs through advertisements or (more often) through word of mouth ("I am informed"; "Accidentally hearing"; "I learnt from Mr. Blackburn"), millworkers of Dudley, Oxford, and Webster may have traveled farther than ever before to reach local factories.[71]

VII

What drew them? Here there had been a rather profound change, for the shifting ethnic composition of factory laborers meant that the pressures and attractions pulling people into southern Massachusetts mill villages were now cast in different proportions than in previous decades. Among the two largest contingents of immigrants, for example, millwork was clearly a solution to a desperate problem. Commonly possessing few resources or marketable skills, the Irish regarded jobs in scattered textile factories as among the few occupational niches that were both accessible to them and capable of facilitating their exit from the port ghettos that had greeted them upon their arrival in the New World. And to French Canadians also, mills were one of the few arenas of available labor; to them, Yankee manufactories comprised a ladder leading down through New England, pointing steadily away from the constraints and scarcities of Quebec. Other immigrants on local factory payrolls – German, Swiss, and English operatives, for instance – were probably less hard-pressed. But the large number of Irish and Canadian recruits must have appreciably raised the fraction of Dudley, Oxford, and Webster millworkers who turned to factory labor out of necessity.

The growing availability of immigrant operatives coincided with the declining availability of natives. As the northeastern economy became more varied and complex, the number of nonfarming jobs available to relatively educated and skilled Americans of the region also increased, with the result that by midcentury the kind of Yankees hitherto drawn toward manufactories often began exploring other opportunities. Even in Dudley, Oxford, and Webster, it will be remembered, the range of nonagricultural, nontextile work expanded for both men and (although to a considerably lesser extent) for women during later antebellum decades.

Once immigrants began penetrating the operative labor force, moreover, this native exodus accelerated. It is impossible to determine for any given mill whether at the outset immigrants displaced Americans or simply filled a vacuum left by already retreating Yankees. But there is little doubt that any factory accepting sizable numbers of immigrants became less attractive to native New Englanders. The novel language and accents of the newcomers, their strange religions and clothes (the Irish workers' "peasant cloaks, red or blue, made with hoods and several capes"),[72] and above all the palpable neediness of the large Irish and Canadian contingents – all this diminished the status of factory work in American eyes. Indeed, the arrival of immigrants also caused alarm among some Yankee mill masters who worried that foreigners generally, and the Irish especially, were too shiftless, too fond of drink and quarreling, to accept factory life or benefit from its corrective discipline. But Yankee operatives felt the most concern. In particular, New Englanders of middling economic status no longer regarded factory stints as enticing interludes, as a means to acquire needed experience or capital for subsequent ventures, or as brief, exciting excursions into a new milieu. Probably by 1850, and certainly by 1860, Yankees who had a choice rarely sought out mills as temporary workplaces.[73]

Some Americans, of course, did remain on local rosters. They appear to have been highly experienced operatives with long strings of mill berths already behind them when they reached southern Worcester County. In 1860, as in 1830, such veterans were often workers with sufficient skill to do well in manufactories or sufficient ambition to push toward higher paying jobs. Upward mobility inside manufactories continued to be rare; and female operatives in particular continued to find their occupational ladders leading only to weaving and drawing-in. But just as overseers were still occasionally recruited from experienced male operatives, so boys who started in the carding room or factory-owned fields occasionally pressed on to better berths inside the mills. Although the number was not large – less than one-seventh of a sample of male Slater operatives employed in the 1840s and 1850s experienced significant promotions – it was likely sufficient to encourage at least some hands to linger in factory work.[74] But then too, just as in earlier years, veterans also included workers who, because of the training they lacked or the temperament they possessed, found other jobs unavailable or unappealing, or who belonged to families headed by such individuals.

The one way Yankee veterans almost certainly diverged from earlier patterns, however, was that they were more numerous. If the letters received by the Slater villages are any proof, virtually all native New Englanders entering local factories during the 1840s and 1850s could claim previous encounters with factory labor.

Thus O. Lacey indicated to the Slater villages in 1841 that he would like "a job as the Shearer or press[er]" in the woolen compound "as I have been the most of my time for the Past 4 years at it my instructors are some of the Best workmen in the country." Joseph France pitched his letter of inquiry closer to home: "In addressing you," he wrote Nelson Slater in late 1840, "it may be proper to say that I Began to work for Almy and Brown and Slaters in 1810 and was in their Employ [as bleacher and dyer] about 20 years." Nor did his family lack seasoning: "My oldest son is in the Carding room and is Capable of taking Charge of a room in first rate manner My second Son is a Machinist and my third son is a giger." Eleven years later H. Eldredge was also able to offer a household well versed in the textile business: "I write to see if you want a family my family consists of three to worke in the Mill a Dresser tender a Weaver a frame [i.e., throstle] spiner if you want write immediately and I will come and see you."[75] Women too occasionally claimed veteran status. In fact, there are hints that by the 1850s the Slater villages were *requiring* their "girls" to have previous experience. So Emily Churle moved quickly to correct the misapprehension that she was new to the business: "You have mistaken the letter [I sent]," she wrote from Worcester in 1855: "I do understand workeing in a coton mill and I understand all girls work [with the] exception of Spinninge and if you have a chance for me I should like to come I have worked in the Factory severile yers."[76]

Indeed, so large was the contingent of veterans that it spilled beyond Yankees to include some immigrants. A few of these experienced foreigners had even held skilled textile jobs before their passage to the United States: "Since many years experienced in this business in Germany," wool sorter August Tachauer wrote the South Village on Independence Day, 1840, "and since 3 years working to the highest Satisfaction in this country, I shall be endeavoured of getting yours too if you should reflect upon me." Writing in 1854, M. McEastum asserted: "I have had 24 years experience as a cotton dyer and acquired my trade in one of the best schools in Glasgow." And an English finisher was recommended by his son "as a fit and proper person he having held A very respectable situation at...Leeds, England for 14 years."[77] Post-1840 Irish and Canadian recruits, by contrast, had rarely entered mills before emigrating. But by the time they reached Worcester County they too could often boast an extensive list of factory posts. Thus, after suggesting that he had actually worked once before in the South village ("you know my abilities"), Irishman James Coyle presented his family:

> i have got threechildren to work in the Mill two Boys and one Girl the oldest Boy is 14 the Girl is 12 and the youngest Boy is 10 my oldest Boy is large enough to work at the Shearsand my Girl is large enough to burl and the other boy to work in the Cardroom.[78]

This still did not signify a permanent factory proletariat. The average engagement for Slater operatives in this second post-1810 generation was slightly less than a single year, or about seven months shorter than for hands employed in 1830; and the odds are good that the full working careers of even the most experienced Slater employees (including engagements before and after their Webster stints) encompassed positions in other trades as well as in other mills. Nonetheless, a substantial proportion of Dudley, Oxford, and Webster operatives evidently did share a common background in mills and mill villages. And more: The evidence suggests that (like James Coyle) an increasing number of operatives entering local mills may have labored in these same establishments at least once before. The fraction of incoming East Village employees – American and non-American – with earlier stints in this specific compound rose from just under one-third in 1830 to one-half during the later period.[79]

But the character of the local operative labor force in this period was also shaped by other changes. The proportion of youngsters inside the factories, for example, fell off sharply during these years. By the fifth and sixth decades of the nineteenth century a consensus had developed in Massachusetts that child labor in textile factories should be restricted, and laws were passed specifying that young millworkers receive both a reduced workday and time off for schooling.[80] Although Dudley, Oxford, and Webster factories did not obey this legislation scrupulously, the cumulative weight of public opinion, probably combined with some loss of confidence in the efficiency of very young workers, led these establishments to prune their staff of children. Factory operatives apparently remained the youngest single contingent of wage laborers in these townships (in 1860 they averaged 25.7 years); and as several of the letters just quoted reveal, operatives continued to arrive with children in hand. But between 1831 and 1860 the proportion of local millworkers under 16 had fallen from one-quarter to just over one-seventh.[81]

The ratio of men and women inside the factories also shifted. The proportion of the latter group dropped from 40 to 31.3 percent, while the fraction of men increased dramatically. Because of the expanded woolen facilities (which continued to hire comparatively more men than cotton factories), probably combined once again with declining confidence in child workers, adult males climbed from 35 to 53.9 percent of the local operative labor force between the creation of Webster and the start of the Civil War.[82]

On the other hand, the proportion of operatives linked by family ties declined. It is true that most millworkers (79.0 percent in Webster in 1860) did coreside with a relative. And it is also true that among the few important shifts in mill regimen to emerge during this later period was management's willingness to accept closer family connections inside the mill buildings. Evidently concluding that earlier restrictions were unnecessary, local manufactories began permitting wives to hold mill jobs and occasionally (again judging mainly from Slater records) even allowed children and parents to work together. Still, considering all three townships, the reduced frequency of youthful operatives meant that the proportion of operatives with a parent, sibling, or child in the mills fell to 45.2 percent by 1860 – close to the proportion previously registered only in woolen mills.[83]

In effect, these family factories were shedding elements of their distinctive labor organization. Still smaller than Waltham-style mills, still rarely (if ever) organized by absentee proprietors, local manufactories were nonetheless edging toward the nonchild, nonfamily format that the early boardinghouse establishments had introduced.[84]

And these trends contributed to another. The rising number of men and the shrinking proportions of children and women inevitably pushed up factory wage scales. Increased productivity also helped here: Like nontextile businesses, cotton and woolen factories took measures (representing one of the only other significant shifts in mill regimens) to promote greater output from their employees. It was a strategy obviously responsive to the steadily stiffening competition manufactories experienced during these later years. But increments in production per worker were also part of the reason behind noticeable (though smaller) increments in wages paid for jobs (like carding and weaving) still performed mainly by women and children.[85] For all these reasons, then, a comparison of average daily payments in all local mills in 1831 with Slater's East and South villages in 1860 reveals an increase of almost 10 percent (from 54.1¢ to 59.4¢), creating a theoretical average annual gross wage (among always-present employees of always-running mills) of $184.14 as the 1850s ended.[86]

Once again, certain distinctions and constraints must be kept in mind. Rates in woolen factories ran about 25 percent above those in cotton mills, and it appears (though precise figures are unavailable) that those family units still on the payrolls continued to earn about twice as much as individual unattached operatives. On the other hand, there also remained expenses. The proportion of earnings needed to rent cows and lodgings may have fallen slightly, and skilled, unattached operatives (machinists, dyers, and wool sorters) still cleared several hundred dollars in a year.[87] But living costs, including payments for clothes and foodstuffs, probably continued to consume the bulk of most workers' incomes. On balance, although net earnings among Dudley, Oxford, and Webster operatives probably improved somewhat during these decades, the average increase through the whole period was most likely small.[88]

In the end, however, these broad trends – the declining number of children and families, the shifting balance of men and women, and the consequent rise in gross, if not net, earnings – all these developments were mediated by the presence of immigrant factory workers. It was clear by 1860 that operatives of non-American ethnicity, and specifically Irish and Canadian operatives, evinced different social structures, and consequently different experiences, compared with millworkers of native heritage. Thus Irish and Canadian factory employees together (though the trend proved more pronounced among the latter) were roughly four times more likely than Americans to place children inside the mills.[89] The proportion of men and women did not reflect any significant ethnic variation,[90] but the jobs held by adult male and female foreigners almost always ranked among the less skilled factory berths.

Which all suggests, of course, that earnings also varied according to national background. Unfortunately, it proves difficult to establish precise wage averages for different ethnic groups. But the general patterns seem readily apparent. Viewing mills as one of their only sources of work, foreign immigrants and their families – and again poor and unskilled Irish and Canadian immigrants in particular – pressed eagerly into the less technically sophisticated, and hence less well paid, openings in local factories. Thus they dispatched children into the carding room, and their women became weavers or spinners rather than tackle the more arcane job of drawing-in.[91]

As for the men, there were (as their letters reveal) some skilled adult males among English, Scots, and German operatives. But they were scarcely typical. In Webster in 1860 every agent and virtually every room overlooker (all but one Englishman) were American. And of twenty-nine machinists and dresser-tenders, just four were of foreign extraction. It is true spinning mules passed from American hands. But because of the diminished skill needed on the new self-acting version of these machines, tending mules had become not only one of the least well paid jobs for men but also one of the few positions earning less in 1860 than in the early 1830s.[92] Taken together, as Table 7.5 indicates, the amount by which wages varied according to the number of Americans holding given jobs was not always large. But the variation always existed and it was always direct.

Immigrants, in sum, did not simply enter local manufactories. The infusion of foreign operatives developed in ways that compressed ethnic Americans into better factory slots and simultaneously concentrated operatives of non-American background toward the bottom of mill hierarchies. The boundary between jobs held by the two groups was not rigid. But mill employees quite obviously comprised the most heterogeneous of all local labor forces. And by 1860 only the thread of previous factory experiences bridged the palp-

Table 7.5. *Average daily wage and percentage of Americans holding selected jobs, Webster cotton mills, 1860*

	Average daily wage	% Ethnic Americans
Machinists	$1.47	89.5
Dresser-tenders	1.44	83.3
Mule spinners	1.29	33.3
Drawers-in	.73	100.0
Weavers	.72	38.6
Carders	.59	23.8

Note: First three jobs held by men, second three held by women and children.
Source: MFCW, 1860; SC: Union Mills, vol. 156.

able gap between operatives of native stock and their immigrant colleagues.

VIII

Of such basic elements was the late antebellum social order in Dudley, Oxford, and Webster constructed: a new demographic landscape in which expanding, older, and increasingly restless populations revealed unprecedented ethnic, occupational, and residential configurations; a smaller, but still significant and essentially unchanging, agricultural sector; a substantially broadened panoply of nontextile businesses, displaying a generally sharpened concern for efficiency and profit; an enlarged slate of textile manufactories embracing some (but not many) shifts in technology, managerial format, and regimen but considerable change in the character of their operative labor force; and finally, an emerging distinction between the social and economic organization of Dudley and Oxford, on the one hand, and the genuine mill town of Webster, on the other.

These were the ingredients. But what were the consequences? It remains to examine how people experienced the inventory of changes – both its extent and its limits – permeating the three communities. It remains to explore, that is, how local inhabitants, considered first as participants within specific work settings and then as citizens of late antebellum New England townships, coped with this second generation of industrialization.

8 Workers: responses new and old

Wage laborers in late antebellum Dudley, Oxford, and Webster had no single, systematic response to their workplace situations. As with the process of economic change in these communities during the 1840s and 1850s, so with the reaction of employees to the conditions they daily faced: evidence of substantial change blended with themes preserved from earlier years.

Yet often enough there did emerge a common denominator, for the behavior and attitudes evinced by several groups of local workers time and again revealed an underlying discontent. Sometimes the workers' unease centered around new issues or new antagonists or both; sometimes it focused on old adversaries and sprang from old conflicts never put to rest. But the salient point remains: To one degree or another, in one form or another, local workers frequently found their situation troubling – and reached for ways to resolve their malaise.

II

In the first generation after 1810 workplace conflicts had boiled up mainly within manufactories. In the second generation, cotton and woolen establishments continued to stand out as arenas of employer–employee joustings. But there is some evidence that in this later period laborers other than those in textile mills also began to express impatience with the status quo.

The clues lie tucked within the voting records of these communities. As an overall pattern, residents throughout the area bounded by Dudley, Oxford, and Webster shifted from offering up occasional majorities for Andrew Jackson in the late 1820s and early 1830s to supporting the comforting moralism and broadly pitched "anti-aristocratic" stand of Republicans in the late 1850s.[1] Between these two points, however, local election results took several curious turns. Textile workers may have played a role here, but the Commonwealth's persisting property and residency requirements for the franchise make it likely – even more likely than in previous decades – that the frequently hard-pressed, transient, and immigrant operatives of this period had difficulty qualifying to vote.[2] Even if the requirements were not enforced with complete consistency, the odds are that whatever employee discontent found expression in voting patterns was mainly the discontent of wage laborers outside manufactories.

The discontent itself was revealed, first of all, in the remarkable support given to the Workingmen's party. Running in 1833 and 1834, Workingmen candidates urged Yankees in all "productive" trades to unite (in the words of a party spokesman) against the unfair " 'monopoly of wealth and income in the hands of the few'," and especially against those few who were unproductive " 'accumulators' ": bankers, lawyers, and investors who provided capital but did no work themselves – men "who manipulated 'associated wealth' and, with it, affairs of public concern." The Commonwealth as a whole demonstrated little enthusiasm for the new political organization, and the party polled no more than 6 percent statewide. Here and there across the countryside, however, workingmen standard-bearers did better. These were areas where yeomen and even well-paid agricultural laborers resented the declining status of husbandry. These were also areas where workshop employees probably faced declining wages and almost certainly confronted stiffer disciplines and more "efficient" divisions of labor. These conditions, of course, were most likely common in Dudley, Oxford, and Webster; and in 1834 the Workingmen's party polled 21.4 percent of the aggregate vote in these three townships.[3]

But a more sustained example of local wage laborers using elections to express dissatisfaction is found in late antebellum support for Massachusetts Democrats. For the most part, Commonwealth residents were decidedly Whiggish in this period: Between 1830 and 1850, Whigs lost the state's governorship only twice. Webster and Dudley followed the dominant pattern, consistently returning majorities, or at least pluralities, in favor of Whig candidates. Oxford, by contrast, tilted toward the Jacksonian Democracy: Eighteen times between the mid-1830s and 1852 the town returned a majority for Jackson's party.[4]

Now it must be admitted that the doctrinal differences between Democrats and Whigs were not always sharp. And it should be conceded too that the Democracy (like both the earlier Jacksonian Republicans and the Workingmen's party) received support from farmers along with wage laborers. Yet in a number of ways – through their support of ten-hour legislation, for example, and their frequently articulated opposition to "special privileges" for business and bank-ing – Democrats at least *seemed* to possess greater sympathy for discontented employees than their more entrepreneurially minded rivals.[5]

Why, then, did the townships end up voting so differently? Some husbandmen and workshop employees in all three communities undoubtedly supported Democrats. But the inclination of Dudley and Webster to give greater support to Whigs probably reflects, first, the frequent inability of the many operatives in these townships to meet franchise requirements, and second (for those millworkers who did qualify), the strong pro-Whig pressure exerted by their em-ployers. (Following the bank veto, proprietors of Yankee manufacto-ries generally – and, in the case of the Slaters, adamantly – opposed Jackson's party.)[6] Oxford had its share of factory workers, as well as its share of anti-Jackson employers. The difference was that this township hosted the largest local concentration of shoemakers.

Although rarely committed to permanent residency in Oxford, most adult male cordwainers would have had little difficulty qualify-ing for elections. Equally important, they would have had little diffi-culty in deciding which candidates to support with their vote. Probably subjected to the same increasing burdens as other local wage laborers but probably also influenced by the example of emphatic shoemaker militancy elsewhere in the Commonwealth, employees in Oxford's boot and shoe trade could easily have felt sufficiently discontented to back Democratic candidates – and sufficiently independent to defy any pressure from employers to do otherwise. Not all shoemakers voted Democratic, of course. But it was almost certainly the town's core of boot and shoe workers that explains Oxford's persistently anti-Whig flavor. For it cannot be overlooked that the voting record of this community rather closely paralleled returns in Lynn, the capital of cordwainer unrest in antebellum Massachusetts.[7]

In the end, however, the ramifications of all these electoral gestures were limited. The constituencies generated by the Workingmen's party and Oxford's defiant commitment to the Democracy are both fair indications that employees of local workshops and stores were less placid than formerly. On the other hand, these employees do not appear to have ever gone beyond voting. More detailed workplace data might expose day-to-day efforts to lighten their situation. But there is no sign of sustained organization; no indication that even skilled workshop employees gave consistent local expression to artisanal culture or self-consciousness;[8] and no hint that anything these workers did – including voting – made much difference.

III

So it was that the resistance of local wage laborers, although more widespread, still found its most significant expression among operatives in textile manufactories. The records are far from comprehensive, but the evidence that exists shows plainly that Dudley, Oxford, and Webster saw no cessation in the tugging back and forth between millworkers and their managers. What changed were simply the elements of their interaction, as factory masters and their hands jockeyed for position in the context of new circumstances.

The continuity of labor relations within the mills reflected the continuity of the regimens mills imposed during these years. There was, throughout New England, a gradual decline in managerial assertions of "kindly and paternal interest." With competition encouraging a steadily heightened emphasis on efficiency and with immigrants (who were often judged poor candidates for "improvement") rapidly replacing Yankees, factory owners began dropping their claim to bolster (or at least preserve) their operatives' "welfare."[9] But in local mills, at least, this was a shift more in the rhetorical coloration of policies than in the policies themselves. In many important ways, the shape of life and work inside the factory compounds of Dudley, Oxford, and Webster remained basically unaltered.

Thus the guidelines for establishing both wage "bargains" and (as noted in Chapter 7) the size of employee rosters continued to reflect market conditions. Moreover, the work schedule in local factories (as in most other Yankee mills as well) remained six days a week, twelve hours a day, with each operative's attendance still measured (at least in the Slater villages) to the nearest ninety minutes.[10] And most workers still found their relationship to management bracketed by the impersonal discipline of waterpowered technologies and the formality of factory bureaucracies.

Outside the mill buildings the story was much the same. Although operatives generally continued to reside within factory enclaves, managers still only sporadically *insisted* that employees purchase supplies at company stores or take lodgings in company-owned boardinghouses and family cottages. Then too, although mill masters remained sympathetic to schools and churches – these were the years George Slater gave support to Webster's Methodists (in 1833), Congregationalists (in 1838), and Baptists (in 1841) – they still did not require the attendance of their hands at either daily classes or sabbath worship.[11]

The only formally stipulated deviations from previous factory regimens involved managerial decisions to raise output and permit
family members to work together. Even here there were precedents,
of course, for the East Village had begun increasing production levels
as early as 1815. Still, the increments imposed during later antebellum years deserve attention. Although data exist only for the Slater
enclaves and only for certain employees, it is clear that North and
East Village throstle spinners, who had worked "four sides" in the
mid-1830s, were obliged in the 1850s to "spin six sides" and "pick
[their] own waste" – that is, clean up fibers thrown off by their
machines and prepare them for subsequent use. Weavers in the East
Village Union Mill had probably also changed from four to six machines in this period. They were in any case turning out an average of
60.2 percent more cloth per day in 1856 than in 1836.[12]

The shift toward permitting increased family collaboration inside
the factories represented a more complete innovation. Management's
evident conclusion that kinship ties would not disrupt mill discipline,
perhaps combined with diminished prejudice against wives (especially immigrant wives) working for wages, served to render millwork available to some thirty married females in Webster by 1860.
Given their likely need to maximize household income, it is not
surprising that Canadians contributed the largest number of these
working wives: ten. The Irish, on the other hand, apparently felt less
need or desire to pursue this opportunity and had only eight wives in
Webster's textile labor force – a number shared by operatives of
American ethnicity.[13]

Husbands and fathers also became more common in factory rooms.
The growing number of slots available to adult males, again combined with management's new policy toward working parents, effected a substantial change on this front: The proportion of East
Village families with fathers working inside the Green or Union mills
stood at just over one-third in 1830; in 1860, 77.0 percent of all
operatives' families in Webster had fathers working inside a factory.
Americans had a slight edge, perhaps because adult male American
employees tended to be somewhat older and therefore somewhat
more likely to have families than their immigrant counterparts. But
Irish and Canadians followed closely behind, and together comprised
almost half (46.0 percent) of the 124 operative household heads.[14]

But it is what followed from this expanded population of millworking
parents that deserves particular attention. Although the evidence
does not permit precise figures for all local factories, there are signs

that parents and children actually worked side by side during the 1840s and 1850s. A sample of forty East Village families in 1850 contained eight fathers and two mothers sharing the same factory room with one or more of their own youngsters.[15] Letters arriving at the Slater villages, moreover, suggest that increasing numbers of workers *expected* to labor near their sons or daughters. Mule spinners from England (where the practice of using relatives as piecers had long been customary) were notably clear on the point: "I am an Englishman about six months in this country," wrote the "Spinner" Thomas Archer from Providence in 1849, "...and have my family here out of which I find my own help."[16]

Thus, what changes there were in the formally promulgated policies of local mills tended to balance out. If proprietors and their deputies pressed for greater output, their increased tolerance for co-working relatives must have simultaneously eased the burden of factory life for at least some operative households. In contrast to the vision of late antebellum Yankee manufactories presented by some historians,[17] the textile factories of Dudley, Oxford, and Webster disclose no sweeping declension into qualitatively harsher conditions and tighter disciplines. Still, declension or not, operatives faced pressures and developments they might have chosen to resist. Did they? Or to put the question more broadly: How did millworkers in fact respond to the regimen of local manufactories?

IV

In effect, antebellum factory employees undertook a balancing of their own: a reckoning up of factors and inclinations – some long familiar, some new – that together shaped attitudes of employees inside local mill villages.

Thus, on the one hand, despite the distancing impact of machines and bureaucratic regulations, some operatives could still feel personally loyal toward their employers. It is unlikely that any second-generation mill master exerted quite the charisma of Samuel Slater. But Nelson Slater in Webster and Dudley's major midcentury factory owner, Henry Stevens, may have come close. Moreover, whatever their feelings toward proprietors, operatives could still grow attached to lower officials: "The most important object in writing this letter," acknowledged a former employee to a Slater agent in 1855, "is to thank you sincerely for your kindness to me as shown in various ways and to let you know that I...appreciate it clearly."[18] Adding further weight to this side of the equation was the lingering perception that mill labor was not physically demanding.[19] And there was probably also often the basic but compelling realization that factory work offered useful wage-paying opportunities to unskilled and semi-skilled employees, including the female and youthful members of needy immigrant households.

Other factors, however, pointed in a different direction. In the first place, there remained a measure of disquieting novelty about factory labor. Even with all the changes overtaking nontextile businesses in communities like Dudley, Oxford, and Webster, no late antebellum workplace confronted employees with quite so many machines as manufactories. And by all accounts, no workshop or store was so large and complex that it needed quite as many rules or supervisory officials as did the average mill.

But the most telling contrast was with the activity that had changed the least: farming. Large numbers of local operatives – including large numbers of immigrants – had some experience with husbandry; and millworkers could in any case scarcely have failed to realize that agriculture outside the factory villages still followed rhythms and priorities distinct from those controlling textile mills. Precisely because of their machines, size, and complexity, manufactories – more than any other businesses – stood out against the persistently traditional ethos of local yeomen. Even for those operatives with extensive familiarity in textile establishments, the gap between mills and farms could only have made factory regimens seem less than inevitable, even suspect.

But veterans – and native veterans in particular – would have had other reservations. Although the order of late antebellum factories in Dudley, Oxford, and Webster actually juxtaposed new stringencies with new flexibilities, experienced workers were probably more concerned about the former than they were grateful for the latter. Bearing memories – either their own or handed down from other long-term hands – of lighter work loads in the past, veterans had reason enough to resent elements of the regimens they confronted. Such disaffection, moreover, was undoubtedly supplemented by the broad political suspicions still surrounding managerial claims of authority in New England: suspicions surely heightened when profactory writers in the late 1840s began defending Lowell (for example) as "a perfect *imperium in imperio*," "an absolute despotism" that was also a "most perfect democracy . . . [since] its subjects can depart from it at pleasure without the least restraint." And finally, of course, there was almost certainly the awareness among veteran operatives (at least by the 1850s) of continuing (indeed, in many cases growing) labor militancy simmering in trades outside manufactories.[20] Although none of this was sufficient to propel these employees out of millwork, it may well have prompted efforts to resist managerial pressures whenever and however they found possible.

These were all considerations shaping the outlook of local operatives. But the behavior of millworkers was also conditioned by the degree of fellowship they felt toward one another. Here again there were factors pulling in different directions. On one side were familiar divisive pressures: the short stints of the workers; their nightly dispersal through separate tenements and cottages; the fact that noisy machines and watchful supervisors at least obstructed – even if they did not preclude – communication during working hours; the continued absence of many (or even any) mill village facilities in which employees could meet outside their residences; the relatively few opportunities workers had to join in town society; and finally, the tendency – at least among operatives still linked to families – for broad workplace loyalties to become deflected by domestic commitments.

By midcentury, of course, there was also the corrosive element of ethnicity. It was not just that American and immigrant millworkers often lived and labored separately. It was also that immigrant groups frequently maintained residential distance from one another and in some instances displayed markedly different social organization inside the factories. Irish and Canadian millworkers, for example, often lived apart. And although the two groups taken together placed more children into the mills than did Americans, Canadian operatives included a considerably larger number of youngsters.[21]

The other side of the ledger is shorter. There is reason to suppose that some immigrants arrived already familiar with, and sympathetic toward, plebian protest and labor organizations. Certainly Irish newcomers would have known about – had perhaps even joined – the secret vigilante societies sprouting up in these years in response to the extraordinary inequities of the Irish countryside. So too, English immigrants had probably often shared exposure to the trade unions developing among British factory operatives.[22] Then too, the millworkers' participation in local churches – their one consistent excursion into town institutions – deserves notice. Undoubtedly making use of nearby Methodist and Congregationalist meetinghouses and certainly using the Catholic churches that had appeared in Oxford and Webster by the 1850s, the workers' demonstrable (though voluntary) religious commitment surely reflected and encouraged some sense of mutuality.[23] And finally, the expanding presence of veterans – whatever their ethnicity – infused into mill village populations the bond of prior factory experience and a shared knowledge of mill culture. But beyond these few centripetal nudges, there was little available to offset the fragmenting forces running through manufactories.

The behavior following from these divergent pressures and perspectives took several forms. There was obedience. In the 1850s, just as in the first generation after 1810, some operatives always, and all operatives sometimes, simply did as they were expected. Yet again this was not the full story. Facing what, by all odds, remained the most stringent work regimen in these communities, factory employees continued to mix docility with resistance and ended up opposing their employers more strenuously and consistently than did other local wage laborers.

The single most dramatic instance of resistance in this period was the turnout of East Village weavers in 1858.[24] Unfortunately for the workers involved, this experiment in late antebellum confrontation was as brief, unsuccessful, and thoroughly anomalous as the South Village strike some thirty years earlier. It is of some moment that willingness to essay a turnout had passed from skilled, male, Yankee woolen employees to semiskilled, female, largely foreign power-loom operatives. But the fact remains that for local millworkers strikes were still not the principal language of resistance. Nor (to reiterate) is there evidence of local operatives advancing meaningful support for the ten-hour movement by which urban operatives in the late 1830s and throughout the 1840s sought to shorten their working days.

Generally speaking, the counterbalance of tugs toward and away from militancy produced a repertory of gestures that picked up precisely where the first generation of factory employees had left off. Thus operatives continued for the most part to resist the daily rigors of mill discipline in ways that did not threaten their employment. Managers were rarely directly challenged by their hands; and although mills continued to burn down, contemporaries did not as quickly assume that workers were setting the fires.[25]

Less disruptive ploys, on the other hand, had not disappeared. Output data for weavers in this period leave uncertain whether these operatives retained their weekly slow-to-fast work rhythms; nor is it certain how "well dressed" women remained in the 1850s. But it is likely that stealing and sabotage persisted, and it is demonstrable that in the Slater villages absenteeism actually grew more pronounced. The average North and East Village employee at midcentury was on hand only 75.4 percent of the hours these two establishments were running: 2.5 percent below the level typical of employees in the

Dudley Woolen Manufacturing Company twenty years earlier and nearly 16 percent below the 1830 norm for the East Village.[26]

There are also signs that collective stratagems continued to play a role. To be sure, there was probably a change in degree. The atomizing pressures of the late antebellum era were sufficiently compelling that – aside from exceptional interludes like the 1858 turnout – operative camaraderie was almost certainly even more "limited" than previously. Yet mutuality by no means entirely vanished. The group exercise of insisting on attending funerals for fellow workers (but not for managers) persisted. And if evidence from Rhode Island manufactories can be applied locally, "lighting up" and "blowing out" festivals still drew large followings. "On... the last night of 'lighting up' for the present," runs a report from Woonsocket in the 1840s, "the younger operatives paraded the streets, bearing torch-lights and shouting at the top of their voices... [for the] little devils... [were] themselves just liberated for a brief season from within the walls of a factory. Who can blame them!"[27]

It is possible, too, that such joint energies sometimes focused directly on conditions "within the walls." Although insistence on "extra pay" for overtime work grew somewhat less rigorous,[28] collaborative standards for tending more and faster machines appear to have survived. The wage hikes in the Slater mills, for example, especially those for female and youthful operatives, were obviously made *possible* by simultaneous increases in output. But managers would have felt little *necessity* to pay more for more work unless they sensed that most employees – just as in earlier decades – shared a broad conviction that higher productivity merited higher recompense.

Yet once again the net impact of these gestures and pressures was limited. Much of the resistance that can be detected or inferred was (like stealing) only sporadic or (like absenteeism) productive of little qualitative change in the factory order. And whatever role Slater workers had in pressuring up wages would have proved equally disappointing, for productivity still climbed faster than pay scales. Weavers and throstle spinners (the only operatives whose output and wage levels are readily accessible in this later period) varied in their ability to get raises comparable to their expanding work loads. For both groups, however, the volume of work turned out continued to rise more rapidly than the level of payments received. In this fundamental sense, operatives at midcentury, like those of twenty and thirty years earlier, were still exploited.[29]

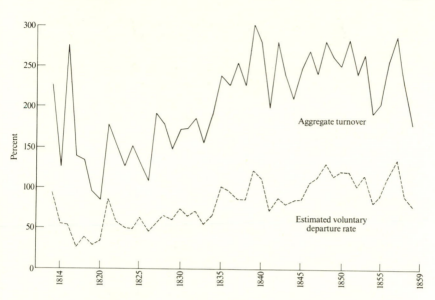

Figure 8.1. Aggregate turnover and estimated voluntary departure rates, Slater employees, 1814–59. Data cover East Village 1814–27; East and North villages, 1828–59. Consistent data unavilable for the South Village. (SC: Slater and Tiffany, vols. 84, 88–91; Phoenix, vols. 24–30; Union Mills, vols. 144–51, 155–6.)

V

The operatives also left. As in the first generation after 1810 so in the second, the most widespread response of millworkers to the conditions of factory life was simply to move on. But there were also significant differences. As Figure 8.1 illustrates, both aggregate turnover and estimated voluntary departure rates of Slater employees picked up sharply in the late antebellum period. Varying widely from year to year and also responding to fluctuating economic conditions, the former measure was nonetheless clearly higher than during the first generation after 1810. Between 1836 and 1859, aggregate turnover of North and East Village employees (the workers covered in Figure 8.1) sagged below 200 percent only three times and averaged 246.7 percent, nearly 90 percent higher than in the earlier period.[30]

To some extent, the increase simply reflected net expansions in the payrolls of these establishments: More workers were arriving because more were being hired. But as the second measure displayed in Figure 8.1 indicates, rising turnover also encompassed rising rates of elective departures. Taking the period as a whole, voluntary leave-takings averaged 101.5 percent, more than 40 percent higher than in the previous generation.[31] On the average, that is, *every* operative chose to leave within twelve months of his or her arrival. And they left not only the factory villages but the surrounding community as well: Only 6.3 percent of a sampling of operatives who quit the Slater establishments in the 1850s were still living in Webster in 1860.[32]

They did not even consistently pause for the four "enthusiasms" washing over this area during the late antebellum era. As in earlier decades, revival years showed no persistent shift in total annual transiency. Unlike the earlier period, however, the months following awakenings in this later era showed little tendency for voluntary departures to rise: Sometimes, in fact, they fell off. Yet this scarcely meant workers had been won over to the moral importance of "steadiness," for *during* at least two revivals – in 1857 and the string of "100 successive evenings" in the winter of 1842–3 – elective exits from the Slater villages actually increased.[33] Among employees in the North and East villages, at least, religion seems to have curbed movement less than ever.

Drawing on both census materials and Slater records, other aspects of late antebellum transiency can be quickly adduced. In the first place, operatives of American ethnicity and high skill levels (the two often overlapping) tended to move less quickly than did immigrant and less skilled workers. At midcentury, just as earlier, employees in better paid jobs appear to have stayed longer.[34] Interestingly, however, this differential was more pronounced among unattached operatives than among family laborers. Typically saddled by a lack of funds, possessing limited occupational choices, and desiring berths where at least some of their children might earn wages, immigrant households evidently found the economic and logistical problems of movement especially burdensome. As a result, foreign-born family operatives and their millworking children tended to linger on factory payrolls. Although taken together, non-American family and unattached workers stayed only about one-third as long as operatives of American ethnicity, English and Canadian family employees averaged stints equal to American family workers: 1.1 years. Irish family operatives actually averaged slightly longer engagements: 1.3 years.[35]

A further characteristic of operative movement in this period was that girls and women shifted around more rapidly than in previous years. Transiency had evidently become sufficiently routine that females felt free to arrive and depart roughly as often as did males with comparable ethnic backgrounds and similar attachments (or lack of attachments) to family units.[36]

Finally, illustrating at least one significant continuity with earlier patterns, kinship tended to retard mobility. It should already be apparent that by the late antebellum period the gap between the transiency of family and unattached employees was largest among immigrants: This is the only way workers of foreign ethnicity could have stayed as long as they did when co-residing with millworking relatives and still register higher overall transiency than American operatives. But even among Americans, domestic attachments sub-stantially curtailed movement, and considering the whole Slater labor force, family workers employed between 1840 and 1860 – like those employed in 1830 – stayed about 50 percent longer (and were 30 percent more likely to return) than nonfamily employees.[37] Indeed, perhaps reflecting the strengthened bonds among relatives now able to labor together inside the mills, the proportion of household heads leaving kinsmen behind when they exited from a Slater village actu-ally declined during the second generation after 1810.[38] This last development did not alter the fact that most operatives still traveled alone or in small groups: Despite the reduced number of fathers departing alone, families rarely moved en masse. At the very least, however, these data imply that the potentially corrosive consequences of movement on households did not grow stronger in the late antebel-lum era.

Yet none of these refinements should blur the central point: The second generation after 1810 saw operatives moving through the Slater villages in southern Massachusetts faster than ever before. Nor is there any reason to suppose these millworkers were exceptional. Precise turnover data from other local manufactories are not avail-able. But the fact (noted in Chapter 7) that millworkers in all three townships ranked among the most transient members of increasingly transient community populations[39] offers strong indication that the extraordinary restlessness registered by Slater employees was typical of factory workers throughout the area.

VI

What lay behind this restlessness? More specifically, what lay behind the almost frantic rate at which operatives voluntarily departed from local mills in this period?

For some workers, exits from local factories probably reflected nothing more complex than a distaste for mill labor. Just as in earlier decades, it seems likely that employees occasionally left manufactories simply because they were tired of factory berths and sought different lines of work. Given the rising proportion of veteran operatives, however, and again drawing heavily on clues from the Slater records, most local employees were probably moving on to other mills. The odds are good, moreover, that a number of them were leaving for precisely the same reason that veteran operatives had begun quitting local factories by the 1820s and 1830s – and for precisely the same reason that late antebellum millworkers from other factories were simultaneously heading toward southern Massachusetts. They wanted better factory jobs: "i am a going to leave heare," E. Chase, Jr., wrote from Northbridge, Massachusetts, to a Slater agent in 1850, "as soon as i can beter my self witch i think that i can sute you if you will give me a chance and i Should like to run that pare of mules over to the east Vilage." Two years earlier, P. L. Brightman had made crystal clear why (with or without his family) he wanted to leave the Massachusetts town of East Douglas: "I have Concluded to com if you want be Cause our wages there is better if you dont want the famely I will Com as a Second hand on in the Cloth room. . . We will come all or part of us."[40]

As had also been true by the 1830s, some operatives sought not only to find but also to create improved situations for themselves. So it was that certain workers in the 1840s and 1850s would agree to a shift in venue only if their terms were met. Thus from a woolen worker in 1845: "I shall be willing to change if I can make a Bargain with you to suite us boath." And nine years later from an Englishman experienced in "covering" carding rollers: "The terms that i should like to come for is those that you finde all Materials [for covering carding rollers] for Working with and Room inside the Mill state what you can aford to give a month."[41]

Women too, some of them apparently immigrants, sometimes asked that "terms" be specified beforehand: If they did not write themselves, they had someone inquire on their behalf. So John Dwyer wrote from Manville in 1851: "I want to know what weavers can make For there is 3 more that wants to go."[42] There even persisted instances of operatives fomenting bidding wars for their services: "I have not received any letter from you yet," begins a marvelously direct message a skilled woolen worker sent to the South Village in 1841: "Mr. Farnum wants to engage me for another year, and I should like to her from you, before I engage with him, . . . if you would like to hire me, you will please write me what you would be willing to give me."[43]

But amid the steady beat of this careful bargaining, a whole new tone, and an entirely new acceptance of conditions and constraints, began to characterize the operatives' transiency. For one thing, the inquiries workers sent off about jobs shifted increasingly from announcing demands to presenting supplications in a manner previously seen only in hard times. Although the change was most noticeable among less skilled employees, some highly trained operatives also adopted the new perspective: "I am willing to stay for but a small salary," a woolen finisher wrote "Messrs. S. Slater and Sons" in 1853, "and can in. . .3 month teach you the newest kind of twill cloth and Doeskin etc. . . .I believe this will be of great interest to you as it will cost you but a trifle to learn it."[44]

Other workers refrained from explicitly soliciting "a small salary" but were equally careful to avoid a priori demands. Another skilled worker, one Thomas Phim, attached no proviso to his letter of inquiry in the 1850s: "If you want a Second hand in Card Room I beg leave to offer my Services, believing myself fully competent of fulfilling the duties required." Similarly, an operative in neighboring Dudley accepted a Slater offer with no hesitation or quibble in 1855: "As I received from Timothy Shanly a letter letting me know that you wanted me to have me to work for you. . .as I am Extremely obliged for your offer. . .I would Except [i.e., accept] of it."[45]

An equally significant emblem of change was the fact that recommendations from previous employers, hitherto only occasionally requested or offered, were becoming de rigueur. Thomas Phim's application, for example, included the assertion: "I can get Recommended from employer." And even a candidate for an overseer's job in 1855 was quick to emphasize: "I can give good references." On some occasions mills evidently commissioned their own reports on applicants: "Respecting Mr. Carpenter he is a very strictly man," begins a cautious review sent to the South Village in 1840, "and his habits are good. . .whether he is a good workman on a Jack or not I cannot say."[46]

But perhaps the most compelling sign of the new atmosphere surrounding transiency was the workers' increasing respect for contractual time commitments. Now it is true that by the end of the 1850s only a faint shadow of the April-to-April work year remained. In the North Village between 1855 and 1859 most operatives continued to concentrate their arrivals in the spring. But a majority (51.4 percent) of employees released by management exited in the fall; and workers making voluntary departures continued a trend (well under way by the 1830s) of scattering their leave-takings throughout the year. Nor did North Village supervisors (or any other Slater agents) make obvious attempts to funnel the operatives' elective departures into a single season: Wage payments, for example, were persistently made on a quarterly or monthly basis.[47] Yet despite all this, worker transiency appears to have grown more manageable in these years because operatives were in certain ways proving more reliable.

Judging from the dispatches they sent Webster, factory employees were less inclined to "take French leave in the night." To a greater extent than at any time since the 1820s, they stayed for the period stipulated by their "bargains" – and their seemingly random departures thus often simply reflected the varying termination dates of their contracts. Or, at the very least, they waited – more faithfully than ever before – to "work [their] notices." So the Dudley operative quoted earlier admitted that, for all his eagerness to start the Webster job, he could not come immediately because "I [am] engaged to work for Mr. . . . alen hancock." So too, in November 1852 another potential Webster recruit told a Slater agent: "i found i could not get my discharge short of four weeks notice."[48] Implicit in this statement is his decision not to leave without a "discharge."

The hints are scattered and at best merely suggestive. Yet it is difficult to escape the impression that by 1860 operatives were experiencing less freedom in, and derived less leverage from, their transiency. It is equally difficult to avoid concluding that this shift stemmed from a fundamental recasting of New England's textile labor market.

It was a market that had apparently shifted in two ways simultaneously. First, it appears to have grown more thoroughly regional. Operatives had always tended to travel long distances before entering local mills. But in late antebellum years, as railroad and highway networks expanded, it is likely that employees drawn to these establishments were no longer restricted to southern New England but arrived from across the entire region. Such wide-ranging circulation, in turn, would have provided a final explanation for the generally upward curve of local factory wage rates. As the structure of family mill work forces tilted increasingly toward the Waltham-style model, and as the two types of manufactory consequently began competing for roughly the same kind of hands, the operatives' broadening orbit of travel could only have helped undercut persistent wage differentials between factories in scattered locations. Rates in small country mills like those in Dudley, Oxford, and Webster would thus have moved up, and the previously higher wage scales in the larger boardinghouse establishments of Lowell and Waltham would have been nudged down.[49]

At the same time, however, the labor market was by all accounts also growing more crowded. There is no way of knowing for sure, because there is no way of calculating how many people may have sought factory jobs at different moments of the antebellum period. But if the Slater correspondence is any indication, small country mill masters by the 1850s had grown less worried about staffing their establishments. As immigrants poured into the region, and as Irish and Canadian newcomers in particular made clear their desire for factory jobs, owners and supervisors of rural manufactories shifted from a chronic concern about finding sufficient employees to a prevailing confidence that there would be enough to go around. Agents complained less often that they were "exceeding short of hands"; and accusations of mills "inveigling" employees from one another fade from the records.[50]

These broad changes in labor market patterns seem to have encouraged an ironic blend of consequences. On the one hand (as already detailed), the money wages of at least several local manufactories did in fact rise during this period. On the other hand, the operatives' ability to move on without managerial approval and – equally important – their ability to win advantages by moving on had declined. As mills grew more certain they could fill empty slots, they were less inclined to offer inducements to get, or keep, particular employees.

Which in turn, of course, raises an obvious question. If late antebellum operatives found their transiency yielding fewer benefits, why were they more restless than ever before? Part of the reason was clearly that movement still produced a *few* concrete advantages. Even with the increasingly populated labor market, factory owners and supervisors were evidently not prepared to discount entirely the utility of wooing employees. After all, there were still *some* instances of operatives successfully transporting themselves into better paying jobs. And there are signs that management still felt *some* need to avoid stringent enforcement of all rules and regulations. Thus, despite its increasing volume, absenteeism in the Slater compounds continued to go unfined and poor work continued to meet few sanctions. Mill managers may have promoted, and surely applauded, the 1849 decision in Webster and the 1857 vote in Dudley to limit the sale of "spirituous liquors" (and in the former town also discourage "the Keeping of Beer shops so called").[51] But the two communities apparently felt little overwhelming pressure from factory proprietors to effect scrupulous enforcement. It is clear, for example, that at least by the early 1860s, and probably earlier, an "illicit" liquor trade flourished throughout this region of Worcester County. (It will be recalled, moreover, that Webster had permitted a brewery to open by 1855.) Bearing in mind that late antebellum temperance campaigns centering around Rhode Island manufactories were widely judged "a very broad farce," it seems likely that strict abstinence of local operatives was far more desired than required.[52]

Yet none of this can fully explain operative mobility in the 1840s and 1850s. Because the fact remains that even if it still produced a number of concessions, the movement of workers was less free and brought fewer concrete material gains than formerly. Why then did transiency increase? Once again the available clues are only suggestive. But in the absence of definitive data it may be proposed that what occurred in this period was, in effect, a transition from an instrumental to an expressive use of movement. The latter designation does not imply diminished rationality or purposefulness. It suggests merely that whereas millworkers by the 1830s were commonly changing berths to "better" themselves, operatives during the generation ending with the Civil War may well have changed jobs largely because the very act of moving was appealing. They may have moved, that is, because nothing held them to one place more than another; because transiency, whatever the constraints placed upon it, signified in itself a kind of independence; because any change of location, even if it offered no material improvement, was intrinsically satisfying.

Using movement in this way would have made particular sense to immigrant operatives – and most particularly to immigrant operatives unattached to households. Yankee millworkers like those in early nineteenth century southern Massachusetts may have felt cut off in their factory villages, may in the end have been regarded by nearby townspeople as distressingly different ("transient and floating") figures – all this may have been true. But such difficulties were heightened for newcomers from other countries. Even after different ethnic groups began clustering into their own residences and even after Catholic immigrants had their own local churches, the mill villages of southern Worcester County were still not home. Whatever their desire to counter the upheavals of international travel by nestling permanently into a new community, newcomers from other lands – especially those without domestic bonds – failed to sink extensive roots in the immediate environs.[53] Lacking not just property ties but also any intuitive cultural bond to the surrounding rural society, immigrant factory employees in hinterland townships like Dudley, Oxford, and Webster could all too easily have seen themselves as permanent strangers.

And also as thoroughly frustrated. In all probability realizing that it was their own pressing need for factory work that undercut their ability to win good bargains, immigrants may have felt blocked from improving their situation. Responding to such pressures and discouragements, immigrants would have had little reason to reject transiency and every reason to accept it as one of the few effective gestures of autonomy available to them.

VII

On the eve of the Civil War, the community of wage laborers in Dudley, Oxford, and Webster was appreciably larger than during the first generation of local industrialization. It was also more restive. Despite the absence of sustained craft organizations, there were indications that, for the first time, nontextile employees were responding through the ballot box to pressures and vexations they met in the workplace. But, of course, the bulk of this discussion has focused on millworkers, partly because more is known about them than about other local employees and partly because, in their own fashion, factory laborers proved especially unsettled. Indeed, if restive is taken to mean physically mobile, local operatives were positively volatile.

To be sure, there were limits to what millworkers would or could do. The rapid turnover of these laborers – and the consequently brief periods they had to develop mutual loyalties – was itself a serious hindrance to more coordinated forms of militancy. But the ethnic fissures among these employees were an even greater obstacle to broad alliances. It is worth noting that a later generation of Slater managers would judge the ethnic heterogeneity of local operatives as *the* critical factor in preventing labor "troubles" throughout the mid and late nineteenth century: "The operatives of [the North, South, and East] villages are made up of seven nationalities," wrote a Slater official in 1902: "This is a very important matter: the large number of the nationalities of operatives makes it well nigh impossible for them to act concertedly. There is no combination or union among the employees, and there *never have been* any labor troubles at these mills."[54]

The image of quiescence is, of course, misleading. Certainly, the ethnically mixed hands of the 1840s and 1850s cannot be accurately described as either calm or stable. Still, in concluding this analysis of employee responses, the issue raised by this agent's pronunciamento has to be confronted more directly: In the final analysis, what was the net impact of immigrants on the desire and capacity of late antebellum millworkers to "act concertedly"?

The question is a difficult one, and it is rendered more difficult by the conflicting historiographical discussion surrounding it. A recent study of Lowell concludes that the "massive entry" of Irish operatives into the mills of that city had a "dampening effect on protest" from the 1840s until almost the end of the 1850s. By contrast, an earlier investigation of factories throughout New England concluded that turnouts grew more numerous, if not more effective, during the decade preceding the Civil War.[55]

The local story bears elements of both patterns. Obviously there was no rise in overt militancy: The data disclose no upsurge of strikes, no rush to join or form ten-hour committees. Just as important, the basic feeling of fellowship among operatives – of camaraderie over and against their employers – had almost certainly grown thinner. Riven by the competing loyalties that inevitably arose among workers of varied national origins, the emergent sense of class that had colored local factory life by the 1830s was surely less palpable by midcentury.

At the same time, however, late antebellum millworkers in southern Worcester County were demonstrably finding ways to assert themselves. They drew on stratagems familiar to an earlier generation of operatives. And if the meaning of their principal weapon – movement – had changed, it was still rarely a neutral act: It still signaled, at the very least, the workers' declaration of their own self-interest. Nor should the decline in fellowship be exaggerated. Certain collective activities (as already noted) almost certainly persisted within the factory compounds. To the extent managers still worried about their mills' reputation, moreover, it was because they believed that operatives still shared not just news but evaluations of berths at various manufactories. And judging from phrases braided into the operatives' letters, the managers were correct. Thus (written by a prospective employee stationed in New York): "From the account I hear of your place, I shall be willing to change."[56] New lines of communication, stretching both along ethnic lines and between them, transmitted the messages ("Mr. Joseph Carter informed me," "Mr. Bates told me"[57]) – and simultaneously offered evidence that the ethnically diverse rural operatives of the 1840s and 1850s were willing to help one another help themselves.

But what did all this amount to? How did these divergent trends and characteristics balance out? Precise reckonings are impossible, but two summary judgments may be offered. First, local operatives evinced less aggressive resistance to mill regimens and managers by the end of the 1850s than they had twenty years earlier. The behavior of late antebellum factory employees thus emerged in counterpoint to the actions of at least some nontextile employees. Overall, operatives remained the single most unruly contingent of local wage laborers. But whereas certain workers outside manufactories seem to have pressed toward unprecedented expressions of independence (if only at the polls), mill hands demonstrated no advance into new forms of militancy, no expression of heightened solidarity.

Yet it is also true that a kind of evolution was taking place inside the factory villages. This is the second judgment to be offered. If the practical gains operatives felt they could win for themselves (especially through movement) had diminished, and if their ability to collaborate had generally weakened, mill employees were nonetheless stirring. Reduced but still significant, the efforts by operatives to push back – and sometimes to aid one another in these exertions – certainly deserve attention. Indeed, after sorting through what these wage laborers managed to do, the impression that remains is not that a community of workers had totally unraveled. Rather, the final impression is that a new constituency of operatives was gradually gaining coherence, slowly learning how to cope – and to some degree to cope together – with factory life.

9   Communities: "the greatest good to the greatest number"

The people of Dudley, Oxford, and Webster did not respond to their second generation of industrialization only as wage laborers. Many of them also perceived – and reacted to – the way developments in this period affected the social, economic, and political organization of their entire communities. Many of them, in short, responded as town citizens.

It was a response that took several forms. Occasionally, it found expression outside formal assemblies: in letters, for example, or in private debates between individuals and groups. Just as in earlier years, however, local inhabitants announced their views as citizens most frequently in "town meetings assembled." Of course, not everyone could join in these civic gatherings. Indeed, given the continued exclusion of women and (as noted in Chapter 8) probably the increased disenfranchisement of textile operatives, the proportion of inhabitants involved as full voting participants in town affairs was likely smaller than during the first generation after 1810. Leaving aside whether qualified voters actually showed up, property and residency standards likely reduced the local polity to, at most, three-quarters of resident adult males, most of them probably yeomen along with some artisans (like shoemakers) and business proprietors.[1] Nonetheless, town meetings were the arenas in which inhabitants most frequently and forcibly vented their feelings about what was happening to their townships, taken as a whole, during the 1840s and 1850s.

What they felt was by no means unaffected by problems encountered during working hours. Disaffections fueling support for state-wide Workingmen and Democratic candidates, for example, were often work related and were also, by definition, reckoned up in ballots cast by the local polity. Just as important, workplace sympathies and antagonisms – probably more often than in previous years – likely colored how at least some town voters came down on the routine questions occupying late antebellum community meetings.

238

In this sense, the gap between residents-as-workers and residents-as-citizens was far from absolute.

Still, it remains true that the topics drawing most attention from town meetings rarely touched directly on conditions inside local workshops and manufactories. Once more, just as in the first few decades after 1810, it was through debates over roads, taxes, and other community-wide "public" issues that the "meetings assembled" reacted to the implications of industrialization.

The reactions themselves were complex. There was acceptance and even approval of what was happening to Dudley, Oxford, and Webster. But there was also concern and occasional resistance. These last, more negative responses were usually less sharp than in earlier years and differed noticeably, both in character and intensity, between Webster and the two older townships. At the same time, however, the negative responses were palpable throughout the period and in all three townships. Widening out to embrace various nonagricultural enterprises but still focusing mainly on textile mills, they reveal a lingering trepidation among local residents over the emerging social order of their communities.

II

But an exploration of townwide attitudes toward late antebellum industrialization must begin by considering two fundamental changes in the way these communities regarded themselves. Virtually every issue – and controversy – faced by Dudley, Oxford, and Webster during the generation ending with the Civil War was conditioned, first, by an expanded and formalized sense of public interest and, second, by a refashioned notion of political leadership.

New England's rural culture had always embraced a conception of public interest. What happened in southern Worcester County in the generation ending with the Civil War was the emergence – in some respects actually a return to colonial patterns – of more extensive and explicit expressions of the commonweal and an inclination to implement these expressions through town government.

Consider once again the illuminations cast by road building. Moving slowly, and admittedly with some inconsistency, town meetings in all three communities had by 1860 largely discarded the postrevolutionary conviction that local highways served mainly private purposes and that residents "more particularly interested" in specific thoroughfares should bear most of their cost. Increasingly, as the decades rolled on, residents resurrected an attitude common during the early and mid-1700s: that roads could, in principle, serve a public good and that when they did the whole community should sponsor their construction and upkeep.[2]

The result was not indiscriminate community backing for every proposed road. Rather, there was simply widespread acknowledgment that the public utility of roads should be assessed and that the "public convenience" thus calculated *might* require the investment of town funds. Thus, in 1844, Dudley's town meeting rejected "a highway in the Northeast part of the Town...till something further may be ascertained as to a publick benefit." Webster, by contrast, determined in 1843 that "the travelling community" using "the road between the blacksmith Shop and rail road [Depot]" comprised a constituency of sufficient size and importance that the town should "remove all difficulties and fill up all excavations etc." on that byway. So also in Oxford: As early as 1835 this town concluded that "both public and private convenience" necessitated bearing the cost of a bridge across the French River and supporting the road over that bridge "as the Town Road."[3]

The altered perspective could make even county roads more acceptable. Since it was now conventional wisdom that *some* highways served the public good, it was plausible that at least *some* routes mapped out by county commissioners could fall within that category. Thus, in the 1830s Oxford – without apparent protests or reservations – had authorized its selectmen "to contract" for the building of a new county road;[4] and in 1838 both Dudley and Webster – probably seeing the move as a definitive reprieve from the irritant of tolls – "voted to assent" (in Webster's words) to transforming the road managed by the Central Turnpike Corporation into a county highway.[5]

There were further, equally significant emblems of broadened civic sensibilities. By 1840 both Dudley and Oxford had assumed responsibility for work farms. Webster waited longer, but by 1849 it too had purchased, and was administering, a "farm for support of [the] poor."[6] Moreover, in two of these townships fire protection came to be judged a community-wide responsibility. Dudley evidently did not take this step. But by 1858 Oxford had organized a "fire company" and spent at least $1,500 for a firehouse, and a "fire engine, as well as a hose cart and 300 feet of hose."[7] Webster had moved more quickly, organizing its own fire company in 1846.[8] So too, the period saw the construction of town halls. Dudley again demurred (continuing throughout the period to use its Congregationalist meeting-

house); and Oxford's efforts to announce heightened civic consciousness with a new building were complicated by wrangles between
northern and southern residents over where the meeting place should
be located. Nonetheless, the latter township did manage in 1839 to
raise a town hall, the first structure in this community intended
expressly for townwide governance.[9] Webster – with substantially
less turmoil – did the same in 1855.[10]

The area least susceptible to broadened community commitments
was education. On the one hand, there clearly developed in these
years a view that schooling was the responsibility of the whole town
toward all town students, which in turn implied an equitable distribution of resources throughout each community's educational system. On the other hand, there persisted the entrenched notion that
each school should draw support only from its own district. The
resulting tension produced what only can be described as baroque
funding arrangements. Webster, for example, decided in 1842 that
three-quarters of its educational budget "be apportioned to the Several Districts according to the valuation thereof. . .and the residu be
divided in Six equal parts and two of the above be given to District
No. 1 and one part to each of the other districts."[11] Using only
different fractions and criteria, Dudley and Oxford experimented
with equally complex formulas.

Still, the overall direction of change was clear enough. For example, townwide school committees, which had actually existed in this
region of Massachusetts as early as 1810, began gaining greater power
over district-based prudential school committees. By 1841, Webster's
central school committee received authority to enforce a "uniformity
of Books" on all town schools.[12] Fourteen years later the same committee wrested from district prudential units the right "to approve
such Teachers only as shall in [its] judgement be qualified." Also in
1855 – indeed, at the meeting immediately following its decision to
centralize teacher hirings – Webster responded to the pressure of
state law (and its own shifting predilections) by voting to include in
its new Town Hall space for a high school: a facility explicitly designed to receive townwide funds and draw students from across
the community.[13]

For its part, Oxford made several efforts in the 1840s to redesign
its school districts "to make them as equal as possible" and to achieve
"the greatest good to the greatest number." In the 1850s – again
despite intratown regional jealousies – this community too launched
a high school. Because it contained the Nichols Academy (which
offered free education to "all pupils of a certain degree of advance-

ment"), Dudley felt no need to construct a supradistrict high school. But this township had moved even more quickly than Webster to standardize school books; and by the end of the 1850s its formula for distributing funds had gone even beyond assigning a portion equally throughout the town. In 1858 Dudley began doling out one-third of its educational budget solely according to the student populations of each school district.[14]

As the towns began accepting wider jurisdictional briefs, town leaders acquired greater authority. The key figures here were selectmen. In a formal sense, these officials had changed little from the second and third decades of the nineteenth century.[15] They were still affluent: Virtually all selectmen elected during the 1840s and 1850s were drawn from the wealthier half of local populations and 76.5 percent came from the upper fifth. At the same time, they also continued to hold office only briefly (about two years during sample decades) and a considerable – indeed, increasing – proportion continued to hold lower jobs both simultaneously and after their selectmanship.[16] Yet amid such ongoing patterns, the role selectmen enjoyed within town government altered significantly.

They gained wider appointive powers. By at least the 1840s local selectmen could name a range of minor officials (Measurers of Wood, for example) hitherto elected by residents. By the 1850s, in Webster at least, selectmen also had the right and duty to replace more important officials – like clerks – who resigned.[17] Then too, it was increasingly expected that selectmen should evaluate the numerous proposals for roads each community received annually. If, during this period, Dudley, Oxford, and Webster indicated willingness to underwrite thoroughfares of "public benefit," it was typically left to selectmen to determine whether a given road actually did serve the public good. Their judgment was sometimes questioned. But usually, and with mounting frequency, residents accepted town ways "as laid out by the selectmen."[18]

And so with other issues. Although ad hoc committees did not disappear, local residents preferred in these years to rely on selectmen to investigate and act upon problems impossible to resolve in town meetings. Thus, in 1848 Oxford charged its selectmen to open negotiations for the town railroad depot.[19] Twelve years later Dudley voted "that the raising of [a] bridge" near a new millsite "be left discretionary with the Selectmen."[20] And Webster too, time and again, gave these officials authority to deal with a broad inventory of subjects "as in their Judgement would be for the best interest of the Town."[21]

Inevitably, given its enlarged responsibilities, the office of selectman also achieved greater status. Although simultaneous and subsequent service in less distinguished posts undoubtedly diluted their
prestige, selectmen seem to have regained during the 1840s and
1850s at least some of the dignity lost since the eighteenth century.
For one thing (drawing from Dudley materials), they acquired a
place to meet and discuss town affairs separate from the town meeting.[22] For another (drawing from Webster records), they began to be
paid. Amid a general firming up of administrative procedures (that
included the routine printing of town reports), selectmen started
receiving per diems. The amounts were by no means sufficient to
turn selectmanships into full-time positions; nor were selectmen the
only high town officials to receive recompense during these decades.[23]
But together with the sharply increased responsibilities flowing to
them, the payments awarded to selectmen surely signaled heightened community respect.

Indeed, taking all their characteristics together, late antebellum
selectmen appear to have achieved a rare blending of several different kinds of eminence. Certain wealthy men (as will be explored
presently) might still have difficulty imposing their economic interests on town meetings, and traditional badges of status – like church
pews and election to high militia rank – might remain problematic.
But to a greater degree than at any time since the Revolution, late
antebellum selectmen often – even typically – combined wealth with
townwide prestige and administrative power.

There were limits to the altered styles and structures of town governance. Law and tradition placed certain areas beyond the jurisdiction of community oversight and hence also beyond the authority of
selectmen. Religion, for example: The several new churches and
"enthusiasms" springing up in Dudley, Oxford, and Webster during these years all remained in private hands. Nor should it be
overlooked that financial constraints limited what the communities
as a whole (and their leaders) could take on. By midcentury, the cost
of public responsibilities weighed heavily on all three townships
(Oxford had to borrow $4,400 between 1848 and 1853 alone),[24] and
new undertakings had to be carefully scrutinized.

Yet on balance a profound change in both the perception and
management of town affairs had obviously occurred. Why it occurred
is tied deeply into the transformations the three towns were experiencing. As the nineteenth century advanced, communities throughout the Northeast attained a density and complexity that created

new problems or cast old problems in a new light. Larger urban settlements discovered that private solutions – to sewage, for example, or fire protection – were no longer feasible.[25] But by the 1840s and 1850s even rural townships had reached levels of demographic concentration and economic interdependence sufficient to promote a heightened sensitivity to communal responsibilities. As a result, despite the transiency and ethnic divisions characterizing local populations, broad notions of public good could be more frequently and explicitly cited by community governments.

There was irony here, of course, for this enlarged notion of commonweal did not connote an enlarged local democracy: The restrictions surrounding the franchise in these communities meant that the public good was being invoked by an all-male minority of town inhabitants. Nonetheless, there had been an important change. In the second post-1810 generation, far more than in the first, Dudley, Oxford, and Webster town meetings could conclude that roads might be "of public benefit," or that some schools should serve all local students, or that adequate fire engines were at once beyond the resources of individual enterprises and yet necessary to forestall the broad community damage threatened if those enterprises burned. And as town meetings expanded their inventory of "public" needs, the necessity grew also for an identifiable, centralized, and effective core of leaders to coordinate community reactions to those needs.

In sum, the late antebellum character of local governance, and the curious reversions to prerevolutionary patterns that it embraced, emerged in response to changes in the social order of the three townships. But it was equally the case that the way Dudley, Oxford, and Webster effected public business provided the vehicle through which these towns, acting as a whole, sought to place some limits on leading local entrepreneurs and enterprises. To some degree a product of the broad weave of developments that comprised industrialization in these communities, late antebellum town governance also went far to shape the way the three townships tried to cope with pivotal elements in the emerging industrial order.

III

The way they coped did not involve confrontation. The period was by no means devoid of conflict between town citizens and important business figures. But the communities moved through the late antebellum era without suffering collisions comparable to the rifts that produced Webster. In part, of course, that was *because* Webster had

appeared. Once Samuel Slater's grievances had received this definitive institutional solution, the most querulous protagonist in earlier
squabbles was silenced – at least so far as Dudley and Oxford were
concerned. But there were also other reasons for greater calm.

Some previously troublesome issues simply faded away. Between
1835 and 1859 no manufactory in any of these communities asked to
be "set into a Separate school district." This was probably because
those factories determined to have their own schools (at least five by
1832) had already achieved their goal, and others evidently judged
participation in a town district an acceptable expense. Similarly, the
transmutation of the Central Turnpike Corporation's highway into a
county road effectively ended controversy surrounding that thoroughfare. The Oxford Bank also disappeared as a bone of contention. Once nestled in Webster, the Slaters made no further efforts to
control or destroy the bank (though they may have still used its
cash-holding facilities); and Dudley and Oxford residents proved
equally accepting of the institution. Oxford's town meeting turned
to the bank for loans, and manufacturers Aaron Tufts and Alexander DeWitt served as successive presidents during the late 1830s and
into the 1840s.[26]

But a more important reason tensions eased off was the influence
that business figures, and mill masters in particular, now exercised
in these townships. Simply put, they could get more of what they
wanted and so had fewer complaints.

It is true such men were not always rich. A good number of those
involved in nontextile projects, and even a few of those backing
textile mills, had moderate resources at best. In fact, considering all
those identified in 1860 as "manufacturers" (mainly shoe and textile
producers), two-fifths stood below the top two deciles in local economic listings.[27] Nor did these individuals control local political structures in any absolute sense: Combining data from all three communities, nearly two-thirds (64.5 percent) of selectmen sampled from
this period whose occupations could be traced turned out to be
farmers.[28] On the other hand, the very wealthiest inhabitants *were* in
business – and most often they were in textiles. On the eve of the
Civil War, Henry Stevens headed the property rankings in Dudley,
Alexander DeWitt paced the list in Oxford, and in Webster shoe
manufacturers H. E. Bugbee and B. A. Corbin joined reigning members of the Slater family at the top of that community's economic
pyramid.[29] More than just rich, of course, these were also individuals whose establishments – again especially those turning out dry
goods – employed sizable proportions of local work forces.

Perhaps inevitably, the mounting economic significance of such men found political expression by the 1840s and 1850s. They could not always have any post simply for the asking: There were several instances of leading textile masters failing to win necessary majorities for positions they coveted.[30] But along with other, only slightly less affluent nonagricultural proprietors, the largest and wealthiest of local business employers received their share of high town offices.

Not surprisingly, the most extensive penetration of local government by major businessmen was in the community created by a factory master: Webster. Whereas the Slaters had served only minimally in Dudley and Oxford town offices before 1832, the new community, at least in its first years, saw active duty from its principal textile family. Up through the early 1840s, scarcely a year passed without John or George Slater standing in as moderator (chairman) of town meetings, representative to the General Court, or selectman. So too, during the 1850s, the wealthy shoe producers Bugbee and Corbin found places in the annually elected list of selectmen in this township.[31] The shift was less dramatic in the two older communities, partly because the inclination to elect farmers was more pronounced in Dudley and Oxford and partly because a few millowners (like Tufts and DeWitt) had won high office in these towns even during the first post-1810 generation. Yet the political involvement of entrepreneurs remained at least constant – both DeWitt and Dudley's Henry Stevens reached important posts in the later period – and even widened out to embrace leading shoe manufacturers: Oxford's Lamont Corbin, for example.[32]

Indeed, there are indications that such men affected town government even out of office. Participating in the occasional ad hoc committees still convened by the three communities, tacitly underscoring both their wealth and usefulness by providing bonds for tax collectors and constables[33] – in such ways, proprietors of important enterprises made their presence felt politically whether or not they held major offices.

But the final factor augmenting the aura of these men – a factor shaping both how they exerted influence and the reasons they could do so – was the evolving character of town governance itself. In the first place, the growing authority of selectmanships meant that any businessmen filling these slots could get results. But there were more general considerations. The acceptance of town officers who combined wealth, power, and prestige inevitably made individuals blending such attributes within their own shops or factories seem less anomalous, less threatening. Just as early nineteenth century mill villages had in some sense seemed throwbacks to earlier versions of Yankee townships, so the reversions in town organization to colonial patterns that occurred during the late antebellum era seemed to narrow the gap between local political culture and nonagricultural enterprises.[34] Even when business leaders "stepped out into the community," either as candidates for office or as participants in town meetings, they did not appear so vividly engaged in "tyranny."

Equally important, however, was the simple fact that widening notions of community good provided local businessmen with enhanced leverage. For if communities were now willing to consider individually sponsored roads and bridges as potentially suitable for town funding, then a central objection to Samuel Slater's earlier dealings with Dudley and Oxford fell away. Whether or not the townships accepted their petitions, it was at least legitimate during the second post-1810 generation for Henry Stevens, or Alexander DeWitt, or the Slaters to describe "improvements" they desired as also advancing the general "convenience and necessity." It was legitimate for mill masters to propose that their interests and the public "benefit" coincided.

This is why no explosive confrontation occurred. But there were still tensions. Dudley and Oxford in particular endured controversies – constrained but repeated – that reflected the unease local citizens felt toward aspects of the emerging social and economic structure. Put briefly, friction persisted in the two older townships because their residents would not grant business proprietors, including prominent millowners, the right *always* to dictate the public weal. If it was less worrisome in 1850 than in 1830 to see factory masters standing for selectmanships or to invest town money in "a road near [a] Factory," it was still the case that Dudley and Oxford were unwilling to act altogether as instruments of entrepreneurial priorities.

The two townships did, after all, contain a variety of constituencies and interests. To start with there were farmers (more, it should be recalled, than in Webster) who retained values different from those guiding many workshops and all manufactories. If the prevailing contrast between husbandry and industry could encourage operatives to question factory regimens, it could surely encourage town-meeting participants, including farmers, to gaze critically upon what businessmen, including factory masters, urged upon the towns as a whole.

Nor should the frustration attributable to nontextile wage laborers in these towns (and especially to Oxford's cordwainers) be overlooked. Their frustrations may not have produced sustained labor militancy; and it bears emphasis once again that these employees did not consistently shift town-meeting agendas from community-wide issues to grievances of the workplace. Still, within the context of town concerns, workshop employees willing and able to participate as citizens may well have found reason enough to spar with local entrepreneurs.

So conflicts arose. The issues were familiar: taxes, for example. In the late 1830s Dudley put through levies that, so far from corroborating Aaron Tufts' notion of public good, roused this longtime textile proprietor into a fury: The episode was resolved only after both sides had begun limbering up for a lawsuit.[35] In the period, as a whole, however, Dudley's most heated quarrels focused once again on roads.

The township by no means always or exclusively opposed business-sponsored thoroughfares. Several highways desired by one or another millowner or workshop proprietor were "accepted" by Dudley's town meetings. By the same token, highways rejected by the community (because the "public would not be so well accommodated") sometimes turn out to have been pushed by farmers.[36] On balance, however, Dudley seems to have been particularly wary of roads backed by businessmen. Systematic quantitative measures are not possible because there is no way of determining who had initially advocated the many roads characterized simply as "recommended by selectmen." But it is safe to say that of highways whose supporters are identifiable, those sponsored by nonagricultural interests excited more frequent and rancorous disapproval than those pushed by husbandmen.[37] For all its broadened embrace of "public benefit" and for all the expanded influence of wealthy business leaders, Dudley apparently found it far easier to equate its common good with the needs of farmers than with the needs of businessmen.

Episodes mined from town-meeting records clearly register the community's leanings. In July 1841 Dudley voted against a road desired by "trader" Moses Barnes.[38] That same year the town meeting concluded that, although county roads were not necessarily inequitable, the particular county highway requested by shoemaker William Corbin should be rejected. Indeed, the county commissioners had to intercede in this case (to certify that the road in fact reflected "common convenience and necessity") before work could begin – and seven years later Corbin met the same local response on another county road he requested.[39] But the most consistent opposition was aroused by highways urged by textile factory masters. "C. Y. [?] Fenner," for example, was granted permission (again in 1841) to "build a dam on [a] road near his Factory," but the town pointedly "Passed over" giving him the money he had requested to reroute the road. Mill master Perry had his highway petition rejected in both March and April 1845. The only way he finally won Dudley's approval (in May) was by reverting to early nineteenth century patterns and agreeing to share the cost with the township.[40] Indeed, even the community's most eminent factory master could count on nothing more: In 1858 Dudley granted a petition by "H. H. Stevens and Others" for relocating a road – but only because Stevens (again following an early nineteenth century format) consented to "give the land and fence it" free of expense to the town.[41]

Oxford's town meeting was no less prickly. There are hints, it is true, that the community-funded fire apparatus was purchased mainly to satisfy concerns raised by local manufactories; and there are signs that the volunteer company mounted to run the apparatus – titled the Col. DeWitt Engine Company – was firmly controlled by leading businessmen (which was why this kind of local fire organization did not follow patterns common in the period and develop into plebeian social clubs).[42] Similarly, a number of roads (like the one built "near the Factory of Davis Bartlett" or another constructed "at the request of [merchant] Stephen Prince"[43] clearly catered to business needs. Yet, once more there is evidence of persisting reluctance to always grant all that nonagricultural proprietors "recommended."

It is notable, for example, that the advice tendered by these men was virtually ignored during Oxford's turmoil over where to locate its town hall and whether to construct a high school. As already indicated, both controversies subsided with time. But while they lasted, the two intracommunity disagreements ran their course despite efforts of factory owner Stephen Barton to specify a logical site for the town hall and equally adamant efforts by Barton and shoemaker Seth Daniels to defend the public "utility, duty, and interest" of a high school.[44]

As in Dudley, however, the most direct barometer of Oxford's skittishness toward nonagricultural priorities took shape in the context of road building. The only way shoe manufacturer Dexter Bugbee got town help for widening a highway in 1849 was to "guarantee that the expence of said road not exceed $50."[45] But (also as in Dudley) Oxford evinced greatest hesitation over projects pressed by millowners. Thus in 1836 the town meeting agreed to "accept of the road" requested by two factory proprietors but only "providing" they agreed to "support and keep in repair free of expense to the Town the bridge over their Canal."[46] Moreover, the only county road to raise serious concern in Oxford during this period was the highway requested in 1851 by mill master (and occasional selectman) Stephen Barton.[47]

Dudley and Oxford were attempting to draw a line. They did not oppose storekeepers or workshop proprietors or even textile factory owners often enough to provoke drastic countermeasures. Given the number, wealth, economic leverage, and political weight such men now enjoyed, continuous community resistance would have been impossible. Indeed, it is likely that the growing dependence of the two communities on nonagricultural employment occasionally encouraged a broad range of town-meeting voters into the sincere belief – at least on some level – that the common good actually *did* involve building roads near a manufactory.

But this perspective had limits. Neither township was so committed to, or dominated by, business enterprises – even large textile enterprises – that it was unable to assess nonfarming ventures with a critical eye. The sparring back and forth produced by this critical perspective did not evolve into rigid community versus entrepreneur antagonisms: For some requests by businesses were honored by town meetings; and just as in earlier decades, business proprietors (including mill masters) often opposed "improvements" sought by brother manufacturers that they themselves had not requested. But the more important point is that, one way or another, the "improvements" often ended up rejected. In the final analysis, Dudley and Oxford town meetings turned down DeWitt and Stevens and Bugbee at least frequently enough to make clear that even leading businessmen could not always dictate the "common convenience."

IV

It was different in Webster. In a significant sense, this township *was* dominated by business and even by a specific company. It is true that the Slater villages were not the community's only nonagricultural undertaking: The range of commercial and handicraft establishments (as earlier documented) was in fact quite considerable. Indeed, the North, South, and East villages did not even represent Webster's only manufactories: At least two other mill complexes operated in the community throughout the 1850s.[48] Yet taken together, the three Slater enclaves unquestionably represented the single most compelling economic power in the township. Containing fewer independent husbandmen than Dudley or Oxford, and with more than 80 percent of its operatives – the largest contingent of the town's nonagricultural employees – listed on Slater payrolls, Webster found it difficult to avoid bending to Samuel Slater and his heirs.[49]

Signs of deference fall thick and fast from the historical record. It is surely suggestive, for example, that shortly after its incorporation Webster "voted unanimously" against a road requested by a group led by a man who, it soon developed, was feuding with Samuel Slater: "that little dirty A. Waters" (as Slater described the resident) who had "not yet removed the encumbrance on the wood lot which he sold to me."[50] A similar convergence of town and Slater interests is indicated in the town's acceptance (in 1842) of a road "Commencing at the East Village and terminating at the Merino Bridge."[51]

Even during the later 1840s and into the 1850s, when the Slater family withdrew from active political leadership of the community and other figures (including wealthy shoemakers H. E. Bugbee and B. A. Corbin) succeeded to selectmanships – even during these years the Slater factories found ways to underscore their abiding importance to the town and so encourage favorable votes in town meetings. In fact, it is undoubtedly precisely because they found ways to remind local residents of their influence that Slater managers concluded they could afford a lower political profile. So it was that representatives of these enclaves continued in this later period to sit on occasional ad hoc committees and to provide bonds for town officials needing posted security. And the Slater mills also persisted in wielding largesse: Just as the company had given land for the "public burying ground" as early as 1836, so it made further property available for Webster's poor farm in 1850. Such generosity could only have reminded the community that it stood to gain considerable benefit by cooperating with its principal manufacturing family.[52]

It is thus scarcely surprising that in 1848, with no Slater sitting among its selectmen, Webster voted to move its "Hook and Ladder House. . . to some central position near the Woolen [i.e., South] Village."[53] Nor is it especially surprising that in 1853 the "legal voters of the Town of Webster" wrote the General Court

> in favor of the Petition of Samuel Slater and Sons for Liberty to construct a Branch Rail Road from this Town to the Southbridge and Blackstone Rail Road in Thompson, Conn. and Respectfully ask that the prayer of the same may be granted for we believe

great benefit will accrue to this Town and the neighboring Towns
in this Commonwealth if said Branch shall be built.[54]

In the end, this petition failed. But the local support it attracted
punctuates the blending of public and Slater "convenience" in late
antebellum Webster.

It was, of course, precisely in this blending that the town disclosed answers to issues first raised in 1832 during the struggle over
its incorporation. Did Webster's town government fulfill the expectation announced by the General Court at the time: Did it serve as a
mechanism providing "salutary check" to the Slaters? Or did the
new township instead validate the prediction articulated by Dudley
and Oxford: that lacking the balancing "influence of a large agricultural community," Webster would inevitably succumb to "one
interest"?[55]

The evidence surely indicates that the latter concern proved more
accurate than the former hope. But it is important to appreciate that
what happened in Webster reflected *both* the emergent political culture of late antebellum rural Yankee townships and a specific economic configuration. It was because there were now throughout the
region formal and frequent acknowledgments that private undertakings might meet public ends that the Slater villages could claim to
serve the common good without having their assertions judged a
priori absurd. But it was also because these same mills were so
central to Webster's economic life – because, that is, there existed
few competing constituencies to offset their influence – that this
township so often (certainly more often than Dudley or Oxford)
ended up actually building "improvements" somewhere "near [a]
Factory." Both factors were necessary to create Webster's situation.
In Dudley and Oxford an enlarged conception of common good
served to provide a standard by which town meetings critically evaluated what businesses – especially manufactories – desired from
their host communities. In Webster, the same conception certified
the power of the Slater factories.

Yet even here, in this most mill dominated of Yankee mill towns,
the Slater compounds confronted murmurings of discontent. They
were never more than murmurings: Webster's protests were on balance more subdued and intermittent than even the nonconfrontational
unrest Dudley and Oxford residents mounted in these years. But
the town's disaffection remains significant simply because it is so
surprising. In cautious, occasional ways, Webster's citizens proved

willing to challenge factories and factory masters on which the community as a whole so obviously, and heavily, depended.

In the 1830s, for example, the town's "Weslean Methodist Society" showed little hesitation in facing off against the "Arkwright of America." Shortly after Webster's incorporation, Samuel Slater (whose son George had already helped these Methodists organize their building committee)[56] entered an arrangement to transfer Slater land to the society for its new meetinghouse. In early 1834, however, Samuel made it clear he wished to retain the church's basement in Slater hands. His intention was to rent this "Basement storey" to Webster as a "Town Hall" – and perhaps (though it remained unstated) in this way symbolize the new community's reliance on Slater family holdings. Webster's town meeting had no objection to the arrangement: It continued to gather within – and pay rent for – the Methodist basement until its new town hall went up in the 1850s. The Methodists, by contrast, were furious. Although willing to grant the town access to the basement for meetings, the "Wesleans" wanted (in fact, believed they had been promised) "control" of the entire church building.[57]

By all indications, Webster's Methodists eventually lost the dispute. But the group's feisty independence is still well worth remarking. At the very least, their struggle reveals that even residents using land provided by Samuel Slater were sometimes prepared to challenge him, directly and strenuously, to get what they wanted.

Another cluster of residents occasionally rose up to tackle the Slaters over the old problem of water rights. Despite an increasing list of judicial decisions favorable to manufacturers' riparian needs, Webster inhabitants could sometimes still convince themselves that certain practices of the North, South, and East villages were unacceptably selfish and prejudicial. "I am instructed to inform you," wrote a lawyer hired by the Bates family in the 1850s to Samuel Slater and Sons, "that the dam [belonging to] the East Village has raised the water above the mark fixed by you...The extra flowage therefore [deserves]...extra damages."[58] Then too, at the very end of the antebellum era, *The Webster Weekly Times* accepted a few circumspectly rebellious contributions. "I do not approve of combinations [i.e., labor unions]," specified the author of a letter to the paper in May 1860. But the long hours faced by Webster operatives gave this "Well Wisher to Both Parties" pause. Signaling virtually the only articulation of ten-hour sensibilities to find local public expression, the correspondent did not "wonder that young people lose their health and break down under the exhaustion of such constant and protracted labors. In my apprehenshion this is a matter for the gravest consideration of manufacturers of great wealth."[59] Given when and where the letter appeared, it is difficult to imagine its target as anyone other than the figure then reigning as proprietor of the North, South, and East villages: Nelson Slater.

The most significant demonstrations of autonomy, however, are found once again in broader community expressions during town meetings. In the first few years of Webster's existence (and hence admittedly before Slater's Whiggish leanings probably achieved full persuasive force), Webster residents gathered in their November assemblies actually gave Workingmen candidates stronger support than did either Dudley or Oxford inhabitants. And there was also some suggestion of the community flexing its muscles in 1854 when Samuel Slater and Sons (along with several other manufacturers sponsoring the project) had to waive "all claims for damages" to win Webster's collective approval for a county road.[60]

But the most vivid expression of Webster's willingness to challenge the Slaters occurred in a town meeting the following year. At that gathering, devoted mainly to bolstering the power of Webster's central school committee, a majority of town citizens had the temerity to authorize an inquiry to determine "if the children are so employed in the Manufacturers as to cut them off from such terms of school as they are by law required to attend."[61]

V

It is useful in the end to recall an observation made early on: that town citizens in this period had several reactions to the emerging industrial order. First, they were less deeply and widely fretful compared with earlier years. Webster presents the clearest case, for nothing this township did between its incorporation and 1860 signified pervasive or permanently effective resistance to the Slater influence. Just as the Methodists ultimately failed to alter Samuel Slater's plans, so residents vexed by sabotaged water privileges or grueling factory hours had little impact on policies implemented by the North, South and East villages. As for broader protests, the town's maverick Workingmen votes ultimately gave way to steady Whig support. And the 1855 query into the schooling of factory children, if it ever actually got under way, had no appreciable impact. No further mention of the investigation is found in Webster records, and there is no evidence that the Slater factories changed their treatment of youthful operatives because of brave words during a town meeting.

But the other two townships also demonstrated less explosive discontent – especially toward textile mills. The advantage of hosting manufactories were now more persuasive; the disadvantages seemed less compelling; and perceived through new conceptions of leadership and community interest, the demands of factory masters appeared less worrisome.

This was one characteristic of late antebellum community attitudes toward industrialization. But within their increased acquiescence the towns also demonstrated a persistent wariness. In a sense, their concerns were what they had always been: They centered less on conditions inside local businesses than on a fear that these establishments might exercise unbridled influence throughout the communities: that these establishments might in every instance get whatever they wanted. The structure of economic change was still sufficiently uneven, and traditional values and practices were still sufficiently resonant (especially in Dudley and Oxford), that large nonagricultural ventures – and manufactories in particular – continued to stand out in clear, sometimes disturbing ways. It followed that roads, bridges, and dams sought by such ventures could occasionally retain irritating or even threatening features.

There is evident in all this a kind of adaptation. All three townships were demonstrably reconciled to an increased presence of stores, workshops, and (above all) textile factories. But in Dudley and Oxford the determination to maintain some independence from local entrepreneurs had been channeled, not surrendered. And even in Webster, the far more overwhelming shadow of the Slater factories could not entirely prevent occasional assertions of autonomy among town residents or occasional resolutions passed by majorities "in town meetings assembled."

PART IV

Afterwards

On this 1st day of January 1866
I place this board under the eaves,
   I am a laborer on the Mill –
   I work at plainning floor boards

   My age is 18 years

   Perhaps when you find This here laid
   My bones perhaps will have decayed

Inscription, Webster Town Historical Society

10   *The war and beyond*

Dudley, Oxford, and Webster embraced the Civil War. Suspicions and divisions running through the local social fabric faded amid the flush of patriotism greeting Lincoln's call to arms. Military companies organized by leading employers (the DeWitt Guards and Slater Guards, for example) drew hundreds of recruits – including operatives and other employees – and were backed by hefty appropriations voted by town meetings.[1]

Some who went to war found excitement – even a vocation. Clara Barton, the 40-year-old spinster daughter of Oxford's manufacturer Stephen Barton, involved herself in nursing Union soldiers and ended up, some twenty years later, helping to found the American Red Cross.[2] But for many, the Civil War had sadder consequences and a grimmer aftermath. Something on the order of one-sixth of all local recruits died in the conflict.[3] And ultimately, as the character and geographical disposition of postbellum American business took shape during the 1890s and early 1900s, the years stretching beyond the Civil War revealed a definitive economic decline in all three communities.

In the short run, it is true, there was prosperity. Shoemaking became less important to Oxford and more important to Webster, but for about thirty years after the war textile manufacturing continued to buoy all three townships.[4] Thereafter, however, the industries central to local economic growth began leaving. Shoemaking, for example, lost out to imports or other, more efficient domestic manufacturing centers. Textiles lost out to the mills of the New South.

The departure of the Slater factories is the best documented of these business exoduses. It was also among the last. From the end of the Civil War up to the turn of the century, the North, South, and East villages did well. In 1865 Samuel Slater and Sons became a corporation (with capital posted at $500,000); and a decision was made to organize an in-house sales department instead of continuing the conventional pattern of retailing products through city-based commission agents.[5] Between 1892 and 1902 the South and East villages piled up annual profits averaging just under a half million dollars; and by the latter date the South and North villages alone employed some 1,600 hands.[6] Throughout this Gilded Age prosperity, moreover, the company continued to exert significant influence over Webster. There was a moment during the early 1870s when, in a delicious turnabout, Nelson Slater complained that the town was using his taxes on projects irrelevant to his interests ("in gross violation of justice and the rights of individuals not benefitting [from the expenditures]"). But by and large the Slater family and its mills appear to have still pulled enormous weight in the community.[7]

The early 1900s, however, soon brought difficulties. When Nelson Slater died in 1888, he was succeeded immediately by his nephew (John Slater's son, whom he had adopted), Horatio Nelson, Jr. But when this grandson of Samuel Slater died in 1899 his own son, Horatio Nelson III, was only 7. The company thus passed to the control of trustees – who, to the dismay of surviving Slaters, promptly undertook to sell the Webster mills.[8] The family managed to beat back this Draconian liquidation – only to discover for itself the need to shed assets. By the early 1920s, the competitive advantage enjoyed by southern factories (largely because of lower labor costs) forced Samuel Slater and Sons to reconsider its position. In 1923, the year Horatio Nelson III finally became president, the firm sold the South Village; four years later it opened a rayon factory of its own in the South. In 1934 parts of the East Village were let go. And finally, in 1936, the company pulled out of Massachusetts completely. In that year, facing both the Great Depression and the first major strike launched by Slater employees (aided by the CIO), Horatio Nelson III shifted operations completely to South Carolina.[9]

Today not a mill remains running in any of the townships, and only a few of the old mill buildings remain standing. A modern visitor schooled in an earlier era of these communities finds the most powerful links to the past confined to local historical societies and to local tombstones bearing names luminous from old records.

II

The story told here from those records has no simple summary and no single conclusion. But a line of sorts may be drawn under certain themes and implications broached along the way.

There is first the nature of the industrializing process. Although a precise, limiting definition of industrialization has been inappropriate to the analysis attempted in this study, it is useful at this juncture to identify the overall shape and range of what the phenomenon came to mean in antebellum Dudley, Oxford, and Webster. The point of departure in these pages has been economic, for it seems evident that local industrialization was tied fundamentally to shifts in the character of work and production. More precisely it was linked to: a trend toward increasing numbers of people earning their keep as free wage laborers, and distributed in increasingly large clusters within individual enterprises; a trend toward increased divisions of labor; a move, in some instances, toward new technologies; and, more broadly, a strengthened emphasis on profit as a central goal of economic life and on new disciplines to promote the efficiency compatible with profits.

But this is *only* the point of departure. The aim here has been to show that industrialization penetrated the northern countryside and that to measure its meaning the entire social order of rural communities must be considered. Different groups of people experienced different kinds and rates of economic change – or in some instances experienced little change at all. But such variation scarcely lessens the need to go beyond simply reviewing economic developments. In the milieu explored by this investigation, industrialization involved the rise of textile manufactories; it also involved (for example) shifts – and sometimes the lack of shifts – in notions of community good, attitudes toward leadership, and patterns of family life. The pace with which "Mr. Thrifty's" sons and daughters left his farm, the chemistry of town meetings – these were as intrinsic to local industrialization as the development of shoe shops and textile mills.

Even when focusing on the economic sphere, moreover, it will not do to depict industrialization simply as a unilinear evolution from one form of production to another. "Modernization" theorists to the contrary notwithstanding, the story of rural Worcester County in this period cannot be reduced to a neat, inevitable "progress" through time from "less" to "more" to "most" industrial: from farms and small, "competency"-minded handicraft works, to larger, more complex and profit-motivated shops, and finally on to cotton and woolen factories. The point is not that the latter shops and mills failed to emerge, for clearly they did. The point is that when they emerged they coexisted – and interacted – with more traditional structures. The coming of industrial order was not *only* a process by which economies moved from "old" to "new." It was also a process by which old and new were bound together, by which old and new proceeded in one another's shadow.

It should be apparent that industrialization in the southern Massachusetts hinterland was complex. It should be equally apparent that its complexity was powerfully conditioned by its setting. Industrialization in Dudley, Oxford, and Webster was not the same as industrialization in other locales. Certainly it was not the same as industrialization in urban settings – in Lowell or Boston or New York, for example – with their larger populations, their wider assortment of social institutions, their involvement with more and more different kinds of manufacturing enterprises, and often their more dense and self-conscious artisanal communities. This geographical variability is the final obstacle to assigning a fixed, concise definition to antebellum "industrialization"; but it need not reduce the rubric to nominalistic vagary. After all, historians continue to derive descriptive and analytic utility from "urbanization" even as they grow sensitive to distinctions in the development of different kinds of cities. What is called for is simply an awareness that early nineteenth century American industrialization bore no single face.

Such, in general terms, is how the industrializing process is treated in this study. As to the implications the process held for Dudley, Oxford, and Webster, the argument has centered on signs of friction. Because industrialization embraced a range of experiences, new developments pressed against – and often compared unfavorably with – institutions and values that remained customary or at least were changing less rapidly. The result was often ambivalence, and sometimes outright hostility, toward innovations taking shape in local society.

There is, to be sure, considerable irony in this response. For the same communities that evinced reservations about what was befalling them were also, simultaneously, providing resources contributing to new shops and manufactories: After all, the forces behind local industrialization were not entirely imported from outside these towns. This kind of paradox scarcely diminishes the extent or importance of tensions winding through local society in the years after 1810. Resistance to change was neither constant nor unanimous; it was only occasionally confrontational and could shade over into forms of adaptation toward what the passing decades were bringing. But in the end, concern about new patterns of life and labor stands as a basic element in the pre–Civil War history of Dudley, Oxford, and Webster.

There was not, of course, just one concern. The previous chapters have been at some pains to stress differences between: on the one hand, reactions to industrialization mounted by employees inside workplaces; and, on the other, responses generated by town residents, who sometimes were wage laborers and sometimes were not, but who in any case expressed disaffections outside working hours (most often in town meetings), and usually as town citizens reflecting worries of their communities as a whole. Workers – particularly factory operatives – focused attention on uneven economic rewards and unprecedented disciplines; now it is clear that workers did not push back in any single manner, but (again especially among mill hands) forms of resistance or at least self-assertion gathered around these workplace issues. By contrast, inhabitants responding as town citizens evaluated new businesses in terms of community issues. They were not distressed by wage scales or "rules or regulations". Rather, they worried about whether new establishments, and once more manufactories in particular, would challenge community norms too sharply.

It followed from these different perspectives that although the towns and workers within these towns had reservations about industrialization, they did not have joint reservations. There was no alliance – but this is not surprising. It was a salient characteristic of New England's rural industrialization that the concerns óf wage laborers and the concerns of town meetings only rarely fused into a common critique.[10]

And yet in one respect their concerns were always linked. Implicit in the exposition presented here – and occasionally remarked explicitly – is the fact that residents-as-workers and residents-as-citizens were both worried about power. It was the new power of the industrial employer (a power expressed not only in personal relations but also through machine disciplines and bureaucratic rules) that provoked factory hands. It was the unprecedented power that business proprietors (especially textile proprietors) claimed within community settings that disturbed town meetings.

This shared anxiety was not surprising. Distrust of power – "the belief that power is evil, a necessary evil perhaps but an evil necessity"[11] – had been integral to revolutionary ideology; and echoes of this view radiated widely across the sensibilities of nineteenth-century America. Indeed, it is fair to say that questions about the legitimacy of power exercised by large, increasingly interwoven economic institutions developed into one of the critical debates of the post–Civil War era. And of later years as well. In many ways we wrestle still with the problems first experienced, during this dawning era of American industrialization, by people who lived and worked in Dudley, Oxford, and Webster, Massachusetts.

Appendixes

Appendix 1   *A note on transiency*

Because geographical mobility, among both members of a given work force and residents of a given community, can be assessed in different ways, it is appropriate to supply a summary discussion of the manner in which transiency is – and is not – treated in this volume. Perhaps the most obvious method of calculating movement is simply to measure the proportion of people *not* moving, that is, persisting, in a particular group over a particular period. A low proportion of persisters (or persistence rate) implies a large degree of transiency and vice versa. This index is frequently applied to historical materials (e.g., see Robert Doherty, *Society and Power: Five New England Towns, 1800–1860.* [Amherst, 1977], p. 31); and I have cited this measure in Tables 1.2, 2.1, and in Chapter 7, II, this volume.

Historians have also used the notion of "turnover." The difficulty is that the term "turnover" is remarkably vague. Thus, it may denote the proportion of people who did not persist in a given group during a given time span; "turnover" would in this instance equal 100 percent minus the persistence rate (corrected for deaths and births as specified in Chapter 1, n. 59, this volume). A more sophisticated version of turnover defines it as a "replacement rate" calculated by dividing the number of departures or arrivals over a year, whichever is smaller, by the average annual size of the population being considered. (See Paul F. Brissenden and Emil Frankel, *Labor Turnover in Industry; A Statistical Analysis* [New York, 1922], p. 2.) Although she seems sometimes to veer toward the first meaning of turnover cited here, Caroline F. Ware apparently generally applied this second notion of the term to antebellum textile factory operatives, including those employed by Slater. (See *The Early New England Cotton Manufacture; A Study in Industrial Beginnings* [Boston, 1931], pp. 224–5.) The relatively low values she derived probably reflect the fact that she gauged "replacement" by comparing payroll listings only once a year.

A third way of calculating turnover is to add up the total number of departures from and arrivals into a given population and divide the sum into the number of people comprising that population – either the number of people at the beginning of the period under review or the average number during a particular period. This is perhaps the most commonly used turnover measure. (See Doherty, *Society and Power*, pp. 32–4; Stephan Thernstrom and Peter R. Knights, "Men in Motion: Some Data and Speculations about Urban Population Mobility in Nineteenth Century America" in Tamara K. Hareven, ed., *Anonymous Americans; Explorations in Nineteenth-Century Social History* [Englewood Cliffs, N.J., 1971], p. 27.) It is also, of course, the version of turnover I used (under the rubric "aggregate turnover") to measure overall transiency among both town residents and factory operatives (Tables 1.2, 2.1; Figures 5.1 and 8.1).

But because the transiency of factory operatives proved particularly important for my analysis, I sought to couple the aggregate turnover of these laborers with an "estimated voluntary departure rate." The rationale and methodology for calculating this latter measure are discussed elsewhere, as is the general relationship between shifts in aggregate turnover and voluntary departures (see Chapter 5, V and n. 35 and n. 36; Chapter 8, n. 31, all this volume). But Table A.1, fleshes out the picture by providing numerical values for the two rates for Slater's North and East villages between 1814 and 1859.

Final leverage on the mobility of factory operatives was provided by gauging the average length of work stints of specific contingents of Slater mill employees. I drew three samples of Slater employees: 71 employees working in the East Village in 1813; 207 employees working in the East and North villages in 1830; and finally a sample of 343 operatives (clustered around midcentury but intended to cover the whole second generation) composed of individuals employed by the East and North villages in 1850 and members of their households working before and/or after that date. These samples were traced forward and (except for the 1813 group) backward in time to generate the estimates of work stints discussed in the text. Derived from SC: Slater and Tiffany, vols. 84, 88–91; Union Mills, vols. 144–51, 155–6; Phoenix, vols. 24–30.

Appendix 2   *Tables*

Table A.1. *Average annual work force, aggregate turnover, and estimated voluntary departure rates, Slater employees, 1814–59*

Year	Average annual work force	Aggregate turnover (%)	Estimated voluntary departure rate (%)
1814	78.3	227.3	94.5
1815	100.5	127.4	56.7
1816	51.0	278.4	54.9
1817	55.5	138.7	27.0
1818	53.8	135.7	40.8
1819	71.8	94.7	30.6
1820	76.0	84.2	34.2
1821	87.3	179.8	87.1
1822	95.0	155.8	58.9
1823	89.5	126.3	52.5
1824	121.5	152.3	50.2
1825	130.8	131.5	63.5
1826	130.0	109.2	47.7
1827	131.0	192.4	54.2
1828	153.5	179.2	65.1
1829	167.8	147.2	61.4
1830	164.0	172.6	75.6
1831	217.1	174.6	66.3
1832	208.8	187.3	72.3
1833	207.3	155.8	55.5
1834	153.8	190.5	65.0
1835	161.3	238.1	101.1
1836	90.6	227.4	96.0
1837	135.5	256.1	87.1
1838	141.6	225.3	86.2
1839	176.8	302.6	122.2
1840	191.4	280.6	111.8
1841	185.6	198.8	73.8
1842	178.0	282.0	87.1
1843	191.3	237.8	81.0
1844	185.6	210.1	84.5
1845	254.3	248.5	86.1
1846	335.0	271.6	106.0
1847	336.3	241.7	113.3
1848	348.6	281.1	130.5
1849	360.6	262.3	115.6
1850	355.6	252.2	120.6
1851	390.8	286.8	120.8
1852	389.1	241.6	103.6
1853	393.1	266.3	116.3
1854	408.8	191.5	82.7
1855	444.3	203.7	92.1
1856	473.6	257.2	116.3
1857	412.3	289.8	135.1
1858	500.8	228.6	88.6
1859	591.3	176.7	78.8

Source: SC: Slater and Tiffany; vols. 84, 88–91; Union Mills, vols. 144–51, 155–6; Phoenix, vols. 24–30. (Data are for East Village alone, 1814–27; East Village and North Village, 1828–59; consistent data unavailable for South Village.)

Table A.2. *Population of Dudley, Oxford, and Webster,*
1790–1860

Year	Dudley	Oxford	Webster
1790	1,114	1,000	
1800	1,240	1,237	
1810	1,226	1,277	
1820	1,615	1,562	
1830	2,155	2,034	
1840	1,352	1,742	1,403
1850	1,443	2,380	2,371
1860	1,736	3,034	2,912

Sources: Return of the Whole Number of Persons Within the Several
Districts of the United States (Philadelphia, 1791); *Return of the*
Whole Number of Persons Within the Several Districts of the United
States (Washington, D.C., 1801); *Aggregate Amount of Persons*
Within the United States in the Year 1810 (Washington, D.C.
1811); *Census for 1820. Published by Authority of an Act of Con-*
gress Under the Direction of the Secretary of State (Washington,
D.C., 1821); *Fifth Census; Or, Enumeration of the Inhabitants of*
the United States. 1830 (Washington, D.C., 1832); *Sixth Census*
or Enumeration of the Inhabitants of the United States, as Corrected
at the Department of State, in 1840. Book I (Washington, D.C.,
1841); *The Seventh Census of the United States: 1850* (Washington,
D.C., 1853); *Population of the United States in 1860; Compiled*
From the Original Returns of the Eighth Census, Under the Direc-
tion of the Secretary of the Interior (Washington, D.C., 1864).

Table A.3. *Nativity of Dudley, Oxford, and Webster inhabitants, 1860, in percentages*

	Dudley	Oxford	Webster	Aggregate
American	73.4	81.2	64.6	73.1
Irish	13.6	10.2	13.1	12.1
Canadian	10.0	4.6	15.4	10.0
English	1.0	2.8	2.7	2.3
German	0.8	0.6	3.4	1.7
Scots	1.2	0.4	0.4	0.6
Others[a]		0.2	0.4	0.2
Total	100.0	100.0	100.0	100.0

Note: Nativity is here determined by place of birth. Because American-born children of foreign-born parents are thus counted as of American nativity, these data reveal a smaller foreign presence than do the ethnicity statistics presented in Table 7.2. Or, to put the same point somewhat differently, the gap between percentages of nativity and ethnicity offers an indication of the extent to which groups of foreign nationality living in Dudley, Oxford, and Webster in 1860 had coresiding offspring born in the United States. Because this gap was largest for the Irish (6.4%), it appears that the Irish – many of whom may have entered America during the famine-spawned emigration of the 1840s – had the largest proportion of American-born children.
[a]Swiss, French, Polish, Italian.
Source: MFCD, MFCO, MFCW, 1860.

Abbreviations used in notes

AAS	American Antiquarian Society.
A & B	Almy and Brown Papers.
Mass. Archives	Archives of the Commonwealth, Massachusetts.
Merino Records	Records of the Merino Mill and the Dudley Woolen Manufacturing Company.
MFCO, MFCD, and MFCW	Manuscript Federal Census, Oxford, Dudley, and Webster Townships, Worcester County (for dates indicated).
DVR	*Vital Records of Dudley, Massachusetts, to the end of the year 1849.*
OVR	*Vital Records of Oxford, Massachusetts, to the end of the year 1849.*
SC	Slater Collection (material on all three Slater villages located originally in Dudley and Oxford and subsequently in Webster).
TRDM I	Town Meeting Records of Dudley, Massachusetts, 1732–54.
TRDM II	Town Meeting Records of Dudley, Massachusetts, 1754–1794.
TRDM III	Town Meeting Records of Dudley, Massachusetts, 1794–1845.
TRDM IV	Town Meeting Records of Dudley, Massachusetts, 1845–60.
TROM I	Town Meeting Records of Oxford, Massachusetts, 1715–53.
TROM II	Town Meeting Records of Oxford, Massachusetts, 1753–99.
TROM III	Town Meeting Records of Oxford, Massachusetts, 1800–31.
TROM IV	Town Meeting Records of Oxford, Massachusetts, 1831–58.
TRWM	Town Meeting Records of Webster, Massachusetts, 1832–63.

Notes

Preface

1. This is not to deny, however, the extraordinary contributions made by several recent studies in the social history of industrialization. Only a few can be cited here: Edward P. Thompson, *The Making of the English Working Class* (New York, 1964); Eric J. Hobsbawm, *Labouring Men; Studies in the History of Labour* (London, 1964); Herbert G. Gutman, *Work, Culture, and Society in Industrializing America: Essays in American Working-Class and Social History* (New York, 1976); David Montgomery, *Beyond Equality; Labor and the Radical Republicans, 1862–1872* (New York, 1967). See also Alex Keyssar, "Men Out of Work: A Social History of Unemployment in Massachusetts, 1870–1916," (Ph.D. diss., Harvard University, 1977).

2. I thus find myself in sharp disagreement with writers who, observing the relative infrequency of "turnouts" among antebellum operatives, have deduced that "labor militancy was rare" and that textile employees "worked hard and for the most part without complaint." See Barbara M. Tucker, "The Family and Industrial Discipline in Ante-Bellum New England," *Labor History* 21 (Winter, 1979–80), p. 55; Anthony F. C. Wallace, *Rockdale: The Growth of an American Village in the Early Industrial Revolution* (New York, 1978), p. 69.

3. Caroline F. Ware, *The Early New England Cotton Manufacture; A Study in Industrial Beginnings* (Boston, 1931), p. 13. I should hasten to add that in thus distancing myself from one element of her treatment I in no way diminish the debt that I (and other students of the period) owe Dr. Ware. After fifty years, her monograph remains the point of departure for any serious discussion of antebellum industrialization.

4. Again only a few can be cited: Alan Dawley, *Class and Community: The Industrial Revolution in Lynn* (Cambridge, Mass., 1976); Paul G. Faler, *Mechanics and Manufacturers in the Early Industrial Revolution: Lynn, Massachusetts, 1780–1860* (Albany, N.Y. 1981); Susan E. Hirsch, *Roots of the American Working Class: the Industrialization of Crafts in Newark, 1800–1860* (Philadelphia, 1978); Bruce Laurie, *Working People of Philadelphia, 1800–1850* (Philadelphia, 1980). See also Robert Sean Wilentz, "Artisan Origins of the American Working Class," *International Labor and Working Class History* 19 (Spring, 1981), pp. 1– 22.

274

5. *Statistical Information Relating to Certain Branches of Industry in Massa-chusetts for the Year Ending June 1, 1855* (Boston, 1856), cited hereafter as *1855 Census*. For populations of the three towns, see Table A.2.
6. See Michael H. Frisch, *Town Into City; Springfield, Massachusetts and the Meaning of Community, 1840–1880* (Cambridge, Mass., 1972), pp. 1–6. Although a population of 2,500 is often used as a benchmark of "urban," this criterion makes little sense applied to communities like the interior townships of Massachusetts, where residents throughout much of the early nineteenth century failed to cluster into any single significant residential concentration. And the standard of 2,500 residents is any case arbitrary. As Frisch points out, "the population level" marking off cities "has been set at anywhere from 1,500 to 15,000 and up."
7. Ibid., p. 24.
8. In 1860, 61.9% of all Massachusetts residents lived outside municipalities with populations of 12,000 or more. Ten years earlier not just a majority of textile operatives but a majority (54.8%) of all Commonwealth inhabitants had lived in communities with populations under 5,000. Derived from *Population of the United States in 1860; Compiled from the Original Returns of the Eighth Census, Under the Direction of the Secretary of the Interior* (Washington, D.C., 1864); *The Seventh Census of the United States: 1850* (Washington, D.C., 1853).
9. Some initial efforts to explore the extent – and limitations – of changes penetrating the late eighteenth and early nineteenth century countryside may be found in Clarence H. Danhof, *Change in Agriculture; The Northern United States, 1820–1870* (Cambridge, Mass., 1969), and in a number of important recent essays: James A. Henretta, "Families and Farms: *Mentalité* in Pre-Industrial America," *William and Mary Quarterly*, 3rd ser. 35 (January 1978):3–32; Michael Merrill, "Cash Is Good to Eat: Self-Sufficiency and Exchange in the Rural Economy of the United States," *Radical History Review* 3 (Winter, 1977):42–71; and Christopher Clark, "The Household Economy, Market Exchange, and the Rise of Capitalism in the Connecticut Valley, 1800–1860," *Journal of Social History* 13 (Winter, 1979):169–89. See also Steven Hahn, "The Roots of Southern Populism: Yeoman Farmers and the Transformation of Georgia's Upper Piedmont, 1850–1890" (Ph.D. diss., Yale University, 1979).
10. See, for example: Hannah G. Josephson, *The Golden Threads; New England's Mill Girls and Magnates* (New York, 1949); Constance McLaughlin Green, *Holyoke, Masschusetts: A Case History of the Industrial Revolution in America* (New Haven, 1939); Howard M. Gitelman, *Workingmen of Waltham: Mobility in American Urban Industrial Development, 1850–1890* (Baltimore, 1974); and the most recent study, Thomas Dublin, *Women at Work: The Transformation of Work and Community in Lowell, Massachusetts, 1826–1860* (New York, 1979). Caroline Ware's study also deals extensively with the Waltham-style factories.

11. The preponderance of Massachusetts mills in rural settings has already been indicated. The exact number of rural mills using the family-style of organization at any given moment in the antebellum era cannot be derived reliably from contemporary data. After reviewing a broad range of sources, however, Caroline Ware concluded that "mills of the boardinghouse [i.e., Waltham] style were few in number compared with... mills...which used 'family' help...[And] their aggregate labor force at any one time amounted to somewhat less than half the total number of mill workers." (*The Early New England Cotton Manufacture*, p. 202.) Ware goes on to suggest that the greater prestige of the boardinghouse factories and the higher transiency of their operatives spread the influence of these larger concerns widely and made them "more important to the community." But even this may overstate the case. For although the fame of the Waltham factories is indisputable, the extraordinary transiency among operatives in family mills is demonstrated in Chapter 5 of this volume.

12. See Laurie, *Working People of Philadelphia*, and Howard B. Rock, *Artisans of the New Republic: The Tradesmen of New York City in the Age of Jefferson* (New York, 1979).

13. Anthony Wallace's *Rockdale* is one study that does treat non-Waltham mills. But Wallace in effect sought to deduce social history from an extensive survey of technological developments and management's intellectual milieu. The result is an important study, but one that is also (as indicated in n. 2) rather unmindful of the complex social dynamics that could emerge in family factories. A briefer, but in many ways more satisfying, treatment is found in Gary Kulik, "Pawtucket Village and the Strike of 1824: The Origins of Class Consciousness in Rhode Island," *Radical History Review* 17 (Spring, 1978):5–37.

14. See Chapter 2, n. 3.

1. The rural order: Dudley and Oxford in 1810

1. TRDM II, June 1774, p. 152; July 1775, p. 165; May 1776, p. 171. For Dudley's contribution to the Revolution, see ibid., April 1774, p. 184; May 1778, p. 194; August 1781, p. 230. Oxford's involvement in these developments is recounted in George F. Daniels, *History of the Town of Oxford, Massachusetts, with Genealogies and Notes on Persons and Estates* (Oxford, 1892), pp. 126–47; cited hereafter as *Oxford*.

2. The reputation of Oxford's General Ebenezer Learned is an example. See Daniels, *Oxford*, pp. 587–9. See also Samuel G. Goodrich, *Recollections of a Lifetime, Men and Things I Have Seen*, 2 vols. (New York, 1856), 1:22–23; cited hereafter as *Recollections*.

3. *History of Worcester County, Massachusetts, Embracing a Comprehensive History of the County from Its First Settlement to the Present Time*, 2 vols. (Boston, 1879), 2: 169–71; cited hereafter as *Worcester County*. Daniels, *Oxford*, pp. 13–14. Mary DeWitt Freeland, *The Records of Oxford*, (Al-

bany, 1894), p. 200. The 1810 population of Dudley was 1,226; the 1810 population of Oxford was 1,277. Aggregate town populations are taken from published federal enumerations. See Table A.2.

4. *Worcester County*, 2:171–3; 1:431–2.

5. Ibid., 1:434, 457. TRDM I, March 1734, p. 36. AAS: Webster, Massachusetts, Papers, Accounts with Indians; Ira Barton Papers, Accounts with Mashpee Indians. This spelling of south Oxford's lake (now Lake Webster) is taken from Holmes Ammidown, *Historical Collections*, 2 Vols. (New York, 1874), 1:461–2; hereafter cited as *Historical Collections*.

6. The proportion of landholding males is derived from the list of the nearly all-male property holders in the Massachusetts and Maine Direct Tax of 1798, New England Historic Genealogical Society (Boston), vol. 16, and the overall number of adult men listed in MFCO and MFCD, 1800. This calculation must be supplemented by the fact that 14.4% of the 354 residents possessing more than house plots in these communities in 1798 nonetheless owned less than the 24–28 acres commonly estimated as necessary for comfortable husbandry. (See Robert A. Gross, *The Minutemen and Their World* [New York, 1976], p. 214.) It is likely some of these individuals combined their plots with those of relatives but at least some were probably effectively cut off from agriculture. Indications that population growth was making it harder for residents to secure real estate is found in a 1771 Oxford list of taxpayers (apparently somewhat incomplete), which shows the landed portion of that community's population running 10% higher than that registered in 1798. (See Daniels, *Oxford*, pp. 261–66.) At the same time, however, it is important to bear in mind that (as is also revealed in the 1798 valuation) twenty-four landless individuals rented acreage. And it is also important to consider how landholding changed over the life cycle. A review of all extant probate records for Dudley and Oxford between 1790 and 1810 (on file at the Worcester County Court House) reveals that at death almost 90% of local inhabitants had acquired at least some property. Thus, although one in three adult men were landless at any particular moment between 1790 and 1810, most who remained in the towns did acquire some real estate, either through inheritance or purchase.

7. Timothy Dwight, *Travels in New England and New York*, 4 vols., ed. Barbara Miller Solomon, with the assistance of Patricia M. King. (Cambridge, Mass. 1969), 1:266.

8. Daniels, *Oxford*, ch. 8.

9. Derived from tracing merchants, craftsmen, and professionals (Daniels, *Oxford*, ch. 8 and pp. 255–6) to landholdings (ibid., pp. 292–363 and the 1798 Oxford valuation. See n. 6).

10. The average size of landholdings is derived from The Massachusetts and Maine Direct Tax of 1798, vol. 16. The average size of households was 5.8 in 1800 and 5.5 in 1810. Derived from MFCO and MFCD, 1800

and 1810. Because the federal censuses for this period list only the names of household heads and provide only the age and sex of all others living within the family dwelling, it is not possible to determine precisely how many farmers hired laborers to live and work with them. An attempt was made to reconstruct a sampling of families from the published vital statistics records of Dudley and Oxford and to compare the age distribution of family members in 1800 and 1810 with the age and sex distribution of the same households revealed by the federal censuses. Theoretically, this should have provided some indication of how many nonfamily members were residing within these households. The results, however, were most inconclusive. The great majority (65%) of the sample households appeared to have extra people living with them, but the excess household members were of all ages, rather than being concentrated in the 10–16 or 16–26 age ranges that would be expected for servants. Many of the deviations between the census listings and the reconstructed families should thus be attributed to problems with the data: underreported births and deaths and the relative carelessness with which the early censuses were compiled. Still, the *lack* of marked deviation between the ages of 10 and 26 does provide at least an indirect suggestion that hired male and female laborers, although certainly not unknown in Dudley and Oxford, were not altogether commonplace. MFCO and MFCD, 1800 and 1810; OVR and DVR.

11. For crop output and livestock, see AAS: Worcester County, Mass., Papers, 1675–ca. 1754, Tax List 1785, box 1, folder 2; Worcester County Valuation Records, oversize vol. 2 (cited hereafter as Worcester County Valuations).

12. See Rolla M. Tryon, *Household Manufactures in the United States, 1640–1860; A Study in Industrial History* (Chicago, 1917), pp. 145–6, n. 1.

13. The only nonreligious social organization of which there is record in either town between the Revolution and 1811 is a Masonic Lodge in Oxford, which ran from 1797 to 1815. See Daniels, *Oxford*, p. 249.

14. The presence of related households in these communities is apparent from the extensive genealogy supplied in Daniels's history (*Oxford*, pp. 365–753) and from the published vital records of both towns (see DVR and OVR). These sources reveal clearly the proliferation of (for example) the Davis and Learned clans in Oxford and the equally dense concentrations of related Corbins and Uphams in Dudley. The more general, if somewhat less reliable, estimate of noncohabiting relatives cited in the text is based on the fact that 97 (21.2%) of the household heads listed in the 1810 manuscript censuses of these townships shared their last names with at least one other household. Obviously, this measure includes people who were not kin and excludes some who were. But it probably provides at least a rough index of noncohabiting relatives. See MFCO and MFCD, 1810.

15. The "berrying parties" and "husking bees" are cited in Nathaniel S. Dodge [John Carver], *Sketches of New England or Memories of the Country* (New York, 1842), p. 13. For comments on "helping," see, for example, AAS: Parker Family Papers, James Parker Diary (1825–9). The building song is found in Benjamin A. Botkin, *A Treasury of New England Folklore; Stories, Ballads, and Traditions of the Yankee People* (New York, 1947), p. 677.

16. Derived from Jeremiah Davis, Account Book, 1787–1822, and Edward K. Wolcott, Ledger and Cash Book, 1774–96, both in Baker Library, Harvard University. Also derived from AAS: Josiah Dean, Account Book, 1804–26; David Nichols and Sons, in Dudley, Mass., Town Records, 1740–1932. See also Daniels, *Oxford*, pp. 237–8.

17. About 80% of local households owned spinning wheels; some 62% owned looms. Derived from surveying Probate Records, 1790–1840, Worcester County Court House. The classic study of household manufacture in this period estimates that in 1810 Worcester County families were producing annually 840,000 yards of cloth, worth a half million dollars. See Tryon, *Household Manufactures in the United States*, p. 170. For a description of household cloth production in Oxford see Freeland, *The Records of Oxford*, pp. 329–30.

18. See AAS: Oxford, Massachusetts, General Store Account Book, 1817–18; David Nichols and Sons, in Dudley, Mass., Town Records, 1740–1932.

19. Colonial Currency Reprints, II, p. 186, quoted in Richard L. Bushman, *From Puritan to Yankee; Character and the Social Order in Connecticut, 1690–1765* (Cambridge, Mass., 1967), p. 27. See James A. Henretta, "Families and Farms: *Mentalité* in Pre-Industrial America," *William and Mary Quarterly*, 3rd ser. 35 (January 1978):3–32. Michael Merrill, "Cash Is Good to Eat: Self-Sufficiency and Exchange in the Rural Economy of the United States," *Radical History Review* 3 (Winter, 1977):42–71.

20. Thomas Jefferson, *Notes on the State of Virginia*, ed., with an introduction and notes by William Peden (Chapel Hill, 1954), p. 165. See also *Plough Boy*, June 1819.

21. Daniels, *Oxford*, pp. 148–9. See David P. Szatmary, *Shays' Rebellion: The Making of an Agrarian Insurrection* (Amherst, 1980).

22. Clarence H. Danhof, *Change in Agriculture: The Northern United States, 1820–1870* (Cambridge, Mass., 1969), p. 17. See also Christopher Clark, "The Household Economy, Market Exchange, and the Rise of Capitalism in the Connecticut Valley, 1800–1860," *Journal of Social History* 13 (Winter, 1979):169–89, esp. p. 176.

23. The evidence here is admittedly largely negative: the absence of recorded conflicts between townspeople over riparian usage. For a general discussion of friction, or the lack of it, over water usage in preindustrial New England, see Gary Kulik, "Opposition to Dam Building: Farmers, Artisans, and Capitalists and the Politics of Water

Rights in the Eighteenth Century" (Paper presented to Smith College Symposium on the "New" New England Working Class History, 1979). In his *Transformation of American Law, 1780–1860* (Cambridge, 1977), Morton J. Horwitz suggests that the conflicts over water rights in the eighteenth century paled in comparison to subsequent battles. See ibid., p. 35, and p. 274, n. 5: "Though there had been controversies involving diversion of water for irrigation or saw and grist mills in the colonial period, the rise of large New England cotton mills after 1815 intensified the conflict."

24. Derived from Probate Records, 1790–1810, Worcester County Court House.

25. Jeremiah Davis, Account Book, 1787–1822, and Edward K. Wolcott, Ledger and Cash Book, 1774–96, both in Baker Library, Harvard University. Also AAS: Oxford, Massachusetts, General Store Account Book, 1817–18.

26. AAS: Worcester County, Mass., Papers, J. P. Aaron Tufts, Record Book, 1801–17, folio vol. 8. In 1801–2, as justice of the peace, Tufts heard nineteen cases involving Dudley and Oxford residents; in 1815 he heard thirty-seven. The cases were often over small amounts of money and involved rich and poor citizens standing as both creditors and debtors. For a description of insolvency cases during the 1790s, see Daniels, *Oxford*, p. 148.

27. Although containing no separate data on landholding, the 1815 valuation (AAS: Worcester County, Mass., Papers, 1815 Valuation, folio vol. 14) remains, with the 1798 valuation, a valuable source on wealth distribution in these townships. In 1798, the richest 10% in the two towns controlled 32.8% of the total community wealth. (Massachusetts and Maine Direct Tax of 1798, vol. 16.) In 1815, the figure stood at 30.2%. Carriage ownership is cited in AAS: Worcester County, Mass., Papers, Account Book of Vehicles Taxed in Worcester County, 1796 and 1801, oversize manuscript box. Half the wealthiest quartile had some involvement in nonagricultural ventures.

28. More than half (51.8%) the residents who owed money when they died were also creditors to residents of their towns. Derived from Probate Records, 1790–1810, Worcester County Court House.

29. See Goodrich, *Recollections*, 1:84.

30. For a thoughtful and provocative, although somewhat schematic, effort to provide such a label, see Merrill's analysis in "Cash Is Good to Eat," pp. 42–71.

31. Derived from Probate Records, 1790–1810, Worcester County Court House. See also Peter F. Copeland, *Working Dress in Colonial and Revolutionary America* (Westport, Conn., 1977), ch. 2.

32. Derived from Jeremiah Davis, Account Book, 1787–1822; Edward K. Wolcott, Ledger and Cash Book, 1774–1796, both in Baker Library, Harvard University. Also AAS: Oxford, Massachusetts, General Store Account Book, 1817–18. Crop output derived from AAS: Worcester

County, Mass., Papers, 1785 Tax List, box 1, folder 2; Worcester County Valuations. See also Gross, *The Minutemen and Their World*, pp. 85–6. William J. Rorabaugh, *The Alcoholic Republic, An American Tradition* (New York, 1979), ch. 1.

33. Daniels, *Oxford*, p. 213 and ch. 8. See Martha Zimiles and Murray Zimiles, *Early American Mills* (New York, 1973), ch. 1.

34. Between 1785 and 1811, the ratio of improved to unimproved acreage in these townships increased from .366 to 1.5 with most of the expansion registered in new fields opened up for pasture. Derived from AAS: Worcester County, Mass., Papers, 1785 Tax List, box 1, folder 2; Worcester County Valuations.

35. Ibid. English hay comprised 23.0% of the total hay crop of these towns in 1801, 30.1% in 1811. Bushels of grain per acre of tillage fell slightly between 1801 and 1811: from 23.0 to 22.2; tons of hay per acre of meadowland remained fixed at .74. Because of the expanded acreage in use, however, the total output of the towns (bushels of grain and tons of hay) rose 3.2% between 1801 and 1811. The number of cows remained fairly constant: 1,992 in 1801 and 1,827 in 1811.

36. Tools used by local farmers are cited in Probate Records, 1790–1810, Worcester County Court House. See also Percy W. Bidwell and John I. Falconer, *History of Agriculture in the Northern United States, 1620–1860* (Washington, D.C., 1925), pp. 90–1, 123–6. Criticism of Yankee farmers is found in Dwight, *Travels in New England and New York*, 1:76. For comments on the customary division of labor, see ibid., 3:142.

37. TROM I, January 1717, p. 10; TRDM I, November 1732, p. 10.

38. Jeremiah Davis, Account Book, 1787–1822, Baker Library, Harvard University. TROM III, April 1802, p. 25. TRDM III, March 1803, p. 102.

39. Town elections were typically held in March; annual budgets and assessments were passed in April.

40. See Joseph F. Kett, "Growing Up in Rural New England, 1800–1840" in Tamara K. Hareven, ed., *Anonymous Americans; Explorations in Nineteenth-Century Social History* (Englewood Cliffs, 1971), pp. 6–10. See also Oscar Handlin and Mary F. Handlin, *Facing Life; Youth and Family in American History* (Boston, 1971), pp. 76–91. Freeland, *The Records of Oxford*, p. 226.

41. Goodrich, *Recollections*, 1:317. Surviving records do not reveal whether local yeomen succumbed to such temptations; they do reveal, however, an annual shift in labor costs that denoted at least the assumption of increased leisure time in the winter. In Oxford in 1801 highway work was pegged at "67 cents per day from the first day of May to the 15th of September, the other parts of the year at 42 cents per day." See TROM III, March 1801, p. 2.

42. Dodge, *Sketches of New England*, pp. 24–6. Goodrich, *Recollections*, 1:86. James Montgomery, *A Practical Detail of the Cotton Manufacture of the United States of America* (Glasgow, 1840), pp. 177–8.

43. Dodge, *Sketches of New England*, p. 15. Dwight, *Travels in New England and New York*, 2:17; 3:42, 334. AAS: Worcester County, Mass., Papers, Court Records, 1675–1864, box 2, folder 7: "March 9, 1792, [four men] did labour and do Business and work on the Lord's Day." Some farmers solved the tensions between religious and economic priorities by working on the sabbath themselves but allowing their hired help to rest. See AAS: Parker Family Papers, James Parker Diary (1825–9).

44. Goodrich, *Recollections*, 1:69. William R. Lawrence, ed., *Extracts from the Diary and Correspondence of the Late Amos Lawrence; with a Brief Account of Some Incidents in His Life* (New York, 1855), pp. 24–6. Patrick Shirreff, *A Tour Through North America; Together with a Comprehensive View of the Canadas and the United States as Adapted for Agricultural Emigration* (Edinburgh, 1835, reprinted, 1971), p. 25. See also Edward P. Thompson, "Time, Work-Discipline, and Industrial Capitalism," *Past and Present* 38 (December 1967):56–97.

45. Distribution of clocks derived from probate records, 1790–1810; see also Carl W. Drepperd, *American Clocks and Clockmakers* (New York, 1947), pp. 24, 76–9.

46. Records of Oxford School District No. 6, 1806–31 (Genealogical Library, microfilm 4694), June 1808 (n.p.), May 1809. Oxford Orders, Receipts, Agreements (Genealogical Library, microfilm 859254), 1796 (n.p.).

47. For a general discussion of eighteenth-century social change focusing largely on New England, see Kenneth A. Lockridge, "Social Change and the Meaning of the American Revolution," *Journal of Social History* 6 (Summer, 1973):403–39.

48. Bushman, *From Puritan to Yankee*, ch. 4. Kenneth A. Lockridge, *A New England Town: The First Hundred Years, Dedham, Massachusetts, 1636–1736* (New York, 1970), ch. 6.

49. Another less serious cause of disruption related to the location of schoolhouses. It was not at all rare in the early nineteenth century for those on the outskirts of Dudley and Oxford to ask permission to "draw out" their school taxes to the adjoining towns of Sturbridge, Charlton, or Douglas simply because of the convenient location of the schoolhouses established by these communities. Ultimately, this practice created so many fiscal and administrative problems that it was prohibited. But it never offered more than an indirect challenge to the notion of town citizenship. See, for example, TROM III, May 1818, p. 182.

50. TRDM I (n.d.), p. 5. Daniels, *Oxford*, pp. 39–41, 53. TROM III, April 1807, p. 73; May 1807, p. 76; October 1807, p. 80. It is also true that Oxford annexed land from neighboring communities.

51. TRDM I, November-December 1733 [sic], pp. 28–30. TRDM III, January 1799, p. 72; November 1814, p. 216; January 1815, p. 220. AAS: Dudley, Mass., Town Records, 1740–1932, Petition, 1796, Oversize vol. 1. *Historical Collections*, 1:419.

52. See, generally, William G. McLoughlin, *New England Dissent, 1630–1833; The Baptists and the Separation of Church and State*, 2 vols. (Cambridge, Mass. 1971), esp. 1: pts. 3–8; 2: pt. 9.

53. Ammidown, *Historical Collections*, 1:221–5, 442–9. TRDM II, May 1772, p. 139. Daniels, *Oxford*, p. 53. TROM II, October 1791, pp. 298–9. The number of churchgoers in these communities is not certain. Besides the estimate of Oxford Universalists cited in the text, the only firm reckoning I have found (Ammidown, *Historical Collections*, pp. 442–3) indicates seventy-one Dudley Congregationalists in 1797.

54. Ammidown, *Historical Collections*, 1:444–7; TRDM II, June 1790, pp. 333–4. TROM II, October 1791, p. 298.

55. Although Dudley's town meeting continued to wrestle for some time with paying off a "dismissed" Congregationalist minister, its growing inclination to leave virtually all religious affairs to individual societies is evident from meetings in the fall and winter of 1795–6, and from the fact that, save for the debt to the departed minister, the town did not subsequently collectively concern itself with the Standing Order. See TRDM III, November-December 1796, pp. 55–8. For Oxford, see TROM III, March 1813, p. 133; May 1813, pp. 137–8. See also Ammidown, *Historical Collections* 1:214, 442–3.

56. Daniels, *Oxford*, p. 60, n. 1. AAS: Josiah Dean, Account Book, 1804–26, entry for 1825. Botkin, *A Treasury of New England Folklore*, p. 600. *Worcester County*, 1:435. Ammidown, *Historical Collections*, 1:448. The concentration of Oxford's Universalists in the southern part of town is inferred from the fact that their meetinghouse was the one chosen by Oxford residents in 1807 for alternate meetings outside the town's regular "northern" meeting place. See n. 49.

57. See Table A.2. To some extent, the towns seem to corroborate Darrett B. Rutman's suggestion that eighteenth-century New England learned to use mobility as a means of maintaining, or reaching, population levels appropriate to available economic resources. See "People in Process: The New Hampshire Towns of the Eighteenth Century," in Tamara K. Hareven, ed., *Family and Kin in Urban Communities, 1700–1930* (New York, 1977), pp. 16–37. A more recent and fuller analysis depicting eighteenth-century migration patterns as an adaptive mechanism by which New Englanders balanced changing demographic patterns to limited resources is found in Douglas Lamar Jones, *Village and Seaport; Migration and Society in Eighteenth-Century Massachusetts* (Hanover, N.H., 1981).

58. Derived from MFCD and MFCO, 1810; OVR and DVR.

59. Derived from MFCD and MFCO, 1800 and 1810. Names of "departing" household heads were compared to local death records to correct for "departures" actually caused by death. And names of "arriving" household heads were compared to local birth records to correct for "arriving" individuals who were actually youngsters coming of age.

60. See Kett, "Growing Up in Rural New England," pp. 6–10. The proportion of sons settling in Dudley and Oxford is derived from MFCD
and MFCO, 1810, and OVR and DVR. The overall mobility in and out
of these townships in this period does not equal that achieved by
urban populations later in the nineteenth century, but the available
scholarship on colonial communities suggests it was probably considerably larger than that common in these townships in the first half of
the eighteenth century. See Stephan Thernstrom and Peter R. Knights,
"Men in Motion: Some Data and Speculations about Urban Population Mobility in Nineteenth Century America," in Hareven, ed., *Anonymous Americans*, pp. 20–1; Philip Greven, *Four Generations: Population,
Land, and Family in Colonial Andover, Massachusetts* (Ithaca, N.Y., 1970),
ch. 6; Charles S. Grant, *Democracy in the Connecticut Frontier Town of
Kent* (New York, 1961), pp. 98–103. The figures cited here for Dudley
and Oxford are roughly comparable (though somewhat lower) than
statistics on 1800–10 mobility recently collected on five other New
England townships. See Robert W. Doherty, *Society and Power: Five
New England Towns, 1800–1860* (Amherst, 1977), ch. 4, esp. pp. 33–5.

61. Thirty-seven of the household heads arriving in these towns between
1800 and 1810 and still resident in 1820 could be traced into the 1815
valuations. The average wealth of these thirty-seven was $130.10,
compared with an average for all residents in these communities of
$148.50. Sixty-four of the household heads leaving these towns be-
tween 1800 and 1810 could be traced to the 1798 valuations. Three-
quarters of these sixty-four had below average landholdings, but their
average total valuation was £60.18 above the community norm for
that year. Derived from MFCD and MFCO, 1800 and 1810; Massachusetts and Maine Direct Tax of 1798, vol. 16; and AAS: Worcester
County, Mass., Papers, 1815 Valuations, folio vol. 14. But see also
Douglas Lamar Jones, "The Strolling Poor: Transciency in Eighteenth
Century Massachusetts," *Journal of Social History* 8 (Spring, 1975):28–54.

62. See Oscar Handlin and Mary F. Handlin, *Commonwealth: A Study of the
Role of Government in the American Economy: Massachusetts, 1774–1861*,
rev. ed. (Cambridge, Mass., 1969), p. 61.

63. For an example of a household head who concluded that it would
"misuse [his] Real Estate [for it] to be divided" into portions for all his
heirs, see the Will of Learned Davis, Probate Records, 1790–1810,
Worcester County Court House.

64. Derived from Probate Records, 1790–1810, Worcester County Court
House.

65. Estimate of remaining children derived from DVR and OVR. See also
Daniels, *Oxford*, pp. 365–753. The economic difficulties faced by
nonmigrating sons is reflected in the fact that of thirty-five young
men who were born between 1771 and 1790 to fathers listed in the
1798 valuation, and who themselves are cited in the 1815 valuation,
most failed to surpass – and 28% failed to match – the quartile their

fathers had occupied seventeen years earlier (see Massachusetts and Maine Direct Tax of 1798, vol. 16; AAS: Worcester County, Mass., Papers, 1815 Valuations, folio vol. 14). This is at best a crude measure of filial economic mobility, making little systematic correction for the life-cycle stages of particular sons. But it offers a rough indication of why propertyless young men may have lacked compelling economic reasons to remain in these townships.

66. Marriage ages derived from DVR and OVR. Among local residents under 26, the proportion of males fell from 52.1% in 1800 to 50.9% in 1810, with the largest decline in the 16–26 age group. In 1800 the proportion of females among all local residents aged 16–45 was 50.7%. By 1810 this figure had risen to 52.1%. Derived from MFCD, MFCO, 1800 and 1800.

67. See Handlin and Handlin, *Commonwealth*, p. 60; Bidwell and Falconer, *History of Agriculture*, p. 204; Daniel Scott Smith, "Parental Power and Marriage Patterns: An Analysis of Historical Trends in Hingham, Massachusetts," *Journal of Marriage and the Family* 35 (August 1973): 419–28.

68. For a discussion of family structures and functions persisting despite limited resources and increased mobility, see: Peter Dobkin Hall, "Family Structure and Economic Organization: Massachusetts Merchants, 1700–1850," in Hareven, ed., *Family and Kin in Urban Communities*, pp. 51–4; James A. Henretta, "The Morphology of New England Society in the Colonial Period," *Journal of Interdisciplinary History* 2 (Autumn, 1971):397.

69. Dwight, *Travels in New England and New York*, 2:34; 1:139. Jones, "The Strolling Poor."

70. Just under half (46.4%) the selectmen serving in Dudley and Oxford between 1800 and 1810 were born in these communities, compared to 51.5% of all household heads living in these towns in 1810. Derived from TROM III, 1800–10, TRDM III, 1800–10, OVR, DVR.

71. Although a considerable proportion (22.2%) of household heads resident in these towns in 1800 persisted until 1820, only 8.6% lasted until 1830 and there is, overall, little evidence in these communities to support Robert Doherty's suggestion that New England towns of this era contained a "stable" core population of leading local families. Data on Dudley and Oxford mobility and changing age distribution patterns do tend to support the contention that young men were more transient than older men. But in these towns the differences appear to have been less than Doherty implies, and movement in general appears to have sooner or later touched the lives of almost every household. See Doherty, *Society and Power*, pp. 43–5.

72. TRDM III, March 1820, p. 290.

73. TROM III, March 1809, p. 91; TRDM III, March 1807, p. 131.

74. Residents of the two gores could join with Oxford's bona fide citizens in meetings dealing with county and state business, but they were

barred from meetings dealing with local affairs. Compare warrants cited in TROM III, April 1808, p. 89, with March 1809, p. 91. The distinction was maintained even after Oxford voted to "receive the lands now belonging to the South Gore" in 1805. See TROM III, April 1805, p. 57.

75. For a useful underscoring of the role of the county, see John Murrin, "Review Essay," *History and Theory* 11 (1972):270–2. In gubernatorial elections, for example, Oxford's support of Federalist candidates averaged 61.7% of votes cast between 1800 and 1810; the comparable figure for Dudley was 73.4%. Voting data courtesy of R. D. Formisano.

76. Although town-meeting minutes were from the outset preserved carefully, it was not until 1808 that Oxford required assessors to transcribe the town's fiscal affairs into a book and deposit that book with the town clerk, a step that Dudley did not take for another nine years. TROM III, March 1808, p. 83; TRDM III, March 1817, p. 250.

77. TRDM I, September 1740, p. 91. TRDM II, December 1760, p. 54; March 1790, p. 325; March 1792, p. 364. Daniels, *Oxford*, pp. 96–8. See Chapter 6, this volume.

78. For auctioning of the poor in this period, see, for example, TROM II, June 1799, p. 346. See Daniels, *Oxford*, p. 223. Generally, the selectmen were charged with overall supervision of the poor. TROM II, May 1799, p. 344.

79. Daniels, *Oxford*, p. 115. TRDM III, March 1801, p. 91.

80. TROM II, August 1799, p. 348. TRDM III, May 1794, p. 23; see also November 1812, p. 187. TROM III, April 1810, p. 107. There were exceptions to the shift described here. As early as 1757, for example, Dudley once charged off a road to a specific individual. And as late as 1793 two Oxford residents gave land for a road "gratis for the good of the publick." (See TRDM II, March 1757, p. 25; TROM II, May 1793, p. 305.) But overall, the trend was in the direction indicated.

81. TROM III, May 1803, p. 3. In this case, work on a county road was "vendered out to the lowest bidder" with the town paying the wages of those to whom the project was awarded. Fourteen years later, the town made labor on a county road part of its general highway work but spent eight months arguing about its necessity. See TROM III, April–November 1817, pp. 169–74.

82. Derived from Daniels, *Oxford*, pp. 272–5, elections cited in TRDM III, 1800–10, and TROM III, 1800–10. These same sources reveal that selectmen were considerably more entrenched in local politics than most officeholders. On the average, individuals elected to some public office in Dudley and Oxford between 1800 and 1810 spent 2.5 years in local government, their involvement often spreading across several decades and embracing several positions. By contrast, selectmen, just as selectmen, and just between 1800 and 1810, averaged 3.1 years in office. For a useful discussion of eighteenth-century local political hierarchies, see Grant, *Democracy in the Connecticut Frontier Town of*

Kent, pp. 145–50. On the continuity of local leadership during and after the Revolution, see Edward M. Cook, Jr., *The Fathers of the Towns: Leadership and Community Structure in Eighteenth-Century New England* (Baltimore, 1976), pp. 185–8; Gross, *The Minutemen and Their World*, pp. 157–70.

83. Derived from Massachusetts and Maine Direct Tax of 1798, vol. 16; the names of the selectmen were extracted from the sources cited in n. 82. The exact proportion of selectmen in the top quartile was 69.6%; the exact proportion in the top two quartiles was 87.0%.

84. Derived from list of Oxford selectmen extracted from sources cited in n. 82 and OVR.

85. TRDM II, March 1790, p. 325. For examples of ad hoc committees, see TROM III, April 1807, p. 73. For a general discussion of the ad hoc committee, see Kenneth A. Lockridge and Alan Kreider, "The Evolution of Massachusetts Town Government, 1640–1740," *William and Mary Quarterly*, 3rd ser. 23 (1966):549–74.

86. Grant, *Democracy in the Connecticut Frontier Town of Kent*, pp. 147, 150.

87. Based on survey of officeholding patterns derived from Dudley and Oxford sources cited in n. 82.

88. Grant, *Democracy in the Connecticut Frontier Town of Kent*, p. 146.

89. AAS: Worcester County, Mass., Papers, Militia, Division Court of Inquiry, Oxford, Massachusetts, 1815, box 5, folder 2.

90. For tradition of "Seating the Meeting House," see Freeland, *The Records of Oxford*, p. 294; TRDM II, March 1781, p. 223. Sales of pews are recorded in TROM III, 1800–10.

91. TROM III, October 1807, p. 80; March 1809, p. 96.

92. TROM III, April 1802, p. 25.

93. Probate Records, 1790–1810, Worcester County Court House.

2. Samuel Slater, textile mills, and a new economic landscape

1. Ammidown, *Historical Collections*, 1:435.

2. AAS: Worcester County Valuations. Louis McLane, *Report of the Secretary of the Treasury, 1832. Documents Relative to the Manufactures in the United States*, 2 vols., *House Executive Documents*, 22d Cong. 1st sess., Doc. No. 308 (Washington, 1833), 1:484–5, 526–7, 576–7; cited hereafter as *Report*.

3. There exists no fully adequate biographical treatment of Slater. Uncritical narrations of his life may be found in George S. White, *Memoir of Samuel Slater* (Philadelphia, 1836; reprinted 1967); Edward H. Cameron, *Samuel Slater, Father of American Manufactures* (Freeport, Me., 1960); and Frederick L. Lewton, "A Biography of Samuel Slater" (Manuscript, Slater Mill Historical Site, Pawtucket, R.I., 1944). A less complete, but more balanced, sketch is scattered through Caroline F. Ware, *The Early New England Cotton Manufacture; A Study in Industrial Beginnings* (Boston, 1931). His role in Dudley and Oxford, as well as

further laudatory accounts of his life, can be derived from Daniels, *Oxford*, pp. 190–1, 198, and large sections of Ammidown's treatment of Webster in his *Historical Collections*, 1:461–97.

4. White, *Memoir of Samuel Slater*, pp. 30–6. Strutt controlled at least three other textile mills in the 1780s, two in Belper itself and one located in the nearby market town of Derby. See R. S. Fitton and Alfred P. Wadsworth, *The Strutts and the Arkwrights, 1758–1830; A Study of the Early Factory System* (Manchester, England, 1958), p. 106.

5. Fitton and Wadsworth, *The Strutts and the Arkwrights*, pp. 60–8. Neil J. Smelser, *Social Change in the Industrial Revolution; An Application of Theory to the British Cotton Industry.* (Chicago, 1959), pp. 85–92. For limitations of the jenny, see Ware, *The Early New England Cotton Manufacture*, p. 24.

6. Fitton and Wadsworth cite the Milford works as undertaking only spinning and bleaching. They acknowledge, however, that the nearby Belper mill did undertake weaving and that Strutt production records are in any case "very weak." (*The Strutts and the Arkwrights*, p. 295.) It is thus at least possible that the Milford factory organized a weaving operation; and even if that were not the case it is plausible that Slater would have been familiar with the weaving activities run out of Belper. Some mill masters had gathered handloom weavers into "factories," or large worksheds, but it seems probable that Strutt would have pursued the more widespread practice of distributing yarn to weavers who labored in their homes. See Smelser, *Social Change in the Industrial Revolution*, pp. 141–2.

7. Fitton and Wadsworth, *The Strutts and the Arkwrights*, pp. 79–80.

8. Ibid., pp. 226–7, 244–5. Jedediah Strutt, Jr., testified in 1816 that the number of hours required in the early mills was not new, for "this had been the invariable practice . . . in the neighborhood for more than 100 years." The precision with which work time was measured, however, was new.

9. *Parliamentary Papers* (Commons), testimony of Martha Chappel in *Factories Inquiry, Royal Commission, Second Report* (1833), Section C34.

10. Stanley D. Chapman, *The Cotton Industry in the Industrial Revolution* (London, 1972), pp. 53–4.

11. Factory Inspector Reports, December 1838, App. 5, p. 98, quoted in Arthur Redford, *Labour Migration in England, 1800–1850*, 2nd ed. Rev. by W. H. Chaloner (Manchester, England, 1964), pp. 22–3. Fitton and Wadsworth, *The Strutts and the Arkwrights*, p. 233.

12. Fitton and Wadsworth, *The Strutts and the Arkwrights*, p. 192.

13. Andrew Ure, *The Cotton Manufacture of Great Britain*, 2 vols. (London, 1836), 2:449. Redford, *Labour Migration in England*, pp. 23–31. Fitton and Wadsworth, *The Strutts and the Arkwrights*, pp. 104–6, 225. Comments by J. Farey and P. Gaskell, quoted in ibid., p. 249. Though written in the nineteenth century, these statements on the Strutt Derbyshire works probably can be safely applied to the 1780s.

14. Fitton and Wadsworth, *The Strutts and the Arkwrights*, pp. 97–105. For Strutt's religious affiliation, see Stanley D. Chapman, *The Early Factory Masters: The Transition to the Factory System in the Midlands Textile Industry* (New York, 1967), pp. 196–7.

15. Sidney Pollard, *The Genesis of Modern Management; A Study of the Industrial Revolution in Great Britain* (Cambridge, Mass., 1965), p. 23. Fitton and Wadsworth, *The Strutts and the Arkwrights*, pp. 75, 111.

16. Fitton and Wadsworth, *The Strutts and the Arkwrights*, pp. 81–5.

17. Cameron, *Samuel Slater, Father of American Manufactures*, pp. 24–30. White, *Memoir of Samuel Slater*, pp. 37–8.

18. Thomas Jefferson, *Notes on the State of Virginia*, ed., with an introduction and notes by William Peden (Chapel Hill, N.C., 1954), p. 165. Ware, *The Early New England Cotton Manufacture*, pp. 7–8.

19. Jacob E. Cooke, *Tench Coxe and the Early Republic* (Chapel Hill, N.C., 1978), pp. 187–8. Ware, *The Early New England Cotton Manufacture*, pp. 9–10. Alexander Hamilton, "Report on the Subject of Manufactures, December 5, 1791," *American State Papers: Finance*, 1:133.

20. Ware, *The Early New England Cotton Manufacture*, pp. 20–1. Mack Thompson, *Moses Brown, Reluctant Reformer* (Chapel Hill, N.C., 1962), pp. 207–9. The first and probably most successful enterprise to use the jenny was Philadelphia's American Manufactory, which ran from 1775 until the early 1780s. See Gary Kulik, "The Beginnings of the Industrial Revolution in America: Pawtucket, Rhode Island, 1672–1829" (Ph.D. diss., Brown University, 1980).

21. James L. Conrad, Jr., "The Evolution of Industrial Capitalism in Rhode Island, 1790–1830: Almy, the Browns, and the Slaters" (Ph.D. diss., University of Connecticut, 1973), p. 30. Thompson, *Moses Brown*, pp. 204–17. Moses Brown to John Dexter, July 22, 1791, in Arthur H. Cole, ed., *Industrial and Commercial Correspondence of Alexander Hamilton, Anticipating His Report on Manufactures* (Chicago, 1928; reprinted, 1968), pp. 72–4. For an able discussion of Moses Brown's background – in shipping, a candle works, a furnace, and stocking weaving – see Kulik, "The Beginnings of the Industrial Revolution in America," pp. 97–100.

22. Thompson, *Moses Brown*, pp. 217–27. Moses Brown to John Dexter, July 22, 1791, in Cole, ed., *Industrial and Commercial Correspondence of Alexander Hamilton*, p. 73.

23. Thompson, *Moses Brown*, pp. 226–7, 230. Moses Brown to John Dexter, July 22, 1791, in Cole, ed., *Industrial and Commercial Correspondence of Alexander Hamilton*, p. 73. Paul E. Rivard, "Textile Experiments in Rhode Island, 1788–1789," *Rhode Island History* 33 (May 1974): 35–45.

24. There are indications that, at least through 1791, Slater concentrated on producing warp yarn. Weft needed for the cloths that Almy and Brown were at this point still turning out continued to be spun on jennies in Providence. Kulik, "The Beginnings of the Industrial Revo-

lution in America," p. 149. Cloth production in these yearly years is discussed in III, this chapter.

25. White, *Memoir of Samuel Slater*, pp. 102–3. Thompson, *Moses Brown*, pp. 225–6.

26. John P. Coolidge, *Mill and Mansion: A Study of Architecture and Society in Lowell, Massachusetts, 1820–1865* (New York, 1942), pp. 29–30, 178–9. Cameron, *Samuel Slater*, pp. 70–7. Estimates of the Old Mill's size vary; I have here followed Coolidge's figures.

27. Moses Brown had actually withdrawn from daily involvement as early as 1789, yielding his place for a brief period to a younger (Quaker) cousin, Smith Brown. By 1791 Smith Brown had given way to Obadiah. The original partnership with Slater was formed in April 1790 but was in no way altered when Obadiah took Smith's place. See Thompson, *Moses Brown*, pp. 219–20, 227–9, 233.

28. Robert Grieve, *An Illustrated History of Pawtucket, Central Falls and Vicinity*. (Pawtucket, 1897), p. 92. There are numerous descriptions of the manufacturing process used in early water-frame mills, but the one I have relied upon heavily here is found in Paul E. Rivard's *Samuel Slater, Father of American Manufactures* (Slater Mill Historical Site, Providence, 1974). See also Anthony F. C. Wallace, *Rockdale: The Growth of an American Village in the Early Industrial Revolution* (New York, 1978), pp. 136–43.

29. See n. 24. Kulik, "The Beginnings of the Industrial Revolution in America," pp. 150, 152, 162–3. Ware, *The Early New England Cotton Manufacture*, pp. 29, 32. Conrad, "The Evolution of Industrial Capitalism in Rhode Island," p. 120.

30. In his *Memoir of Samuel Slater*, White notes that Slater introduced "such regulations, as his previous observations of cotton mills in Derbyshire had shown to be useful and applicable to the circumstances of an American population" (p. 107).

31. Conrad, "The Evolution of Industrial Capitalism in Rhode Island," pp. 72–3, 99–104, 273. See also Moses Brown to John Dexter, July 22, 1791, in Cole, ed., *Industrial and Commercial Correspondence of Alexander Hamilton*, p. 77: "The Manufacture of the Mill yarn is done by Children from 8 to 14 years old."

32. Thompson, *Moses Brown*, pp. 204–6. Josiah Quincy, "Account of Journey of Josiah Quincy," *Massachusetts Historical Society Proceedings*, 2nd ser. 4 (1887–9), p. 124.

33. See White, *Memoir of Samuel Slater*, p. 52; Gary Kulik, "Opposition to Dam Building: Farmers, Artisans, and Capitalists and the Politics of Water Rights in the Eighteenth Century" (paper presented to Smith College symposium on the "New" New England Working Class History, 1979), pp. 1, 12–18; and Kulik, "The Beginnings of the Industrial Revolution in America," pp. 154–9. As Kulik explains, the initial controversy over the Slater, Almy, and Brown dam spawned other ripar-

ian disputes, resulting in squabbles both between farmers and artisans and among different groups of artisans. But the precipitating event was the construction of the Old Mill dam; and the Old Mill proprietors emerged as the chief victors of the whole crisis. See also Conrad, "The Evolution of Industrial Capitalism in Rhode Island," pp. 34, 90–1.

34. Conrad, "The Evolution of Industrial Capitalism in Rhode Island," pp. 110, 276–7. A & B: box 1, no. 15, Slater to Almy and Brown, March 29, 1791: "This day have sent the above cotton Yarn as it is very dangerous to keep a quantity of Yarn here." Slater may have been worried about fire, but thievery was almost certainly also on his mind.

35. A & B: box 1, no. 126, Slater to Almy and Brown, November 23, 1794; box 2, no. 184, Slater to Almy and Brown, February 3, 1795; box 2, no. 227, Slater to Almy and Brown, June 2, 1795; box 2, no. 243, Slater to Almy and Brown, August 17, 1795; box 2, no. 256, Slater to Almy and Brown, September 25, 1795; box 3, no. 352, Slater to Almy and Brown, July 19, 1795. *Providence Journal*, September 29, 1890.

36. A & B: box 2, no. 271, Slater to Almy and Brown, October 30, 1795.

37. A & B: box 7, no. 945, Slater to Almy and Brown, January 28, 1811. Conrad, "The Evolution of Industrial Capitalism in Rhode Island," pp. 112–13. White, *Memoir of Samuel Slater*, p. 107. Brendan F. Gilbane, "A Social History of Samuel Slater's Pawtucket, 1790–1830" (Ph.D. diss., Boston University, 1969), pp. 307–9.

38. A & B: box 3, no. 318, Slater to Almy and Brown, February 19, 1796; box 1, no. 126, Slater to Almy and Brown, November 23, 1794.

39. *Providence Journal*, September 29, 1890.

40. Evidence for the lack of fines and blacklists is largely negative but still compelling: The total absence of any mention of these managerial tools in all documents or descriptions of the factory run by Slater, Almy, and Brown in the 1790s. Indications that Slater himself did all the supervising in the early days of this establishment are found in Quincy, "Account of Journey of Josiah Quincy," p. 124, and Coolidge, *Mill and Mansion*, p. 179.

41. Gilbane, "A Social History of Samuel Slater's Pawtucket," pp. 123–4. A & B: box 2, no. 253, Slater to Almy and Brown, September 8, 1795; box 1, no. 126, Slater to Almy and Brown, November 23, 1794; box 10, no. 1443, Sally Brown to Almy and Brown, November 14, 1794.

42. Ware, *The Early New England Cotton Manufacture*, pp. 32–4. See also James B. Hedges, *The Browns of Providence Plantation*, vol. 2: *The Nineteenth Century* (Providence, 1968), pp. 167–8.

43. Ware, *The Early New England Cotton Manufacture*, pp. 27–8, 37–8. This count, based on Secretary of the Treasury Louis McLane's 1832 *Report on manufactures*, is almost certainly a minimal estimate. One prominent observer of American manufactures suggested that in 1809 alone more than fifty factories were under construction in New England,

and a British report put the total number of United States cotton factories in 1810 at eighty-nine. Both these estimates undoubtedly reflect the post-1807 expansion noted later, but they also suggest that more than twenty new mills may have been built in the Northeast in the fourteen years after 1793. See Victor Clark, *History of Manufactures in the United States*, 3 vols. (New York, 1929), 1:536.

44. Ware, *The Early New England Cotton Manufacture*, p. 37. Hedges, *The Browns of Providence Plantations*, 2:169–73. Conrad, "The Evolution of Industrial Capitalism in Rhode Island," pp. 198–200.

45. Arthur H. Cole, *The American Wool Manufacture*, 2 vols. (Cambridge, 1926), 1:86–116; 2: app. B.

46. William R. Bagnall, "Contributions to American Economic History" (manuscript, 4 vols., Baker Library, Harvard University, 1908), 2:998–9.

47. A & B: box 1, no. 30, Slater to Almy and Brown, June 2, 1791.

48. Quincy, "Account of Journey of Josiah Quincy," p. 124. Samuel Slater to John Slater, December 23, 1808, in Samuel Slater, Original Letters, Invoices, etc. (Rhode Island School of Design). A & B: box 1, no. 30, Samuel Slater to Almy and Brown, June 2, 1791.

49. A & B: box 28, Moses Brown to Elisha Waterman, February 23, 1802. Conrad, "The Evolution of Industrial Capitalism in Rhode Island," pp. 154–5, 209–10.

50. Conrad, "The Evolution of Industrial Capitalism in Rhode Island," pp. 142–4. Lewton, "A Biography of Samuel Slater," pp. 44–5. Other incidents had already begun to create friction between Slater and his two associates. In 1797 Slater had deeply resented (and apparently vetoed) Almy's suggestion that he take on a foreman. Almy claimed he made the proposal because Slater was overworked, but Slater viewed the suggestion as an attempt to undermine his authority. He was equally suspicious of an effort to shift to Almy and Brown a greater ownership of the water privilege serving the Old Mill. See ibid., pp. 50–1.

51. Lewton, "A Biography of Samuel Slater," pp. 46–8. Technically, Slater's position in the White Mill was "superintendent," but his preeminence in the venture is signaled by the name of the operating authority: Samuel Slater and Company.

52. Matching Slater's irritation with their own, Almy and Brown also unsuccessfully opposed the Rehoboth venture. See ibid., p. 47. For Rehoboth's objections, see Town Meeting Records, May 1799 (Town Clerk's Office, Rehoboth, Mass.), vol. 5 (1793–1808), p. 148. Slater ultimately won his exemption in Rehoboth, and the town became reconciled to providing factories with this privilege at the outset of their careers. See ibid., May 1805, pp. 202–3. Conrad, "The Evolution of Industrial Capitalism in Rhode Island," p. 147. Rhode Island was generally reluctant to grant such exemptions to early mills. See Peter J. Coleman, *The Transformation of Rhode Island, 1790–1860* (Providence, 1963), pp. 75–6. For the attitude of postrevolutionary Massachusetts

legislators toward the question, see Oscar Handlin and Mary F. Handlin, *Commonwealth: A Study of the Role of Government in the American Economy: Massachusetts, 1774–1861*, rev. ed. (Cambridge, Mass., 1969), pp. 79–80, 103–5, 126–7.

53. Lewton, "A Biography of Samuel Slater," pp. 63–5. Joseph Brennan, *Social Conditions in Industrial Rhode Island: 1820–1860* (Washington, D.C., 1940), p. 9. Conrad, "The Evolution of Industrial Capitalism in Rhode Island," pp. 176–8.

54. Lewton, "A Biography of Samuel Slater," pp. 68–71.

55. Ammidown, *Historical Collections*, 1:464–6. Almy and Brown helped Slater finance his move to Massachusetts, though he gave them no control over his new property. See Conrad, "The Evolution of Industrial Capitalism in Rhode Island," pp. 229–30. For Hannah Slater's death, see Lewton, "A Biography of Samuel Slater," pp. 76, 82–3. Ammidown, *Historical Collections*, 1:496. Hannah was survived by six children. Two daughters (Elizabeth and Mary) and one son (William) died in infancy.

56. J. D. Van Slyck, *Representatives of New England Manufacturers* (Boston, 1879), p. 418. In 1803 Slater, Almy, and Brown divided $18,000 at the ten-year accounting of the Old Mill. See Lewton, "A Biography of Samuel Slater," pp. 51–2. Estimates of profits earned by the Slater brothers during this period range up to $40,000. See Conrad, "The Evolution of Industrial Capitalism in Rhode Island," p. 227. For an estimate of Slater's holdings in 1817, see White, *Memoir of Samuel Slater*, p. 215.

57. TRDM III, January 1812, pp. 191–2; March 1813, p. 194. TROM III, May 1812, p. 127.

58. Daniels, *Oxford*, p. 191. SC: Slater and Tiffany, vol. 89. Ammidown, *Historical Collections*, 1:437. For the geographical configuration of his mills, see also AAS: Slater Family Papers, 1824–1911, Amos Bartlett to Messrs. Kidder, Peabody and Co., January 11, 1902, octavo vol. 11. See also SC: Slater and Tiffany, vol. 178. In his *Memoir of Samuel Slater*, White notes that in 1831 the Slaters had "seven mills" in Dudley and Oxford (p. 263). The distribution was probably: two mills (The Green and Union mills) in the East Village; three separate woolen spinning and weaving buildings in the South Village; and two separate buildings for processing thread in the North Village.

59. See references to central "villages" in Mass. Archives: Petition of George B. Slater and 173 Others praying for the incorporation of a town to be formed of Oxford south Gore and a part of the Towns of Oxford and Dudley, June 3, 1831, Original Papers of Ch. 93, Acts of 1832; cited hereafter as Petition of George B. Slater and 173 Others.

60. Ammidown, *Historical Collections*, 1:466–7, 469, 498. White, *Memoir of Samuel Slater*, p. 215.

61. Ammidown, *Historical Collections*, 1:467–72.

62. For treatment of Waltham-style mills, see the Preface, n. 10. For the

development of power looms, see Smelser, *Social Change in the Industrial Revolution*, pp. 144–7.

63. The prevalence of rural mills following the family-style format is discussed in the Preface, esp. n. 11.

64. Dudley grew from 1,226 to 2,155; Oxford increased from 1,277 to 2,034. See Table A.2.

65. Average size of landholdings derived from Probate Records, 1810–32, Worcester County Court House, and Daniels, *Oxford*, pp. 294–363. Lacking any tax listing showing landholdings for 1810–30, it is not possible to calculate the precise proportion of landless residents at any given time. Probate records reveal that at death most (83.8%) residents did own property, suggesting that (just as had been true before 1810) residents generally managed to acquire real estate if they remained in these towns to the end of their lives. (In the previous generation, almost 90% of those dying in these towns held land. See Chapter 1, n. 6, this volume.) But the rapid increase in populations pressing against overall community land supplies and the high rates of transiency (see V, this chapter) both imply the presence of large numbers of inhabitants who possessed little or no arable property and who moved on before dying.

66. MFCD and MFCO, 1820. A total of 573 residents, most of them household heads, placed themselves in three broad occupational categories: agriculture, manufacturing, and commerce.

67. Local farms continued to produce barley, Indian corn, fruit, cider, peas, beans, and at least some wheat. Data on overall exports from these towns suggest that most nondairy goods were consumed rather than traded. See AAS: Worcester County Statistics, 1769–1837 (n.p.), and Worcester County Valuations; Worcester County, Mass., Papers, 1675–ca. 1954, "A Statement From the Following Towns in the County of Worcester of Their Annual Imports and Exports," box 1, folder 3. Local wheat cultivation is not shown in the 1831 valuation but is recorded in 1840. See *Commonwealth of Massachusetts, General Court Committees, Valuation: 1840* (Boston, 1840). *Old Farmer's Almanack*, September 1837.

68. AAS: Worcester County Valuations. Clarence H. Danhof, *Change in Agriculture; The Northern United States, 1820–1870* (Cambridge, Mass., 1969), pp. 9–13.

69. McLane, *Report*, 1:69. The per capita value of goods turned out by households throughout all Worcester County plummeted from $7.50 for dry goods alone in 1810 to 25¢ in 1840 for all products. See Rolla M. Tryon, *Household Manufactures in the United States, 1640–1860; A Study in Industrial History* (Chicago, 1917), pp. 170, 314.

70. Carroll D. Wright, *History of Wages and Prices in Massachusetts, 1752–1883* (Boston, 1885), pp. 77–105. For the particular volatility of wool prices see Danhof, *Change in Agriculture*, p. 166.

71. Data on local debts are derived from Probate Records, 1810–30, Worcester County Court House. Aaron Tufts reported in 1831 that Dudley

farms "will not rent over 3% after deducting expenses of repairs in buildings, etc." And a report from nearby Uxbridge in the same year suggested agricultural profit levels holding at 3% or lower. See McLane, *Report*, 1:68–9, 81. See also Danhof, *Change in Agriculture*, pp. 148–9.

72. Derived from Probate Records, 1810–32, Worcester County Court House. The increase was not so much in outright insolvency, which grew only 5%, but in the number of solvent estates required to sell land. As in the years before 1810, there is no evidence of children gaining special access to the land being auctioned off.

73. As in the treatment of transiency between 1800 and 1810 (see Chapter 1, IV, this volume), firm statistics are available only for household heads. Figures were corrected for births and deaths by procedures described in Chapter 1, n. 59, this volume. In Dudley between 1820 and 1830, persistence for all household heads was 49.3%; for household heads declaring themselves in "agriculture" it was 51.0%. Derived from MFCD, 1820 and 1830.

74. Derived by tabulating household heads who were known to have had children, who specified their occupation as agriculture, who were over age 45, and who had no coresiding household members other than spouse in 1820.

75. For proportion of sons settling in these towns between 1790 and 1810, see Chapter 1, IV, this volume. Proportion of sons settling between 1810 and 1830 derived from OVR, DVR, and MFCD, MFCO, 1830.

76. Lady Emmeline Stuart-Wortley, *Travels in the United States, etc., During 1849 and 1850* (New York, 1851), p. 73.

77. About four-fifths (82.3%) of the increase in household heads between 1810 and 1830 appears to have resulted from immigration into these townships. Derived from MFCD, MFCO, 1810 and 1830; DVR, OVR.

78. More precisely, the overall turnover of household heads ran 28.7% higher between 1810 and 1820 than between 1800 and 1810, and 39.4% higher between 1820 and 1830 than between the 1800 and 1810 enumerations. The number of arriving and departing household heads traveling with their families in tow was probably lower during these years than between 1800 and 1810; but even if only three-quarters were thus accompanied, something on the order of 1,800 people may have moved through these communities between 1810 and 1820, and more than 2,500 may have passed through between 1820 and 1830.

79. The variegated character of economic activities in post-1810 Dudley and Oxford is explored in Chapter 4, this volume. The points raised here about families facilitating youthful nonagricultural investments cannot be demonstrated quantitatively, for the total number of young men, both newcomers and locally born, who used parental aid to invest in local businesses is not known. But cash settlements to sons of local yeoman households were relatively common and at least some of these young men subsequently invested, at least briefly, in nonagricultural enterprises. Moreover, at least fourteen proprietors

of nonagricultural ventures operating in Oxford between 1810 and the early 1830s inherited their shares in these businesses from their fathers. See Probate Records, 1820–30, Worcester County Court House; Daniels, *Oxford*, ch. 8. See also, Joseph F. Kett, *Rites of Passage: Adolescence in America, 1790 to the Present* (New York, 1977), p. 31; and Christopher Clark, "The Household Economy, Market Exchange, and the Rise of Capitalism in the Connecticut Valley, 1800–1860," *Journal of Social History* 13 (Winter, 1979), pp. 176–7.

80. Daniels, *Oxford*, ch. 8.
81. Ibid.
82. Ibid. McLane, *Report*, 1:484–5, 526–7, 576–7.
83. Ibid. Precise capitalization figures are not known, but a survey of comparable establishments cited in McLane's *Report* suggests fairly low start-up costs. For details on the local textile machine and nail-making works, see Chapter 4, this volume.
84. Of sixty-two nontextile businesses started in Oxford between 1810 and 1830, twenty-two were partnerships. At least six of these partnerships joined kinsmen in common enterprises, and at least two newcomers from the same town collaborated in business. Derived from Daniels, *Oxford*, ch. 8.
85. See Chapter 6, II, this volume.
86. Names of nontextile proprietors are derived from Daniels, *Oxford*, ch. 8. Residency and landholdings of these men are derived from MFCO, 1800, and Daniels, *Oxford*, "Genealogy" and ch. 12. Estimated wealth is derived from AAS: Worcester County, Mass., Papers, 1815 Valuations, folio vol. 14; and Oxford School Taxes, in "Roads and Taxation," Town of Oxford, Mass., Records, box 7, Old Sturbridge Village; cited hereafter as Oxford School Taxes.
87. Derived from Daniels, *Oxford*, ch. 8.
88. Ibid., pp. 210, 214–15. McLane, *Report*, 1:526–7.
89. Derived from Daniels, *Oxford*, ch. 8; Ammidown, *Historical Collections*, 1:435–8; McLane, *Report*, 1:484–5, 526–7, 576–7.
90. Daniels, *Oxford*, pp. 192, 205.
91. Derived from AAS: Worcester County Valuations, and McLane, *Report*, 1:484–5, 526–7, 576–7. The McLane data date from 1832, after Webster was carved out of Dudley and Oxford (see Chapter 6, this volume), and the mill villages cited under the new community in this document must thus be added to compounds listed for Dudley and Oxford to find the correct number extant in the latter two towns in 1831. The factory counted here as Oxford's woolen works and one of the three woolen mills in Dudley actually produced satinet (a cheap cloth made with cotton warps). See Cole, *The American Wool Manufacture*, 1:199–200.
92. Names of textile proprietors are derived from Daniels, *Oxford*, ch. 8; Ammidown, *Historical Collections*, 1:435–8. These names were traced to MFCD, MFCO, 1800, and OVR and DVR.

93. Daniels, *Oxford*, ch. 8.
94. Ibid. Ammidown, *Historical Collections*, 1:435–8.
95. Tax quartiles of textile proprietors are derived from AAS: Worcester County, Mass., Papers, 1815 Valuations, folio vol. 14; and Oxford School Taxes. Of the thirty-eight textile investors who could be traced to these records, eighteen (47.3%) were in the middle two quartiles and nine (23.7%) were in the lowest quartile.
96. See McLane, *Report*, 1:69.
97. Precise capitalization figures for all local mills are not known, but general data on the issue are cited in Coleman, *The Transformation of Rhode Island*, pp. 93, 98. Estimates for local manufactories cited in McLane's *Report* (cf. 1:484–5, 526–7, 576–7) give higher figures, but these are not for original capitalization. At least six of these mills were incorporated by the General Court under the law of 1809, which declared the Commonwealth willing, on petition, to create manufacturing corporations. See Handlin and Handlin, *Commonwealth*, pp. 125–8. See also: Chs. 5, 101, Acts of 1812; Ch. 65, Acts of 1814, all in *Laws of the Commonwealth of Massachusetts*, vol. 6 (Boston, 1812–15). Ch. 3, Acts of 1815; Ch. 61, Acts of 1816, all in *Laws of the Commonwealth of Massachusetts*, vol. 7 (Boston, 1818). The other mills, including the Slater ventures, were evidently organized as joint partnerships. Slater's hesitation to seek incorporation probably reflects his experience in Rhode Island, where both the state legislature and businessmen had been notably reluctant to adopt this form of business organization. See Coleman, *The Transformation of Rhode Island*, pp. 110–19.
98. Daniels, *Oxford*, p. 235 and ch. 8.
99. AAS: Oxford, Massachusetts, General Store Account Book, 1817–18. For operations of stores directly connected to mills, see AAS: Craggins and Andrews, Account Book, 1820–7; William Law, Account Book, 1819–23.
100. For Slater's contribution on roads, see, for example, AAS: Dudley, Massachusetts, Town Records, 1740–1932, 1824 Central Turnpike Corporation folio. For his role in the Oxford Bank, see Daniels, *Oxford*, p. 232, and Chapter 6, this volume.

3. People and work: the social structure of occupations

1. Differences in age classifications used in the third and fifth federal censuses create some statistical blurring, but it is suggestive that in 1810, 17.2% of the residents in Dudley and Oxford were aged 45 or over, whereas in 1830, 21.6% of the two local populations were over 40. Derived from MFCD and MFCO, 1810, 1830. In 1820 the proportion of females among local residents aged 16 to 45 was 53.6%.
2. See Chapter 2, V, this volume.
3. A sampling of Dudley and Oxford household heads describing themselves as farmers and linked to the 1815 tax enumeration of this com-

munity reveals 26.5% in the top quartile, 18.4% in the lowest, and 55.1% in the middle two. Derived from MFCO, 1820, and AAS: Worcester County, Mass., Papers, 1675–ca. 1954, 1815 Valuations, folio vol. 14.

4. The ratio of improved to unimproved land in Oxford shifted from 1.67 in 1801 to 7.6 in 1831. Data on the latter year are not available for Dudley, but the trend toward cultivating greater fractions of homesteads was clear in earlier years and almost certainly continued. AAS: Worcester County Valuations. See Chapter 1, III, this volume.

5. The ratio of horses and oxen to polls remained virtually unchanged in Dudley and Oxford: 1.3 in 1811 and 1.0 in 1831. See AAS: Worcester County Valuations. Average size of households in Dudley and Oxford in 1810, when occupations were not specified but farming was the dominant local undertaking, came to 5.5. The average size for households identified in the 1820 census as primarily committed to agriculture was 5.31. MFCO, MFCD, 1810, 1820.

6. *Old Farmer's Almanack*, April 1837.

7. McLane, *Report*, 1:576. See also, Clarence H. Danhof, *Change in Agriculture; The Northern United States, 1820–1870* (Cambridge, Mass., 1969), pp. 73–9.

8. Danhof, *Change in Agriculture*, pp. 74–8.

9. Caroline F. Ware, *The Early New England Cotton Manufacture; A Study in Industrial Beginnings* (Boston, 1931), pp. 240–2. Edith Abbott, *Women in Industry; A Study in American Economic History* (New York, 1910; reprinted, 1969), pp. 63–80. Abbott contends (p. 66) that "there were more than one hundred industrial occupations open to women at this time." But she subsequently acknowledges (p. 80) that "a large proportion of the industries enumerated...employed only a very few women."

10. TRDM III, 1820–30, pp. 283–442. TROM III, 1820–30, pp. 211–341. Abbott, *Women in Industry*, p. 68. Admittedly impressionistic, the suggestion that the labor force of local small businesses was largely male is derived from McLane, *Report*, 1:526–7, and Daniels, *Oxford*, ch. 8.

11. Estimate of total labor force is based on the forty-nine individuals cited in McLane (*Report*, 1:526–7), as working in several of these establishments and by assuming, on the basis of data cited elsewhere in *Report* and in Daniels (*Oxford*, ch. 8), that other ventures employed about four workers each.

12. Daniels, *Oxford*, ch. 8. Also Alan Dawley, *Class and Community: The Industrial Revolution in Lynn* (Cambridge, Mass. 1976), pp. 48–50. George S. Gibb, *The Saco-Lowell Shops; Textile Machinery Building in New England, 1813–1949* (Cambridge, Mass., 1950), p. 89.

13. Daniels, *Oxford*, ch. 8. Joseph F. Kett, *Rites of Passage: Adolescence in America, 1790 to the Present* (New York, 1977), p. 26. McLane, *Report*, 1:526–7. Evidence of shorter apprenticeships in textile machine-making shops is found in Gibb, *The Saco-Lowell Shops*, p. 89.

14. Daniels, *Oxford*, ch. 8.
15. The factory labor force was 816. See VI, this chapter.
16. Merino Records: series I, A, vol. 2. SC: Slater and Howard, vol. 22.
17. The New England straw-hat industry made wide use of outwork and may have recruited households in Dudley and Oxford. See Abbott, *Women in Industry*, p. 72.
18. Derived from SC: Slater and Tiffany, Weave Books A and D.
19. Ibid.
20. Sample of eighty-eight names derived from SC: Slater and Tiffany, Weave Books A and D. Names compared with those in Daniels, *Oxford*, pp. 365–753, and AAS: Worcester County, Mass., Papers, 1815 Valuations, folio vol. 14, and MFCO, 1820.
21. Henry B. Fearon, *Sketches of America* (London, 1818), p. 100.
22. Sample compared to Daniels, *Oxford*, ch. 8.
23. Ware, *The Early New England Cotton Manufacture*, pp. 73–4.
24. Bruce Laurie, *Working People of Philadelphia, 1800–1850* (Philadelphia, 1980), p. 29. Ware, *The Early New England Cotton Manufacture*, p. 76. Edward P. Thompson, *The Making of the English Working Class* (New York, 1964), ch. 9.
25. Derived from SC: Slater and Tiffany, Weave Book A. Output figures are close to the 100-yard weekly production of Philadelphia journeymen cited in David Montgomery, "The Shuttle and the Cross: Weavers and Artisans in the Kensington Riots of 1844," *Journal of Social History* 5 (Summer, 1972):417.
26. SC: Slater and Tiffany, Weave Books A and D.
27. Ibid.
28. Ibid.
29. See Christopher Clark, "The Household Economy, Market Exchange, and the Rise of Capitalism in the Connecticut Valley, 1800–1860," *Journal of Social History* 13 (Winter, 1979):178–80.
30. Samuel Ogden, *Thoughts, What Probable Effect the Peace with Great Britain Will Have on the Cotton Manufacture of this Country* (Providence, 1815), p. 15; cited hereafter as *Thoughts*.
31. Thomas Steere, *History of the Town of Smithfield* (Providence, 1881), pp. 134–5.
32. McLane, *Report*, 1:928–9. The words are Slater's own.
33. Merino Records: Series IV, Part I, A, vol. 1. The Dudley Woolen Manufacturing Company took over the property of the defunct Merino Mill in 1823 and ran it until 1845. Data bearing on its operation are contained in the collection here referred to as Merino Records.
34. Frederick L. Lewton, "A Biography of Samuel Slater" (manuscript, Slater Mill Historical Site, Pawtucket, R.I., 1944), pp. 80–4. Slater had six sons who survived infancy: Samuel, Jr. (born, 1802), George B. (born, 1804), John (born, 1805), Horatio Nelson (born, 1808), William (born, 1809), and Thomas G. (born, 1812). Samuel, Jr., died of tuberculosis in 1821. William, after losing his foot in a waterwheel accident,

apparently grew into a wild youth. He ran away from home at least once and died of yellow fever in Georgia a month short of his seventeenth birthday. Slater's youngest son, Thomas, never became interested in his father's business affairs. After receiving his legacy in 1833, he traveled widely and apparently in considerable luxury. He died of pneumonia in West Sutton, Mass., in 1844. See Ammidown, *Historical Collections*, 1:496; Lewton, "A Biography of Samuel Slater," pp. 83, 118–22, 187–9. For subsequent history of John, George, and Nelson, see Chapter 7, this volume.

35. Lewton, "A Biography of Samuel Slater," pp. 130, 132. George S. White, *Memoir of Samuel Slater* (Philadelphia, 1836; reprinted 1967), p. 215.

36. SC: Samuel Slater and Sons, vol. 235, Samuel to John Slater, March 5, 1826; March 30, 1826; October 23, 1827; November 11, 1827; July 15, 1828; July 21, 1831. Slater and Tiffany, vol. 93.

37. Ammidown, *Historical Collections*, 1:474, 476–7. SC: Samuel Slater and Sons, vol. 235, Samuel to John Slater, June 7, 1826; January 13, 1826. Lewton, "A Biography of Samuel Slater," p. 135.

38. *Massachusetts Spy*, June 24, 1829. Lewton, "A Biography of Samuel Slater," pp. 108, 180, 182–4. At this point the South Village woolen mill took the title Dudley Manufacturing Company. Lewton, "A Biography of Samuel Slater," p. 138.

39. For criticism of the American tendency to hire inexperienced managers, see Ogden, *Thoughts*, pp. 9–10. Daniels, *Oxford*, ch. 8. Ammidown, *Historical Collections*, 1:462–3, 466, 476.

40. Before his dismissal, Edward Howard evidently occupied a residence that adjoined the South Village boardinghouse (see Map 3.3). But there is evidence to suggest that other agents occupied dwellings that were entirely separate from those of the operatives and at least sufficiently well appointed to provide temporary quarters for one or another visiting Slater (SC: Samuel Slater and Sons, vol. 235, Samuel to John Slater, November 17, 1820). Moreover, even Howard (as Map 3.3 indicates) had his own garden.

41. William R. Bagnall, "Contributions to American Economic History" (manuscript, 4 vols., Baker Library, Harvard University, 1908), 3:2121. Merino Records: Series IV, Part I, A, vol. 1. Ammidown, *Historical Collections*, 1:467. SC: Slater and Kimball, vol. 3.

42. Examples may be found in Bagnall, "Contributions to American Economic History," 2:1042–3; 3:1827–8, 1952–4.

43. A & B: References to overseers in boxes 4 and 5.

44. Ogden, *Thoughts*, p. 29. Henry A. Miles, *Lowell, As It Was, And As It Is* (Lowell, 1846; reprinted, 1972), p. 140. SC: Slater and Kimball, vol. 3.

45. SC: Slater and Kimball, vol. 3. For examples of overseers promoted, see n. 42.

46. Daniels, *Oxford*, pp. 533, 200 (n. 1), 572, 615.

47. *Massachusetts Spy*, April 11, 1821; June 2, 1824. Statistics on promotions are derived from SC: Slater and Tiffany, vols. 88–9; Slater and Kimball, vol. 3.
48. SC: Samuel Slater and Sons, vol. 235, Samuel to John Slater, July 21, 1831.
49. Compare role of overseers supporting workers in ten-hour movement in Lowell during the 1840s (cited in *Voice of Industry*, January 20, 1846; reference courtesy of Thomas Dublin) with beating incident noted in *Manufacturers' and Farmers' Journal and Providence and Pawtucket Advertiser*, September 22, 1823. See also Chapter 5, II, this volume.
50. Number of operatives derived from McLane, *Report*, 1:484–5, 526–7, 576–7. For the size of Slater mills, see SC: Slater and Tiffany, vol. 178. The populations of the North and East villages are estimates based on the ratio between the known populations of these villages and their roster of operatives in 1844 and the number of operatives laboring in 1832. SC: Slater and Tiffany, vols. 90–1, 178; Phoenix, vols. 24, 28; Union Mills, vols. 156, 144.
51. For a general discussion of economic conditions facing the textile industry in these years, see Ware, *The Early New England Cotton Manufacture*, pp. 66–7, 88–99.
52. SC: Slater and Kimball, vol. 3. Thomas Dublin, *Women at Work: The Transformation of Work and Community in Lowell, Massachusetts, 1826–1860* (New York, 1979), pp. 63–4.
53. McLane, *Report*, 1:484–5, 526–7, 576–7.
54. Ibid. I have assumed that there were roughly as many girls as boys, whose numbers are given. Ware cites a statewide average of 21% child workers in Massachusetts cotton mills in 1832. See Ware, *The Early New England Cotton Manufacture*, p. 210.
55. See Chapter 4, V, this volume.
56. Derived from SC: Slater and Tiffany, vols. 90–1; Slater and Kimball, vol. 3. Merino Records; Series IV, Part I, D, vol. 75.
57. For apprentices at the woolen mill at Humphreysville, see Timothy Dwight, *Travels in New England and New York*, ed. Barbara Miller Solomon with the assistance of Patricia M. King (Cambridge, Mass. 1969), 3:275. Merino Records: series I, A, vol. 2.
58. The letters indicating that operatives came mainly from southern New England were culled from SC: Slater and Tiffany, vol. 101; Slater and Howard, vol. 26. Merino Records: Series IV, Part II, E, boxes 20–3. Household names were derived from SC: Slater and Tiffany, vols. 88–9, 93; Slater and Kimball, vol. 3. Merino Records: Series IV, Part I, D, vols. 74–5, 80. These were compared to MFCD, MFCO, 1810, 1820, and to the third and fourth manuscript federal enumerations of Ward, Millbury, Sutton, Douglas, Woodstock, and Southbridge. The nonlocal origins of Dudley and Oxford operatives conflicts with the scholarly convention that "the comparatively few hands [family mills] at first required were found in their immediate neighborhood." Victor S.

Clark, *History of Manufactures in the United States*, 3 vols. (New York, 1929), 1:397. In all, 24.19 of pre-1830 operative households were local.

59. *Massachusetts Spy*, April 11, 1824; August 14, 1822. SC: Webster Woolen, vol. 110, Ashron Loring to D. W. Jones, September 4, 1836.

60. Waltham-style mills sometimes had difficulty filling empty berths, but the comparatively easier recruitment experience of these establishments is suggested in Ware, *The Early New England Cotton Manufacture*, pp. 201, 227. Recruitment policies of a Lowell mill in this period are treated in Dublin, *Women at Work*, ch. 3. Dublin even suggests (p. 28) that in the 1830s the Hamilton Mill may have drawn large numbers of workers from Lowell itself. There are provocative indications both in Dublin's monograph and in his collection of millworkers' correspondence (Thomas Dublin, ed., *Farm to Factory: Women's Letters, 1830–1860* [New York, 1981]) as well as Ware's study (*The Early New England Cotton Manufacture*, p. 220) that mills in Lowell – and perhaps many of the other Waltham-style factories clustered in northern New England – attracted most of their hands from the region's northern tier of states. But it must be stressed that any north-south division between Waltham and family mills in the early antebellum textile labor market was at most a trend, not a firm or inevitable policy implemented by proprietors of family and Waltham factories. There are numerous instances of Vermont girls working in family mills in Connecticut and Rhode Islanders working in Lowell. See, for example, Nell W. Kull, "I Can Never Be Happy There in Among So Many Mountains – The Letters of Sally Rice," *Vermont History* 38 (1970): 49–57.

61. Derived from SC: Slater and Tiffany, vols. 88–91. Merino Records: Series IV, Part I, D. vols. 74–5. The majority of operatives could have had shorter stints than the average engagement because some workers (18.7% employed by the East Village in 1830) worked sufficiently long (from two to five years) to raise the latter measure above the former.

62. Merino Records: Series IV, Part II, E, box 21, Phebe N. Larned to Mr. Permans (?), February (?), 1827.

63. SC: Slater and Tiffany, Vols. 89, 93.

64. McLane, *Report*, 1:484–5, 526–527, 576–7. There were typically 310 working days after subtracting Sundays and holidays. See Chapter 4, VI, this volume.

65. Ibid. SC: Phoenix, vol. 24. Unattached workers earned on the average 23.5% more than the average family workers; families as a unit earned 2.1 times more than unattached workers.

66. SC: Phoenix, vol. 24.

67. In the North Village 79.8% of all workers and 85.7% of family workers rented housing.

68. Merino Records: Series I, A, vol. 2.

69. SC: Phoenix, vol. 24. The exact statistics are: for unattached workers, 16.4%; for families, 25.8%.

70. SC: Slater and Tiffany, vols. 10, 93; Slater and Howard, vol. 26, Joseph W. Collier to Slater and Howard, March 26, 1829. The general arrangement seems to have been for the mills to lease their stores to merchants (see Map 3.3).

71. SC: Slater and Tiffany, vol. 93.

72. See Ware, *The Early New England Cotton Manufacture*, pp. 240–2. Lowell wage rates are derived from data on the Hamilton Mill presented in Dublin, *Women at Work*, p. 66. The differential between wages in the Waltham and the family-style mills indicated here did not, in this period, undermine the autonomy of the two factory labor systems or contract the possible geographical division in the two labor markets cited in n. 60. In the first place, Waltham-style mills made handsome profits even with their higher wages (see Chapter 4, IV, this volume) and thus were not constrained to change tactics. Moreover, the fact that this differential revolved largely around children's wages meant that, although the higher overall wage rate quoted by Waltham establishments probably facilitated their recruiting efforts, it could not systematically draw away all the employees sought by family mills. Differences in average wages paid to adults by Hamilton and local factory managers seem to have resulted mainly from differing proportions of specific kinds of jobs; men and women doing comparable tasks in Lowell and in southern Worcester County in this era earned roughly the same amount. And the Hamilton Mill was not interested in hiring youngsters.

73. Derived by tracing names cited in SC: Slater and Tiffany, vols. 88–91 to AAS: Worcester County, Mass., Papers, 1815 Valuations, folio vol. 14; and the genealogy in Daniels, *Oxford*, pp. 365–753; Probate Records, 1810–1830, Worcester County Court House. Some data were found on a total of sixty-nine names.

74. Quoted in Dublin, *Women at Work*, p. 36. See ibid., chap. 3.

75. A & B: box 10, no. 1443, Sally Brown to Almy and Brown, November 14, 1794. See n. 73. Of the eighteen Slater workers traced to the 1815 tax list, nine were in the last quartile, fourteen in the bottom two. Altogether, I found thirteen cases of children apparently dispatched to the East Village by parents who did not come to the compound themselves. Nine of these cases involved Oxford parents, of whom six were in the lowest quartile of the 1815 tax listing (AAS: Worcester County, Mass., Papers, 1815 Valuations, folio vol. 14).

76. White, *Memoir of Samuel Slater*, p. 127. Daniels, *Oxford*, pp. 365–753.

77. White, *Memoir of Samuel Slater*, p. 127. Average number of working children (between eight and sixteen) in the East Village households during this period was 4.9. Derived from SC: Slater and Tiffany, vols. 88–9, Slater and Kimball, vol. 3.

78. See James L. Conrad, Jr., "The Evolution of Industrial Capitalism in Rhode Island, 1790–1830: Almy, the Browns, and the Slaters" (Ph.D. diss., University of Connecticut, 1973), p. 293.

79. Merino Records: Series IV, Part II, E, box 20, John Sykes to John Brown, October 15, 1823; box 21, Phebe H. Larned to Mr. Permans (?), February (?), 1827; SC: Slater and Howard, vol. 26, John Brierly to Edward Howard, March 5, 1829.
80. See V, this chapter.
81. *Massachusetts Spy*, May 27, 1818.
82. Figures on returning workers derived from SC: Slater and Tiffany, vols. 84, 88–9. Samuel Slater and Sons, vol. 234, P. Pond to H. N. Slater, July 31, 1839.
83. SC: Slater and Howard, vol. 26, James Green to Samuel Slater, July 14, 1829.
84. SC: Slater and Howard, vol. 26, William Shaw to Edward Howard, February 28, 1827; Joseph Collier to Slater and Howard, March 12, 1829; John Brierly to Edward Howard, March 5, 1829.
85. SC: Slater and Tiffany, vol. 178; *Lowell Offering* 4 (June 1844):170.
86. Plan to Boarding House in Merino Records: Series IV, Part I, D, box 1, Miscellaneous.
87. The first Masonic Lodge actually ran from 1797 to 1815; the second, from 1825 to 1831. See Daniels, *Oxford*, pp. 248–50. A careful comparison of Dudley and Oxford town-meeting days with factory schedules reveals no effort to close the mills to permit workers to attend these gatherings. Militia membership of mule spinners derived from SC: Slater and Tiffany, vol. 73; Oxford Military Records, (Genealogical Library, microfilm 859224).
88. Marriages derived from SC: Slater and Tiffany, vols., 84, 88–91, DVR, OVR. The marriage ages of these workers were 21.1 years for women and 25.4 years for men, slightly below the average for the towns as a whole. Eric J. Hobsbawm, *Labouring Men; Studies in the History of Labour* (London, 1964), p. 9.
89. See Chapter 5, this volume.

4. The industrial order

1. Chapter 2, V, this volume; Chapter 3, II, this volume.
2. Joseph F. Kett, *Rites of Passage: Adolescence in America, 1790 to the Present* (New York, 1977), p. 31.
3. *New England Farmer* 17 (1838–9):406.
4. *Old Farmer's Almanack*, May 1834; March 1838; February 1850.
5. Ibid., April 1837.
6. Clarence H. Danhof, *Change in Agriculture; The Northern United States, 1820–1870* (Cambridge, Mass., 1969), p. 74, n. 1.
7. Patrick Shirreff, *A Tour Through North America* (Edinburgh, 1835), pp. 25, 16.
8. *Old Farmer's Almanack*, February 1844.
9. References to neighbors and relatives sharing labor cited in Chapter 1, n. 15, this volume, apply generally to these later decades as well.

The estimate of kin living in Dudley and Oxford is a rough index only, derived from MFCD, MFCO, 1820, by the method cited in Chapter 1, n. 14, this volume.

10. See, for example, Alis Rosenberg Wolfe, ed., "Letters of a Lowell Mill Girl and Friends: 1845–46," *Labor History* 17 (Winter, 1976):96–102; Nell W. Kull, "I Can Never Be Happy There in Among So Many Mountains – the Letters of Sally Rice," *Vermont History* 38 (1970):49–57. For the continuing strength of farming kinship patterns generally, see Peter Dobkin Hall, "Family Structure and Economic Organization: Massachusetts Merchants, 1700–1850," in Tamara Hareven, ed. *Family and Kin in Urban Communities, 1700–1930* (New York, 1977), pp. 51–4.

11. Cast-iron ploughs began to be widely marketed at least by 1817. Although the hill-planting method for corn continued until the 1850s, cultivators for the crop existed by the 1820s. Hay rakes (for gathering mown grass) were retailed from 1823 on. Danhof, *Change in Agriculture*, pp. 188, 214–15, 204, 219. Percy W. Bidwell and John I. Falconer, *History of Agriculture in the Northern United States, 1620–1860* (Washington, D.C., 1925), pp. 210–11.

12. Quoted in Danhof, *Change in Agriculture*, p. 135.

13. Bidwell and Falconer, *History of Agriculture*, p. 232. Danhof, *Change in Agriculture*, p. 138. AAS: Worcester County Valuations. English hay rose from 30.1% to 63.2% of the total hay production in the two townships between 1811 and 1831.

14. Ch. 140, Acts of 1812, *Laws of the Commonwealth of Massachusetts*, vol. 6 (Boston, 1812–15). Danhof, *Change in Agriculture*, pp. 220, 189, 279.

15. Danhof, *Change in Agriculture*, pp. 189, 204, 220, 257, 271.

16. Ibid., pp. 257, 279–80.

17. Ibid., p. 279. See Chapter 2, V, this volume.

18. Asher Robbins, *Address to the Rhode Island Society for the Encouragement of Domestic Industry* (Pawtucket, 1822), pp. 10–11.

19. *New England Farmer* (1832), p. 149.

20. Connecticut State Agriculture Society, *Transactions* (Hartford, 1855), p. 300.

21. Henry Colman, *Second Report on Agriculture of Massachusetts* (Boston, 1838), pp. 61–2.

22. See Chapter 6, III, this volume.

23. References cited in Chapter 1, n. 44, this volume, apply generally to these later decades as well. See also Alan Dawley, *Class and Community: The Industrial Revolution in Lynn* (Cambridge, Mass., 1976), pp. 46, 48; Paul G. Faler, *Mechanics and Manufacturers in the Early Industrial Revolution: Lynn, Massachusetts, 1780–1860* (Albany, 1981), p. 78.

24. Stanley Lebergott, *Manpower in Economic Growth: The American Record Since 1800* (New York, 1964), p. 169. Thomas B. Hazard, *Nailer Tom's Diary: Otherwise, the Journal of Thomas B. Hazard of Kingstown, Rhode*

Island, 1778 to 1840. Printed as Written and Introduced by Caroline Hazard (Boston, 1930), entry for July 28, 1821, p. 562.

25. George S. Gibb, *The Saco-Lowell Shops; Textile Machinery Building in New England, 1813–1949* (Cambridge, Mass., 1950), p. 53; see also pp. 146–7. Anthony F. C. Wallace, *Rockdale: The Growth of an American Village in the Early Industrial Revolution* (New York, 1978), p. 149.

26. See, for example, the agreement of E. White to build the "new meeting house" for a flat fee of $525 and "board himself." AAS: Dudley, Massachusetts, Town Records, 1740–1932, E. White to Col. Learned or Anyone of the Meetinghouse Committee, May 18, 1833, oversize vol. 2.

27. Wallace, *Rockdale*, pp. 147–8. On the general importance of the division of labor in the industrializing process, see Susan E. Hirsch, *Roots of the American Working Class: The Industrialization of Crafts in Newark, 1800–1860* (Philadelphia, 1978), pp. 21–2.

28. The system could encourage a heightened division of labor and a dilution of craft skills, especially among "assistants" hired by the contractor. But even where this happened – in the small-arms industry, for example – machinist-contractors remained highly proficient and generally in control of their own labor. See Felicia J. Deyrup, *Arms Makers of the Connecticut Valley; A Regional Study of the Economic Development of the Small Arms Industry, 1798–1870* (Northampton, Mass., 1948), pp. 100–2, 160–4; Merritt Roe Smith, *Harpers Ferry Armory and the New Technology: The Challenge of Change* (Ithaca, N.Y., 1977), pp. 239–40, 273. Textile machine shops of the period probably remained even more closely tied to traditional craft norms. See Gibb, *The Saco-Lowell Shops*, pp. 88–90.

29. Daniels, *Oxford*, pp. 191, 202, 197.

30. J. R. Chapin, "Among the Nail-Makers," *Harper's New Monthly Magazine* 21 (1860):163.

31. Dawley, *Class and Community*, p. 42. Wallace, *Rockdale*, p. 148.

32. Chapter 2, V, this volume.

33. For nonlocal sales, see McLane, *Report*, 1:484–5, 526–7, 576–7. For lawsuits, see Merino Records: Series III, A, vol. 4, Ledgers, Writs Served 1813–14; Series IV, Part II, A, box 1, Writs, 1828–34; AAS: Worcester County, Mass., Papers, 1675–ca. 1954, Record Book, 1801–17, of J. P. Aaron Tufts, folio vol. 8.

34. Daniels, *Oxford*, p. 204. AAS: Craggins and Andrews, Account Book, 1820–7; William Law, Account Book, 1819–23.

35. Caroline F. Ware, *The Early New England Cotton Manufacture; A Study in Industrial Beginnings* (Boston, 1931), pp. 140–1. McLane, *Report*, 1: 71, 74.

36. SC: Slater and Tiffany, Weave Book A; vol. 234, Samuel to John Slater, December 31, 1825. McLane, *Report*, 1: 577. Ware, *The Early New England Cotton Manufacture*, p. 164.

37. See Chapter 6, III, this volume.

38. Virtually all the testimony from textile manufacturers in McLane's *Report* complained of high overhead and raised arguments favoring a tariff. For contemporary invocations of greater efficiency, see James Montgomery, *A Practical Detail of the Cotton Manufacture of the United States of America* (Glasgow, 1840); Ogden, *Thoughts.*

39. *Derby Mercury*, August 25, 1785, quoted in R. S. Fitton and Alfred P. Wadsworth, *The Strutts and the Arkwrights, 1758–1830; A Study of the Early Factory System* (Manchester, England, 1958), pp. 102–3. Michael Ignatieff, *A Just Measure of Pain: The Penitentiary in the Industrial Revolution, 1750–1850* (New York, 1978), p. 63.

40. See Chapter 2, II, this volume. Quoted in James L. Conrad, Jr., "The Evolution of Industrial Capitalism in Rhode Island, 1790–1830: Almy, the Browns, and the Slaters" (Ph.D. diss., University of Connecticut, 1973), pp. 15–16.

41. Thomas Steere, *History of the Town of Smithfield* (Providence, 1881), p. 105. George S. White, *Memoir of Samuel Slater* (Philadelphia, 1836; reprinted, 1967), p. 108.

42. Harriet Martineau, *Society in America*, 2 vols. (New York, 1837), 2:138.

43. White, *Memoir of Samuel Slater*, p. 108. Wallace, *Rockdale*, pp. 327–31. SC: Slater and Kimball, vol. 3. Ignatieff, *A Just Measure of Pain*, pp. 66–71.

44. David J. Rothman, *The Discovery of the Asylum; Social Order and Disorder in the New Republic* (Boston, 1971), chs. 3–8, but esp. pp. 62–71, 124–9, 165–79. Michael B. Katz, *The Irony of Early School Reform; Educational Innovation in Mid-Nineteenth Century Massachusetts* (Cambridge, Mass., 1968), parts 1 and 2. *Common School Journal* 12 (August 1850):236, quoted in ibid., p. 124.

45. Ogden, *Thoughts*, p. 7.

46. Henry A. Miles, *Lowell, As It Was, And As It Is*, (Lowell, 1846; reprinted, 1972), pp. 130–1. "Article II [Review of *A History of the Cotton Manufacture in Great Britain* by Edward Baines and *Memoir of Samuel Slater* by George S. White]," *North American Review* 52 (January 1841):50.

47. *Manufacturers' and Farmers' Journal and Providence and Pawtucket Advertiser*, October 30, 1820. See Conrad, "The Evolution of Industrial Capitalism in Rhode Island," pp. 2–4.

48. White, *Memoir of Samuel Slater*, p. 117.

49. Ibid., pp. 116–17. Ignatieff, *A Just Measure of Pain*, pp. 60–2. See also, Chapin, "Among the Nail-Makers," p. 146. The notion of contagion (and the related concern about workers "crowding" together) invaded many of the arguments defending and criticizing the health of textile operatives. See Miles, *Lowell, As It Was*, pp. 120–2. Martineau, *Society in America*, 2:139–40.

50. McLane, *Report*, 1:930–1.

51. Interestingly enough, asylums themselves – despite their ideological overlap with factories – were often judged so harsh as to make military, rather than paternalistic, metaphors seem appropriate. See

Rothman, *The Discovery of the Asylum*, pp. 62–78, 90–7, 105–8, 120–2, 165–6.

52. Erastus Richardson, *History of Woonsocket* (Woonsocket, 1876), p. 140.
53. White, *Memoir of Samuel Slater*, p. 108. William R. Bagnall, *Samuel Slater and the Early Development of the Cotton Manufacture in the United States* (Middletown, Conn., 1890), pp. 68–9.
54. Ammidown, *Historical Collections*, 1:502. Scholarly acknowledgments of paternalism include: John P. Coolidge, *Mill and Mansion: A Study of Architecture and Society in Lowell, Massachusetts, 1820–1865* (New York, 1942), pp. 114–15, 164; George Rogers Taylor, *The Transportation Revolution, 1815–1860* (New York, 1951), pp. 275–6; and (though they mean the term more critically) Norman Ware, *The Industrial Worker, 1840–1860; The Reaction of American Industrial Society to the Advance of the Industrial Revolution* (Boston, 1924), chs. 6–8, and Thomas Dublin, *Women at Work: The Transformation of Work and Community in Lowell, Massachusetts, 1826–1860* (New York, 1979), pp. 77–8, 142–3.
55. The proportion of family workers in the East Village stood at 68.8% in 1813, rose to 87.9% during the depression of 1819, and fell back to 69.8% in 1830. SC: Slater and Tiffany, vols. 84, 88–90.
56. Derived from SC: Slater and Tiffany, vol. 88; Slater and Kimball, vol. 3; Slater and Howard, vol. 22.
57. A sampling of 175 youngsters working in the East Village during the 1820s reveals that 56% left the village, evidently on their own, for periods of roughly a year. See Chapter 5, this volume, for a discussion of workers' leaving.
58. SC: Slater and Kimball, vol. 3.
59. Some married women "washed towels," others turned out candlewicks in their living quarters, and widows frequently ran the boardinghouses. The point here is simply that married women and mothers did not hold berths inside the factories. SC: Slater and Tiffany, vols. 73, 88–91, 93. It should also be acknowledged that some operatives arrived at the mills evidently expecting to work with their children (see SC: Samuel Slater and Sons, vol. 237, Joseph Gregory to John Slater, June 7, 1829). But the segregation pressed ahead anyway. On mule spinners and piecers, see especially SC: Slater and Kimball, vol. 3, Contract (1837) with [?] Dilworth and Samuel Bronaugh under which S. Slater and Sons agreed "to find him piecers"; also contracts of Thomas Twiss, Jr. (1828) "to piece on mules for E. Emerson"; and with Isaac Amidown (1829) "to work for mule spinners as they agree."
60. Seven out of ten East Village male household heads had berths in 1817; by 1830 the proportion was 35.3%. Out of eleven mule spinners and dressers in 1830, eight (72.7%) had been promoted or hired as unmarried men. Derived from SC: Slater and Tiffany, vols. 73, 88–91, 93; Slater and Kimball, vol. 3.
61. *Manufacturers' and Farmers' Journal and Providence and Pawtucket Advertiser*, September 22, 1823.

62. *Pawtucket Chronicle*, August 29, 1829. On republican ideology, see generally, Bernard Bailyn, *The Ideological Origins of the American Revolution* (Cambridge, Mass., 1967), and Gordon S. Wood, *The Creation of the American Republic, 1776–1787* (Chapel Hill, N.C., 1969).
63. Ogden, *Thoughts*, p. 6. *Pawtucket Chronicle*, August 29, 1829.
64. Sui Generis: Alias Thomas Man, *Picture of a Factory Village: To Which are Annexed Remarks on Lotteries* (Providence, 1833), pp. 8–9.
65. Dublin, *Women at Work*, ch. 6.
66. SC: Samuel Slater and Sons, vol. 110, S. Slater and Sons to D. W. Jones, May 1, 1837.
67. SC: Samuel Slater and Sons, vol. 235, Samuel to John Slater, August 4, 1828; Samuel to John Slater, September 14, 1828.
68. Merino Records: Series IV, Part I, A, vol. 1, p. 10. SC: Slater and Howard, vol. 22.
69. A & B: box 1, no. 18, Samuel Slater to Almy and Brown, April 4, 1791. Neil J. Smelser, *Social Change in the Industrial Revolution; An Application of Theory to the British Cotton Industry* (Chicago, 1959), p. 66.
70. Ware, *The Early New England Cotton Manufacture*, pp. 70–2.
71. Ibid., pp. 73–4. SC: Slater and Tiffany, Weave Books B–D.
72. Derived from SC: Slater and Tiffany, Weave Book D.
73. Victor S. Clark, *History of Manufactures in the United States*, 3 vols. (New York, 1929), 1:422. SC: Slater and Tiffany, Weave Book B.
74. See n. 34 and Daniels, *Oxford*, pp. 198, 204. SC: Slater and Tiffany, vol. 84; Weave Book D. There is thus little evidence for the hypothesis (suggested by Ware) that Slater clung to handloom weaving after it became costly simply because he had long familiarity with this method of cloth production (see Ware, *The Early New England Cotton Manufacture*, p. 74). Robert Brooke Zevin has distinguished between cost-cutting and labor-saving motivations for introducing power looms, arguing that the former were more consequential; see *The Growth of Manufacturing in Early Nineteenth Century New England* (New York, 1975), p. 8. It is worth emphasizing, too, that adopting the integrated spinning-weaving production format of Waltham factories did not lead mills like those in Dudley and Oxford to adopt the all-adult labor force of large northern New England establishments. Small country mills continued to hire families.
75. See Edward P. Thompson, *The Making of the English Working Class* (New York, 1964), ch. 9.
76. See Chapter 5, IV, this volume.
77. SC: Slater and Howard, Daybook 11; Samuel Slater and Sons, vol. 191.
78. Merino Records: Series IV, Part II, E, box 20, Perez B. Wolcott to Major John Brown, October 25, 1824; Part I, D, vols. 80–1; E, vols. 91–3. Aaron Tufts testified in 1828 that whereas his cassimeres were still woven entirely by hand, broadcloths in the Tufts Woolen Mill "are wove partly by the hand and partly by the power loom." *American State Papers: Finance*, 3:810.

79. SC: Slater and Howard, vol. 22.
80. "Work Diary" (12 vols.) in Gordon Papers, Baker Library, Harvard University, vol. 5, June 21, 1831; cited hereafter as N. B. Gordon, "Diary."
81. See Chapter 6, IV, this volume.
82. SC: Slater and Kimball, vol. 3. The numerous letters sent by operatives to the mills would suggest that this was a labor force with at least preliminary experience in reading and writing. The point here is simply that so long as they remained within local mill villages, their children were not likely to receive formal schooling.
83. Derived from Daniels, *Oxford*, ch. 4; Ammidown, *Historical Collections*, 1:214–34, 439–52, 503–22; *Worcester County*, 1:430–7; 2:171–9, 456–64.
84. Ware, *The Early New England Cotton Manufacture*, p. 285. Dudley's Baptist Church may have independently launched a Sunday school in 1827. See *Worcester County*, 2:460.
85. Derived from Daniels, *Oxford*, ch. 4.
86. Derived from Daniels, *Oxford*, chs. 4, 8; Ammidown, *Historical Collections*, 1:214–34, 439–52, 503–22; *Worcester County*, 1:430–7; 2:171–9, 456–64.
87. Brendan F. Gilbane, "A Social History of Samuel Slater's Pawtucket, 1790–1830" (Ph.D. diss., Boston University, 1969), pp. 430–5. Conrad, "The Evolution of Industrial Capitalism in Rhode Island," pp. 262–4. Frederick L. Lewton, "A Biography of Samuel Slater" (manuscript, Slater Mill Historical Site, Pawtucket, R.I., 1944), pp. 185–6. *Worcester County*, 2:461; Ammidown, *Historical Collections*, 1:511.
88. Ammidown, *Historical Collections*, 1:448.
89. Derived from "Constitution of the Methodist Episcopal Church, 1830–1840," manuscript, United Church of Christ, Webster, Mass.
90. See Chapter 5, VI, this volume.
91. Clark, *History of Manufactures in the United States*, 1:426–9. Arthur H. Cole, *The American Wool Manufacture*, 2 vols. (Cambridge, Mass., 1926), 1:92–118. Cole notes that John Goulding's "American Card" and Gilbert Brewster's "Globe-Spinner" for woolen mills were both known by the 1820s but found little favor before 1830 and were specifically rejected by Slater. For greater emphasis on jacks, see Merino Records: Series IV, Part I, B, vols. 45–6.
92. Dublin, *Women at Work*, pp. 67–8. Cole, *The American Wool Manufacture*, 1:93–118, 128–31. Wallace, *Rockdale*, pp. 148–50. Wallace notes (p. 195) that the self-acting (power-driven) mule did not reach America until 1840.
93. See Dublin, *Women at Work*, pp. 62–8. Harriet H. Robinson, *Loom and Spindle, or Life Among the Early Mill Girls* (New York, 1898), p. 30.
94. Andrew Ure, *The Philosophy of Manufactures* (London, 1835), p. 155. SC: Slater and Howard, vol. 22; Slater and Kimball, vol. 3.
95. Robinson, *Loom and Spindle*, p. 30; *New England Offering* 1 (April 1848):5. Mass. House Documents, No. 50, March 1843, quoted in John R.

Commons et al., eds., *Documentary History of American Industrial Society*, 11 vols. (Cleveland, 1910–11), 8:137.

96. Derived from SC: Slater and Tiffany, vols. 73, 84, 88–91, 93; Slater and Kimball, vol. 3.

97. See Wallace, *Rockdale*, p. 179; Ware, *The Early New England Cotton Manufacture*, p. 263.

98. N. B. Gordon, "Diary," vol. 5, November 10–17, 1830.

99. Montgomery, *A Practical Detail*, pp. 177–8.

100. Merino Records: Series IV, Part I, D, vols. 74, 78. SC: Slater and Tiffany, vols. 84, 88–91. For highway work by the hour, see Chapter 1, this volume.

5. How the operatives responded

1. DVR, OVR.

2. SC: H. N. Slater, vol. 33, (?) Hedges to H. N. Slater, April 11, 1838.

3. SC: Webster Woolen, vol. 111, James Carter to D. W. Jones, February 22, 1839.

4. See Chapter 2, III, this volume. A & B: box 2, no. 256, Samuel Slater to Almy and Brown, September 25, 1795.

5. Autumn dips in attendance and Slater attendance figures derived from SC: Slater and Tiffany, vols. 88–91; Dudley Woolen Mill figures derived from Merino Records: series IV, Part I, D, vols. 74 and 75. It should be pointed out that the fall harvesting in which Slater's southern Massachusetts workers engaged may have been in fields owned by Slater and undertaken at his orders. To some degree, of course, these attendance figures may reflect managerial decisions to run the machines more continuously. Generally speaking, the improved reliability of machines, the more consistent access to raw materials, and the strengthened linkage to retail outlets – all undoubtedly permitted millowners to maintain a more continuous schedule (during good times) in the 1820s and 1830s than in the 1790s. But to separate out absenteeism somewhat more precisely from managerial determinations to shut down for a few days or to run short time, an operative was counted absent only if more than half his or her department was simultaneously at work. As a further indication that resulting attendance figures cited in the text are reflective of operatives' attitudes, it may be noted that punctuality increased even within the post-1810 generation and even after correcting for economic conditions and shutdowns. Thus, East Village operatives were 2.5% more punctual at the end of this period than at its start; Dudley Woolen workers "improved" 8.7% during the 1820s alone.

6. SC: Slater and Tiffany, vols. 88 and 89.

7. SC: Slater and Kimball, vol. 3.

8. Joseph Brennan, *Social Conditions in Industrial Rhode Island: 1820–1860* (Washington, 1940), pp. 32–3. A & B: box 7, no. 944, Samuel Slater to

Almy and Brown, October 9, 1811. For a general discussion of arson in antebellum mills, see Gary Kulik, "Pawtucket Village and the Strike of 1824; The Origin of Class Conflict in Rhode Island," *Radical History Review* 17 (Spring, 1978):5–37.

9. Daniels, *Oxford*, pp. 191, 193, 207, 209.

10. See Caroline F. Ware, *The Early New England Cotton Manufacture; A Study in Industrial Beginnings* (Boston, 1931), p. 290.

11. Thomas Dublin occasionally hints at comparable tensions among the Lowell workers. See *Women at Work: The Transformation of Work and Community in Lowell, Massachusetts, 1826–1860* (New York, 1979), ch. 6 esp. pp. 94–5.

12. SC: Slater and Tiffany, vols. 88–91. Merino Records: Series IV, Part I, D, vols. 74 and 75.

13. SC: Slater and Tiffany, vol. 101, (?) to John Slater, August 8, 1834.

14. N. B. Gordon, "Diary," vol. 4, June 8, 1829.

15. Derived from SC: Slater and Tiffany, vol. 84. The pattern cited in the text was not caused by absenteeism: Neither weavers nor any other Slater operatives showed consistent proclivity to avoid work on Mondays and show up on Saturdays. Nor is it likely that the trend reflected managerial decisions, for if that had been the case the pattern would have appeared more consistently. The most likely explanation for the slow-to-fast rhythm is that the weavers themselves – when they could, to the degree they could – were altering their output by varying the pace of piecing on their looms. For an analysis of comparable inclinations among British handloom weavers, see E. P. Thompson, *The Making of the English Working Class* (New York, 1964), p. 306. See also the same author's "Time, Work-Discipline, and Industrial Capitalism," *Past and Present* 38 (December 1967):56–97.

16. Harriet Martineau, *Society in America*, 2 vols. (New York, 1837), 2:56. Charles Dickens, *The Works of Charles Dickens: American Notes* (London, 1929), 16:85.

17. Brennan, *Social Conditions in Industrial Rhode Island*, p. 39.

18. SC: Slater and Howard, vol. 26.

19. See Hannah G. Josephson, *The Golden Threads: New England's Mill Girls and Magnates* (New York, 1949), p. 83. There are hints of such parties in SC: Samuel Slater and Sons, vol. 235, Samuel to John Slater, October 23, 1830.

20. Relations of operatives during working hours derived from SC: Slater and Tiffany, vol. 94. An excellent discussion of social relations of workers within the Lowell mills is found in Dublin, *Women at Work*, ch. 4. Mention of the sign language used by modern textile workers is found in Betty Messenger, *Picking Up the Linen Threads: A Study in Industrial Folklore* (Austin, Texas, 1978), pp. 148–9. Testimony among antebellum New England operatives that they could communicate despite their machines is taken from *The Harbinger*, November 14, 1846, quoted in Norman Ware, *The Industrial Worker, 1840–1860: The*

Reaction of American Industrial Society to the Advance of the Industrial Revolution (Boston, 1924), p. 106.

21. SC: Samuel Slater and Sons, vol. 235, Samuel to John Slater, April 4, 1820.

22. Funeral attendance is noted in SC: Slater and Tiffany, vols. 88–91; Samuel Slater and Sons, vol. 235, Samuel to John Slater, August 6, 1834. Time books reveal that managers never closed down the East Village to mark a death or a funeral, even when a manager, or even a Slater, died. These records also show, however, that although workers unilaterally decided to take days off to attend funerals of other operatives, they did not do so when a manager, including Samuel Slater himself, was interred in the local cemetery.

23. Old Slater Mill Collection (Pawtucket, R.I.), Caleb Farnum to Samuel Slater, June 9, 1814 (reference courtesy of Gary Kulik). Merino Records: Series IV, Part I, D, vols. 74–78. SC: Slater and Tiffany, vols. 88, 91, 93. For examples of other mills that started to pay "something extra" for work past normal quitting times, see Ware, *The Early New England Cotton Manufacture*, p. 69.

24. Derived from SC: Slater and Tiffany, vols. 73, 89, 93; Slater and Kimball, vol. 3.

25. Merino Records: Series IV, Part II, E, box 20, Slater and Howard to Major John Brown, March 10, 1827.

26. Useful treatments of labor militancy in this period include: Alan Dawley, *Class and Community: The Industrial Revolution in Lynn* (Cambridge, Mass., 1976); Bruce Laurie, *Working People of Philadelphia, 1800–1850* (Philadelphia, 1980); Philip S. Foner, *History of the Labor Movement in the United States*, 4 vols. (New York, 1947), vol. 1; Norman Ware, *The Industrial Worker*; Paul G. Faler, *Mechanics and Manufacturers in the Early Industrial Revolution: Lynn, Massachusetts, 1780–1860* (Albany, N.Y., 1981). For the Pawtucket strike, see Kulik, "Pawtucket Village and the Strike of 1824."

27. For indications of this pattern elsewhere in the textile industry, see Ware, *The Early New England Cotton Manufacture*, p. 273; Foner, *History of the Labor Movement in the United States*, 1:105. For the context surrounding confrontations among antebellum shoemakers, see Dawley, *Class and Community*.

28. For the shift to power looms, see Chapter 4, VI, this volume. Although some handweaving persisted in the South Village until 1830, it is clear that this factory had stopped turning out cassimere by handlooms considerably before that. SC: Samuel Slater and Sons, vol. 191.

29. SC: Union Mills, vol. 119. Oxford tilted to Jackson's party in 1829 and 1831; Dudley in 1829, 1830, and 1831. (Local voting data kindly supplied by R. D. Formisano.) General political trends in Massachusetts in this period are treated in Arthur B. Darling, *Political Changes in Massachusetts, 1824–1848; A Study of Liberal Movements in Politics* (New

Haven, 1925), pp. 49–58; 75, n. 79; 93, n. 14. For failure to attend regional mechanics' meetings, see *Providence Journal*, October 25, 1831.

30. Some brief confrontations in rural mills undoubtedly escaped the public record, but the perspective argued here is generally substantiated by Carroll D. Wright, *Strikes in Massachusetts, 1830–1880 (Being Part I of the Eleventh Annual Report of the Massachusetts Bureau of Statistics of Labor [1880])* (reprinted, Boston, 1889). For patterns of developing militancy among Lowell workers, see Dublin, *Women at Work*, esp. chs. 6 and 7. A general treatment of labor strikes, along with a suggestion that they did not become important in America until after the mid-1840s, is found in David Montgomery, "Strikes in Nineteenth Century America," *Social Science History* 4 (February 1980):81–104, esp. 86–7.

31. Derived from SC: Slater and Tiffany, vols. 73, 84; Slater and Kimball, vol. 3.

32. Aggregate turnover was 94.7% and 84.2% in 1819 and 1820, respectively (see Table A.1). The number of arrivals and departures used to compute aggregate turnover was established by comparing payroll listings four times each year; April, July, October, and January. Departures were treated as distinct from absenteeism: Workers were counted as having departed only if they failed to appear at any point in a monthly payroll listing. Names of household heads among departing workers were compared to 1820 and 1830 enumerations, Fourth and Fifth Federal Censuses, of Dudley, Oxford, Charlton, Ward, Millbury, Sutton, Woodstock, and Southbridge, all in Worcester County, Massachusetts.

33. Derived by comparing transiency of households found in SC: Slater and Tiffany, vols. 88 and 89, between 1820 and 1830, with transiency of household heads not cited as "manufacturing" in MFCO, MFCD, 1820 and 1830.

34. See Chapter 3, VI, this volume.

35. Voluntary exits were estimated by subtracting departures coinciding with net reductions in the work force from each year's total exits and computing the remainder as a percentage of the average annual work roster. (The rate of voluntary departure could exceed 100% of the average annual labor force because the calculations for this rate are derived from measurements of movement taken quarterly.) The assumption behind this methodology is that net reductions reflected managerial decisions. This, in turn, assumes that management succeeded in finding the number of workers it wanted during any given quarter. As indicated in the following discussion, local managers worried constantly about being shorthanded and often had difficulty filling their berths. Nonetheless, available evidence indicates that these mills were not short of workers often or long enough to distort the estimates revealed in Figure 5.1.

36. Aggregate turnover and estimated voluntary departure rates do move

in opposite directions in 1816, when the East Village dropped fifty workers and those with jobs chose to remain in place. The two rates also diverge in 1824 when an increase in the size of the East Village roster pushed up aggregate turnover but voluntary departures remained almost unchanged. And the same was true in 1827, when the shift to power-loom operatives pushed up aggregate turnover but only slightly increased voluntary exits. Generally, however, the two rates tended to move in parallel. The average voluntary departure rate for the 1814–35 period was 59.8%.

37. SC: Slater and Tiffany, vols. 73, 84.
38. SC: Slater and Tiffany, vols. 88 and 89; Slater and Kimball, vol. 3.
39. Merino Records: Series IV, Part II, E, box 23, Tyler Chamberlain to Major John Brown, March 11, 1831.
40. SC: Slater and Tiffany, vols. 88 and 89; Slater and Kimball, vol. 3.
41. *Massachusetts Spy*, November 27, 1816.
42. Derived from William R. Bagnall, "Contributions to American Economic History" (manuscript, 4 vols., Baker Library, Harvard University, 1908) and Daniels, *Oxford*, pp. 365–753. N. B. Gordon, "Diary," vol. 5, May 21, 1830.
43. See SC: Slater and Howard, vol. 26. There is no evidence, however, that workers generally traded longer contracts for lower rates.
44. SC: Samuel Slater and Sons, vol. 236, (?) Hedges to John Slater, August 18, 1834. Merino Records: Series IV, Part I, A, vol. 5, September 1, 1841. Desire for nonfinancial improvements is indicated in SC: Webster Woolen, vol. 110, Ashron Loring to D. W. Jones, September 4, 1836; Slater and Howard, vol. 25, Thomas Haygood to Edward Howard, May 28, 1827. For Slater's earlier experience with intermill mobility, see James L. Conrad, Jr., "The Evolution of Industrial Capitalism in Rhode Island, 1790–1830: Almy, the Browns, and the Slaters" (Ph.D. diss., University of Connecticut, 1973), p. 292.
45. Henry A. Miles, *Lowell, As It Was, And As It Is* (Lowell, 1846; reprinted, 1972), p. 129. "Article II [Review of *A History of the Cotton Manufacture in Great Britain* by Edward Baines and *Memoir of Samuel Slater* by George S. White]," *North American Review* 52 (January 1841): 50.
46. See, for example, SC: Samuel Slater and Sons, vol. 235, Samuel to John Slater, July 13, 1822.
47. See Ware, *The Early New England Cotton Manufacture*, pp. 201, 227. SC: Webster Woolen, vol. 76, Phoenix Mill to Mr. James Cook, June 30, 1831.
48. Merino Records: Series IV, Part II, E, box 21, S. H. Babcock to Mr. Clemons, August 9, 1834.
49. SC: Samuel Slater and Sons, vol. 236, Hedges to John Slater, August 18, 1834.
50. SC: Webster Woolen, vol. 110, George Hanson to D. W. Jones, November 22, 1836.

51. SC: Webster Woolen, vol. 110, Christy Davis to D. W. Jones, December 4, 1836.

52. SC: Webster Woolen, vol. 26, J. M. Gibbs to Edward Howard, November 30, 1827.

53. SC: Webster Woolen, vol. 110, Anne Smith to D. W. Jones, January 15, 1838.

54. Merino Records: Series IV, Part II, E, box 23, S. A. Hitchcock to John Brown, February 26, 1831; Ansel Crosby to [Dudley Woolen Mill], January 29, 1831; Ansel Crosby to [Dudley Woolen Mill], February 17, 1831.

55. Samuel Slater, Original Letters, Invoices, etc., Relating to the Cotton Industry in Rhode Island, 1804–45 (Rhode Island School of Design): Samuel to John Slater, December 23, 1808.

56. A & B: box 3, no. 398, Samuel Slater to Almy and Brown, January (?), 1796. For contracts during the 1810–35 period, see Merino Records: Series I, A, vol. 2; SC: Slater and Howard, vol. 22; Slater and Kimball, vol. 3.

57. Slater and Tiffany, vol. 93; Slater and Howard, vol. 22.

58. Stanley Lebergott, *Manpower in Economic Growth: The American Record Since 1800* (New York, 1964), p. 237. SC: Slater and Tiffany, vol. 101, (?) to S. Slater and Sons, March 7, 1836.

59. Between 1825 and 1830 the season with the most layoffs (50.5% of the total) was fall. Between 1831 and 1835 the season with the most layoffs (40.3% of the total) was summer. Derived from SC: Slater and Tiffany, vols. 88–91.

60. SC: Webster Woolen, vol. 26, William Shaw to Edward Howard, February 28, 1827.

61. Derived from Merino Records: Series IV, Part I, D, vols. 74 and 75; SC: Slater and Tiffany, vols. 88–91; Phoenix, vols. 24–5.

62. A & B: box 8, no. 1092, Samuel Slater to Almy and Brown, March 3, 1814. Merino Records: Series IV, Part II, E, box 23, Nancy Gossett to [Merino Factory], March 26, 1831. SC: Slater and Howard, vol. 25, William Buckminster to Edward Howard, May 29, 1827.

63. For continuing threats not to pay workers who left precipitously, see SC: Slater and Kimball, vol. 3. For indications of payment schedules more rapid than once every twelve months, see SC: Slater and Tiffany, vols. 89–91, and vol. 101, Samuel Slater to (?) Sales and (?) Hitchcock, April 25, 1827. For contracts that permitted giving "notice," see SC: Slater and Kimball, vol. 3. Even with these clauses, workers continued to leave "unexpectedly." See SC: Webster Woolen, vol. 114, (?) Hedges to S. Slater and Sons, October 25, 1838. For workers persisting in signing for, and honoring, yearlong contracts, see Merino Records: Series IV, Part II, E, box 20, Josiah Moulton to Dudley Woolen Mfg. Co., March 16, 1829.

64. SC: Samuel Slater and Sons, vol. 236, (?) Hedges to John Slater, April 11, 1834; Webster Woolen, vol. 110, Christy Davis to D. W. Jones, December 4, 1836.

65. See Chapter 2, III, this volume. James Montgomery, *A Practical Detail of the Cotton Manufacture of the United States of America* (Glasgow, 1840), p. 41. See also Paul F. McGouldrick, *New England Textiles in the Nineteenth Century; Profits and Investments* (Cambridge, Mass., 1968), p. 37. Ware, *The Early New England Cotton Manufacture*, pp. 223–4.

66. Merino Records: Series IV, Part II, E, box 20, James Wolcott to Perez B. Wolcott, September 5, 1825.

67. Samuel Slater, Original Letters, Invoices, etc., Relating to the Cotton Industry in Rhode Island, 1804–45, (Rhode Island School of Design): P. C. Bacon to John Slater, March 20, 1831.

68. Dates of revivals and construction of new churches derived from: Daniels, *Oxford*, ch. 4; Ammidown, *Historical Collections*, 1:213–34; 439–52; 503–22. Transiency of operatives derived from SC: Slater and Tiffany, vols. 88–91; Phoenix, vols. 24 and 5.

69. The first revival was in Dudley and occurred in the winter of 1813–14. The other three took place in Oxford: in 1822 during the spring, peaking in July; in 1831 during the fall; and in 1835 in the late fall, peaking in December.

70. The postrevival surge in 1822 amounted to an autumnal increment of only 5.0%. This was more than matched by a 13.8% increment in voluntary departures in the same season during 1820–5 as a whole. In 1813 and 1835, however, postrevival increases (during first and fourth quarters of these years, respectively) outpaced increases in parallel months during surrounding years by 15.1% (in 1813–14) and 28.9% (in 1835). In 1831 the postrevival upswing (again in the fourth quarter) was smaller than the 1830–5 average for that season. But voluntary departures fell off through 1831, and the upswing that did occur after that year's revival sufficed to make the wintertime exit rate the second highest for that year. During the 1830–5 period as a whole, by contrast, fourth-quarter voluntary departure rates ranked third.

71. Though often suggesting that revivals provided a desired sense of rootedness, several authors have noted the particularly sympathetic chord religious "enthusiasm" struck among antebellum America's transient citizens. See Philip Greven, *The Protestant Temperament: Patterns of Child-Rearing, Religious Experience, and the Self in Early America* (New York, 1977), p. 25, and the classic study by Whitney Cross, *The Burned Over District; The Social and Intellectual History of Enthusiastic Religion in Western New York, 1800–1850* (Ithaca, N.Y., 1950), p. 6. Somewhat different views of the intersection of religious revivals and antebellum workers are found in Paul E. Johnson, *A Shopkeeper's Millennium: Society and Revivals in Rochester, New York, 1815–1837* (New York, 1978), and especially in Anthony F. C. Wallace, *Rockdale: The Growth of an American Village in the Early Industrial Revolution* (New York, 1978), pts. 3 and 4. See also Laurie, *Working People of Philadelphia*.

72. Miles, *Lowell, As It Was*, pp. 128–40. Carl Gersuny, " 'A Devil in Petticoats' and Just Cause: Patterns of Punishment in Two New England Textile Factories," *Business History Review* 50 (Summer, 1976): 131–52.

73. The contrast to Waltham mills should not be overdrawn. These larger establishments did occasionally find transiency sufficiently troubling to offer bonuses to "steady" workers; and they likely did not always enforce all their rules. See McGouldrick, *New England Textiles in the Nineteenth Century*, p. 273; Ware, *The Early New England Cotton Manufacture*, p. 264. The point here is that the larger mills on balance appear to have enforced rules and to have used disciplinary techniques that were characteristically avoided by smaller, rural factories.

74. Peter J. Coleman, *The Transformation of Rhode Island, 1790–1860* (Providence, 1963), p. 232. Thomas Steere, *History of the Town of Smithfield* (Providence, 1881), p. 105. Brennan, *Social Conditions in Industrial Rhode Island*, p. 67.

75. SC: Slater and Tiffany, vol. 101, (?) to Russel Hill, January 18, 1827; Slater and Tiffany, vol. 8, vol. 84. Merino Records: Series IV, Part II, E, box 20, Edward Howard to Chester Clemons, July 8, 1830.

76. SC: Samuel Slater and Sons, vol. 235, Samuel to John Slater, August 19, 1825.

77. Brennan, *Social Conditions in Industrial Rhode Island*, p. 67.

78. SC: Webster Woolen, vol. 111, Hannah Mathews to D. W. Jones, August 12, 1839; Webster Woolen, vol. 114, John A. Wheelock to J. Wilson, February 6, 1840.

6. How the towns responded

1. See Chapter 2, V, this volume.
2. TRDM III, May 1821, p. 309.
3. TROM III, November 1823, p. 259; TRDM III, November 1822, pp. 323–5.
4. Mass. Archives: Report of the Viewing Committee on petition of Geo. B. Slater and others, January 17, 1832, Original Papers of Ch. 93, Acts of 1832, pp. 4–5; cited hereafter as Report of the Viewing Committee.
5. TROM III, March 1821, p. 223; TRDM III, March 1828, p. 403.
6. TROM III, December 1819, p. 205. TRDM III, April 1817, p. 251; March 1839, p. 591. Daniels, *Oxford*, p. 223.
7. TRDM III, April 1827, p. 390–1.
8. TRDM III, November 1816, pp. 246–7; May 1818, pp. 265–6; March 1822, p. 319. Oxford's reluctance was the more notable because by the late 1820s the town's school districts had annual incomes ranging very widely (from a low of $27.41 to a high of $135.36). Derived from 1827 and 1829 Oxford School Taxes.
9. Derived from Oxford School Taxes. Data cover eight of the nine school districts.
10. The tax bills levied on all local mills have not survived, but extant records indicate that the Slater family was paying around 10% of Oxford's total tax assessment in 1832. See Report of the Viewing

Committee, p. 4. For a discussion of the Oxford Bank, see discussion in IV, this chapter, and Daniels, *Oxford*, p. 232.

11. See III, this chapter.

12. Selectmen are cited in TRDM III, 1820–30; TROM III, 1820–30. Names were compared to AAS: Worcester County, Mass., Papers, 1675–ca. 1954, 1815 Valuations, folio vol. 14; and (for Oxford) Oxford School Taxes.

13. The average length of service for selectmen in both towns fell from 3.1 years between 1800 and 1810 to 2.2 years between 1820 and 1830. The proportion of selectmen born outside these towns remained just under half the total (46.5%), but the proportion of men preceded into the post by a close relative fell from three-quarters to just over one-fifth. See Chapter 1, V, this volume. Derived from TRDM III, 1820–30; TROM III, 1820–30, DVR, OVR.

14. See Chapter 1, V, this volume.

15. Derived from TRDM III, 1820–30; TROM III, 1820–30.

16. SC: Samuel Slater and Sons, vol. 235, Samuel to John Slater, February 7, 1825.

17. See Morton J. Horwitz, *The Transformation of American Law, 1780–1860* (Cambridge, Mass., 1977), pp. 40–2.

18. J. D. Van Slyck, *Representatives of New England Manufacturers* (Boston, 1879), p. 415. TRDM III, April 1826, p. 375. Such, at least, is the inference that may be drawn from the fact that the town refused to spend its own money to repair the damage Tufts had caused.

19. Merino Records: Series IV, Part II, E, box 21, S. H. Babcock to Mr. Clemons, May 28, 1834.

20. SC: Samuel Slater and Sons, vol. 235, Samuel to John Slater, February 7, 1825 (emphasis in original).

21. TRDM III, November 1832, p. 486.

22. SC: Samuel Slater and Sons, vol. 235, Samuel to John Slater, February 7, 1825. For further disputes with the Oxford Bank, see IV, this chapter.

23. TRDM III, November 1832, p. 490.

24. Mass. Archives: Petition for the Oxford Bank (n.d.) in Original Papers of Ch. 68, Acts of 1823. Daniels, *Oxford*, p. 232. Slater's family controlled 17.1% of the 144 shares listed by Daniels. For Slater's use of the bank, see James L. Conrad, Jr., "The Evolution of Industrial Capitalism in Rhode Island, 1790–1830: Almy, the Browns, and the Slaters" (Ph.D. diss., University of Connecticut, 1973), p. 250.

25. See Daniels, *Oxford*, p. 232. Conrad cites Samuel's son John as a director of the bank ("The Evolution of Industrial Capitalism in Rhode Island," p. 248), but this is not confirmed by Daniels.

26. Merino Records: Series IV, Part II, E, box 23, S. Barton to Dudley Woolen Manufacturing Company, June 4, 1833.

27. SC: Samuel Slater and Sons, vol. 235, Samuel to John Slater, April 11, 1828; Samuel to John Slater, August 7, 1828.

28. Mass. Archives: Petition of the President and Director of Oxford Bank

for a Renewal of Their Charter, Jan. 1, 1830; Remonstrances of Samuel
Slater, et al. Against the Renewal of Charter of the Oxford Bank, Jan.
12, 1831, both in Original Papers of ch. 73, Acts of 1830. Slater declined "to detail at length in this memorial" the reasons for his protest, but his previous complaints about bank policy suggest his
motivation fairly clearly.

29. Slater's response to losing the battle seems to have been a decision to
sell his bank stock. See SC: Samuel Slater and Sons, vol. 236, Agreement Between John Slater of Oxford and H. N. Slater of Rhode Island
on the One Hand, and Jonathan Davis of Oxford, on the Other,
February 3, 1831.

30. TRDM III, April 1815, p. 226.
31. TRDM III, November 1816, p. 246.
32. TRDM III, November 1831, p. 477.
33. TRDM III, April 1815, p. 226.
34. TROM III, March 1815, pp. 147–9.
35. TROM III, March 1823, pp. 251–2; April 1823, p. 253; May 1823, p.
256.
36. TRDM III, November 1824, p. 347.
37. TROM III, March 1829, p. 329; April 1829, p. 332.
38. TROM IV, November 1831, p. 17; TRDM III, November 1831, p. 477.
39. Conrad, "The Evolution of Industrial Capitalism in Rhode Island,"
pp. 240–1, 244. Conrad notes that Slater invested in "seven different
turnpikes in Rhode Island, Massachusetts, and Connecticut."
40. TROM III, November 1814, p. 145. TRDM III, April 1812, p. 180.
41. TRDM III, May 1816, p. 241. TROM III, May 1819, p. 197.
42. Old Sturbridge Village, Town of Oxford, Mass., Papers, box 1, Misc.:
Petition from Slater and 63 Others to the General Court (n.d.); Petition of Slater and 63 Others to the General Court, May 23, 1824. These
appear to be for two sections of the same turnpike road. For stockholders of the Central Turnpike Corporation, see AAS: Dudley, Mass.,
Town Records, 1740–1932, 1824 Central Turnpike Corporation folio.
43. Slater held 65 out of 228 shares (28.5%), the largest single block. See
AAS: Dudley, Mass., Town Records, 1740–1932, 1824 Turnpike Corporation folio.
44. Conrad, "The Evolution of Industrial Capitalism in Rhode Island," p.
240. It was perhaps the imposition of tolls on local residents in Connecticut that caused a "labourer" of that state to comment: " 'Roads, I
guess, are unpopular in this state: we think, I guess, that they are
invasions of our liberties: we were mightily toiled [vexed] when they
were first cut, and we always spoiled them in the night!' " quoted in
Henry B. Fearon, *Sketches of America: A Narrative of a Journey of Five
Thousand Miles Through the Eastern and Western States of America* (London, 1818), p. 96.
45. TRDM III, November 1828, p. 418. For subsequent dealings over the
Corporation, see Chapter 9, II, this volume.

46. Daniels, *Oxford*, pp. 116–17.
47. TROM III, May 1817, p. 170; June 1817, p. 171; November 1817, p. 174; May 1818, p. 182.
48. *Pawtucket Chronicle*, September 29, 1829.
49. TROM III, June 1829, p. 334.
50. TROM III, August 1830, p. 347.
51. William R. Bagnall, "Contributions to American Economic History" (manuscript, 4 vols., Baker Library, Harvard University, 1908), 2:998–9. Seekonk Town Records (Town Clerk's Office, Seekonk, R.I.), vol. 2 (October 1827), p. 6. Brendan F. Gilbane, "A Social History of Samuel Slater's Pawtucket, 1790–1830" (Ph.D. diss., Boston University, 1969), pp. 39–40.
52. SC: Samuel Slater and Sons, vol. 235, Samuel to John Slater, April 11, 1828; November 19, 1828; March 5, 1826. The town meeting he wanted to invade may have been discussing the poor farm, and Slater may have had some hope of selling Oxford one of his properties. But the episode seems to reflect less his desire to make a real estate deal than his general lack of faith in Oxford's judgment. Restrictions on the franchise of South Gore residents are noted in Chapter 1, V, this volume.
53. Quoted in Frederick L. Lewton, "A Biography of Samuel Slater" (manuscript, Slater Mill Historical Site, Pawtucket, R.I., 1944), p. 161.
54. SC: Samuel Slater and Sons, vol. 235, Samuel to John Slater, January 29, 1829.
55. Ammidown, *Historical Collections*, 1:473–6. Lewton, "A Biography of Samuel Slater," pp. 136–41.
56. Lewton, "A Biography of Samuel Slater," pp. 136–44. Conrad, "The Evolution of Industrial Capitalism in Rhode Island," pp. 325–7. In 1833 Slater and his brother bought out the interest of Almy and Brown in the Smithfield works.
57. See SC: Samuel Slater and Sons, vol. 235, Samuel to John Slater, July 21, 1831; January 19, February 3, May 28, 1834; January 7, 1835.
58. Petition of George B. Slater and 173 Others.
59. TRDM III, November 1831, pp. 474–6.
60. See listings for establishments in Webster cited in McLane, *Report*, 1:576–7, and in Petition of George B. Slater and 173 Others.
61. Petition of George B. Slater and 173 Others.
62. Report of the Viewing Committee, p. 7.
63. It was acknowledged by all sides that 487 (or 67.5%) of the 722 prospective Webster inhabitants hitherto living in Dudley were on Slater's payroll. The proportion of Slater employees among the 446 Oxford and Oxford, South Gore, residents within the projected township is not certain. It is known, however, that the East Village annual payroll in 1831 averaged out to 186 operatives. Combining these data with the number of nonworking wives and children (especially in the East Village) connected to operatives makes it reasonable to assume that

no less than two-thirds of Webster's prospective population had a direct connection to "Messrs. Slater." See Report of the Viewing Committee, pp. 4, 6. SC: Slater and Tiffany, vols. 84, 90 and 91. See also Chapter 3, VI, this volume.

64. There were enough roads in "that portion [of Dudley] now sought to be taken off" to cause Dudley residents in the town's "western portion" to grow indignant, for they had (so they argued) paid a substantial share in building these "improvements." Report of the Viewing Committee, pp. 4, 7. TRDM III, November 1831, p. 475.

65. Report of the Viewing Committee, p. 1. TRDM III, November 1831, p. 474. TROM IV, September 1831, pp. 13–14.

66. TRDM III, November 1831, p. 474. TROM IV, September 1831, pp. 13–14.

67. Report of the Viewing Committee, p. 6.

68. TRDM III, November 1831, p. 477.

69. Ibid.

70. Report of the Viewing Committee, p. 8.

7. Society and economy in three towns

1. Erastus Richardson, *History of Woonsocket* (Woonsocket, 1876), p. 184.

2. See Table A.2. Michael H. Frisch, *Town into City; Springfield, Massachusetts, and the Meaning of Community, 1840–1880* (Cambridge, Mass., 1972), p. 24.

3. The aggregate proportion of females 16–45 years of age in the towns underwent a net shift of only 0.89 (from 53.6% to 52.8%) between 1820 and 1860. Derived from MFCD, MFCO, MFCW, 1830, 1860. See Chapter 3, n. 1, this volume.

4. Although the overall proportion of Americans in these three towns was 77.4% at midcentury, the proportion of Americans under 16 in the aggregate local populations was 74.2%; the proportion aged 16–45 was 75.6%, and the figure for those over 45 was 89.1%. Unless otherwise indicated, national affiliations always refer to ethnicity. Ethnicity is here defined by father's nativity or, if that is unknown, by the individual's own nativity. Data on ethnicity are thus, inevitably, somewhat less reliable than statistics on nativity themselves would be. (For figures on nativity, see Table A.3.) But I have chosen to use ethnicity because it is a more accurate depiction of the contemporary view. In this region and period, American children of foreign parentage usually viewed themselves, and were viewed, as foreigners.

5. See Oscar Handlin, *Boston's Immigrants: A Study in Acculturation*, rev. and enlarged ed. (Cambridge, Mass., 1969) pp. 38–51. Marcus Lee Hansen, *The Mingling of the Canadian and American Peoples* (New Haven, 1940), 1:115–16, 122–6.

6. Derived from Webster Tax Book (marked "1855"; Town Clerk's Office, Webster, Mass.); cited hereafter as Webster Tax Book. Valuation

of Oxford for 1859 (Town Assessor's Office, Oxford, Mass.); cited hereafter as Oxford Valuation. Dudley Assessments, 1860 (Town Assessor's Office, Dudley, Mass.); cited hereafter as Dudley Assessments. The first two listings cite total property valuations; the last gives only tax assessments. The concentration of wealth cited in the text for Webster may actually understate the situation. In that township in 1860, one-quarter of all community wealth was controlled by fourteen people; one-half of all community ratable resources belonged to fifty-one residents. Moreover, whereas in Dudley and Oxford one-half and nine-tenths of local residents, respectively, were above minimal valuations or assessments, only three-tenths of Webster's population paid anything more than poll taxes.

7. *Worcester County*, 2:181, 473.
8. Data on 1831 and 1840 derived from AAS: Worcester County Valuations; *Commonwealth of Massachusetts, General Court Committees, Valuation: 1840* (November 1840). The 1840 data reveal a drop in the number of Dudley's shops and tanneries, probably because the creation of Webster put them outside Dudley. Overall, however, nontextile ventures in the area covered by the three townships increased from 128 to 211 between 1831 and 1840. Daniels, *Oxford*, ch. 8. 1855 Census.
9. The *1855 Census* shows 1,013 shoemakers: 526 men and 487 women. The women are not explicitly specified as outworkers, but this would have been the usual arrangement. See Paul G. Faler, *Mechanics and Manufacturers in the Early Industrial Revolution: Lynn, Massachusetts, 1780–1860* (Albany, 1981), p. 23. The 1860 federal enumerations (MFCD, MFCO, MFCW, 1860) list 450 male shoemakers for the three townships, indicating both a contraction after the 1857 depression and the apparent disinclination of the latter survey to count female outworkers. Because of this disinclination, the number of shoemakers in local work forces cited in the 1860 manuscript censuses, and reflected in Table 7.3, is almost certainly an undercount. If the proportion of male and female shoemakers remained about the same, the overall proportion of shoemakers in 1860 may have run roughly 15% higher than indicated in the census. The 1832 count is of men in shoe shops.
10. The number of mills derived from Daniels, *Oxford*, ch. 8, and *1855 Census*. The latter document lists 1,168 textile employees for the three towns but fails to specify rosters for two woolen mills. The 1860 census cites 978 operatives, indicating a contraction after 1857 but perhaps also an undercount of the highly transient operatives. MFCD, MFCO, MFCW, 1860.
11. If shoemakers were undercounted in the 1860 census by roughly 15% (see n. 9, this chapter), then shoemaking could have edged out mill-work as the largest occupation in Oxford. Taking the three towns together, however, operatives would still have been the most sizable occupational group. For 1850, see MFCD, MFCO, MFCW, 1850. In that year, the proportion of farmers listed in the all-male work forces

polled by the federal census was 51.5% for Dudley, 27.9% for Oxford, and 13.8% for Webster, for an aggregate figure of 28.2%. The statistics for operatives at midcentury were: 17.5% for Dudley, 18.1% for Oxford, and 34.5% for Webster, for an aggregate figure of 24.2%.

12. In 1855 the Slater labor force represented 54.4% of all local operatives and 84.7% of all Webster millworkers. Derived from SC: Union Mills, vol. 150; Webster Woolen, vols. 66–9; *1855 Census*. Residents of native American descent were spread widely through the local labor force, with none of the largest occupations in 1860 drawing more than a quarter of this ethnic group's working members. On the other hand, 71.8% of all working Canadians and 58.6% of all working Irish were operatives, and about a third (30.7%) of the latter group were laborers. Though somewhat smaller (19.2%), the proportion of Canadians serving as laborers was still nearly 8% larger than the proportion of Americans. Looked at from another side, the proportion of Americans among local operatives and laborers was only 27.1% and 46.7%, respectively, with most American "laborers" actually concentrated among farm laborers. Residents of Irish and Canadian ethnicity comprised 66.1% of all millworkers and 49.9% of all laborers in the three townships. On the other hand, 95.1% of all farmers and 82.4% of all shoemakers were Americans. Derived from MFCD, MFCO, MFCW, 1860.

13. Derived from MFCD, MFCO, MFCW, 1850 and 1860.

14. The precise figures were: Dudley, 44.5%; Oxford, 40.0%; Webster, 25.3%. The average for the three towns was 35.4%. Derived from Webster Tax Book, Oxford Valuation, and Dudley Assessments.

15. Considering all three towns, 44.9% of residents who remained between 1850 and 1860 changed occupations, but only 21.5% moved into obviously improved jobs; i.e., from unskilled to skilled or white-collar work. (This is roughly the same rate of occupational mobility a classic study of the period has ascribed to an urban population during the same decade. See Stephan Thernstrom, *Poverty and Progress; Social Mobility in a Nineteenth Century City* [Cambridge, Mass., 1964], p. 96.) And only 20.9% shifted into higher economic levels. Because an analysis organized by quartiles would mask widening income distributions, valuation and tax listings of this period were separated into deciles. Although the economic mobility data extrapolated from this classification is not precisely comparable to data based on interquartile movement, and although (once again) the economic mobility cited here is uncorrected for age, interdecile movement should – if anything – emphasize economic mobility. The fact that the upward mobility rate that emerges (20.9%) is no higher than the interquartile figure obtained earlier in the nineteenth century (see Chapter 1, II, this volume) is thus notable. Even if the level of economic mobility remained about the same, it clearly demonstrates that economic growth did not produce accelerated economic advancement. Combined with

the modest rate of upward occupational mobility, the picture that emerges is of constrained opportunity. Derived from MFCD, MFCO, MFCW, 1850 and 1860; Webster Tax Book.

16. Derived from MFCD, MFCO, MFCW, 1850 and 1860. Persistence rates are cited here by themselves, rather than in conjunction with aggregate turnover rates as formerly, because it proved difficult to correct all arrivals and departures for births and deaths in this later period.

17. In Webster between 1850 and 1860, persistence rates by occupation were: farmers, 23.8%; handicraft and workshop employees (including shoemakers), 21.1%; textile operatives, 10.0%; laborers, 4.4%. Persistence rates in the same community and during the same period by ethnicity were: Americans, 25.4%; Irish, 10.9%; Canadians, 7.7%; other, 10.6%.

18. Persistence rates by town were: Dudley, 26.5%; Oxford, 30.0%; Webster, 20.5%.

19. In 1860, 63.9% of all residents lived in single-family dwellings; 31.9% in multiple-family dwellings; and 5.9% were quartered in boardinghouses.

20. A total of 680 individuals – some of them servants, others linked to their own family members – appear to have boarded with individuals or households unrelated to themselves.

21. Derived from MFCD, MFCO, MFCW, 1860. About 60% of all household heads not living in the same building shared a common surname. This crude measure of kinship among non-coresiding inhabitants is rendered even more suspect in the late antebellum period because of the frequency among the Irish of a relatively few last names. Still, it probably remains true that non-coresiding kinsmen were relatively common in the three townships in the late 1850s.

22. For Oxford and Webster, see *Worcester County*, 2:181, 473. For Dudley, the evidence lies in references to civic and educational activities centering around the Congregationalist meetinghouse and in later maps showing "Dudley Centre" to have emerged precisely in this area. See TRDM III; TRDM IV, June 1849, p. 80; *Official Topographical Atlas of Massachusetts* (Boston, 1871), pp. 24–5.

23. Of a sample of 65 multiple-family dwellings, 59 (90.8%) were ethnically homogeneous, and only 9 (13.8%) were not obviously dominated by one or another ethnic group. Of 190 ethnic Americans boarding with other families, 67.4% lived only among Americans. The comparable figure for Canadians was 68.3%, and for Irish, 31.6%. Irish and Americans tended to dominate the boardinghouses in which they lived roughly half the time; Canadians *averaged* 71.2% residency in the boardinghouses in which they bedded down. The high proportions registered by Canadians makes clear that the phenomenon of ethnic clustering did not simply reflect the size of given ethnic groups in local populations. These data, and the propinquity of ethnically similar residences, derived from MFCD, MFCO, MFCW, 1860.

24. The four revivals known to have occurred in this period were in 1840, 1842–3, 1850, and 1857. See Daniels, *Oxford*, pp. 69, 81. For new churches, see *Worcester County*, 1:435–7; 2:178–9, 458–63.

25. A sample of fifty-nine yeomen was drawn from Dudley and Webster (the towns with the most and least farmers, respectively). Of this sample, 28.8% (42.0% in Webster) were in the wealthiest decile, 13.6% in the bottom two strata, and more than a third (33.9% for both townships and 48.5% in Dudley) were clustered in the middle five deciles. Derived from MFCD, MFCW, 1860; Dudley Assessments; Webster Tax Book. For earlier income distribution of husbandmen, see Chapter 3, n. 3, this volume.

26. *Old Farmer's Almanack*, February 1851.

27. Considering only Dudley and Webster, twenty-four farmers aged 45 or older and known to have had children were without coresiding youngsters in 1860. The figure for 1820 was thirteen households (see Chapter 2, V, this volume). Data on occupations of family members is sketchy in the early nineteenth century, but the proportion of coresiding youngsters in farming households who were not engaged in farming appears to have grown from about 35.0% in 1820 to 68.0% in 1860. Derived from MFCD, MFCO, 1820 and 1860, and MFCW, 1860; DVR; Webster Births, Marriages, and Deaths (Town Clerk's Office, Webster, Mass.).

28. Derived from MFCD, MFCO, MFCW, 1820 and 1860.

29. A total of 123 farm laborers are listed in the 1860 censuses of the two townships. The difficulty is that textile mills used some of these laborers on the farms they operated. The precise number that factories thus employed is not certain, but the Slater mills alone were hiring around 40 during the 1850s. The estimate of 60 to 70 farm laborers for all mills (leaving 50 to 60 for local yeomen) may thus be on the low side. See MFCD, MFCW, 1860. SC: Union Mills, vols. 144–5; Phoenix, vol. 30.

30. MFCD, MFCW, 1860. Clarence H. Danhof, *Change in Agriculture; The Northern United States, 1820–1870* (Cambridge, Mass., 1969), p. 77.

31. Derived from *1855 Census* and AAS: Worcester County Valuations. The average bushels of grain per acre jumped from 18.3 (for Dudley and Oxford) in 1831 to 30.1 for all three towns in 1855.

32. *Plough, Loom, and Anvil* 5 (1852):141.

33. AAS: Worcester County, Mass., Papers, 1675–ca. 1954, Record of Factories and Farms, 1840, oversize mss. box. *1855 Census*.

34. SC: Samuel Slater and Sons, vol. 200, Douglas Noune (?) to S. Slater and Sons, July 7, 1855; Samuel Slater and Sons, vol. 199, Dexter Baldwin to "Mr. Agent Sir," September 27, 1854.

35. Danhof, *Change in Agriculture*, pp. 189–91, 215–16, 224–6, 235, 240–2, 259, 263, 268–71. *1855 Census*. *Old Farmer's Almanack*, April 1854.

36. Danhof, *Change in Agriculture*, ch. 11.

37. *Old Farmer's Almanack*, February 1855.

38. For crop selection, see *1855 Census*. SC: Webster Woolen, vol. 114, Charles Waite to John Slater, April 5, 1837. Average acreage in Dudley and Webster (for all landholders owning more than home and business lots) was 68.9 acres. This was down from the 100-acre average earlier in the century (see Chapter 1, II; Chapter 2, V) but still larger than the minimum historians have estimated as necessary simply to support a household. See Robert A. Gross, *The Minutemen and Their World* (New York, 1976), p. 214.
39. Derived from Daniels, *Oxford*, ch. 8; MFCO, 1850. Thirty-five of fifty-eight proprietors (60.3%) were not in the town in 1850.
40. Derived from Daniels, *Oxford*, ch. 8; *Worcester County*, 2:473–5; MFCD, MFCW, 1860; Webster Tax Book; Dudley Assessments; Oxford Valuation.
41. Between 1810 and 1830, 35.5% of nontextile businesses were partnerships; between 1850 and 1860, 60.3% of these businesses had more than one proprietor. See Daniels, *Oxford*, ch. 8.
42. A total of 792 laborers is estimated to have been working in local nontextile establishments in 1860 (this does not include outworking female shoeworkers laboring in their homes). See MFCD, MFCO, MFCW, 1860. For estimates of this work force in earlier years, see Chapter 3, III, this volume.
43. Derived from MFCD, MFCO, MFCW, 1860; Oxford Valuation, Webster Tax Book, Dudley Assessments. Faler, *Mechanics and Manufacturers*, pp. 171, 173.
44. MFCD, MFCO, MFCW, 1860.
45. Felicia J. Deyrup, *Arms Makers of the Connecticut Valley; A Regional Study of the Economic Development of the Small Arms Industry, 1798–1870* (Northampton, Mass., 1948), pp. 146–61. Merritt Roe Smith, *Harpers Ferry Armory and the New Technology: The Challenge of Change* (Ithaca, N.Y., 1977), pp. 104–5, 247. See also George S. Gibb, *The Saco-Lowell Shops; Textile Machinery Building in New England, 1813–1949* (Cambridge, Mass., 1950), p. 217. "Inside contracting" is discussed in Chapter 4, III, this volume.
46. *1855 Census*. Smaller establishments included forges, brick- and chair-making works, the tinware manufactures, as well as stores and taverns.
47. Ibid. There were fifteen shoe shops and 391 male shoemakers in Oxford in 1855. If, as seems reasonable, at least two-thirds of these men worked in shops (the remaining third laboring at home), there would have been 17.5 employees per shop.
48. Faler, *Mechanics and Manufacturers*, p. 78. Smith, *Harpers Ferry Armory and the New Technology*, pp. 272–4.
49. Deyrup, *Arms Makers of the Connecticut Valley*, pp. 144–6, ch. 11.
50. See Faler, *Mechanics and Manufacturers*, pp. 22–3, ch. 4; *Worcester County*, 2:473. The 1860 census shows 3 shoe manufacturers, 18 cutters, and 129 shoemakers for Webster. See MFCW, 1860.

51.   Of the twenty-four individuals engaged in nontextile businesses in Oxford in the 1850s who could be traced to the 1850 federal enumeration of that community, three listed themselves as farmers. See Daniels, *Oxford*, ch. 8. MFCO, 1850. See also Christopher Clark, "The Household Economy, Market Exchange, and the Rise of Capitalism in the Connecticut Valley, 1800–1860," *Journal of Social History* 13 (Winter, 1979): 182.

52.   The Northampton Editor is quoted in Clark, "The Household Economy," p. 183. Faler, *Mechanics and Manufacturers*, pp. 17–19, ch. 4.

53.   The changing size of local mills is derived from McLane, *Report*, 1:484–5, 526–7, 576–7; *1855 Census*. For introduction of self-acting mules, see Anthony F. C. Wallace, *Rockdale: The Growth of an American Village in the Early Industrial Revolution* (New York, 1978), pp. 195–6. A discussion of major changes in woolen technology is found in Arthur H. Cole, *The American Wool Manufacture*, 2 vols. (Cambridge, Mass., 1926), 1:306–14, 358.

54.   Burring machines in woolen mills are noted in Cole, *The American Wool Manufacture*, 1:310–12, and in the South Village in SC: Samuel Slater and Sons, vol. 199, J. Kinsman by C. S. Goddard to S. Slater and Sons, March 22, 1853. Shearing machines (also in woolen mills) are noted in Cole, *The American Wool Manufacture*, 1:307–14, 350–64, and more locally in SC: Samuel Slater and Sons, vol. 196, Reuben Daniels to S. Slater and Sons, March 3, 1845. Capitalization figures from the *1855 Census* show $38,833.33 for cotton mills and $45,625.00 for woolen mills. The average for both groups was $40,531.25. Rhode Island figures cited in Peter J. Coleman, *The Transformation of Rhode Island, 1790–1860* (Providence, 1963), pp. 129, 140. For figures for earlier mills, see Chapter 2, VI, this volume.

55.   Derived from Daniels, *Oxford*, ch. 8; *Worcester County*, 1:439–41; MFCO, MFCD, MFCW, 1850 and 1860.

56.   Proprietors derived from Daniels, *Oxford*, ch. 8; *Worcester County*, 1:439–41; 2:182–3.

57.   Derived from Daniels, *Oxford*, ch. 8; *Worcester County*, 1:439–41; MFCD, MFCO, MFCW, 1860; Webster Tax Book; Oxford Valuation; Dudley Assessments. See Chapter 2, VI, this volume.

58.   Daniels, *Oxford*, ch. 8. Ten of twenty-two Oxford textile proprietors during the 1850s rented their facilities.

59.   Frederick L. Lewton, "A Biography of Samuel Slater" (manuscript, Slater Mill Historical Site, Pawtucket, R.I., 1944), pp. 147–8, 155–6.

60.   James L. Conrad, Jr., "The Evolution of Industrial Capitalism in Rhode Island, 1790–1830: Almy, the Browns, and the Slaters" (Ph.D. diss., University of Connecticut, 1973), p. 328. *Providence Journal*, April 22, 1835. *Pawtucket Chronicle*, May 1, 1835.

61.   Lewton, "A Biography of Samuel Slater," pp. 144, 183–5.

62.   Ibid., p. 184.

63.   The issue of when and why steam was used in the Slater mills is

murky. A "boiler for the Woolen mills" is cited in 1849 (SC: Samuel Slater and Sons, vol. 202, E. W. Fletcher to S. Slater and Sons, August 17, 1849). And coal "for manufacturing purposes" is mentioned as early as 1840 (SC: Samuel Slater and Sons, vol. 196, W. J. B. Smith to S. Slater and Sons, March 14, 1840). On the other hand, references to specific applications of steam are confined to heating, gigging, and dyeing (SC: H. N. Slater, vol. 33, M. Bartlett to H. N. Slater, April 5, 1841; Webster Woolen, vol. 115, H. N. Slater to Webster Woolen, September 26, 1856). On balance, the Slater correspondence of this period suggests that the North, South and East villages did not shift to consistent use of steam for motive power until after the Civil War. And the same seems to have been true for other local manufactories.

64. SC: Slater and Tiffany, vol. 101, Agent to Samuel Slater and Sons, January 26, 1836. Barbara M. Tucker, "Samuel Slater and Sons: The Emergence of an American Factory System, 1790–1860" (Ph.D. diss., University of California, Davis, 1974), p. 116. SC: Webster Woolen, vol. 114, J. Carter to J. Robinson, December 6, 1856.

65. Daniels, *Oxford*, ch. 8; SC: Slater and Kimball, vol. 3.

66. MFCD, MFCO, MFCW, 1860. SC: Union Mills, vols. 144–51, 155–6; Phoenix, vols. 24–30. For hints relating to the labor force needed to construct the Stevens Linens Works in Dudley in the late 1850s, see *Worcester County*, 1:439.

67. Only 11.6% of a sample of 121 male Slater workers employed between 1840 and 1860 moved between field and factory positions. Derived from SC: Union Mills, vols. 144–51, 155–6; Phoenix, vols. 26–30.

68. One-fifth of all "laborers" and farm laborers in these towns had a coresiding relative, usually a child, working inside the mills. Some of these laborers may have worked for nontextile employers, of course, and simply sent their youngsters to the factories. But it seems likely that most of them lived inside the mill villages and worked for manufactories in nonoperative positions. See MFCD, MFCO, MFCW, 1860. For Nelson's letter see SC: Samuel Slater and Sons, vol. 203, H. N. Slater to Webster, December 5, 1845.

69. For economic conditions in the textile industry during this period, see, generally, Caroline F. Ware, *The Early New England Cotton Manufacture; A Study in Industrial Beginnings* (Boston, 1931), pp. 98–118. I have once again assumed that, through the course of a given year, the Slater mills were able to recruit the workers they needed. See Chapter 8, this volume.

70. Derived from SC: Union Mills, vols. 144–51, 155–6. MFCW, 1850. See Chapter 3, VII, this volume.

71. MFCW, 1860. SC: Samuel Slater and Sons, vol. 196, James Greenwood to Mr. Slater, February 3, 1845; Samuel Slater and Sons, vol. 198, Thomas Archer to S. Slater and Sons, August 2, 1849; O. Whitney, Jr., to Messrs. Slater, June 10, 1850.

72. Harriet H. Robinson, *Loom and Spindle: or, Life Among the Early Mill Girls* (New York, 1898), p. 12.
73. On the declining proportion of native workers in New England, see, generally, Thomas Dublin, *Women at Work: The Transformation of Work and Community in Lowell, Massachusetts, 1826–1860* (New York, 1979), pp. 138–40. Ware, *The Early New England Cotton Manufacture*, pp. 228–32. Cole, *The American Wool Manufacture*, 1:369–70. On the concern about the poor working habits of immigrants, see Stephan Thernstrom, *Poverty and Progress*, p. 101.
74. Rates of upward mobility drawn from a sample of 121 males derived from SC: Union Mills, vols. 144–51, 155–6. Estimates of promotions within wage laboring ranks of local factory payrolls are facilitated in this period by the more accurate job listings used in Slater records after 1840. At the same time, however, it should be recognized that the statistic cited in the text does not take into account employees who left and found better jobs in other mills.
75. SC: H. N. Slater, vol. 33, O. Lacey to H. N. Slater, December 4, 1841; Joseph France to H. N. Slater, November 15, 1840; Samuel Slater and Sons, vol. 198, H. Eldredge to S. Slater and Sons, November 12, 1851.
76. SC: Samuel Slater and Sons, vol. 200, Miss Emily L. Churle to "Dear Sir," (?), 1855.
77. SC: H. N. Slater, vol. 33, August Tachauer to H. N. Slater, July 4, 1840; Samuel Slater and Sons, vol. 199, M. McEastum to S. Slater Esq., May 10, 1854; Slater Woolen Mill, vol. 112, James Dixon to L. Robinson, March 27, 1845.
78. SC: Samuel Slater and Sons, vol. 196, James Coyle to Mr. Slater, January 30, 1841. It must be admitted that Irish and Canadian immigrants were not as typically literate as native Americans, and those who sent letters testifying to their experience were thus perhaps less representative than letter-writing Americans of the period. On the other hand, there is no particular reason to suppose that illiterate immigrants were inexperienced by the time they reached Dudley, Oxford, and Webster. See n. 79.
79. See Chapter 3, VII, VIII, this volume. The average of all stints undertaken by operatives on the East Village payroll in 1850 was 0.8 years. The proportion of workers staying less than nine months was slightly higher than it had been in 1830: 53.1%. Derived from SC: Union Mills, vols. 144–51, 155–6.
80. Ware, *The Early New England Cotton Manufacture*, pp. 282–90.
81. See Chapter 3, VI, this volume; MFCD, MFCO, MFCW, 1860. The exact figure was 14.8%.
82. See Chapter 3, VI, this volume. Cole, *The American Wool Manufacture*, 1:371. MFCD, MFCO, MFCW, 1860.
83. The figure of 79.0% for the proportion of millworkers coresiding with some relative is derived from MFCW, 1860. This statistic is not precisely comparable to data for previous decades, because earlier re-

cords indicate only relatives on the factory payrolls (see Chapter 3, VI). Presence of wives and the overall proportion (45.2%) of related operatives in local mills in the late antebellum period (which is comparable to earlier estimates) derived from MFCD, MFCO, MFCW, 1860. For children and parents working together, see Chapter 8, III, this volume and SC: Union Mills, vols. 144–51, 155–6; Phoenix, vols. 24–30.

84. Ironically, Waltham-style mills were simultaneously moving toward the family-style mills during this era by taking on more children and men. See Dublin, *Women at Work*, pp. 140–2.

85. On increased output of late antebellum mills, see Dublin, *Women at Work*, pp. 109–12; Ware, *The Early New England Cotton Manufacture*, pp. 111–13, 272. For further discussion of falling profit rates (and hence increasing pressure for productivity) among New England mills in this period, See John Michael Cudd, *The Chicopee Manufacturing Company, 1823–1915* (Wilmington, Del., 1974), p. 83.

86. See Chapter 3, VII, this volume. Derived form SC: Union Mills, vol. 156. Webster Woolen, vol. 69.

87. Ibid. By the 1850s, the cost of renting lodgings and cows amounted to 13.4% of the average Slater operative's wages.

88. Though focusing on Waltham and Lowell mills (where money wages fell off in this period), Robert G. Layer's survey of *Earnings of Cotton Mill Operatives, 1825–1914* (Cambridge, Mass., 1955) lends support to this conclusion. Layer suggests that although real wages of operatives probably underwent an overall rise in the antebellum segment he considered, the increment was marked by several "dips": between 1835 and 1837 and again between 1851 and 1858. Moreover, he found that the relative position of operatives compared with wage laborers in nontextile industries declined after 1840 (pp. 45, 51). See also Cudd, *The Chicopee Manufacturing Company*, p. 90.

89. The proportion of American operatives who were under 16 in Dudley, Oxford, and Webster in 1860 was 7.5%. The figures for Irish and Canadian operatives were 10.8% and 30.3%, respectively, averaging out to 19.6% for the whole population of Irish and Canadian workers. Derived from MFCD, MFCO, MFCW, 1860.

90. Overall adult Irish and Canadian operatives of both sexes outnumbered their American counterparts. (Only 29.2% of all local women operatives and 25.8% of all local men operatives were American.) But this simply reflected the absolute majority of these immigrants in the local factory labor force. The proportions of men and women *within* the populations of ethnic natives, on the one hand, and Irish and Canadians, on the other, were much closer. Thus 38.3% of American operatives were women and 56.6% were men, while 32.7% of Irish and Canadians combined were women and 47.7% were men (with Canadians having 1% fewer women and 11% fewer men compared to Irish operatives).

91. MFCW, 1860.
92. Ibid.

8. Workers: responses new and old

1. See Chapter 5, IV. this volume. Local voting data kindly supplied by R. D. Formisano. For statewide voting patterns, see Paul Goodman, "The Politics of Industrialism: Massachusetts, 1830–1870," in Richard L. Bushman et al., eds., *Uprooted Americans: Essays to Honor Oscar Handlin* (Boston, 1979), pp. 161–207.
2. For voting requirements and potential disenfranchisement of wage laborers like those in local mills, see, generally, Chilton Williamson, *American Suffrage; From Property to Democracy, 1760–1860* (Princeton, New Jersey, 1960), pp. 268–73; Robert W. Doherty, *Society and Power: Five New England Towns, 1800–1860* (Amherst, Mass., 1977), pp. 92–102. Requirements surrounding local elections and state and federal contests seem to have been generally similar, although participation in local elections commonly ran lower. Unfortunately, there exist no precise counts of local inhabitants "qualified to vote" on any level. There are, however, strong indications by the 1840s and 1850s of the kind of exclusion suggested in the text. First, in 1840, Whig supporters in the three communities estimated that only 70% to 75% of adult men were "eligible" to vote in state elections (see Letters of Whig State Central Committee to Dudley, Oxford, and Webster, in AAS: Worcester County, Mass., Papers, 1675–ca. 1954, box 7, folder 3). Second, a comparison of votes cast in the few polls detailed in town records with the number of adult males resident in the three townships provides a rough indication that actual political participation (in both state and local affairs) hovered just below 40%. (Oxford registered the highest, Webster the lowest.) (Derived from: TRDM IV, April 1849, p. 75; TROM IV, February 1852, p. 355; TRWM, May 1859, p. 352; MFCD and MFCO, 1850; MFCW, 1860.) Third, these towns swung (with the rest of the state) over to nativist Know-Nothing candidates in the mid-1850s, an unlikely development if immigrant operatives had participated broadly in elections. (Derived from: voting data from R. D. Formisano; Goodman, "The Politics of Industrialism," pp. 192–4.)
3. Arthur B. Darling, *Political Changes in Massachusetts, 1824–1848; A Study of Liberal Movements in Politics* (New Haven, 1925), p. 98. Christopher Clark, "The Household Economy, Market Exchange, and the Rise of Capitalism in the Connecticut Valley, 1800–1860," *Journal of Social History* 13 (Winter, 1979):184. Local voting data from R. D. Formisano.
4. Carl Siracusa, *A Mechanical People: Perceptions of the Industrial Order in Massachusetts, 1815–1880* (Middletown, Conn., 1979), p. 80. Goodman, "The Politics of Industrialism," p. 166. Local voting data from R. D. Formisano.

5. Siracusa, *A Mechanical People*, pp. 122–4, 200.

6. SC: Samuel Slater and Sons, vol. 235, Samuel to John Slater, January 6, 1834; February 14, 1834; March 3, 1835. Evidence of Whiggish sympathies among Dudley and Oxford employers (including Aaron Tufts in the former town and Alexander DeWitt in the latter) is found in Letters of the Whig State Central Committee, May 1, 1840, in AAS: Worcester County, Mass., Papers, box 7, folder 3.

7. Siracusa, *A Mechanical People*, p. 252.

8. Masonic lodges started up in Webster and (once again) in Oxford during this period. But they appeared only in 1859 and (just as in Oxford's earlier lodges) evidently catered more to employers than employees. (See Chapter 3, III, and n. 87, this volume. Daniels, *Oxford*, p. 250; *Worcester County*, 2:477.) Similarly, the available indications are that the local fire companies, which took shape during this period, were too firmly controlled by local businesses to develop (as they did in some cities of the era) into organizations expressing artisanal or, indeed, any kind of work-based cultural solidarity. See Chapter 9, III, this volume.

9. See statements quoted in Paul F. McGouldrick, *New England Textiles in the Nineteenth Century; Profits and Investments* (Cambridge, Mass., 1968), pp. 206–7. See also Thomas Dublin, *Women at Work: The Transformation of Work and Community in Lowell, Massachusetts, 1826–1860* (New York, 1979), p. 143.

10. For indications of the market affecting wage bargains, see SC: Samuel Slater and Sons, vol. 109, S. Slater and Sons to (?) Jones, December 30, 1839. For economic conditions influencing size of the labor force, see Chapter 7, VI, this volume. For length of workdays, see, generally, Caroline F. Ware, *The Early New England Cotton Manufacture; A Study in Industrial Beginnings* (Boston, 1931), pp. 279–82. There were reports of local mills even running up to thirteen hours per day in the late 1850s. See *Webster Weekly Times*, May 19, 1860. For calibration of attendance records, see SC: Union Mills, vols. 144–51, 155–6.

11. Residence patterns derived from MFCW, 1860. For George Slater's religious support, see Chapter 4, VI, this volume; *Worcester County*, 2:461; Ammidown, *Historical Collections*, 1:511.

12. Derived from SC: Union Mills, vols. 144–51. See Chapter 4, VI, this volume.

13. Derived from MFCW, 1860.

14. Ibid.

15. Derived form SC: Union Mills, vol. 151.

16. SC: Samuel Slater and Sons, vol. 198, Thomas Archer to S. Slater and Sons, August 2, 1849.

17. For example, see Hannah G. Josephson, *The Golden Threads; New England's Mill Girls and Magnates* (New York, 1949), ch. 10, and Norman Ware, *The Industrial Worker, 1840–1860; The Reaction of American Industrial Society to the Advance of the Industrial Revolution* (Boston, 1924), ch.

7. Though she sees more a "retention of earlier standards" amid a milieu of rising expectations, Caroline Ware does suggest that "far from bringing a lightening of the worker's lot, the last years of the [antebellum] period witnessed a tendency toward the depression of wages, [and] the extension of hours" (see *The Early New England Cotton Manufacture*, p. 269).

18. SC: Samuel Slater and Sons, vol. 114, H. Conant to "Brother James," November 21, 1855. The salutation may signal a religious connection, for James J. Robinson was a deacon in Webster's Congregational Church. *Worcester County*, 2:462.

19. For the suggestion that factory work was not difficult, see *New England Offering* 1 (April 1848):5.

20. Quoted in Josephson, *The Golden Threads*, p. 288. For a general treatment of labor unrest in this period see Ware, *The Industrial Worker*, chs. 14 and 15.

21. See Chapter 7, II, VI, this volume.

22. Robert Sean Wilentz, "Review Essay: Industrializing America and the Irish: Towards the New Departure," *Labor History* 20 (Fall, 1979):586–7. Neil J. Smelser, *Social Change in the Industrial Revolution; An Application of Theory to the British Cotton Industry.* (Chicago, 1959), ch. 12, esp. pp. 336–41.

23. *Worcester County*, 2:174, 462.

24. See Chapter 5, IV, this volume. The 1858 turnout followed a wage cut.

25. Erastus Richardson, *History of Woonsocket* (Woonsocket, 1876), p. 173. Five mills burned in Oxford between 1840 and 1860. Daniels, *Oxford*, ch. 8.

26. Derived from SC: Union Mills, vol. 151; Phoenix, vol. 30. Again an attempt was made to distinguish voluntary absenteeism from managerial decisions to shut down briefly or run short time. As with earlier measures of absenteeism, the technique followed was to count an operative absent only when more than half his or her co-workers were simultaneously at work (see Chapter 5, n. 5, this volume).

27. *Providence Daily Gazette*, March 24, 1845, quoted in Joseph Brennan, *Social Conditions in Industrial Rhode Island: 1820–1860* (Washington, D.C., 1940), p. 48. These workers' high spirits were flavored by Rhode Island's excitement at this time over reform leader Thomas Dorr.

28. SC: Union Mills, vols. 150–1.

29. For earlier evidence of production rising faster than wages, see Chapter 5, IV, this volume. In the second post-1810 generation, weavers' wages fell behind their hikes in output only slightly – about 2%; but the differential between production and wage hikes for spinners was 17.6%. Derived from SC: Union Mills, vol. 151; Phoenix, vol. 30. Because of differences in data, it is difficult to compare these differentials with what workers experienced in the 1820s. Weavers probably did better, spinners less well, and mule spinners (recalling that they

suffered an absolute decline in wages) much worse. But see also Ware, *The Early New England Manufacture*, p. 113.

30. For methods of calculating these rates see Chapter 5, n. 32, 35, this volume.

31. The data for 1837 are somewhat suspect (see Chapter 7, VI, this volume), but the rise in aggregate turnover in that year may reflect layoffs; the decline in 1838 measures both the small net increase in operatives as the villages kept their rosters stable until conditions improved, combined with the low voluntary departures that commonly occurred in depressions. The dip of both rates in the early 1840s probably reflects a business stagnation that was insufficient to cause large layoffs but enough to discourage workers from choosing to leave. The impact of the 1857 depression on workers' voluntary movements appears to have been felt mainly in 1858: Although layoffs had occurred the previous year (pushing up aggregate turnover), it was in 1858 that operatives chose to hold on to their jobs, depressing both turnover and voluntary departure figures.

32. Sampling derived from SC: Union Mills, vols. 151, 155–6. Names compared with MFCW, 1860.

33. For earlier pattern, see Chapter 5, VI, this volume. For revivals in the second post-1810 generation, see Chapter 7, III, and n. 24, this volume. Data on voluntary departures derived from SC: Union Mills, vols. 144–51, 155–6; Phoenix, vols. 24–30. Voluntary departures rose 2.8% during the 1842–3 revival, reaching the highest rate (28.3%) for any quarter of the surrounding twelve months. Only the East Village was examined for the 1857 revival, because the economic downturn of this year was already causing the North Village to reduce its payroll. In the East Village during this latter revival, voluntary departures rose by 21.9%, reaching 47.6%, the highest rate for that year.

34. For earlier patterns of movement referred to in this and the two following paragraphs, see Chapter 5, V, this volume.

35. This profile of transient operatives was derived from two sources: a comparison of millworkers listed in the Webster manuscript censuses of 1850 and 1860 and a sample of Slater operatives in the 1850s (SC: Union Mills, vols. 144–51, 155–6. See Table A.3 for discussion of this sample). The former source provides reliable data on ethnic background. Because they do not reflect the intrayear movement shown in the payrolls, however, censuses tend to overstate the persistence for all groups. Nonetheless, the census-derived figures are probably acceptable for comparisons between different ethnic and occupational groupings and have been used for that purpose. They show that between 1850 and 1860, Americans were 3.3 times less mobile than foreigners and that machinists were half as mobile as the average operative. Data derived from the payroll sample offer a far more reliable guide to the actual length of work stints, but unfortunately only the ethnicity of sampled family workers could be determined

with sufficient frequency to be useful. (Precisely because unattached operatives moved more quickly, they can rarely be traced in local censuses, and hence their ethnicity remains unknown.) As a result, only the ethnic breakdown of family-worker stints cited in the text is derived from this sample.

36. Derived from SC: Union Mills, vols. 144–51, 155–6.
37. Ibid. See Chapter 5, V, this volume.
38. Ibid. The proportion declined from 56% to 35%.
39. See Chapter 7, II, this volume.
40. SC: Samuel Slater and Sons, vol. 198, E. Chase, Jr., to [S. Slater and Sons], June 10, 1850; Samuel Slater and Sons, vol. 197, P. L. Brightman and Son-in-Law to [S. Slater and Sons], December 2, 1848.
41. SC: Samuel Slater and Sons, vol. 196, Thomas Midgley to Mr. Slater, July 21, 1845; Samuel Slater and Sons, vol. 199, (?) to [S. Slater and Sons], May 5, 1854.
42. SC: Samuel Slater and Sons, vol. 198, John Dwyer to "Dear Sir," March 20, 1851.
43. SC: H. N. Slater, vol. 33, James Waterhouse to H. N. Slater, April 19, 1841.
44. SC: Samuel Slater and Sons, vol. 199, Francis Dentz to Messrs. S. Slater and Sons, January 13, 1853.
45. SC: Samuel Slater and Sons, vol. 200, Thomas Phim to "Sir" (n.d.); James Newman to "Sir," July 29, 1855.
46. Ibid. SC: Samuel Slater and Sons, vol. 200, A. J. Nelson to "Dear Sir," September 21, 1855; Samuel Slater and Sons, vol. 201, Erastus Wolcott to Messrs. Slater and Sons, October 21, 1840.
47. Derived from SC: Union Mills, vols. 146, 155–6.
48. SC: Samuel Slater and Sons, vol. 197, P. L. Brightman and Sons-in-Law to [S. Slater and Sons], December 2, 1848; Samuel Slater and Sons, vol. 200, James Newman to "Sir," July 29, 1855; Samuel Slater and Sons, vol. 198, Riley Thayer to "Dear Sir," November 1, 1852.
49. See Chapter 3, VII, and n. 72; Chapter 7, VI, this volume. See also Stanley Lebergott, *Manpower in Economic Growth: The American Record Since 1800* (New York, 1964), pp. 131–5. For declining wage levels in Waltham-style mills, see Dublin, *Women at Work*, pp. 158–64.
50. The new perspective did not rule out all recruiting headaches, especially for employers still seeking Yankee operatives. See Dublin, *Women at Work*, p. 139. But judging from the Slater records, the managerial attitude in local mills was more relaxed.
51. TRWM, November 1849, p. 211. TRDM IV, March 1857, p. 207.
52. *Webster Weekly Times*, September 9, 1865; *1855 Census*. The comment on Rhode Island law is quoted in Brennan, *Social Conditions in Industrial Rhode Island*, p. 87. It took several tries before the local temperance lobby managed to persuade Webster to go dry. See TRWM, April 1842, pp. 138–9; March 1844, p. 158.

53. See Chapter 6, VI, this volume. Perhaps because their milieu was more dense and supportive, stints of operatives in urban textile centers, by contrast, actually grew longer in this period. See Dublin, *Women at Work*, p. 161.
54. AAS: Slater Family Papers, 1824–1911, octavo vol., Amos Bartlett to Messrs. Kidder, Peabody, and Co., January 11, 1902, p. 20.
55. Dublin, *Women at Work*, pp. 200, 203–7. Ware, *The Early New England Cotton Manufacture*, p. 276.
56. SC: Samuel Slater and Sons, vol. 196, Thomas Midgley to Mr. Slater, July 21, 1845.
57. SC: Samuel Slater and Sons, vol. 196, E. J. Lacey to [S. Slater and Sons], March 11, 1845; Samuel Slater and Sons, vol. 200, James Crosin to Mr. Allen, April 1, 1855.

9. Communities: "the greatest good to the greatest number"

1. See Chapter 8, II, and n. 2.
2. For earlier attitudes, see Chapter 1, V; Chapter 6, II, both this volume.
3. TRDM IV, March 1857, p. 207; April 1844, p. 704. TRWM, April 1843, p. 151. TROM IV, November 1835, p. 80.
4. TROM IV, November 1833, p. 50.
5. TRWM, November 1838, p. 86. TRDM III, September 1838, p. 574. Efforts in 1836 to find a way to travel the road "toll free" had failed. See TRWM, March 1836, p. 61; TRDM III, November 1836, p. 538.
6. TRDM III, March 1839, p. 591. TROM IV, November 1831, p. 17. TRWM, March 1849, p. 209.
7. Daniels, *Oxford*, p. 245.
8. TRWM, June 1846, p. 182.
9. Daniels, *Oxford*, pp. 228–9. There was also a later installment of the controversy in 1851. See ibid., pp. 229–30.
10. *Worcester County*, 2:465.
11. TRWM, March 1842, p. 134.
12. Ibid., March 1841, p. 120.
13. Ibid., March-April 1855, pp. 284–5; *Worcester County*, 2:465. For a discussion of the legal and social dimensions surrounding the emergence of high schools in antebellum Massachusetts (and the opposition they frequently met from advocates of the antecedent district system), see Michael B. Katz, *The Irony of Early School Reform; Educational Innovation in Mid-Nineteenth Century Massachusetts* (Cambridge, Mass., 1968), pp. 53–7; 227–9.
14. TROM IV, March 1845, pp. 212–13; May 1845, p. 220. Daniels, *Oxford*, pp. 99–100. *Worcester County*, 1:437. TRDM III, March 1839, pp. 585–8; TRDM IV, March 1858, p. 221.
15. See Chapter 6, II, this volume.

16. Sample of selectmen derived from TRDM IV, 1845–55; TROM IV, 1845–55; TRWM, 1850–60. Names compared with Dudley Assessments, Oxford Valuation, Webster Tax Book.
17. TRDM III, March 1840, p. 608. TRWM, January 1852, p. 240.
18. TRWM, November 1851, p. 239.
19. TROM IV, April 1848, p. 283.
20. TRDM IV, June 1860, p. 262.
21. TRWM, August 1854, p. 270.
22. TRDM IV, April 1846, p. 15.
23. TRWM, March 1842, p. 136; March 1840, p. 102.
24. TROM IV, November 1848, p. 295; April 1849, p. 306; April 1852, p. 363; November 1852, p. 367; March 1853, p. 379; April 1853, p. 381.
25. I have here drawn generally on: Michael H. Frisch, *Town into City; Springfield, Massachusetts, and the Meaning of Community, 1840–1880* (Cambridge, Mass., 1972); Sam Bass Warner, Jr., *The Private City; Philadelphia in Three Periods of Its Growth* (Philadelphia, 1968); Constance McLaughlin Green, *Holyoke, Massachusetts; A Case History of the Industrial Revolution in America* (New Haven, 1939).
26. TROM IV, March 1853, p. 379; Daniels, *Oxford*, p. 232.
27. Derived from MFCD, MFCO, MFCW, 1860; Dudley Assessments, Oxford Valuation, Webster Tax Book. See Chapter 7, IV and V, this volume.
28. Names of selectmen derived as indicated in n. 16. Occupations of selectmen derived from MFCD, MFCO, 1850; MFCW, 1860. However, the agricultural vocation of selectmen was more pronounced in Dudley and Oxford than in Webster. See n. 32.
29. Dudley Assessments, Oxford Valuation, and Webster Tax Book.
30. For example: TRDM IV, November 1849, p. 83; November 1850, p. 100 (though in the latter case Stevens did ultimately win a slot as representative).
31. TRWM, 1832–45; March 1856, p. 295; March 1857, p. 316.
32. In Dudley and Oxford, of twenty-four selectmen sampled whose occupation could be traced, seventeen (70.8%) appear to have been farmers; in Webster the proportion was three out of seven (42.9%). Stevens reached the selectmanship in 1849 and 1851; DeWitt was elected moderator in 1833 and 1842, served as representative in 1834, and was Oxford's delegate to a state Constitutional Convention in 1853. See Daniels, *Oxford*, pp. 271–2, 276; TRDM IV, March 1849 and 1851, pp. 72, 107. Lamont Corbin was evidently unrelated to Webster's B. A. Corbin. See Daniels, *Oxford*, p. 451.
33. For example: TROM IV, March 1850, p. 317; TRDM III, May 1841, p. 632; TRDM IV, March 1851, p. 107.
34. See Chapter 4, V, this volume.
35. TRDM III, April–June 1838, pp. 570–1.
36. TRDM IV, June 1848, p. 51. See also ibid., March 1857, p. 207.

37. Virtually every highway known to have been advocated by a millowner met at least some opposition or had conditions placed around its "acceptance."
38. TRDM III, July 1841, p. 647. The road was finally accepted in November (ibid., November 1841, p. 651).
39. See ibid., March 1842, pp. 658–63. (This town meeting refers to a county commissioners' report from the previous September.) TRDM IV, July 1848, p. 68.
40. TRDM III, May 1841, p. 645. Ibid., March-May 1845, pp. 728, 734–9.
41. TRDM IV, November 1858, p. 230.
42. Daniels, *Oxford*, p. 245. See Chapter 8, n. 8, this volume.
43. TROM IV, April 1845, p. 217; November 1836, p. 88.
44. Ibid., May 1838, p. 110; March 1854, p. 401.
45. Ibid., March 1849, pp. 305–6.
46. Ibid., November 1836, p. 88.
47. Ibid., September 1851, p. 344.
48. See Chapter 7, II, this volume. McLane's *Report* cites Zera Preston's mill as existing in Webster in 1832 (1:576–7). Data on the 1850s derived from *1855 Census*, pp. 552–4.
49. See Chapter 7, II, and n. 12, this volume.
50. TRWM, November 1832, p. 16. SC: Samuel Slater and Sons, vol. 235, Samuel to John Slater, August 6, 1834.
51. TRWM, March 1842, p. 136.
52. Ibid., March 1836, p. 58; March 1850, p. 220.
53. Ibid., November 1848, p. 205.
54. Ibid., April 1853, p. 256.
55. See Chapter 6, VI, this volume.
56. *Worcester County*, 2:461.
57. SC: Samuel Slater and Sons, vol. 235, Samuel to John Slater, January 6, 19, 24, 27, 1834. For indications that Webster's town meeting continued to meet in the Slater-owned chapel, see TRWM, March 1851, p. 233. Eventually, in 1869, Nelson Slater sold the chapel to French Catholics. *Worcester County*, 2:462.
58. SC: Samuel Slater and Sons, vol. 198, F. H. Underwood to [H. N. Slater], September 16, 1850. Further criticism of the Slater water politics is found in ibid., Samuel H. Foskett to S. Slater and Sons, August 11, 1851.
59. *Webster Weekly Times*, May 10, 1860.
60. TRWM, September 1854, pp. 275–7. The road was also supported by H. H. Stevens.
61. Ibid., March 1855, pp. 284–5. There is also a hint in town-meeting records that during the fall of this year Webster declined an offer by Samuel Slater and Sons for a free "Deed...of land upon which the High School is located." See ibid., September-November 1855, pp. 289–91.

10. The war and beyond

1. Daniels, *Oxford*, p. 160. *Worcester County*, 2:185–6, 465–6.
2. Daniels, *Oxford*, pp. 391–4.
3. *Worcester County*, 2:186, 466–7.
4. *Census of the Commonwealth of Massachusetts: 1895* (Boston, 1900), pp. 1104–7, 1162–4, 1203–6.
5. Frederick L. Lewton, "A Biography of Samuel Slater" (Manuscript, Slater Mill Historical Site, Pawtucket, R.I., 1944), p. 194.
6. AAS: Slater Family Papers, 1824–1911, octavo vol., Amos Bartlett to Messrs. Kidder, Peabody, and Co., January 11, 1902, pp. 11–16.
7. AAS: Slater Family Papers, 1824–1911, H. N. Slater to P. C. Bacon, September 18, 1873. Ammidown, *Historical Collections*, 1:502.
8. AAS: Slater Family Papers, 1824–1911, octavo vol., Amos Bartlett to Messrs. Kidder, Peabody, and Co., January 11, 1902, p. 56.
9. Lewton, "A Biography of Samuel Slater," pp. 194–6.
10. For an exception, see discussion of the 1853 strikes at the Salisbury cotton and flannel mills in Carroll D. Wright, *Strikes in Massachusetts, 1830–1880 (Being Part I of the Eleventh Annual Report of the Massachusetts Bureau of Statistics of Labor [1880])* (reprinted, Boston, 1889), pp. 9–13.
11. Bernard Bailyn, "The Central Themes of the American Revolution: An Interpretation," in Stephen G. Kurtz and James H. Hutson, eds., *Essays on the American Revolution* (Chapel Hill, 1973), p. 26.

Bibliography

Primary sources

Published

"Article II [Review of *A History of the Cotton Manufacture in Great Britain* by Edward Baines and *Memoir of Samuel Slater* by George S. White]." *North American Review* 52 (January 1841):31–56.

Chapin, J. R. "Among the Nail-Makers." *Harper's New Monthly Magazine* 21(1860):145–64.

Cole, Arthur H., ed. *Industrial and Commercial Correspondence of Alexander Hamilton, Anticipating His Report on Manufactures.* Chicago, 1928; reprinted, 1968.

Colman, Henry. *Second Report on Agriculture of Massachusetts.* Boston, 1838.

Colman, Henry. *Third Report of the Agriculture of Massachusetts in Wheat and Silk.* Boston, 1840.

Commons, John R., Gilmore, Eugene A., Sumner, Helen L., Andrews, John B., Phillips, Ulrich B. eds. *Documentary History of American Industrial Society,* 11 vols. Cleveland, 1910–11.

Connecticut State Agriculture Society. *Transactions.* Hartford, 1855.

Coxe, Tench. *A Statement of the Arts and Manufactures of the United States of America, for the Year 1810: Digested and Prepared by Tench Coxe, esquire, of Philadelphia.* Philadelphia, 1814.

Dickens, Charles. *The Works of Charles Dickens,* vol. 16: American Notes. London, 1929.

Dodge, Nathaniel S. [John Carver]. *Sketches of New England, or Memories of the Country.* New York, 1842.

Duncan, John M. *Travels Through Part of the United States and Canada in 1818 and 1819.* New York, 1823.

Dwight, Timothy. *Travels in New England and New York,* 4 vols. Edited by Barbara Miller Solomon, with the assistance of Patricia M. King. Cambridge, Mass., 1969.

Fearon, Henry B. *Sketches of America. A Narrative of a Journey of Five Thousand Miles Through the Eastern and Western States of America; Contained in Eight Reports Addressed to the Thirty-Nine English Families by Whom the Author was Deputed, in June 1817, to Ascertain Whether Any, and What Part of the United States Would be Suitable for Their Residence. With Remarks on Mr. Birbeck's "Notes" and "Letters."* London, 1818.

Goodrich, Samuel G. *Recollections of a Lifetime, or Men and Things I Have Seen: In a Series of Familiar Letters to a Friend, Historical, Biographical, Anecdotical, and Descriptive,* 2 vols. New York, 1856.

Great Britain, *Parliamentary Papers* (Commons), Royal Commission, Second Report. 1833.

Hamilton, Alexander. "Report on the Subject of Manufacturers, December 5, 1791," *American State Papers: Finance,* 1:123–45.

Hazard, Thomas B. *Nailer Tom's Diary: Otherwise, the Journal of Thomas B. Hazard of Kingstown, Rhode Island, 1778 to 1840, which Includes Observations on the Weather, Records of Births, Marriages, and Deaths, Transactions by Barter and Money of Varying Value, Preaching Friends, and Neighborhood Gossip. Printed as Written and Introduced by Caroline Hazard.* Boston, 1930.

Jefferson, Thomas. *Notes on the State of Virginia.* Edited, with an introduction and notes, by William Peden. Chapel Hill, N.C., 1954.

Larcom, Lucy. "Among Lowell Mill Girls: A Reminiscence." *Atlantic Monthly* 48 (1881):593–612.

Lawrence, William R., ed. *Extracts from the Diary and Correspondence of the Late Amos Lawrence; with a Brief Account of Some Incidents in His Life.* New York, 1855.

Leavitt, Thomas, ed. *The Hollingworth Letters; Technical Change in the Textile Industry, 1826–1837.* Cambridge, Mass., 1969.

McLane, Louis. *Report of the Secretary of the Treasury, 1832. Documents Relative to the Manufactures in the United States. House Executive Documents,* 22d Cong., 1st sess., Doc. No. 308, 2 vols. Washington, D.C., 1833.

Mann, Horace. *Slavery: Letters and Speeches.* Boston, 1853.

Martineau, Harriet. *Society in America,* 2 vols. New York, 1837.

Massachusetts State Censuses (in chronological order)

Statistics of the Condition and Products of Certain Branches of Industry in Massachusetts, for the Year Ending April 1, 1845. Boston, 1846.

Statistical Information Relating to Certain Branches of Industry in Massachusetts, for the Year Ending June 1, 1855. Boston, 1856.

Abstract of the Census of the Commonwealth of Massachusetts Taken with Reference to Facts Existing on the First Day of June, 1865. Boston, 1867.

Census of Massachusetts: 1875. Prepared Under the Direction of Carroll D. Wright, Chief of the Bureau of Statistics of Labor. Boston, 1877.

Census of the Commonwealth of Massachusetts: 1895. Boston, 1900.

Massachusetts State Legislation, published volumes (in chronological order)

Laws of the Commonwealth of Massachusetts Passed at the Several Sessions of the General Court, Holden in Boston, Beginning 26 May, 1812 and Ending on 2d March, 1815. Vol. 6. Boston, 1812–15.

Laws of the Commonwealth of Massachusetts Passed at the Several Sessions of the General Court, Beginning May 31, 1815, and Ending on the 24th of February, 1818. Vol. 7. Boston, 1818.

Laws of the Commonwealth of Massachusetts Passed at the Several Sessions of

the General Court, Beginning May, 1822 and Ending February, 1825.
Vol. 9. Boston, 1825.

Massachusetts State published valuation

Commonwealth of Massachusetts, General Court Committees, Valuation: 1840
Boston, 1840.

Metcalf, John G. *Annals of the Town of Mendon, from 1659 to 1880.* Providence,
1880.

Miles, Henry A. *Lowell, As It Was, And As It Is.* Lowell, Mass., 1846; reprinted, 1972.

Montgomery, James. *A Practical Detail of the Cotton Manufacture of the United
States of America; and the State of Cotton Manufacture of that Country
Contrasted and Compared with that of Great Britain; with Comparative Esti-
mates of the Cost of Manufacturing in Both Countries.* Glasgow, 1840.

Official Topographical Atlas of Massachusetts. Boston, 1871.

Ogden, Samuel. *Thoughts, What Probable Effect the Peace with Great-Britain Will
Have on the Cotton Manufactures of this Country: Interspersed with Remarks
on Our Bad Management in the Business; and the Way to Improvement,
so as to Meet Imported Goods in Cheapness, at our Home Market, Pointed
Out.* Providence, 1815.

Pilkington, J. *A View of the Present State of Derbyshire, with an Account of Its
Most Remarkable Antiquities, Illustrated with Accurate Map and Plates.*
Derby, 1789.

Quincy, Josiah. "Account of Journey of Josiah Quincy." *Massachusetts Historical Society Proceedings,* 2nd ser. 4 (1887–9):123–35.

*A Review of "The Necessity of Sabbath Labor" on Corporations. By a Citizen of
Lowell.* Lowell, 1847.

Robbins, Asher. *Address to the Rhode Island Society for the Encouragement of
Domestic Industry, Delivered at Pawtuxet, October 16, 1822.* Pawtucket, 1822.

Robinson, Harriet H. *Loom and Spindle: or, Life Among the Early Mill Girls.
With a Sketch of "The Lowell Offering" and of Its Contributors.* New York,
1898.

Shirreff, Patrick. *A Tour Through North America; Together with a Comprehensive
View of the Canadas and the United States, as Adapted for Agricultural Emigration.* Edinburgh, 1835; reprinted, 1971.

Stuart-Wortley, Lady Emmeline. *Travels in the United States, etc., During 1849
and 1850.* New York, 1851.

Sui Generis: Alias, Thomas Man. *Picture of a Factory Village: To Which are
Annexed Remarks on Lotteries.* Providence, 1833.

Thoreau, Henry David. *The Writings of Henry David Thoreau,* vol. 2: *Walden;
or Life in the Woods.* Reprinted, Boston, 1954.

Town Records of Dudley, Massachusetts, 1732–1794, 2 vols. in 1. New York,
1842; Pawtucket, 1893.

United States, published censuses (in chronological order)

*Return of the Whole Number of Persons Within the Several Districts of the
United States.* Philadelphia, 1791.

Return of the Whole Number of Persons Within the Several Districts of the United States. Washington, D.C., 1801.

Aggregate Amount of Persons Within the United States in the Year 1810. Washington, D.C., 1811.

Census for 1820. Published by Authority of an Act of Congress Under the Direction of the Secretary of State. Washington, D.C., 1821.

Fifth Census; Or, Enumeration of the Inhabitants of the United States. 1830. Washington, D.C., 1832.

Sixth Census or Enumeration of the Inhabitants of the United States, as Corrected at the Department of State, in 1840. Book I. Washington, D.C., 1841.

The Seventh Census of the United States: 1850. Washington, D.C., 1853.

Population of the United States in 1860; Compiled From the Original Returns of the Eighth Census, Under the Direction of the Secretary of the Interior. Washington, D.C., 1864.

Ure, Andrew. *The Cotton Manufacture of Great Britain Systematically Investigated and Illustrated. With an Introductory View of Its Comparative State in Foreign Countries*, 2 vols. London, 1836.

Ure, Andrew. *The Philosophy of Manufactures: or an Exposition of the Scientific, Moral, and Commercial Economy of the Factory System of Great Britain*. London, 1835.

Van Slyck, J. D. *Representatives of New England Manufacturers*. Boston, 1879.

Vital Records of Dudley, Massachusetts, to the End of the Year 1849. Worcester, 1908.

Vital Records of Oxford, Massachusetts, to the End of the Year 1849. Worcester, 1905.

White, George S. *Memoir of Samuel Slater, The Father of American Manufactures; Connected with a History of the Rise and Progress of the Cotton Manufacture in England and America, With Remarks on the Moral Influence of Manufacturies in the United States*. Philadelphia, 1836; reprinted, 1967.

Unpublished (arranged by location)

Archives of the Commonwealth of Massachusetts, State House, Boston.
  Petition of George B. Slater and 173 Others praying for
      the incorporation of a town to be formed of Oxford
      south Gore and a part of the Towns of Oxford
      and Dudley, June 3, 1831; in Original Papers of Ch.
      93, Acts of 1832.
  Report of the Viewing Committee on petition of Geo. B. Slater and others, Jan. 17, 1832; in Original Papers of Ch. 93, Acts of 1832.
  Petition for the Oxford Bank (n.d.); in Original Papers of Ch. 68, Acts of 1823.
      Petition of the President and Director of Oxford Bank for a Renewal of Their Charter of the Oxford Bank, Jan. 1, 1830; in Original Papers of Ch. 73, Acts of 1830.

Remonstrances of Samuel Slater et al. Against the Renewal of Charter of the Oxford Bank, Jan. 12, 1831; in Original Papers of Ch. 73, Acts of 1830.
American Antiquarian Society, Worcester, Mass.
  Ira Barton Papers.
  Craggins and Andrews, Account Book, 1820–27.
  Josiah Dean, Account Book, 1804–26.
  Dudley, Mass., Town Records, 1740–1932.
  William Law, Account Book, 1819–23.
  Oxford, Mass., General Store Account Book, 1817–18.
  Parker Family Papers.
  Samuel Slater Papers, 1824–1911.
  Webster, Mass., Papers.
  Worcester County, Mass., Papers, 1675–ca. 1954.
Baker Library, Harvard University, Cambridge, Mass.
  Jeremiah Davis, Account Book, 1787–1822.
  Gordon Papers
  Slater Collection (arranged by divisions of the collection)
    Almy and Brown
    Phoenix
    Samuel Slater and Sons
    Slater and Howard
    Slater and Kimball
    Slater and Tiffany
    Union Mill
    Webster Woolen
  Edward K. Wolcott, Ledger and Cash Book, 1774–96.
Dudley, Mass.
  Dudley Assessments, 1860, Town Assessor's Office.
  Town Meeting Records, 1794–1845, Town Clerk's Office.
  Town Meeting Records, 1845–1860, Town Clerk's Office.
Genealogical Library (Boston and Atlanta branches).
  Oxford Orders, Receipts, Agreements, microfilm 859254.
  Oxford Military Records, microfilm 859224.
  Records of Oxford School District No. 6, 1806–31, microfilm 4694.
  Town Meeting Records, 1715–53, microfilm 859252.
  Town Meeting Records, 1800–31, microfilm 859224.
  Town Meeting Records, 1831–58, microfilm 859225.
New England Historic Genealogical Society, Boston.
  Massachusetts and Maine Direct Tax of 1798.
Old Slater Mill Historical Site, Pawtucket, R.I.
  Old Slater Mill Collection.
Old Sturbridge Village, Sturbridge, Mass.
  Records of the Merino Mill and Dudley Woolen Manufacturing Co.
  Town of Oxford Records. (Town Meeting Records, 1753–99.)

Oxford, Mass.
  Valuation of Oxford for 1859, Town Assessor's Office.
Rehoboth, Mass.
  Town Meeting Records, Town Clerk's Office.
Rhode Island Historical Society, Providence, R.I.
  Almy and Brown Papers.
Rhode Island School of Design, Providence, R.I.
  Samuel Slater, Original Letters, Invoices, etc., Relating to the
      Cotton Industry in Rhode Island, 1804–45.
Seekonk, R.I.
  Town Meeting Records, Town Clerk's Office.
United States Manuscript Censuses
  First-Eighth Manuscript Federal Censuses, Worcester County: Dudley
      and Oxford.
  Sixth-Eighth Manuscript Federal Censuses, Worcester County: Webster.
  Third-Fourth Manuscript Federal Censuses, Worcester County: Ward,
      Millbury, Sutton, Douglas, Woodstock, and Southbrige.
Webster, Mass.
  Constitution of the Methodist Episcopal Church, 1830–40. Manuscript,
      United Church of Christ.
  Webster Births, Marriages, and Deaths, Town Clerk's Office.
  Webster Tax Book, 1855, Town Clerk's Office.
  Town Meeting Records, 1832–63, Town Clerk's Office.
Worcester County Court House, Worcester, Mass.
  Probate Records, 1790–1840.

Newspapers

Lowell Offering, Lowell, Mass.
Manufacturers' and Farmers' Journal and Providence and Pawtucket Advertiser
      Providence, R.I.
Massachusetts Spy, Worcester, Mass.
New England Farmer, Boston.
New England Offering, Lowell, Mass.
Old Farmer's Almanack, Woburn, Mass.
Pawtucket Chronicle, Pawtucket, R.I.
Plough Boy, Albany, N.Y.
Plough, Loom, and Anvil, Philadelphia and New York.
Providence Journal, Providence, R.I.
Voice of Industry, Lowell, Mass.
The Webster Weekly Times, Webster, Mass.

Secondary sources

Published

Abbott, Edith. *Women in Industry; A Study in American Economic History*. New
      York, 1910; reprinted, 1969.

Ammidown, Holmes. *Historical Collections: Containing I. The Reformation in France; The Rise, Progress and Destruction of the Huguenot Church. II. The Histories of Seven Towns, Six of Which are in the South Part of Worcester County, Massachusetts, namely: Oxford, Dudley, Webster, Sturbridge, Charlton, Southbridge, and the Town of Woodstock, Now in Connecticut, But Originally Granted and Settled by People from the Province of Massachusetts, and Regarded as Belonging to Her for About Sixty years*, 2 vols. New York, 1874.

Anderson, Michael. *Family Structure in Nineteenth Century Lancashire*. Cambridge, England, 1971.

Bagnall, William R. *Samuel Slater and the Early Development of the Cotton Manufacture in the United States*. Middletown, Conn., 1890.

Bagnall, William R. *The Textile Industries of the United States, Including Sketches and Notices of Cotton, Woolen, Silk, and Linen Manufactures in the Colonial Period*. Cambridge, Mass., 1893.

Bailyn, Bernard. "The Central Themes of the American Revolution: An Interpretation," in Stephen G. Kurtz and James H. Hutson, eds., *Essays on the American Revolution*. Chapel Hill, N.C., 1973.

Bailyn, Bernard. *The Ideological Origins of the American Revolution*. Cambridge, Mass., 1967.

Bidwell, Percy W., and Falconer, John I. *History of Agriculture in the Northern United States, 1620–1860*. Washington, D.C., 1925.

Botkin, B. A. *A Treasury of New England Folklore; Stories, Ballads, and Traditions of the Yankee People*. New York, 1947.

Bowen, C. W. *The History of Woodstock, Connecticut*. 6 vols. Norwood, Mass., 1926.

Brennan, Joseph. *Social Conditions in Industrial Rhode Island: 1820–1860*. Washington, D.C., 1940.

Brissenden, Paul F., and Frankel, Emil. *Labor Turnover in Industry; A Statistical Analysis*. New York, 1922.

Bushman, Claudia L. *"A Good Poor Man's Wife": Being a Chronicle of Harriet Hanson Robinson and Her Family in Nineteenth-Century New England*. Hanover, N.H., 1981.

Bushman, Richard L. *From Puritan to Yankee; Character and the Social Order in Connecticut, 1690–1765*. Cambridge, Mass., 1967.

Bushman, Richard L.; Harris, Neil; Rothman, David; Solomon, Barbara Miller; and Thernstrom, Stephan eds. *Uprooted Americans: Essays to Honor Oscar Handlin*. Boston, 1979.

Cameron, Edward H. *Samuel Slater, Father of American Manufactures*. Freeport, Me., 1960.

Chapman, Stanley D. *The Cotton Industry in the Industrial Revolution*. London, 1972.

Chapman, Stanley D. *The Early Factory Masters: The Transition to the Factory System in the Midlands Textile Industry*. New York, 1967.

Clark, Christopher. "The Household Economy, Market Exchange, and the Rise of Capitalism in the Connecticut Valley, 1800–1860." *Journal of Social History* 13 (Winter, 1979):169–89.

Clark, Victor S. *History of Manufactures in the United States*, 3 vols. New York, 1929.

Cole, Arthur H. *The American Wool Manufacture*, 2 vols. Cambridge, Mass., 1926.

Coleman, Peter J. *The Transformation of Rhode Island, 1790–1860*. Providence, 1963.

Cook, Edward M., Jr. *The Fathers of the Towns: Leadership and Community Structure in Eighteenth-Century New England*. Baltimore, 1976.

Cooke, Jacob E. *Tench Coxe and the Early Republic*. Chapel Hill, N.C., 1978.

Coolidge, John P. *Mill and Mansion: A Study of Architecture and Society in Lowell, Massachusetts, 1820–1865*. New York, 1942.

Copeland, Peter F. *Working Dress in Colonial and Revolutionary America*. Westport, Conn., 1977.

Cowley, Charles. *Illustrated History of Lowell*, rev. ed. Boston, 1868.

Cross, Whitney. *The Burned Over District; The Social and Intellectual History of Enthusiastic Religion in Western New York, 1800–1850*. Ithaca, N.Y. 1950.

Cudd, John Michael. *The Chicopee Manufacturing Company, 1823–1915*. Wilmington, Del., 1974.

Danhof, Clarence H. *Change in Agriculture; The Northern United States, 1820–1870*. Cambridge, Mass., 1969.

Daniels, George F. *History of the Town of Oxford, Massachusetts, with Genealogies and Notes on Persons and Estates*. Oxford, Mass., 1892.

Darling, Arthur B. *Political Changes in Massachusett, 1824–1848; A Study of Liberal Movements in Politics*. New Haven, 1925.

Dawley, Alan. *Class and Community: The Industrial Revolution in Lynn*. Cambridge, Mass., 1976.

Demos, John. *A Little Commonwealth; Family Life in Plymouth Colony*. New York, 1970.

Deyrup, Felicia J. *Arms Makers of the Connecticut Valley; A Regional Study of the Economic Development of the Small Arms Industry, 1798–1870*. Northampton, Mass., 1948.

Doherty, Robert W. *Society and Power: Five New England Towns, 1800–1860*. Amherst, Mass., 1977.

Drepperd, Carl W. *American Clocks and Clockmakers*. New York, 1947.

Dublin, Thomas. *Women at Work: The Transformation of Work and Community in Lowell, Massachusetts, 1826–1860*. New York, 1979.

Dublin, Thomas, ed., *Farm to Factory: Women's Letters, 1830–1860*. New York, 1981.

Engels, Friedrich. *The Condition of the Working Class in England*. Edited and translated by W. O. Henderson and W. H. Chaloner. Stanford, Calif., 1968.

Faler, Paul G. *Mechanics and Manufacturers in the Early Industrial Revolution: Lynn, Massachusetts, 1780–1860*. Albany, N.Y., 1981.

Fitton, R. S., and Wadsworth, Alfred P. *The Strutts and the Arkwrights, 1758–1830; A Study of the Early Factory System*. Manchester, England, 1958.

Foner, Eric. *Tom Paine and Revolutionary America*. New York, 1980.

Foner, Philip S. *History of the Labor Movement in the United States*. 4 vols. New York, 1947.

Freeland, Mary DeWitt. *The Records of Oxford; Including Chapters of Nipmuck, Huguenot and English History from the Earliest Date, accompanied with biographical sketches and notes, 1630–1890. With Manners and Fashions of the Time*. Albany, N.Y. 1894.

Frisch, Michael H. *Town into City; Springfield, Massachusetts, and the Meaning of Community, 1840–1880*. Cambridge, Mass., 1972.

Genovese, Eugene D. *Roll, Jordan, Roll; The World the Slaves Made*. New York, 1974.

Gersuny, Carl. " 'A Devil in Petticoats' and Just Cause: Patterns of Punishment in Two New England Textile Factories." *Business History Review* 50 (Summer, 1976):131–52.

Gibb, George S. *The Saco-Lowell Shops; Textile Machinery Building in New England, 1813–1949*. Cambridge, Mass., 1950.

Gitelman, Howard M. *Workingmen of Waltham: Mobility in American Urban Industrial Development, 1850–1890*. Baltimore, 1974.

Goodman, Paul. "The Politics of Industrialism: Massachusetts, 1830–1870," in Richard L. Bushman, Neil Harris, David Rothman, Barbara Miller Solomon, Stephan Thernstrom, eds., *Uprooted Americans: Essays to Honor Oscar Handlin*, pp. 161–207. Boston, 1979.

Grant, Charles S. *Democracy in the Connecticut Frontier Town of Kent*. New York, 1961.

Green, Constance McLaughlin. *Holyoke, Massachusetts: A Case History of the Industrial Revolution in America*. New Haven, 1939.

Greven, Philip. *Four Generations: Population, Land, and Family in Colonial Andover, Massachusetts*. Ithaca, N.Y., 1970.

Greven, Philip. *The Protestant Temperament: Patterns of Child-Rearing, Religious Experience, and the Self in Early America*. New York, 1977.

Grieve, Robert. *An Illustrated History of Pawtucket, Central Falls and Vicinity*. Pawtucket, 1897.

Gross, Robert, A. *The Minutemen and Their World*. New York, 1976.

Gutman, Herbert G. *Work, Culture, and Society in Industrializing America: Essays in American Working-Class and Social History*. New York, 1976.

Hall, Peter Dobkin. "Family Structure and Economic Organization: Massachusetts Merchants, 1700–1850," in Tamara K. Hareven, ed., *Family and Kin in Urban Communities, 1700–1930*, pp. 38–61. New York, 1977.

Handlin, Oscar. *Boston's Immigrants: A Study in Acculturation*, rev. and enlarged ed. Cambridge, Mass., 1969.

Handlin, Oscar, and Handlin, Mary F. *Commonwealth: A Study of the Role of Government in the American Economy: Massachusett, 1774–1861*, rev. ed. Cambridge, Mass., 1969.

Handlin, Oscar, and Handlin, Mary F. *Facing Life; Youth and Family in American History*. Boston, 1971.

Hansen, Marcus Lee. *The Mingling of the Canadian and American Peoples.* Vol 1: *Historical.* New Haven, 1940.

Hareven, Tamara K., ed. *Anonymous Americans; Explorations in Nineteenth-Century Social History.* Englewood Cliffs, N.J., 1971.

Hareven, Tamara K., ed. *Family and Kin in Urban Communities, 1700–1930.* New York, 1977.

Hedges, James B. *The Browns of Providence Plantations*, vol. 2: *The Nineteenth Century.* Providence, 1968.

Henretta, James A. "Families and Farms: *Mentalité* in Pre-Industrial America." *William and Mary Quarterly*, 3rd ser. 35 (January 1978):3–32.

Henretta, James A. "The Morphology of New England Society in the Colonial Period." *Journal of Interdisciplinary History* 2 (Autumn, 1971):379–98.

Hirsch, Susan E. *Roots of the American Working Class: The Industrialization of Crafts in Newark, 1800–1860.* Philadelphia, 1978.

History of Worcester County, Massachusetts, Embracing a Comprehensive History of the County from Its First Settlement to the Present Time, with a History and Description of Its Cities and Towns, Illustrated. 2 vols. Boston, 1879.

Hobsbawm, Eric J. *Labouring Men; Studies in the History of Labour.* London, 1964.

Horwitz, Morton J. *The Transformation of American Law, 1780–1860.* Cambridge, Mass., 1977.

Ignatieff, Michael. *A Just Measure of Pain: The Penitentiary in the Industrial Revolution, 1750–1850.* New York, 1978.

Johnson, Paul E. *A Shopkeeper's Millennium: Society and Revivals in Rochester, New York, 1815–1837.* New York, 1978.

Jones, Douglas Lamar. "The Strolling Poor: Transiency in Eighteenth Century Massachusetts." *Journal of Social History* 8 (Spring, 1975):28–54.

Jones, Douglas Lamar. *Village and Seaport; Migration and Society in Eighteenth-Century Massachusetts.* Hanover, N.H., 1981.

Josephson, Hannah G. *The Golden Threads; New England's Mill Girls and Magnates.* New York, 1949.

Katz, Michael B. *The Irony of Early School Reform; Educational Innovation in Mid-Nineteenth Century Massachusetts.* Cambridge, Mass., 1968.

Kett, Joseph F. "Growing Up in Rural New England, 1800–1840," in Tamara K. Hareven, ed., *Anonymous Americans; Explorations in Nineteenth-Century Social History*, pp. 1–16. Englewood Cliffs, N.J., 1971.

Kett, Joseph F. *Rites of Passage: Adolescence in America, 1790, to the Present.* New York, 1977.

Knowlton, Evelyn. *Pepperell's Progress; History of a Cotton Textile Company, 1844–1945.* Cambridge, Mass., 1948.

Kulik, Gary. "Pawtucket Village and the Strike of 1824: The Origins of Class Conflict in Rhode Island." *Radical History Review* 17 (Spring, 1978):5–37.

Kull, Nell W. "I Can Never Be Happy There in Among So Many Mountains – The Letters of Sally Rice." *Vermont History* 38 (1970): 49–57.

Kurtz, Stephen G., and Hutson, James H., eds. *Essays on the American Revolution*. Chapel Hill, N.C., 1973.

Laurie, Bruce. *Working People of Philadelphia, 1800–1850*. Philadelphia, 1980.

Layer, Robert G. *Earnings of Cotton Mill Operatives, 1825–1914*. Cambridge, Mass., 1955.

Lebergott, Stanley, *Manpower in Economic Growth: The American Record Since 1800*. New York, 1964.

Lockridge, Kenneth A. *A New England Town: The First Hundred Years, Dedham, Massachusetts, 1636–1736*. New York, 1970.

Lockridge, Kenneth A. "Social Change and the Meaning of the American Revolution." *Journal of Social History* 6 (Summer, 1973):403–39.

Lockridge, Kenneth A., and Kreider, Alan. "The Evolution of Massachusetts Town Government, 1640–1740." *William and Mary Quarterly*, 3rd ser. 23 (1966):549–74.

McGouldrick, Paul. *New England Textiles in the Nineteenth Century; Profits and Investment*. Cambridge, Mass., 1968.

McLoughlin, William G. *New England Dissent, 1630–1833; The Baptists and the Separation of Church and State*. 2 vols. Cambridge, Mass., 1971.

Main, Jackson Turner. *The Social Structure of Revolutionary America*. Princeton, 1965.

Merrill, Michael. "Cash Is Good to Eat: Self-Sufficiency and Exchange in the Rural Economy of the United States." *Radical History Review* 3 (Winter, 1977):42–71.

Messenger, Betty. *Picking Up the Linen Threads: A Study in Industrial Folklore*. Austin, Texas, 1978.

Montgomery, David. *Beyond Equality; Labor and the Radical Republicans, 1862–1872*. New York, 1967.

Montgomery, David. "The Shuttle and the Cross: Weavers and Artisans in the Kensington Riots of 1844." *Journal of Social History* 5 (Summer, 1972):411–46.

Montgomery, David. "Strikes in Nineteenth Century America." *Social Science History* 4 (February 1980):81–104.

Montgomery, David. "The Working Classes of the Pre-Industrial City, 1780–1830." *Labor History* 9 (Winter, 1968):3–22.

Morison, Samuel Eliot. *A History of the Constitution of Massachusetts*. Boston, 1917.

Murrin, John. "Review Essay." *History and Theory* 11 (1972):226–75.

Pollard, Sidney. *The Genesis of Modern Management; A Study of the Industrial Revolution in Great Britain*. Cambridge, Mass., 1965.

Redford, Arthur. *Labour Migration in England, 1800–1850*, 2nd ed. Rev. by W. H. Chaloner. Manchester, England, 1964.

Richardson, Erastus. *History of Woonsocket*. Woonsocket, R.I., 1876.

Rivard, Paul E. *Samuel Slater, Father of American Manufactures*. Slater Mill Historical Site. Providence, 1974.

Rivard, Paul E. "Textile Experiments in Rhode Island, 1788–1789." *Rhode Island History* 33 (May 1974):35–45.

Rock, Howard B. *Artisans of the New Republic: The Tradesmen of New York City in the Age of Jefferson.* New York, 1979.

Rorabaugh, William J. *The Alcoholic Republic, An American Tradition.* New York, 1979.

Rothman, David J. *The Discovery of the Asylum; Social Order and Disorder in the New Republic.* Boston, 1971.

Rutman, Darrett B. "People in Process: The New Hampshire Towns of the Eighteenth Century," in Tamara K. Hareven, ed., *Family and Kin in Urban Communities, 1700–1930*, pp. 16–37. New York, 1977.

Siracusa, Carl. *A Mechanical People: Perceptions of the Industrial Order in Massachusetts, 1815–1880.* Middletown, Conn., 1979.

Smelser, Neil J. *Social Change in the Industrial Revolution; An Application of Theory to the British Cotton Industry.* Chicago, 1959.

Smith, Daniel Scott. "Parental Power and Marriage Patterns: An Analysis of Historical Trends in Hingham, Massachusetts." *Journal of Marriage and the Family* 35 (August 1973):419–28.

Smith, Merritt Roe. *Harpers Ferry Armory and the New Technology: The Challenge of Change.* Ithaca, N.Y. 1977.

Steere, Thomas. *History of the Town of Smithfield From Its Organization, in 1730–1, to Its Division, in 1871, Compiled in accordance with the votes of the Towns of Smithfield, North Smithfield, Lincoln and Woonsocket, R.I.* Providence, 1881.

Szatmary, David P. *Shays' Rebellion: The Making of an Agrarian Insurrection.* Amherst, Mass., 1980

Taylor, George Rogers. *The Transportation Revolution, 1815–1860.* New York, 1951.

Thernstrom, Stephan. *Poverty and Progress; Social Mobility in a Nineteenth Century City.* Cambridge, Mass., 1964.

Thernstrom, Stephan, and Knights, Peter R. "Men in Motion: Some Data and Speculations about Urban Population Mobility in Nineteenth Century America," in Tamara K. Hareven, ed., *Anonymous Americans; Explorations in Nineteenth-Century Social History*, pp. 17–47. Englewood Cliffs, N.J., 1971.

Thompson, Edward P. *The Making of the English Working Class.* New York, 1964.

Thompson, Edward P. "Time, Work-Discipline, and Industrial Capitalism." *Past and Present* 38 (December 1967):56–97.

Thompson, Mack. *Moses Brown, Reluctant Reformer.* Chapel Hill, N.C., 1962.

Tryon, Rolla M. *Household Manufactures in the United States, 1640–1860; A Study in Industrial History.* Chicago, 1917.

Tucker, Barbara M. "The Family and Industrial Discipline in Ante-Bellum New England." *Labor History* 21 (Winter, 1979–80):55–74.

Walkowitz, Daniel J. "Working Women in the Gilded Age: Factory, Community and Family Life Among Cohoes, New York, Cotton Workers." *Journal of Social History* 5 (Summer, 1972):464–90.

Walkowitz, Daniel J. *Worker City, Company Town: Iron and Cottonworker Protest in Troy and Cohoes, New York, 1855–1884.* Urbana, Ill. 1978.

Wallace, Anthony F. C. *Rockdale: The Growth of an American Village in the Early Industrial Revolution. An Account of the Coming of the Machines, the Making of a New Way of Life in the Mill Hamlets, the Triumph of Evangelical Capitalists Over Socialists and Infidels, and the Transformation of the Workers into Christian Soldiers in a Cotton-Manufacturing District in Pennsylvania in the Years Before and During the Civil War.* New York, 1978.

Ware, Caroline F. *The Early New England Cotton Manufacture; A Study in Industrial Beginnings.* Boston, 1931.

Ware, Norman. *The Industrial Worker, 1840–1860; The Reaction of American Industrial Society to the Advance of the Industrial Revolution.* Boston, 1924.

Warner, Sam Bass, Jr. *The Private City; Philadelphia in Three Periods of Its Growth.* Philadelphia, 1968.

Wilentz, Robert Sean. "Review Essay: Industrializing America and the Irish: Towards the New Departure." *Labor History* 20 (Fall, 1979):579–95.

Wilentz, Robert Sean. "Artisan Origins of the American Working Class." *International Labor and Working Class History* 19 (Spring, 1981):1–22.

Williamson, Chilton. *American Suffrage; From Property to Democracy, 1760–1860.* Princeton, 1960.

Wolfe, Allis Rosenberg, ed. "Letters of a Lowell Mill Girl and Friends: 1845–46." *Labor History* 17 (Winter, 1976):96–102.

Wood, Gordon S. *The Creation of the American Republic, 1776–1787.* Chapel Hill, N.C., 1969.

Wright, Carroll D. *History of Wages and Prices in Massachusetts, 1752–1883, Including Comparative Wages and Prices in Massachusetts and Great Britain: 1860–1883 (Being Parts III and IV of the Sixteenth Annual Report of the Massachusetts Bureau of Statistics of Labor).* Boston, 1885.

Wright, Carroll D. *Strikes in Massachusetts, 1830–1880. (Being Part I of the Eleventh Annual Report of the Massachusetts Bureau of Statistics of Labor [1880]).* Reprinted, Boston, 1889.

Zevin, Robert Brooke. *The Growth of Manufacturing in Early Nineteenth Century New England.* New York, 1975.

Zimiles, Martha, and Zimiles, Murray. *Early American Mills.* New York, 1973.

Unpublished

Bagnall, William R. "Contributions to American Economic History: Sketches of the Manufacturing Establishments in New York City and of Textile Establishments in the Eastern States." Edited by Victor Clark. Manuscript, 4 vols., Baker Library, Harvard University, Cambridge, Mass., 1908.

Conrad, James L., Jr. "The Evolution of Industrial Capitalism in Rhode Island, 1790–1830: Almy, the Browns, and the Slaters." Ph.D. dissertation, University of Connecticut, 1973.

Gilbane, Brendan F. "A Social History of Samuel Slater's Pawtucket, 1790–1830." Ph.D. dissertation, Boston University, 1969.

Hahn, Steven. "The Roots of Southern Populism: Yeoman Farmers and the Transformation of Georgia's Upper Piedmont, 1850–1890." Ph.D. dissertation, Yale University, 1979.

Keyssar, Alexander. "Men Out of Work: A Social History of Unemployment in Massachusetts, 1870–1916." Ph.D. dissertation, Harvard University, 1977.

Kulik, Gary. "The Beginnings of the Industrial Revolution in America: Pawtucket, Rhode Island, 1672–1829." Ph.D. dissertation, Brown University, 1980.

Kulik, Gary. "Opposition to Dam Building: Farmers, Artisans, and Capitalists and the Politics of Water Rights in the Eighteenth Century." Paper presented to Smith College symposium on the "New" New England Working Class History, 1979.

Lebergott, Stanley. "Wage Trends, 1800–1900." National Bureau of Economic Research, Conference on Research in Income and Wealth, Papers. Williams College, 1957.

Lewton, Frederick L. "A Biography of Samuel Slater." Manuscript, Slater Mill Historical Site, Pawtucket, R.I., 1944.

Tucker, Barbara M. "Samuel Slater and Sons: The Emergence of an American Factory System, 1770–1860." Ph.D. dissertation, University of California, Davis, 1974.

Index

absenteeism, 44, 137, 140, 225–6
agents
  in nontextile businesses, 200
  in textile factories, 78–81, 82,
    83–4, 134, 206, 215
aging
  of farmers, 194
  of local populations, 25, 67,
    185t, 185–6
agriculture
  as basis of rural life in 1810, 6–8
  and commerce, 10–11, 39–40,
    52–4, 104–5, 195–6, 197
  increasing intensity of, 68, 196
  products of, 8, 53, 195–6
  technology and work processes
    of, 103–4, 196
  see also farmers
Almy, William, 40, 48
Almy and Brown, 42, 44, 45, 46,
  48, 135, 153
  and Slater, 42, 43
Ammidown, Mrs. Samuel, 93
Amoskeag Mill, 79, 175
apprentices, 13, 35, 37
  absence of 43, 70, 87
Arkwright, Richard, 35, 37, 38
  technologies developed by, 35,
    39, 40–1
  see also water frames
arson, 136, 225
artisans, xi, 121, 143, 262
  culture of, 71, 133, 219, 235
Athol, Massachusetts, 73

Ballow, Dexter, 115
Baltimore, 46
Baptists, 20–1, 40, 125, 126, 220
  and meetinghouses, 193
Barnes, Moses, 248
Barton, Clara, 259
Barton, Stephen, 249, 250, 259

Bellingham, Massachusetts, 83
Belper (England), 35, 37, 38
Blackstone Mill, 47
Blackstone River, 41, 44, 48
boardinghouse-style factories, *see*
  Waltham-style factories
Boston, 141, 176, 177, 204
Brierly, John, 94, 96
Brightman, P.L., 230
Brown, Charles, 72
Brown, John, 79
Brown, Obadiah, 42, 48
Bugbee, Dexter, 249
Bugbee, H.E., 245, 246, 251
Butler, James, 9

Campbell, Samuel, 9, 32
Canadians
  as factory employees (occa-
    sional), 207
  as farm laborers, 194
  as laborers, 190
  occupational patterns of, 190
  as operatives, 190, 210, 212, 215,
    221, 224, 228, 233
  residential patterns of, 192–3
  as town residents, 186, 187t
  transiency of, 191
Carter, James, 134–5
cash
  meaning of, 12
  scarcity of, 9, 109
Catholics
  churches of, 193, 224
  and immigrants, 186
Central Falls, Rhode Island,
  175
Central Turnpike Corporation,
  171–2, 240, 245
Chabanakongkomun, Lake, 6, 49
Charlton (Massachusetts), 19
Chase, E., Jr., 230

Chatman, Thomas W., 60, 106, 107, 108
children
  connection to parents inside textile factories, 117–18, 136, 221–2
  and independence, 25, 101
  leaving the community, 24–5, 54, 56, 191, 192, 194
  and outwork, 73, 77
  and resistance as operatives, 137–8 (*see also* transiency)
  and tasks in farming households, 8, 14, 15, 68
  in textile factories, 36, 37, 38, 43, 86, 94, 128, 213, 214, 215
  and wages as operatives, 90, 91–2, 214
  see also family
churches, *see listings under separate denominations*; meetinghouses
Churle, Emily, 212
Civil War, 259
class
  and operatives' camaraderie, 96, 98, 224–5, 236–7
  and relationship of operatives to textile factory managers, x, 157
Clemons, Chester, 79
clothing, 13–14
  household production of, 9, 68, 77
  of operatives, 139, 225
Congregationalists, 19–21, 125–6, 220
  and meetinghouses, 125, 160, 192, 193, 224, 240–1
Connecticut, operatives arrive from, 88
Corbin, B.A., 245, 246, 251
Corbin, Lamont, 246
Corbin, William, 248
cotton factories
  cost of 62, 203
  labor force in, 86–7
  spread of through New England, 46–7
  technology and work processes of, 35–6, 42–3, 126–9, 202–3

(*see also* power looms; spinning jenny; spinning mule)
  see also textile factories
country mills, *see* family-style factories
Coyle, James, 212
Coxe, Tench, 40, 111
credit, 11–12, 24, 54, 109, 159
  see also debt
currency, *see* cash

Daniels, Seth, 249
Davis, Abijah, 12, 30, 32, 166
Davis, Elijah, 59
Davis, Ezra, 59
Davis, Jonathan, 12, 166, 171
Davis, Learned, 170
Day, Jonathan, 30, 92, 177
debt, 11, 54, 110
  and transiency, 24, 191
Delaware, operatives arrive from, 88
Democrats, 218–19
  candidates of, 238
Derbyshire (England), 36, 38, 42, 45, 47, 125
DeWitt, Alexander, 61, 62, 162, 177, 178, 203, 245, 246, 247, 250
  and Oxford Bank, 167, 245
DeWitt, Stearns, 61, 62, 170, 203
  and Oxford Bank, 167
Dudley, Abel, 125
Dudley, William, 24
Dudley
  and changes in governance and hierarchy, 239–44
  and continuities in governance and hierarchy, 159–63
  and creation of Webster, 175–80
  and friction with mills, 164–73, 247–50, 255
  growth of nontextile businesses in, 58t, 58–9, 188–90
  growth of textile factories in, 60, 188–90
  lack of confrontations in, 244–7
  origins of, 4, 6
  political leanings of, 27, 217–19

population of, 6, 21, 52, 184–6,
187t, 271 (*see also* residential
patterns; transiency)
postbellum developments in,
259–60
and Slater's holdings, 49–50
and temperance, 233
as typical setting of antebellum
textile factories, xii
see also elite; operatives; town
government
Dudley Woolen Manufacturing
Company, 79, 81, 87, 89, 94,
116–17, 121, 124, 135, 137,
140, 225–6
and enforcement of discipline,
155
and Oxford Bank, 167
threatened lawsuit against, 164
and transiency of workers, 89,
147, 148, 150, 152, 153
Dwight, Timothy, 16, 25
Dwyer, John, 230

East Douglas, Massachusetts,
230
East Village, 50, 52, 60, 61, 116,
117, 118, 121–2, 124, 126, 129,
173, 174, 175, 221, 222, 225
and creation of Webster, 175–6,
179
and enforcement of discipline,
155–6
management of, 79–83
postbellum developments in,
260
and relation to Webster, 250–3,
254
and roads, 171–3
and school districts, 168–70
strike against, 142, 225
and transiency of operatives,
144–5, 145f, 146–8, 150–4,
227f, 227–9, 270
see also operatives;
outworkers
economic mobility, 12, 191
and promotions in textile
factories, 81, 82, 94, 206, 211
Eldredge, H., 211

elite
in towns, 12–13, 29–31, 161–3,
242–3
and factory managers, 83–4,
161–3, 245–7
English
as handloom weavers, 76
as operatives, 94, 210, 215, 224,
228
occupational patterns of, 190
as town residents, 186, 187t
Episcopal churches, Slater's
support for, 126
ethnicity
and nontextile employees, 199
and occupational patterns of
town residents, 189–90
and operatives, 214–16, 224,
235–7
and residential patterns, 192–3
and town residents, 185–6, 187t
and transiency, 191, 228, 229,
234–5
Exeter, Massachusetts, 124

factory discipline
enforcement of, 45–6, 130,
155–7, 233
and machines, 126–9
and moral amelioration, 112–
13
and policies toward families,
116–18, 213, 221–2
relation of to profit, 116
and resistance of operatives,
36–7, 135–44, 225–6 (*see also*
transiency)
and time, 36–7, 43, 130–1, 202,
220
factory employees (occasional),
71–2, 121–2, 207–8
see also outworkers
factory proprietors, 46, 60–2, 177,
203–4
and agents, 78–9
and town elite, 83–4, 161–3,
245–7
Fall River, Massachusetts, 149
family
and farms, 8

family (*cont.*)
　operatives attached to, 27, 43,
　　86–7, 90, 91, 116–18, 213–14,
　　215, 221–2
　and transiency of members,
　　21–5, 54–6, 101–2, 146–7,
　　191, 194, 228–9
　see also children; households;
　　kinship
family-style factories
　characteristics of, xiii, 51–2, 78–9
　convergence toward Waltham-
　　style factories, xiii, 214, 232
　critiques of, 119–20
farmers
　ethnicity of, 190
　image of, 105
　laborers hired by, 6–7, 13, 25,
　　68–9, 102, 189, 189t, 194–5,
　　218
　number of, 52, 188–9, 189t
　relation to textile mills, 40,
　　105–6, 111, 114
　response to departing children,
　　101–2
　wealth of, 67–8, 194
　and Workingmen's party, 218
　see also agriculture
Federalists, 27, 142
food, 9, 14, 90–1
Framingham, Massachusetts, 94
France, Joseph, 211

General Court, 19, 162, 167, 175,
　　177, 179–80, 246, 251, 252
generations, defined, xiv
Germans
　occupational patterns of, 190
　as operatives, 210, 215
　as town residents, 186, 187t
Googins, William, 93
Green Mill, 49, 50, 72–3, 79, 83,
　　87, 110, 118, 122, 123, 138,
　　145, 221

Hall, Nathan, 92
Hall, Thaddeus, 61
Hamilton, Alexander, 40, 111
handloom weavers, 36, 42, 43, 49,
　　51, 138

and handlooms, 9
　and South Village strike, 141–2
　and woolen mills, 86, 123–4
　see also outworkers
Hanson, George, 149
Harris, Jonathan, 32
Hartley, David, 112
Harwood, Stephen, 72
holidays, 16, 130
households
　distribution of tasks within, 15,
　　68
　and manufacturing, 9, 53, 77
　size of, 8, 68
　see also children; family;
　　operatives
Howard, Edward, 80, 81, 175
Howland, Willard, 83
Huguenots, 4
husbandmen, *see* farmers
husbandry, *see* agriculture

immigrants, *see listings under
　separate national groups;*
　ethnicity
industrialization
　arguments for and against,
　　39–40, 111–16
　meaning of, ix–x, 99, 260–1
　not confined to urban settings,
　　xi–xii, 262
industrial order, xi–xii, 261
Irish
　as factory employees (occa-
　　sional), 207
　as farm laborers, 194
　as handloom weavers, 76
　as laborers, 190
　occupational patterns of, 190
　as operatives, 94, 190, 210,
　　212–13, 215, 221, 224, 228,
　　233, 236
　residential patterns of, 192–3
　as town residents, 186, 187t
　transiency of, 191
Italians
　as town residents, 186, 187t, 247

Jackson, Andrew, 217
　and Democratic party, 143

Jefferson, Thomas, 10, 39–40
  embargo issued by, 46
Jewett City, Connecticut, 79, 175

King Philip's War, 4
Kingsbury, Alfred, 82
Kingsbury, Jeremiah, 12, 30
Kingsbury, Mary, 117
kinship
  and business partnerships, 59,
    62
  drawing operatives to mills, 89
  households linked by, 8, 103,
    159
  and political office, 30
  and residential patterns, 192
  see also family

labor scarcity, 16, 43, 89
  aggrevated by transiency, 148
  diminished after 1840, 233
  and effect on factory discipline,
    155–6
Lacey, O., 211
Lancashire (England), 35, 36, 38
Law, William
  store owned by, 109
Learned, Ebenezer, 24
Learned, Thomas, 12, 30
Locke, John, 112
Lowell, xii–xiii, 51, 236
  see also Waltham-style factories
Ludlow, Massachusetts, 79
Lyon, Nathaniel, 79, 81
Lynn (Massachusetts), 219

McEastum, M., 212
McIntire, Sylvester, 62
McKnight, Reuben, 31
Mackwell, John, 17
Manchester, New Hampshire, 51
manufactories, *see* textile factories
Manville mills, 155, 230
marriage age, 25
Martineau, Harriet, 112
Mashpee (Indians), 6
Masonic Lodges, 98
Massachusetts, operatives arrival
  from, 88, 209
Massachusetts Spy, 147

Mayo, Peter, 136
meetinghouses
  awarding of pews in, 31
  location of, 18–19
  *see also listings under separate
    denominations*
men
  as agents, 78
  as factory employees (occa-
    sional), 71–2, 207
  and nontextile workforce, 69,
    199
  and outwork, 73
  as overseers, 82
  in textile factories, 36, 86, 94,
    213–14, 215
  in textile factories as fathers,
    118, 221–2
  and wages in textile factories,
    90, 91, 214, 216t
Merino Wool Factory, 34, 49, 60,
  72, 79, 80, 98, 150, 156
  Slater agent arrives from, 81
  and roads, 170
Methodists, 125, 126, 220
  chapels of, 193, 224
  quarrel with Slater, 253, 254
Middlefield, Massachusetts, 82–3
Milford (England), 35, 37, 38, 39,
  46
militia, 31, 98, 162
mill masters, *see* factory
  proprietors
Millar, James, 82
Moore, Rufus, 107, 110, 199

National Republicans, 142–3
  dispute over candidate of, 174
New Jersey, operatives arrive
  from, 88
New York (city), 46, 141
New York (state), operatives
  arrive from, 88
Nichols, David, 9
Nipmucks (Indians), 4, 6
nontextile businesses
  employees of, 69–71, 188–9,
    189t, 190, 198–9
  expansion of, 7, 7t, 52, 58t,
    58–9, 188, 189t, 189–90

nontextile businesses (*cont.*)
goals of, 56–7, 108–10, 201–2
proprietors of, 59–60, 61, 62, 198
and relation to employees, 133,
217–19, 237
technology and work processes
in 14, 70, 106–8, 199–201
wages in, 70, 107, 199
Northbridge, Massachusetts, 230
North Providence, Rhode Island,
163, 164, 175
North Village, 50, 52, 60, 61, 116,
126, 134, 173, 174, 175, 221,
225
and creation of Webster, 175–6,
178–9
and enforcement of discipline,
155–7
management of, 79–83
postbellum developments in,
260
and relation to Webster, 250,
252, 253, 254
and school districts, 169
and transiency of operatives,
144–5, 145f, 146–8, 150, 152–4,
227f, 227–9, 270
see also operatives
Norwich and Worcester Railroad,
170, 188

Ogden, Samuel, 78, 113, 120
Old Farmer's Almanack, 53, 68, 102,
197
Old Mill, 41, 42–4, 46, 48, 57, 79,
82, 92, 135, 138, 175
Olney, Richard, 170
Olney, Wilson, 198
operatives
in Dudley, Oxford, and
Webster, 84–5, 85t, 86–96,
98, 188–9, 189t, 203, 208t,
208–14
in England, 36–8
and ethnicity, 87, 190, 215–16,
216t
and franchise, 98, 148, 217–18
and labor market, 232
in Old Mill, 43, 46
others' perceptions of, 178–9

religious interests of, 126
resistance to textile factories,
36–7, 44, 135–44, 225–6 (*see
also* transiency)
workloads of, 128–9, 144, 222–3
see also factory employees
(occasional); outworkers
Ormsbee, Erastus, 198
outworkers, 70, 107, 188, 200, 201
dismissal of, 122–3
employed by East Village, 72–3,
74m, 75m, 76–8
see also handloom weavers;
pickers
overseers
in textile factories, 37, 45, 82–4,
117, 130, 134, 206–7, 215
in nontextile businesses, 70,
107, 200
Oxford
as center of Shays' Rebellion,
10
and changes in governance and
hierarchy, 239–44
and continuities in governance
and hierarchy, 159–63
and creation of Webster, 175–80
and friction with mills, 164–73,
247–50, 255
growth of nontextile businesses
in, 7, 7t, 58t, 58–9, 188–90
growth of textile factories in, 60,
188–90
lack of confrontations in, 244–7
origins of, 4, 6
political leanings of, 27, 217–19
population of, 6, 21, 52, 184–6,
187t, 271 (*see also* residential
patterns, transiency)
postbellum developments in,
259–60
and sample of outworkers, 73,
76
and Slater's holdings, 49–50
and Slater's home, 80
as typical setting of antebellum
textile factories, xii
see also elite; operatives; town
government
Oxford, North Gore, 27

Oxford, South Gore, 27, 35, 49, 50, 52, 72, 79, 98, 168, 174, 175
Oxford Bank, 63, 161, 164, 165, 245
and textile factories, 166–7
Oxford Cotton Manufacturing Company, 61, 62
Oxford General Store, 62

paupers, 12, 26, 27, 28, 160, 177, 240
Pawtucket (Rhode Island), 41, 45, 48, 79, 81, 82, 140
and 1824 strike, 141
and hostility to textile factories, 43–4, 46, 47
and mill fire, 136
Pawtucket Chronicle, 172, 205
Peace Dale factory, 155
Perry Mill, 170
Philadelphia, 39, 41, 46, 76, 141
Phim, Thomas, 231
Phipps, Calvin, 92
Phoenix Thread Factory, 50, 85, 91 (*see also* North Village)
pickers, 42
see also outworkers
Plough, Loom, and Anvil, 195
Poles, as town residents, 186, 187t
Porter, Andrew W., 166
power looms, 85, 86, 92, 127, 128, 146
in Waltham-style factories, xiii, 51
in weave shops, 123
women operating, 138–9, 140, 144, 146, 148, 221, 225
in woolen mills, 123–4, 203
Pratt, Sylvanus, 60
Preston, Zera, 175
profit
and agriculture, 10–11, 53, 104–5, 195–6
limited influence of, 10–13
and nontextile businesses, 56–7, 108–10, 201–2
and outworkers, 77–8
and textile factories, 44, 56–7, 110–11, 121–4, 150, 202

property
distribution of, 6–7, 52 (*see also* farmers)
inheritance of, 24, 54, 191, 194
size of holdings, 8, 52, 104, 197
and transiency, 23–5
Providence, Rhode Island, 16, 40, 43, 46, 81, 120, 204, 206
Providence Journal, 205
Providence Steam Cotton Company, 79, 175, 205
Provincetown, 16

Quakers, 20
involvment in early textile industry, 40, 41, 46, 47, 125

Rehoboth, Massachusetts, 48, 82
republican ideology, and critiques of textile factories, 119–20, 136
Republican Party, local support for, 217
residential patterns, 18, 159–60
after 1840, 192–3
of operatives, 50, 51, 96–8, 117
revivals, 20, 125, 160, 193
and transiency, 154, 228
Rhode Island, operatives arrival from, 88
Rhode Island-style factories, *see* family-style factories
riparian usage, 11, 44, 109, 110, 159, 164, 165, 253
roads, 28–9, 160, 239–40
and textile factories, 165–6, 170–3, 248–50, 254
Robinson, James, 206
Rush, Benjamin, 112

schools, 27–8, 161, 241–2
and textile factories, 124–5, 165–6, 167–70, 245, 254
Scots
as operatives, 215
as town residents, 186, 187t
Seekonk (Rhode Island), 173
selectmen, 29, 31, 162–3, 242–3, 245
Shaw, William, 95

Shays' Rebellion, 10, 12
shoemakers, 60, 69, 102, 106, 188,
    189t, 190, 200, 219, 249
  shops for, 58, 59, 69, 70, 72,
    107, 108, 133, 200–1
Sigourney, Andrew, 9, 12, 166
Slater, Esther (Mrs. Samuel
    Slater), 79
Slater, George, 80, 126, 163, 167,
    175, 205, 220, 246, 253
Slater, H. Nelson, 80, 167, 205–6,
    207, 209, 211, 232, 254, 260
Slater, John (Samuel's brother),
    53, 79
Slater, John (Samuel's son), 80,
    156, 163, 164, 167, 174, 175,
    205, 246
Slater, Samuel, xiv, 60, 61, 62, 63,
    111, 114, 115, 116, 122, 134,
    135, 148, 150, 155, 163, 164,
    165, 222, 245, 251, 253, 254
  arrival in America, 39, 41
  and creation of Webster, 175–80
  death of, 205
  and development of Dudley and
    Oxford holdings, 49–50
  early American experiences of,
    42–6
  English training of, 35–9
  and expanding textile industry,
    46–9
  managerial strategy of, 79–80,
    82–3
  and Oxford Bank, 166–7
  and roads, 170–3
  and school districts, 168–70
  and support of religion, 125–6
  temperament of, 173–5
  see also North, South, and East
    villages
Slater, William, 35
Slatersville, 48, 50, 140, 205
Smith, Anne, 150
Smithfield, Rhode Island, 48, 79,
    82, 175, 205
South Village, 50, 52, 60, 61, 72,
    116, 121, 124, 134, 173, 174,
    175, 196, 212
  and creation of Webster, 176,
    178–9

and enforcement of discipline,
    155–6
  law suit against, 164
  management of, 79–83
  postbellum developments in, 260
  and relation to Webster, 250,
    251, 254
  and school districts, 169
  strike against, 141–4, 225
  and transiency of operatives,
    150–4
  see also operatives
Southbridge, Massachusetts, 150
spinning jacks, 47, 127, 203
spinning jenny, 36, 43
  early American use of, 40
  in woolen mills, 47, 127
spinning mule, 48
  operatives using, 86, 94, 98, 118,
    127–8, 140, 144, 146, 215, 216t,
    222
  self-acting, 203
spinning wheels, 9, 36, 43
Springfield (Massachusetts), 51
Springfield Manufacturing Com-
    pany, 79
Stockwell, Nathaniel, 17
Stevens, Henry H., 203, 222, 245,
    246, 247, 249, 250
strike
  in East Village, 142, 225
  rare use by antebellum
    operatives, x, 143, 225, 236
  in South Village, 141–4, 225
Strutt, Jedediah, 35–9, 41, 42, 49,
    51, 111, 125, 130
Sturbridge (Massachusetts), 19
"Sui Generis: Alias Thomas Man",
    120
Sunday schools, 38, 45, 111, 125
Sutton, Massachusetts, 61
  and county road, 172–3
Sutton Manufacturing Company,
    205
Swiss
  as operatives, 210
  as town residents, 186, 187t

Tachauer, August, 212
ten-hour movement

and Democrats, 218–19
lack of local support for, 143,
  225, 236
letter approving, 253–4
textile factories
and bureaucracy, 129–31, 220
community opposition to, 36,
  43–4, 158–9, 164–80
cost of, 62, 203
in Dudley, Oxford, and
  Webster, 34, 60, 188 (*see also*
  specific companies; North,
  South, and East villages)
early growth of in New
  England, 46–7
in England, 35–9
and ideology surrounding, 40,
  111–16
limits of ideology surrounding,
  120–31
and meaning of industrialization, xi
nonlocal investment in by
  Samuel Slater, 48, 79, 175, 205
  (*see also* Old Mill; White
  Mill)
and profit, 44, 56–7, 110–11,
  120–4, 150, 202
promotions within, 81, 82, 94,
  206, 211
purpose and success of ideology
  surrounding, 116–20
resistance to by operatives,
  36–7, 135–44, 225–6 (*see also*
  transiency)
technology and work processes
  of, 35–6, 42–3, 47, 126–9,
  202–3 (*see also* power looms;
  spinning jacks; spinning
  jenny; spinning mule)
see also factory discipline;
  operatives; wages
Thompson, Connecticut, 73
Tiffany, Bela, 49, 50, 81, 168
time
and factory discipline, 36–7, 43,
  130–1, 202, 220, (*see also*
  absenteeism)
and industrial calendar, 150–1,
  231–2

and work rhythms in nontextile
  businesses, 106–7, 200
and work rhythms in rural life,
  15–17, 103
town government
jurisdiction of, 27–9, 159–61,
  239–45
requirements of participation in,
  27, 217–18, 238, 244
see also elite
transiency
effects on children, 101–2
of nontextile employees, 69, 71
of operatives, 37, 44–5, 89, 90,
  144, 145f, 145–56, 179, 191,
  227f, 227–35, 236, 270
and social deviancy, 112–13
of townspeople, 21–6, 54–6,
  190–1
(*see also* A Note on Transiency)
Tufts, Aaron, 12, 30, 34, 60, 62,
  162
and creation of Webster, 177
as factory manager, 79, 80–1,
  164, 203, 246, 248
and Oxford Bank, 166–7, 245
Tufts, George, 162, 177
Tufts Woolen Mill, 86
turnouts, *see* strikes
turnover, *see* transiency
Tyson, John, 81

unemployment, 16, 43
Union Mill, 50, 85, 87, 118,
  221
Unitarian chapel, built by Strutt,
  38
Universalists, 20–1, 125

wages
and agents, 81, 206
of agricultural laborers, 25, 68,
  195
basis of in countryside, 17
and guidelines in textile
  factories, 48, 153
of operatives, 37, 44, 89–92, 93,
  214, 215–16, 216t, 226, 232
of outworkers, 76–7
and overseers, 82, 206

wages (*cont.*)
    and timing of payments in
        textile factories, 151
    and town officers, 29, 243
Waltham, Massachusetts, 51, 110
Waltham-style factories
    availability of operatives for, 88,
        149
    characteristics of, xii-xiii, 51, 73,
        78–9, 81, 86–7, 92, 96, 115,
        122
    convergence toward family-style
        factories, xiii, 214, 232
    criticism of, 120
    ideology of, 113–14
Warwick, Rhode Island, 48
water frames, 36, 41, 48, 127, 128,
    140
Waterman, Fisher, 204
weavers, *see* handloom weavers;
    outworkers; power looms
wealth
    distribution of, 12, 161, 186
    and factory proprietors, 61–2,
        204
    and nontextile proprietors, 59,
        198
    and status, 32–3
    and town elite, 29–30, 162, 242
Webster
    and changes in governance and
        hierarchy, 239–44
    creation of, 175–80
    and nontextile businesses in,
        188–90
    political leanings of, 217–19
    population of 184–6, 187, 271,
        (*see also* residential patterns;
        transiency)
    postbellum developments in,
        259–60
    relation of to Slater mills, 250–5
    and temperance, 233
    textile factories in, 188–90

as typical setting of antebellum
    factories, xii
Webster Weekly Times, The, 193, 253
Whigs, 143, 218
    support for, 254
White Mill, 48
Whitmore, Nathaniel, 32
Wilkinson, Hannah (Mrs. Samuel
    Slater), 41, 49
Wilkinsonville, 175
women
    exclusion from mills if married,
        118
    and outwork, 73, 77, 188, 201
    and resistance as operatives,
        137–8 (*see also* transiency)
    tasks of in farming households,
        15, 68
    in textile factories, 36, 85–6, 94,
        211, 212, 213, 215, 221, 222
    and wages as operatives, 90, 91,
        214, 216t
    and work in nontextile
        businesses, 69, 199
Wood, Asa, 72, 121
Woodstock, Connecticut, 153
woolen factories
    and absence of outworkers, 72
    cost of, 62, 203
    labor force of, 86–7
    spread of through New
        England, 47
    technology and work processes
        of, 47, 127, 203
    wages in, 90, 214
    see also textile factories
Woonsocket, Rhode Island, 47,
    173, 226
Workingmen's party, 218
    candidates of, 238
    support for in Webster, 254

yeomen, *see* farmers